DATE DUE

D0481963

GAYLORD — PRINTED IN U.S.A.

WORMHOLES

c. 2

WORMHOLES

Essays and Occasional Writings

JOHN FOWLES

EDITED AND INTRODUCED
BY JAN RELF

Henry Holt and Company
New York

Henry Holt and Company, Inc.
Publishers since 1866
115 West 18th Street
New York, New York 10011

Henry Holt ® is a registered trademark of
Henry Holt and Company, Inc.

Library of Congress Cataloging-in-Publication Data
Fowles, John, 1926–
Wormholes : essays and occasional writings / John Fowles ; edited
and introduced by Jan Relf.—1st ed.
p.   cm.
ISBN 0-8050-5867-2 (alk. paper)
I. Relf, Jan.   II. Title.
PR6056.085W6   1998   97-42986
824'.914—dc21   CIP

Henry Holt books are available for special promotions and premiums.
For details contact: Director, Special Markets.

First Edition 1998

Book design by Claire Naylon Vaccaro

Printed in the United States of America
All first editions are printed on acid-free paper.∞

1   3   5   7   9   10   8   6   4   2

CONTENTS

When this book was first mooted I was truly not very keen on the idea. I realized that it was marred not only by a somewhat cynical, essentially cultural lack of sympathy for myself as a publicly known writer ("John Fowles"), but also by a similar distaste for the climate in which literature is generally valued and judged nowadays. This might suggest that I am a model puritan and lack all vanity, but that really can't stand against what is, in my experience, a truth about all writers, male or female. They are professionally, often foolishly and blindly, egocentric. Somewhere, it may be deep down, they all believe that no one can—or could—write so well as they. The vanity of this self-belief is really what distinguishes and specifies our kind. An excessive case of consciousness of personal individuality, it is a condition shared by all artists; a kind of clinging, in the savage typhoon of existence with its seemingly mindless rage against all religion and philosophy, to the one spar that promises to float. We cannot escape this archetypal need, often against all social and political belief, to cling to our eachness, our very own individuality. It is in a sense that "noble rot" which we esteem in certain wines, fruits, and cheeses. It must frequently seem, in the limitless gray sea of those largely without creative gifts, to be a hogging of too much elbow room in the (rat) race for a prize that at heart most of us know neither can nor does exist: immortality.

All my life an image has haunted me against this bleak view of existence: the mosaic. An early book I tried to write was entitled *Tesserae*; to be of minor relationships, dabs of color. I always felt then that I was best understood and seen—or felt—as a sequence of very small happenings, little brick squares of opinion and feeling. Perhaps that was why the title we first toyed with here was *Fragments*, based on T. S. Eliot's well-known line, "These fragments I have shored against my ruins." I was next persuaded to reuse a line very loosely based on Descartes, "I write therefore I am." In one bearing it was vain in the obsessively individual sense hinted at above; in another I hope it is true in a more rational, psychological way. At least since my early twenties I haven't been able to think, like a condemned man in his cell, that I am not ineluctably a writer, more specifically a novelist; but perhaps the condemned man is altogether too Camusian a simile. This seeming incarceration does of course bring some very different—and far happier—moods and moments. I express myself, sell myself, best through narration, not (as I would sometimes prefer to imagine) as a poet or playwright. In the past I often used to dismiss the novel as a *faute de mieux*. So I dropped the second title.

Title choosing is always both a thrill and a nightmare. In the end I appealed to my fellow novelist and friend Peter Benson, who knows me well as he lives in the next village here in Dorset. He proposed *Wormholes*. It immediately pleased me. He was, of course, using the word in the sense of the new physics, as defined in the *OED*: "A hypothetical interconnection between widely separated regions of space-time." That seemed at least metaphorically appropriate, since the complex space-time I live in is, though perhaps remote from that of any modern physicist, that of my own imagination. Its burden was what I had sensed and approved in an essay by Katherine Tarbox in a special number of *Twentieth-century Literature* (spring 1996) devoted to my work. It was my favorite piece there. All serious writers are endlessly seeking for the wormholes that will connect them to other planes and worlds. I spasmodically collect old books; I live in an old house; I know the other sort of wormhole only too well: thus the title. I shouldn't like one, in any case, at which I could not sometimes smile.

So I offer or proffer (a little as they do in an even older profession) these little bits of what I am, only too aware that there are many they will not please—and perhaps strictly in relation to how clumsily they fall from acceptable academic and journalistic standards of knowledge and expertise. I hope the reader will at least realize the importance that nature and natural history, though I so seldom write directly about them, have played in my life, and why I have usually cited them when asked to name influences. *Tenthredinifera, tenthredinifera, tenthredinifera . . .* those *tesserae* shall be explained later.

This first clutter of mosaics will probably infuriate any decent academic, and I must in part apologize for their higgledy-piggledy nature, but anything that laid me out like a corpse for dissection would very profoundly not be me. I feel one place where I may have misled my readers is on insufficiently emphasizing the importance for *The French Lieutenant's Woman* of that strange little French novel by Claire de Duras, *Ourika* (1824), now published in my English translation by the Modern Language Association of America.[1]

I am lucky in one thing, which is that my friend Jan Relf has greatly helped me in assembling or excerpting what is here. I have always liked Jan both as a woman and as a human being, not only for her shrewd intelligence but for her equally shrewd independence. I hope I should always have tried to become a feminist, but her humor and scholarship have made it certain that at least I know how inadequate a one I am.

JOHN FOWLES

---

1. New York, 1994.

INTRODUCTION

*There is a curious spiral rhythm, and the mind approaches again
and again the point of concern, repeats itself, goes back, destroys
the time-sequence entirely. . . .*

D. H. LAWRENCE

As a novelist, John Fowles needs no introduction. His popularity and his
place in the English literary canon have been assured for at least the past
two decades. His nonfiction writings are less well known, in part because
their appearance has been scattered in ephemeral periodicals, in academic
journals, and (in the case of his introductions and forewords) in books by
others which have enjoyed a considerably smaller circulation and less popularity than his own novels, and which, in some cases, are now out of
print. Here, then, for the first time, is a representative gathering of Fowles's
fugitive and intensely personal writings: essays, literary criticism, commentaries, autobiographical statements, memoirs, and musings.

The selection in this volume comprises some thirty pieces, ranging
from a single page to substantial essays, and covers the period from 1963
and the appearance of Fowles's first novel, *The Collector*, to the present. It
thus represents the writer's developing views on the art of fiction, and the
relationship of literature to life and morality, throughout the mature, fertile period of his career.

The process of selection was not an easy one. Most of the essays here
are reproduced in full, but in some cases—the long essay entitled "Islands,"
for instance—the inclusion of the full text would have meant the exclusion of some important shorter pieces. My aim in making the selection,
and the inevitable editorial cuts that followed, has been always to give the
reader a sense of the diversity of Fowles's interests, and of what Coleridge
called the "passion and the life that are within." (I am, incidentally, the
"academic friend" referred to in the last essay, "The Nature of Nature"—
the friend who, quoting William Hazlitt on Coleridge, and probably mo-

mentarily maddened by John's wildly digressive habits of thought and speech, suggested that Fowles himself had a tangential and Coleridgean mind! It was taken, fortunately, as an oblique compliment.)

The essays collected here represent a chronicle of the various matters that have plagued, preoccupied, or delighted Fowles throughout his life, and the thread that connects them is inevitably an autobiographical one. All writing, of course, is to some extent autobiographical—"true lies"— whether it is fiction or nonfiction. The writer's obsessions and passions permeate his work, and readers who are familiar with Fowles's novels will find in these essays frequent resonances and reflections of themes that they may already have met in the fiction: the lost *domaine*, the woman as *princesse lointaine*; evolution and natural history; freedom and responsibility, randomness and hazard; literature, literariness, and the role of the writer. They also reflect his lifelong commitment to left-wing politics, conservation, and "green" issues. And the gift for narrative, for which Fowles's novels are so justly celebrated, is evident in many of these essays. In "Shipwreck," for instance, the opening lines have all the qualities of a compelling story: the feeling of "once upon a time," the powerful sense of place, and the way the first-person narrator draws the reader into the here and now of the tale he is telling.

Fowles's style is lively, scholarly, frequently provocative, and occasionally contentious—as, for instance, in his statement that "writing is like eating or making love: a natural process, not an artificial one"! Above all, it is extremely accessible. He writes primarily for "you the reader who is neither critic nor writer" ("Notes on an Unfinished Novel"). At the same time, these essays must be of great interest to scholars and writers everywhere, affirming as Fowles himself so often does the importance of the novel, and taking issue with those critical Cassandras who prophecy its imminent demise.

The writings also bear witness to Fowles's grumblingly ambivalent relationships with the literary academy and with the wilder shores of literary theory and criticism, and to his adamant refusal to concede what Roland Barthes famously called the "death of the author." He constantly claims that he is utterly baffled by the intellectual flights of literary theorists—as, for instance, in "A Modern Writer's France": "What very skimpy reading I have done of Derrida, Lacan, Barthes, and their fellow *maîtres* has more often left me baffled and frustrated than enlightened," he complains. In an earlier piece on Kafka, the literary academy is referred to as a "college of morticians," who murder to dissect. Scholars, he says, will not be impressed by his "quasi-academic" views on literature; and yet, in spite of the tongue-in-cheek insults, they *are*, it seems, impressed. Moreover, his strangest novel, *Mantissa*, bears witness to his more-than-competent grasp of deconstruction and poststructuralist theory. Nevertheless, the continuing stream of academic visitors and thesis writers who find their way to the writer's home in Lyme Regis—which might reasonably be regarded as the price of being taken seriously as a writer—seems to inspire in him a kind of terror. Is it, one wonders, that terror familiar to many academics as well as to writers and other artists—the terror of being disarmed or found out? "Novelists," says Fowles, "are like conjurors, always expert at misleading"; and the last thing a conjuror (or magus) wants is for his shamanistic tricks, his particular magic, to be rumbled.

Fowles's writings reflect the diversity and overlapping nature of his interests. Neither the writings nor the interests fall into neat, convenient categories, and the task of ordering the essays was not an easy one. The reader looking for references to Fowles's views on a particular subject will find it easier to work through the index than to scan the contents page for clues. Eventually the material seemed to sort itself out into four main groups, and I have ordered it accordingly; within each section, the essays are presented chronologically. It may be tempting to read them as an exposition of linear intellectual development, but for me they represent something far more interesting: the "curious spiral rhythm" of a mind returning again and again to its main points of concern, always moving on, and yet blurring or destroying the idea of time as sequence, so that the fragments, the *tesserae* that at one time were to have given this book its title, combine to form a kaleidoscopic pattern: a shake, or a reordering, and a new image takes shape. A shoring-up against the ruins, perhaps, but as the essay "Behind the Magus" affirms, "such fragments make good shoring" indeed. As Fowles himself tells us in the interview with Dianne Vipond, each piece of his nonfiction writing, whatever its subject matter, is a "little square of mosaic in my general portrait"; but given the shape-shifting nature of this particular writer's persona, each reader will find in this text a different mosaic, a different John Fowles.

Just as the author-persona of *The French Lieutenant's Woman* self-consciously reminds us of the inevitably split nature of the writer—the way in which he, or she, is both the "I" who writes and the "I" who is written, the self who is both within and without the fiction—so here we find recurrent meditations on the same theme. The tribute to William Golding, for instance, juxtaposes the private man, gentle, elderly, unknown and perhaps unknowable, with the publicly owned and constructed figure "Golding," a semimythical entity "made purely of words." The briefest essay in this collection, "The J. R. Fowles Club," similarly reflects on the fractured nature of the writer-beast. It was written in response to a request from the Ecco Press, which, in the spring of 1995, published an issue of *Antæus* devoted to writers' senses of themselves as writers. Ecco had asked for a "little experimental/mock-autobiographical prose on the experience of writing." The model was Borges's famous mini-essay "Borges and I," an early postmodernist statement on the act of writing, in which Borges speaks of himself as his "other," as a split subject: the "I" who writes, acts, speaks, and has "produced a few worthwhile pages," and the "I" who watches and is "doomed to oblivion." The most startling difference between the Borges piece and John's is that whereas Borges sees himself as split in two—self and other, subject and object, the seeing and the seen—the Fowlesian self is multiply fractured, a shambolical disunity of many, often reluctantly coexisting parts. This self—the "club"—is composed of many members, some of whom are in constant, querulous disagreement with each other: the would-be feminist, for instance, who's consumed with male guilt over the sins committed against women by an earlier, younger self—a self who had much in common with Nicholas of *The Magus*.

At the same time, certain recurrent motifs do accumulate and cohere: the writer's sense of himself as dislocated, as a romantic in exile; the technophobe at odds with a world of computers and virtual reality; the need for solitude and for the green, regenerative retreat; the sacred combe that is part of and fundamental to his passionate love of the natural world ("Solitude—in exile geographically and socially—is essential for me").[1]

The interview with Dianne Vipond with which this book ends is the most recent of the many interviews given by Fowles over the years. Here we find him reflecting upon and amplifying many of the issues and concerns that have emerged in the preceding pages. In some matters, Fowles's

---

1. Journal entry for July 7, 1951.

views have remained remarkably consistent since he first became known as a writer in the 1960s; but where his views have changed or shifted ground, this interview provides a useful and illuminating update.

The first section—Writing and the Self—includes the most explicitly autobiographical of Fowles's nonfiction writing, and it is here (though not only here) that we find his most confessional statements about the guilty pleasures of what he calls the godgame of writing fiction. Writing, it seems, is a sexy business. Fiction making, the creating of another world, is a "haunting, isolating, and guilt-ridden experience"; his characters need "constant caressing"; he falls in love with his heroines and is, if only imaginatively, unfaithful to his wife with every novel he writes. His relationship with the novel, for the duration of its writing, is like an affair, full of guilts, anxieties, secret delights. "Such pleasures," he says, "are unholy."

There are more infidelities in the travel writing—with *la sauvage* and *agria Ellada*, both shatteringly beautiful, remote, and bounteous in their offerings. The first, of course, is France, the France of "endless obscure countrysides and lost villages," where Fowles first discovered the lost domain that was to haunt him, and his fiction, forever: the Sologne of Alain-Fournier's *Le Grand Meaulnes*, the wild France of Fowles the latter-day Romantic. With *agria Ellada*, or "wild Hellas," he has had, since falling "hopelessly, overwhelmingly in love on the first day of arrival," a lifelong love affair. Although there may be some repetition and echoes between the two pieces on Greece here, this was clearly an experience that was so important, so impressive—in the sense of making a mark, an impress—that I had no hesitation in including both.

The title of the second section, Culture and Society, is a conscious allusion to the work of the great Marxist critic and writer Raymond Williams, and here I have included John's most openly political commentary. It is, in fact, rare for him to make overt political statements, though he is quite open—trenchantly so—in his adherence to left-wing politics, socialism, and republicanism, even while declaring a pox on all political parties!

In his essay on the Falklands war, Fowles deplores the way in which party politics have been reduced by the media to low-grade public entertainment, and laments the irresponsible use of language for party-political ends. "The one thing we [writers] learn from our profession (and share with the politicians) is the frightening capacity of the image and the word to trigger buried things, and to drown sober reason," he writes. History indeed has provided us with ample evidence of that power and the horrors it can unleash. But then there is a recoil, prompted perhaps by memories of that evidence—an unwillingness to stand so close to the politician: "Bad and self-indulgent art hurts few; bad and self-indulgent politics hurts millions." Few of us would disagree with the latter part of this statement, but I for one do not believe that bad art is innocuous, any more than I believe that good art is impotent. Fowles's art is a committed art; it is neither morally nor politically neutral. The duty of all art, he asserts in his "Recollections of Kafka," "is in some way to improve society at large," and this is affirmed in the Vipond interview. Writers, he says, have inherited a moral and ethical function from the clerics of the Middle Ages, whose domain was also literature. Like D. H. Lawrence, whom he so much admires (in spite of my efforts as a good feminist to persuade him otherwise!), Fowles is a self-confessed didact. Lawrence believed that the purpose of the novel was to teach, which is largely why F. R. Leavis canonized and elevated him to one of the "great tradition." Would Leavis, one wonders, have done the same for John Fowles? Certainly Fowles writes, as Lawrence wrote, to be heard; and as he writes of Lawrence, he himself is constantly trying, like a good preacher, to save us, and wringing his hands at our apparent collective unwillingness to be saved.

The writers who seem to speak most strongly to Fowles, with whom he seems to feel the greatest sense of connection, are those who for one reason or another have shared his own sense of exile, his sense of being an outsider of some kind, or, in his own words, a "crusty recluse, a hermit." As I assembled the essays for the third section here, I was intrigued by the accumulation of evidence of John's predilection for literary "sports," historical odd-bods, dissenters of one sort or another, whether in their choice of subject matter or in their personae.

With Ebenezer Le Page, the subject and "fictional alter ego" created by G. B. Edwards, Fowles shares a "querulousness over the new" and a sense of being excluded from the modern world. For Fowles, this is the postindustrial world of virtual reality and information technology; for Edwards himself it was a "kind of againstness, or bloody-mindedness," the characteristics of the lifelong dissenter with whom Fowles clearly identifies. The Channel Island world of Ebenezer Le Page becomes a metaphor for the "island of the self," with its fierce resistance to anyone or anything attempting occupation or colonization.

John Aubrey, best known for his *Brief Lives*, was another lonely maverick, fervent conservationist, fellow magpie, and dissenter from all orthodoxies. And with his contemporary William Golding, Fowles also seems to share a sense of being a kind of intellectual expatriate. "Ideas," as he quotes from another writer in an earlier essay, "are the only motherland."[2] Nor is this identification with his subjects confined to members of his own sex. Ann Lee, the subject of Fowles's most recent novel, *A Maggot*, and founder of the Shakers, was one of the great dissenters of the eighteenth century and, though not represented in this collection, has long been one of John's heroines. Another heroine who *is* included here is Marie de France, the twelfth-century writer of the *Lais*, about whose life we know very little, but whose writing tells us that she was highly educated, extremely successful, very wise, and rather wicked. Almost certainly, whatever her professed allegiances, she was another intellectual expatriate.

Alain-Fournier, the writer to whom Fowles "still feel[s] closer" than to any other novelist, living or dead, was clearly a fellow nympholept. The importance of his only novel, *Le Grand Meaulnes* (irreverently referred to as "The Great Moan" by some of the less reverent of John's friends), to the life and work of Fowles has been fully and ably documented by critics and scholars, as well as by John himself, and this is not the place for yet another critical analysis. Yet something must be said here, since its central theme, the idea of the lost *domaine*, constitutes what I believe we may call John's life myth. It speaks of something always already lost—a mythical Garden of Eden, some golden age of childhood innocence, or, in psychoanalytic terms, the idealized mother of infancy, as suggested by Gilbert Rose in Fowles's revealingly autobiographical essay "Hardy and the Hag." In the same essay, Fowles universalizes this state—"The universal condition of mankind [is] a state of loss," he writes—but in his revised foreword to *The Magus* he speaks, also, of its special importance to the writer. "Loss is essential for the novelist," he says, and "immensely fertile for his books, however painful to his private being." He is not the only writer to have made this observation and connection. Günter Grass, for instance, has written similarly of his own sense of exile and loss: "Language didn't compensate me for my loss, but by stringing words together I was able to make something in which my loss could be declared. . . . Loss has given me a voice. Only what is entirely lost demands to be endlessly named: there is a

---

2. Claire de Duras, *Ourika* (1824). See "Notes on an Unfinished Novel" in section I.

mania to call the lost thing until it returns. Without loss there would be no literature."[3]

Paradise lost, then. But Paradise is regained, time and again, in the green retreats, the sacred combes and *bons vaux* that figure so significantly in the fictional work and in the life. Fournier's hero is an adolescent when he finds his lost *domaine* in the French countryside, as John was when he had what was then called a nervous breakdown and, at the same time, moved to Devon, where he discovered his own private Eden in his relationship with nature, wildlife, and the landscape. It's a relationship that has sustained him throughout his life, as his journals testify. Undoubtedly it has provided some kind of check or balance to the sense of loss: a solace, a refuge, a sense of evolutionary continuity. In the novels, it's at the very point where the two things converge—the driving sense of loss and the consolatory green retreat—that we find the lost *domaine*. In the life, it's the daily contact with the wild as well as the cultivated parts of his garden, and his intimate, "hands-on" experience of nature—the year's first snowdrop, a sighting of a rare bird or bug, a new colony of orchids to be visited—that clearly provide the wellspring of the writer's life force and creativity.

The haunting presence that inhabits the lost *domaine* is, of course, the figure of the *princesse lointaine*, the archetypally unattainable woman, and its supplement is John's self-confessed nympholepsy—that perverse but persistent condition of desire for the unattainable which in his case is so paradoxically productive.

These writers and their subjects, then, tend to reflect the quirks and preoccupations—the obsessional maggots—of Fowles himself. The subject of two of the essays in this collection, Thomas Hardy, is perhaps rather a special case. Again there is an identification with a fellow self-exile, and again there is a recognition of the sense of loss and its corollary, literary fertility. Of Hardy's attempt to cut himself off from his past, Fowles writes that the "deep sense of loss this self-exile engenders, the guilt, the sense of the wasteful futility of human history, are a very valuable thing for a writer, since they are also a deep source of energy in creation." But Hardy is a literary giant, one whose shadow (in the metaphorical and the Jungian sense) cannot be avoided—a literary mentor and father figure who, according to Fowles, shared the experience of writing as an "onanistic and taboo-laden pursuit." More guilty pleasures. Indeed, the Hardy poem with which

---

3. "Losses," *Granta* 42 (Winter 1992).

Fowles prefaces his essay "Hardy and the Hag"—a metaphorical striptease whereby the young goddess attained and enjoyed during the night emerges with the dawn as loathsome, rotten, haglike—speaks disturbingly of a terror that goes beyond pleasure. If the satisfaction of the desire is also (as it must be, however temporarily) the death of the desire, and if that death is experienced, as Hardy's poem suggests, as a foul and shameful corruption, then nympholepsy—the rejection of the attainable (from the "need to avoid consummation") in favor of the unattainable object of desire that may be gazed upon but never carnally enjoyed—is an obvious psychological response. Fowles's essay on Hardy's novel *The Well-Beloved* probably reveals at least as much about himself as about his subject; and if the "shared predicament" has, as he tells us, been painful and problematic in daily life, it has also been, for both writers, extraordinarily and indispensably important for the imaginative and creative life.

John Fowles's main private interest—passion, even—is, and has always been, natural history and (as the title of the final essay in this collection indicates) the nature of nature. In recent years that passion has been fueled by anger, as the last group of essays bears witness. It is an anger born out of the rage and despair of the ardent conservationist who sees what he loves desecrated and dying; it is directed at those who are seen to be "murdering nature and natural landscape the world over."

In "Land," Fowles takes on the more complex question of nature and representation, speaking of his suspicion of landscape photography. What he seeks in landscape is, he says, the "personal and direct experience of it," that intimate connection which is so professionally generative and personally regenerative. There is anger, too, at the spurious sentimentality of those who would purvey only prettiness and nostalgia in their views of the English countryside—the legacy of a decadent romanticism. Fowles, like Hardy—and like the poet John Clare, that other nature writer whom he so admires—never forgets that "rural life can be obscene, stupid, and cruel," so that even as he cherishes the myth of the sacred combe, *les bons vaux*, he always insists on an honest recognition of the often harsh realities of rural, agricultural life. He reckons that his experience of practical farming all through the 1940s, though far more poetic than practical, has deeply marked his life, and he is most proud of having written the first chapter of *Daniel Martin* in honor of that closeness. Nature, for Fowles, commands respect above all things; not sentimentality, not nostalgia, not romantic representation. When not angry, the writings about nature often take on an elegiac tone, a mourning for what is already lost, a pleading for the conservation and survival of what is left. Reading these pieces is like listening to the "loud lament of the disconsolate chimera," as Eliot puts it in his "Four Quartets"; as if the voice that speaks had a strong sense of crying in the wilderness, of being "the Word in the desert." One of the bees in Fowles's bonnet is the "lethal perversion" of the collector—another of the themes that inflect and inform his fiction. Clegg, the repellent hero of *The Collector*, is the archetype of all those natural-history collectors who "in the end collect the same thing: the death of the living"—a statement central to Fowles's relationship to nature and the natural world.

More than once in these writings, Fowles makes contrite reference to his own early collecting habits, and confesses that he first came to nature "through hunting it with both gun and rod." Later, he not only relinquished all such pursuits, but came to despise most "collecting and hoarding activities . . . however useful they may claim to be scientifically," since they bring out the very worst in man. Here the gendered language is conscious and deliberate. (Gendered language has been something of an editorial difficulty; wherever possible without changing the sense or sacrificing the elegance of Fowles's prose, I have altered gender-specific language—*man* meaning "humanity," for instance—to more politically correct usage.) Throughout his extended (over a lifetime) critique of *man's* iniquitous collecting habits, Fowles exempts woman from blame. Women, for Fowles, are natural conservationists; man, that "vicious parasitical predator," is the greedy, guilty party. Perhaps it is not surprising that this should be so. Nature, after all, is consistently identified as female (problematically so, for many feminists), and so long as this is the case, "man" will probably continue to treat nature as he has traditionally treated women—as semisentient, unpredictable, something to be tamed, colonized, exploited, and occasionally placated—whereas women's fellow feeling for nature may continue to keep them on the side of the angels, ecologically speaking.

Natural historian he may be, but what Fowles advocates in the final essay here is the cultivation of the poetic and Keatsian (or MacCaigian), rather than the scientific and Linnaean, relationship to nature. For Fowles, the only (possibly) forgivable form of collecting is bibliophily, and even then, a certain puritanism forbids him the purchase of first editions and expensive rare books. Here at least, though, the thrill of the chase, and of the find, is permissible.

.   .   .

But I have said enough of guilty pleasures. It is time now for the reader's pleasure—the pleasure of the text. The writings that follow may have a didactic function, may be controversial, may have a "use value," but they are also superbly entertaining, vital, varied, and beautifully crafted. For having myself been a kind of collector in assembling them, I make no apology whatsoever, since they are not to keep but to offer; not to hoard but to share.

JAN RELF
MAY 1997

WORMHOLES

I

AUTOBIOGRAPHICAL: WRITING AND THE SELF

All my life, though sometimes all too erratically and spas-modically, I have kept a diary, in which I perhaps foolishly imagine the real me, as opposed to the phony John Fowles, the public pseudo-person, may be found. But to say that all the essays here are "not really me" is a sort of shamefaced ex-cuse I do not seek. I do believe everything that is said here, and I know it is absurd to say I wish it had been expressed better. I hope that one day the diaries will be published. They are now in the safekeeping of Exeter University, and I trust will finally be in the Harry Ransom Humanities Research Center at Austin, Texas. That is where my ego, my self, for what it is worth, will lie.

J. F.

I WRITE THEREFORE I AM
(1964)

I have never really wanted to be a novelist. For me the word carries a load of bad connotations—like *author* and *literature* and *reviewer*, only worse. It suggests something factitious as well as fictitious, insipidly entertaining; train-journeyish. One can't imagine a "novelist"'s ever saying what he actually means or feels—one can hardly even imagine his meaning or feeling.

These words have bad connotations because they suggest that in some way writing and being a writer aren't central human activities.

I've always wanted to write (in this order) poems, philosophy, and only then novels. I wouldn't even put the whole category of activity—writing—first on my list of ambitions. My first ambition has always been to alter the society I live in; that is, to affect other lives. I think I begin to agree with Marx-Lenin: writing is a very second-rate way of bringing about a revolution. But I recognize that all I am capable of is writing. I am a writer. Not a doer.

Society, existing among other human beings, challenges me, so I have to choose my weapon. I choose writing; but the thing that comes first is that I am challenged.

A publisher accepted *The Collector* in July 1962. I had been deliberately living in the wilderness; that is, doing work I could never really love, precisely because I was afraid that I might fall in love with my work and then forever afterwards be one of those sad, faded myriads among the intelligentsia who have always had vague literary ambitions but have never quite made it. I chose ten years ago to be a writer—chose in the existentialist sense of the act of choosing; that is, I have constantly had to renew the choice and to live in anguish because I so often doubted whether it was the right one. So I have turned down better jobs; I have staked everything on this one choice. Partly it had been a conscious existentialist choice, partly something in my blood, in the Cornish quarter of me, perhaps. I think, now, that even if the book had not been accepted, even if I should never have had any book accepted, I was right to live by such a choice. Because I am surrounded by people who have not chosen themselves, in this sense, but who have let themselves be chosen—by money, by status symbols, by jobs—and I don't know which are sadder, those who know this or those who don't. This is why I feel isolated from most people—just isolated, most of the time. Occasionally content to be so.

Stained glass, engraved glass, frosted glass: give me plain glass.

At a literary party. Frogs and oxen. The frogs are the magazine and newspaper men, the agency men, the publishers, who rather pathetically try to equate knowing writers with actually creating something; the oxen are the writers, who are castrated by their own self-interest, their own vanities, their "shop." Both frogs and oxen are very well by themselves; but the syzygy is fatal. Their chatter deafens me, and I feel like Alice at the tea party. They are not even good "material."

Money makes me happy to the extent that it brings me more time to write. But it also brings me proportionately sharper doubts about my ability to write; existentialist doubts about whether I have *really* earned the freedom to write. The present perfect is the appropriate tense here because these doubts are about both past and present performance. I always have to write something every day. A day when I write nothing is a desert.

In January of 1963 I decided to leave work. I can't imagine myself as a professional writer. Writing has always been with me a semireligious occupation, by which I certainly don't mean that I regard it with pious awe, but rather that I can't regard it simply as a craft, a job. I know when I am writing well that I am writing with more than the sum of my acquired knowledge, skill, and experience; with something from outside myself.

Inspiration, the muse experience, is like telepathy. Nowadays one hardly dares to say that inexplicable phenomena exist for fear of being kicked in the balls by the positivists and the behaviorists and the other hyperscientists. But there is a metatechnics that needs investigating.

I don't think of myself as "giving up work to be a writer." I'm giving up work to, at last, *be*.

To a career man, I suppose, the decision would seem lunatic; perhaps even courageous. But a bank vault is secure; an atomic shelter is secure; death is secure. Security is one of the prison walls of the affluent society; even since the *pax Romana*, being safe has been an unhealthy mega-European obsession.

Why have I got it in for the novel? Because it has been shifted away from life, whatever, as Wittgenstein put it, is the case, these last fifty years. Circumstances have imposed this shift. It is not the novelists' fault. In the eighteenth and nineteenth centuries the novel was at one remove from life. But since the advent of film and television and sound recording it is at two removes. The novel is now generally about things and events which the other forms of art describe rather better.

All the purely visual and aural sequences in the modern novel are a bore, both to read and to write. People's physical appearance, their movements, their sounds, places, moods of places—the camera and the microphone enregister these twenty times better than the typewriter. If the novel is to survive it must one day narrow its field to what other systems of recording can't record. I say "one day" because the reading public still isn't very aware of what I call mischanneling—that is, using the wrong art form to express or convey what you mean.

In other words, to write a novel in 1964 is to be neurotically aware of trespassing, especially on the domain of the cinema. Of course, very few of us ever get the chance to express ourselves on film. (Having one's book filmed is equivalent to having a luxury illustrated edition; it is *not* expressing oneself on film.) So over the novel today hangs a *faute de mieux*. All of us under forty write cinematically; our imaginations, constantly fed on films, "shoot" scenes, and we write descriptions of what has been shot. So for us a lot of novel writing is, or seems like, the tedious translating of an unmade and never-to-be-made film into words.

I don't know which is worse, having the words and lacking the ideas, or the reverse. I think the former, not just because the latter happens to be my case but because I believe (as in most other things, against Pascal) that if it comes to the crunch—in great novels it never does—good ideas are more important than good words. That is what I dislike about some post-war American novels. Almost all the younger American novelists write technically so much better than we (the British) do. They have much more skill at describing, at cutting, at dialogue, at all the machinery; and then at the end one takes the sunglasses off, and something's gone wrong. One hasn't a tan. The whole process with them seems (even when it isn't) artificial, frozen-food; cleverly mixed, à-la-modish (even when it's not meant to be); sound, in creative-writing terms. But humanly, or in some other vague old European way, unsound.

Perhaps I'm simply justifying my own technical deficiencies. I sweat from ideas (ideas proper, symbolism, plots) to words (the page); and maybe there are writers in America who feel that they are sweating their way from their easily composed pages to their hard-come-by ideas.

It is the dramatic psychosexual implications of isolating extreme situations[1] that excite and interest me; I have never found them very important as aids to analysis from Freudian or Jungian points of view. Perhaps this is because I have for many years worked in predominantly female environments and I am a feminist—that is, I like women and enjoy their company, and not only for sexual reasons. Quite apart from this, the only sort of relationship, with men or women, that has ever had any interest for me is the I-thou one. I am an ochlophobe; for me three is always a potential mob.

In *The Collector* I tried to write in terms of the strictest realism; to go straight back to that supreme master of the fake biography, Defoe, for the surface "feel" of the book. To Jane Austen and Peacock for the girl. To Sartre and Camus for the "climate." It is only very naïf critics who think that all one's influences must be contemporary. In the noosphere there are no dates; only sympathies, admirations, allergies, loathings.

The kind of British novel I have no time for is what I call the *novel of fun*—variations on the old picaresque novel done in the debased contemporary rococo. I don't blame the writers of such novels—not much, anyway—but I do blame the reviewers and literary publicity men who seem

---

1. Imprisonment is only the most extreme of a whole group of allied situations: the stuck lift (as used brilliantly by Bergman in *A Lesson in Love*), the shipwreck or aircrash (Golding), the desert island (Defoe to Antonioni), the jungle, the yacht, the room (Ionesco and Pinter), the lonely house (the Brontës), the car in the fog, and so on.

to have erected Fun (from funny farce to funny satire) as the great dipstick of literary worth. For this reason I class all writers as either entertainers or preachers; I'm not against entertainers, but I am against their present hegemony.

I think this trend in the British novel springs not only from our endemic refusal to take writing in general seriously, but in particular from a contemporary refusal to take European writing seriously. I see no future in the sort of isolationist attitude that Kingsley Amis has popularized. I loathe John Bull at the best of times; but John Bull in blue jeans is the bloody end. I'm sick to death of the inarticulate hero. To hell with the inarticulate. Pity the slobs, but don't glorify them.

I was on jury duty at the Old Bailey in May 1961. The law may be very fine, but there is no justice. A mental defective with five children, who had thrown the incestuously begotten baby of his eldest daughter into a furnace, stood fumbling and weeping in the dock. A nakedness of suffering and horror filled the court; all his children were imbeciles, his wife had left him, he had no money, no relations, nothing except his heavy dirty-nailed hands and his tears. I wanted to jump up and cry out. We did not judge him; he was the judge, and he judged the whole of existence. I know by reason that there cannot be a God; I felt it, with my whole being, before that bowed figure. Being an atheist is a matter not of moral choice, but of human obligation.

I feel I have three main politicosocial obligations. First to be an atheist. Second, not to belong to any political party. Third, not to belong to any bloc, organization, group, clique, or school whatever. The first because even if there is a God, it is safer for humankind to act on the assumption that there is not (the famous Pascalian *pari* in reverse); and the second and the third because individual freedom is in danger, and as much in the West as in the East. The virtue of the West is not that it is easier to be free here, but that if one is free one doesn't have to pretend, as one does behind the Iron Curtain, that one is not.

I read French at Oxford and, historically, still know French literature rather better than English. Gradually I have come to feel that this is a blessing, not a liability. It makes me by acquired instinct more interested in what I say than in how I say it; it makes me impatient with the feeble insularity of so much English writing (France is, among other things, what we were always too hypocritical or too puritanical or too class-ridden or too empire-spirited to be). And at the same time it makes me proud of certain aspects of England and English literature. Great cultures reflect each other; and even if the only reason for getting to know France and the French mind were to rediscover one's Englishness, it would still be a sufficient reason; and a sufficient reason to despise all those eternal Anglo-Saxon provincials who think of France as a trivial Petit Trianon beside the solid gray magnificence of our Windsor Castle.

I don't want to be an English writer; I want to be a European one, what I call a mega-European (Europe plus America plus Russia plus wherever else the culture is essentially European). This isn't vaulting ambition o'er-leaping itself, but plain common sense. What is the point of writing just to be read in England? I don't even want to be English. English is my language, but I am a mega-European.

The Atlas situation: carrying the world on one's shoulders. Every writer must feel this: the world he or she has created crushing down, piling him or her into the ground. Sometimes you feel it as you read the book. The novel has steamrollered the novelist. Or the reverse happens: the world is a bubble of air, and the Atlas-novelist stands flexed like a Mack Sennett weight lifter, magnificently upholding nothing. What I look for is the poise, the concord, the exact agreement between the strength of the Atlas and the weight of his or her world. Flaubert, for example. Or Jane Austen.

I very much dislike having to document, as if climbing a pitch where the rock is treacherous. I dislike all the places where the imagination is helpless and mere documentation takes over. I want to be "true to life"—but by "life" I mean my limited knowledge of objective reality, not necessarily the scientific, linguistic, or statistical reality I might get if I spent months interviewing people and swotting up textbooks. It seems to me that this is a new problem (or an old one much aggravated) for writers: just how much use they should make of all the modern means of recording what objects actually look like, how people sound, and so on. Some American creative-writing courses apparently encourage the documentary approach. For me this will always represent a fundamental heresy. A novel is one person's view of life, not a collage of documentations.

. . .

The *nouveau roman* school makes me ashamed to be a Francophile. Its adherents have done nothing that Sartre did not do better in a couple of paragraphs in *La Nausée*, For me there are four great post-1918 French novels—Céline's *Voyage au bout de la nuit*, Malraux's *La Condition Humaine*, *La Nausée*, and Camus's *La Peste*. The are all novels that face life in some way, even though in the *Voyage* it is only to attack it. There is no back-turning, no commitment to total noncommitment. I suspect the *nouveau roman* is best treated as one of the periodic French fugues across the Rhine; as cultural amnesia, in other words. Of course these writers sense, as we all do, that the novel has got itself into a dangerous situation. But the way out of an impasse is not to sit down and describe the wall at the end.

The one thing a modern writer should not be committed to: a style. The next great mega-European writer will write in all the styles, as Picasso has painted and Stravinsky composed. This does not mean a loss of identity. The loss of identity occurs in the sacrifice of everything to the fear of loss of identity. The first English writer to accept this was Defoe.

This is the wretched loneliness of writing: constantly having to judge between judgments—other people's and one's own—and never really knowing what standards others judge by. But fearing the worst.

I have a special complaint. It is that so many practicing novelists review novels. In music and art such judgment by interested rivals is almost unheard-of, and I wish it were so with books.

The really bad reviewers so stand and posture in front of the books they are supposed to be reviewing that the books themselves are totally obscured; and on the principle that naked devils aren't dangerous, one needn't worry too much about them. The reviewers I can't stand are the ones who give the impression that all novel writing is a more or less reprehensible exhibition of infantilism. Adults write reviews; children write novels.

I don't want some passive thing: to be sold, to be read. Writing is active, and the kind of writing I have always admired, and shall always want to achieve, makes reading active too—the book reads the reader, as radar reads the unknown. And the unknown ones, the readers, feel this.

·   ·   ·

In this money-and-amusement-mad Western world of ours, all the creative acts of preacher-artists (their declarations about themselves as well as their artefacts) are suspect—every false or clumsy move they make is pounced on as hypocrisy, as arrogance, as naïveté—and the pressures on them, inner as well as outer, are all such as to destroy whatever authenticity they have tried to establish in their ways of living and writing; and this is so whether they are in economic terms "successes" or "failures." When Miranda talks about the Few, in *The Collector*, this is the kind of people I meant her to mean: preeminently creators, not simply highly intelligent or well-informed people, nor people who are simply skilled with words.

Such writers can't help being what they are, nor do they cease to belong to the Few if they reject the concept. They are of the Few as this man is born left-handed and this, Chinese. They have no choice about freedom; they have to be free. And this is what isolates them, still, even when all the other barriers between them and the Many, the Profane Mob, are down.

NOTES ON AN
UNFINISHED NOVEL
(1969)

The novel I am writing at the moment (provisionally entitled *The French Lieutenant's Woman*) is set about a hundred years back. I don't think of it as a historical novel, a genre in which I have very little interest. It started four or five months ago, as a visual image. A woman stands at the end of a deserted quay and stares out to sea. That was all. This image rose in my mind one morning when I was still in bed half asleep. It corresponded to no actual incident in my life (or in art) that I can recall, though I have for many years collected obscure books and forgotten prints—all sorts of flotsam and jetsam from the last two or three centuries, relics of past lives—and I suppose this leaves me with a sort of dense hinterland from which such images percolate down to the coast of consciousness.

These mythopoeic "stills" (they seem almost always static) float into my mind very often. I ignore them, since that is the best way of finding whether they really are the door into a new world.

So I ignored this image; but it recurred. Imperceptibly it stopped coming to me. I began deliberately to recall it and to try to analyze and hypothesize why it held some sort of immanent power. It was obviously mysterious. It was vaguely romantic. It also seemed, perhaps because of the latter quality, not to belong to today. The woman obstinately refused to stare out of the window of an airport lounge; it had to be this ancient quay—and as I happen to live near one, so near that I can see it from the bottom of my garden, it soon became a specific ancient quay. The woman had no face, no particular degree of sexuality. But she was Victorian; and since I always saw her in the same static long shot, with her back turned, she represented a reproach on the Victorian age. An outcast. I didn't know her crime, but I wished to protect her. That is, I began to fall in love with her. Or with her stance. I didn't know which.

This (not literally) pregnant female image came at a time (the autumn of 1966) when I was already halfway through another novel and had three or four others planned to follow it. It was an interference, but of such power that it soon came to make the previously planned work seem the intrusive element in my life. This accidentality of inspiration has to be allowed for in writing, both in the work one is on (unplanned development of character, unintended incidents, and so on) and in one's work as a whole. Follow the accident, fear the fixed plan—that is the rule.

Narcissism, or pygmalionism, is the essential vice a writer must have. Characters (and even situations) are like children or lovers: they need constant caressing, concern, listening to, watching, admiring. All these occupations become tiring for the active partner—the writer—and only something akin to love can provide the energy. I've heard people say, "I want to write a book." But wanting to write a book, however ardently, is not enough. Even to say "I want to be possessed by my own creations" is not enough; all natural or born writers are possessed, and in the old magical sense, by their own imaginations long before they even begin to think of writing.

This fluke genesis must break all the rules of creative writing, must sound at best childlike, at worst childish. I suppose the orthodox method is to work out what one wants to say and what one has experience of, and then to correlate the two. I have tried that method and started out with an analytically arrived-at theme and a set of characters all neatly standing for something; but the manuscripts have all petered out miserably. *The Magus* (written before *The Collector*, which also originated in a single image) sprang from a very trivial visit to a villa on a Greek island; nothing in the least unusual happened. But in my unconscious I kept arriving at the place again and again; something wanted to happen there, something that had not happened to me at the time. Why it should have been at *that* villa, *that* one visit, among so many thousands of other possible launching pads, I do not know. Only a month ago someone showed me some recent photographs of the villa, which is now deserted; and it was just a deserted villa. Its mysterious significance to me fifteen years ago remains mysterious.

Once the seed germinates, reason and knowledge, culture and all the rest have to start to grow it. You cannot create a world by hot instinct; only by cold experience. That is one good reason so many novelists produce nothing until, or do all their best work after, the age of forty.

I find it very difficult to write if I don't know I shall have several days absolutely clear. All visits, all intrusions, all daily duties become irksome. This is during the first draft. I wrote the first draft of *The Collector* in under a month; sometimes ten thousand words a day. Of course a lot of it was poorly written and had to be endlessly amended and revised. First-draft and revision writing are so different they hardly seem to belong to the same activity. I never do any "research" until the first draft is finished; all that matters to begin with is the flow, the story, the narrating. Having research material then is like swimming in a straitjacket.

During the revision period I try to keep some sort of discipline. I make myself revise whether I feel like it or not; in some ways, the more disinclined and dyspeptic one feels, the better—one is harsher with oneself. All the best cutting is done when one is sick of the writing.

But all this advice from senior writers to establish a discipline always, to get down a thousand words a day whatever one's mood, I find an absurdly puritanical and impractical approach. Writing is like eating or making love: a natural process, not an artificial one. Write, if you must, because you feel like writing; never because you feel you ought to write.

I write memoranda to myself about the book I'm on. On this one: *You are not trying to write something one of the Victorian novelists forgot to write; but perhaps something one of them failed to write.* And: *Remember the etymology of the word. A novel is something new. It must have relevance to the writer's now— so don't ever pretend you live in 1867; or make sure the reader knows it's a pretense.*

In the matter of clothes, social manners, historical background, and the rest, writing about 1867 is merely a question of research. But I soon get into trouble over dialogue, because the genuine dialogue of 1867 (insofar as it can be heard in books of the time) is far too close to our own to sound convincingly old. It very often fails to agree with our psychological picture of the Victorians—it is not stiff enough, not euphemistic enough, and so on—so here at once I have to start cheating and pick out the more formal and archaic (even for 1867) elements of spoken speech. It is this kind of "cheating," which is intrinsic to the novel, that takes the most time.

Even in modern-novel dialogue, the most real is not the most conformable to actual current speech. One has only to read a transcribed tape of actual conversation to realize that it is, in the literary context, not very real. Novel dialogue is a form of shorthand, an *impression* of what people actually say; and besides that it has to perform other functions—keep the narrative moving (which real conversation rarely does), reveal character (real conversation often hides it), and so on.

This is the greatest technical problem I have; it is hard enough with modern characters, and doubly so with historical ones.

Memorandum: *If you want to be true to life, start lying about the reality of it.*

And: *One cannot describe reality; only give metaphors that indicate it. All human modes of description (photographic, mathematical, and the rest, as well as literary) are metaphorical. Even the most precise scientific description of an object or movement is a tissue of metaphors.*

Alain Robbe-Grillet's polemical essay "Pour un nouveau roman" (1963) is indispensable reading for the profession, even where it produces no more than total disagreement. His key question: *Why bother to write in a form whose great masters cannot be surpassed?* The fallacy of one of his conclusions—that we must discover a new form to write in if the novel is to survive—is obvious. It reduces the purpose of the novel to the discovery of new forms, whereas its other purposes—to entertain, to satirize, to describe new sensibilities, to record life, to improve life, and so on—are clearly just as viable and important. But his obsessive pleading for new form places a kind of stress on every passage one writes today. To what extent am I being a coward by writing inside the old tradition? To what extent am I being panicked into avant-gardism? Writing about 1867 doesn't lessen the stress; it increases it, since so much of the subject matter must of its historical nature be "traditional." There are apparent parallels in other arts: Stravinsky's eighteenth-century rehandlings, Picasso's and Francis Bacon's use of Velázquez. But in this context, words are not nearly so tractable as musical notes or brushstrokes. One can parody a rococo musical ornament, a baroque face. Very early on I tried, in a test chapter, to put modern dialogue into Victorian mouths. But the effect was absurd, since the real historical nature of the characters is hopelessly distorted; the only people to get away with this (Julius Caesar speaking with a Brooklyn accent, and so on) are the professional funny men. One is led inevitably, by such a technique, into a comic novel.

My two previous novels were both based on more or less disguised existentialist premises. I want this one to be no exception; and so I am trying to show an existentialist awareness before it was chronologically possible. Kierkegaard was, of course, totally unknown to the British and American Victorians; but it has always seemed to me that the Victorian age, especially from 1850 on, was highly existentialist in many of its personal dilemmas. One can almost invert the reality and say that Camus and Sartre have been trying to lead us, in their fashion, to a Victorian seriousness of purpose and moral sensitivity.

Nor is this the only similarity between the 1960s and the 1860s. The great nightmare of the respectable Victorian mind was the only too real one created by the geologist Lyell and the biologist Darwin. Until then man had lived like a child in a small room. They gave him—and never was a present less welcome—infinite space and time, and a hideously mechanistic explanation of human reality into the bargain. Just as we "live with the bomb," the Victorians lived with the theory of evolution. They were hurled into space. They felt themselves infinitely isolated. By the 1860s the great iron structures of their philosophies, religions, and social stratifications were already beginning to look dangerously corroded to the more perspicacious.

Just such a man, an existentialist before his time, walks down the quay and sees that mysterious back, feminine, silent, also existentialist, facing the sea and turned on him.

Magnificent though the Victorian novelists were, they almost all (an exception, of course, is the later Hardy) failed miserably in one aspect: nowhere in "respectable" Victorian literature (and most of the pornography was based on the brothel—or on eighteenth-century accounts) does one see a man and a woman described together in bed. We do not know how they made love, what they said to each other in their most intimate moments, what they felt then.

Writing, as I have been today, about two Victorians making love—with no guides except my imagination and vague deductions from the spirit of the age and so on—is really science fiction. A journey is a journey, backwards or forwards.

. . .

The most difficult task for a writer is to get the right "voice" for his or her material; by "voice" I mean the overall impression one has of the creator behind what he or she creates. I've always liked the ironic voice that the line of the great nineteenth-century novelists, from Austen through to Conrad, all used so naturally. We tend today to remember the failures of that tone—the satirical overkill in Dickens, the facetiousness of Thackeray, the strained sarcasm of Mark Twain, the priggishness in George Eliot— rather than its virtues. The reason is clear enough: irony needs the assumption of superiority in the ironist. Such an assumption must be anathema to a democratic, egalitarian century like our own. We suspect people who pretend to be omniscient; and that is why so many of us twentieth-century novelists feel driven into first-person narration.

I have heard writers claim that this first-person technique is a last bastion of the novel against the cinema, a form where the camera dictates an inevitable third-person point of view of what happens, however much we may identify with one character. But the matter of whether a contemporary novelist uses "he" or "I" is largely irrelevant. The great majority of modern third-person narration is "I" narration very thinly disguised. The real "I" of the Victorian writers—the writer himself or herself—is as rigorously repressed there (out of fear of seeming pretentious, etc.) as it is, for obvious semantic and grammatical reasons, when the narration is in literal first-person form.

But in this new book I shall try to resurrect this technique. It seems in any case natural to look back at the England of a hundred years ago with a somewhat ironical eye—and "I"—though it is my strong belief that history is horizontal in terms of the ratio between understanding and *available* knowledge, and (far more important) horizontal in terms of the happiness the individual gets from being alive. In short, there is a danger in being ironic about the apparent follies and miseries of any past age. So I have written myself another memorandum: *You are not the "I" who breaks into the illusion, but the "I" who is a part of it.*

In other words, the "I" who will make the first-person commentaries here and there in my story, and who will finally even enter it, will not be my real "I" in 1967, but much more just another character, though in a different category from the purely fictional ones.

An illustration. Here is the beginning of a minor novel (*Lovel the Wid-ower* [1861]) by Thackeray:

> *Who shall be the hero of this tale? Not I who write it. I am but the Chorus*
> *of the Play. I make remarks on the conduct of the characters: I narrate their*
> *simple story.*

Today I think we should assume (not knowing who the writer was) that the "I" here is the writer's "I." For three or four pages more we might still just believe this; but then suddenly Thackeray introduces his eponymous hero as "my friend Lovel," and we see we've been misled. "I" is simply an-other character. But then a few pages on, the "I" cuts in again in the de-scription of a character:

> *She never could speak. Her voice was as hoarse as a fishwoman's. Can that*
> *immense stout old-box-keeper at the* —————— *theatre . . . be the once bril-*
> *liant Emily Montanville? I am told there are no lady box-keepers in the*
> *English theatres. This, I submit, is a proof of my consummate care and arti-*
> *fice in rescuing from a prurient curiosity the individual personages from*
> *whom the characters of the present story are taken. Montanville is not a box-*
> *opener. She may, under another name, keep a trinket-shop in the Burling-*
> *ton Arcade, for what you know: but this secret no torture shall induce me to*
> *divulge. Life has its rises and downfalls, and you have had yours, you hob-*
> *bling old creature. Montanville, indeed! Go thy ways! Here is a shilling for*
> *thee. (Thank you, sir.) Take away that confounded footstool, and never let*
> *us see thee more!*

We can just still suppose that the "I" is another character here; but the strong suspicion is that it is Thackeray himself. There is the characteristic teasing of the reader, the shocking new angle of the present tense, the compensatory self-mocking in the already revealed "secret no torture shall induce me to divulge." But clearly he doesn't mean us to be sure; it is not the whole Thackeray.

Lovel rates poorly by Thackeray's own standards elsewhere; it is never-theless a brilliant technical exercise in the use of "voice." I cannot believe that it is a dead technique. Nothing can get us off the charge of omni-science—and certainly not the *nouveau roman* theory. Even that theory's most brilliant practical demonstrations—as exemplified by, say, Robbe-Grillet's own *La Jalousie*—fail to answer the accusation. Robbe-Grillet may have removed the writer Robbe-Grillet totally from the text; but he has never denied he wrote it. If the writer really believes in the statement "I know nothing about my characters except what can be tape-recorded and photographed (and then 'mixed' and 'cut')," the logical step is to take up tape recording and photography, not writing. But if he still writes, and writes well, as Robbe-Grillet does, then he is self-betrayed; he belongs to La Cosa Nostra, and is transparently far more deeply implicated than he will admit.

September 2, 1967. Now I am about two thirds of the way through. Always a bad stage, when one begins to doubt major things like basic motivations, dramatic design, the whole bloody enterprise; in the beginning one tends to get dazzled by each page, by one's fertility, those nice Muses always at one's shoulder . . . but then the inherent faults in the plot and characters begin to emerge. One starts to doubt the wisdom of the way the latter make things go; the stage in an *affaire* when one begins to thank God that marriage never raised its ugly head. But here one is condemned to a marriage of sorts—I have the woman on the quay (whose name is Sarah) for better or for worse, so to speak; and all seems worse.

I have to break off for a fortnight to go down to Majorca, where they're filming *The Magus*. I have written the script, but like most scripts it's really a team effort. The two producers have had their say, and the director; and a number of nonhuman factors, such as the budget, the nature of the locations, and the casting of the main roles, have had theirs. Most of the time I feel like a skeleton at the feast: this isn't what I had imagined, either in the book or in the script.

Yet it is interesting to watch, on a big film production, how buttressed each key man is by the other key men; to see how often one will turn to another and say, "Will it work?" I compare this with the loneliness of the long-distance writer; and I come back with a sort of relief, a reaffirmation in my faith in the novel. For all its faults, it is a statement by one person. In my novels I am the producer, director, and all the actors; I photograph it. This may seem a megalomania beside which the more celebrated cases from Hollywood pale to nothingness. There *is* a vanity about it, a wish to play the godgame, which all the random and author-removing devices of avant-garde technique cannot hide. But there must be a virtue, in an age that is out to exterminate both the individual and the enduring, in the individual's attempt to endure by his or her own efforts alone.

The truth is, the novel is a free form. Unlike the play or the film script, it has no limits other than those of the language. It is like a poem; it can be what it wants. This is its downfall and its glory; and it explains why both forms have been so often used to establish freedom in other fields, social and political.

A charge that all of us who sell film rights have to answer is that we wrote our books with this end in view. What has to be distinguished here is the legitimate and the illegitimate influence of the cinema on the novel. I saw my first film when I was six; I suppose I've seen on average—and discounting television—a film a week ever since; let's say some two and a half thousand films up to now. How can so frequently repeated an experience not have indelibly stamped itself on the *mode* of imagination? At one time I analyzed my dreams in detail; again and again I recalled purely cinematic effects: panning shots, close shots, tracking, jump cuts, and the rest. In short, this mode of imagining is far too deep in me to eradicate—and not only in me, but in all my generation.

This doesn't mean we have surrendered to the cinema. I don't share the general pessimism about the so-called decline of the novel and its present status as a minority cult. Except for a brief period in the nineteenth century, when a literate majority and a lack of other means of entertainment coincided, it has always been a minority cult.

One has in fact only to do a film script to realize how inalienably in possession of a still-vast domain the novel is; how countless the forms of human experience only to be described in and by it. There is too an essential difference in the quality of image evoked by the two media. The cinematic visual image is virtually the same for all who see it; it stamps out personal imagination, the response from individual *visual* memory. A sentence or paragraph in a novel will evoke a different image in each reader. This necessary cooperation between writer and reader—the one to suggest, the other to make concrete—is a privilege of *verbal* form; and the cinema can never usurp it.

Nor is that all. Here (the opening four paragraphs of a novel) is a flagrant bit of writing for the cinema. The man has obviously spent too much time on film scripts and can now think only of his movie sale.

> *The temperature is in the nineties, and the boulevard is absolutely empty.*
> *Lower down, the inky water of a canal reaches in a straight line. Midway between two locks is a barge full of timber. On the bank, two rows of barrels.*
> *Beyond the canal, between houses separated by workyards, a huge, cloudless, tropical sky. Under the throbbing sun, white facades, slate roofs, and granite quays hurt the eyes. An obscure distant murmur rises in the hot air. All seems drugged by the Sunday peace and the sadness of summer days.*
> *Two men appear.*

It first appeared on March 25, 1881. The writer's name is Flaubert. All I have done to his novel *Bouvard et Pecuchet* is to transpose its past historic into the present.

I woke in the small hours, and the book tormented me. All its failings rose up in the darkness. I saw that the novel I'd dropped in order to write *The French Lieutenant's Woman* was much better. This one was not my sort of book; it was an aberration, a folly, a delusion. Sentences from vitriolic reviews floated through my mind: "a clumsy pastiche of Hardy," "a pretentious imitation of an inimitable genre," "a pointless exploration of an already overexplored age . . . ," and so on and so on.

Now it is day, I am back on it again, and it denies what I felt in the night. But the horror of such realizations is that someone, some reader or reviewer, *will* realize them. The nightmare of the writer is that all his or her worst private fears and self-criticisms will be made public.

The shadow of Thomas Hardy, the heart of whose "country" I can see in the distance from my workroom window, I cannot avoid. Since he and Thomas Love Peacock are my two favorite male novelists, I don't mind the shadow. It seems best to use it; and by a curious coincidence, which I didn't recall when I placed my own story in that year, 1867 was the crucial year in Hardy's own mysterious personal life.[1] It is somehow encouraging that while my fictitious characters weave their own story in their 1867, only thirty miles away, in the real 1867, the pale young architect was entering his own fatal life-incident.

The female characters in my books tend to dominate the male ones. I see man as a kind of artifice, and woman as a kind of reality. The one is cold idea, the other is warm fact. Daedalus faces Venus, and Venus must win. If the technical problems hadn't been so great, I should have liked to make Conchis in *The Magus* a woman. The character of Mrs. de Seitas at the end of the book was simply an aspect of his character, as was Lily. Now Sarah exerts this power. She doesn't realize how. Nor do I yet.

I was stuck this morning trying to find a good answer from Sarah at the climax of a scene. Characters sometimes reject all the possibilities one offers. They say, in effect: *I would never say or do a thing like that.* But they don't say what they *would* say; and one has to proceed negatively, by a very tedious coaxing kind of trial and error. After an hour over this one wretched sentence, I saw that she had in fact been telling me what to do: silence from her was better than any line she might have said.

By the time I left Oxford, I found myself much more at home in French than in English literature. There seems to me to be a vital distinction between the French and Anglo-Saxon cultures in this field. Since 1650 French writers have assumed an international audience, and Anglo-Saxons a national one. This may be no more than a general tendency; the literatures of the two cultures offer hundreds of exceptions, even among the best-known books. Nevertheless, I have always found this French assumption that the proper audience of a book is one without frontiers more attractive than the extreme opposite view, which is still widely held in both Britain and America, that the proper job of a writer is to write of and for his or her own country and countrymen.

I am aware of this when I write, and especially when I revise. English

---

1. In 1867, Hardy, plagued by ill health, left London, returned to Bockhampton, and began writing his first novel.

references that will mean nothing to a foreigner I usually cut out, or avoid in the first place. In the present book I have the ubiquity in the West of the Victorian ethos; that helps greatly.

Various things have long made me feel an exile in England. Some years ago I came across a sentence in an obscure French novel: "Ideas are the only motherland."[2] Ever since I have kept it as the most succinct summary I know of what I believe. Perhaps *believe* is the wrong verb—if you are without national feeling, if you find many of your fellow countrymen and most of their beliefs and their institutions foolish and antiquated, you can hardly *believe* in anything, but only accept the loneliness that results.

So I live completely away from other English writers and the literary life of London. What I have to think of as my "public" self is willy-nilly absorbed into or rejected by (mostly the latter, in my case) the national literary "world." Even to me that public self seems very remote and often distastefully alien and spurious; just one more thing that I feel my real self in exile from.

My real self is here and now, writing. Whenever I think of this (the writing, not the written) experience, images to do with exploring, single-handed voyages, lone mountain ascents always spring unwanted to my mind. They sound romantic, but they're not meant to. It's the damned solitude, the fear of failure (by which I do *not* mean bad reviews), the tedium of the novel form, the often nauseating feeling that one is prey to an unhealthy obsession. . . .

When I go out and meet other people, become mixed in their lives and social routines, my own solitude, routinelessness, and freedom (which is a subtle imprisonment) from economic "worries" often make me feel like a visitor from outer space. I like earthmen, but I'm not quite sure what they're at. I mean, we regulate things better at home. But there it is—I've been posted here. And there's no transport back.

Something like this lies behind all I write.

This total difference between the written and the writing worlds is what nonwriters never realize about us. They see us as we were; we live with what we are. What matters to writers is not subjects, but the experience of

---

2. Claire de Duras *Ourika* (1824): "L'opinion est comme une patrie." I gave it thus when I translated the book, in 1977. The Modern Language Association edition of 1995 proposes "A view of life is like a motherland."

handling them; in romantic terms, a difficult pitch scaled, a storm survived, the untrodden moon beneath one's feet. Such pleasures are unholy; and the world in general does right to regard us with malice and suspicion.

I loathe the day a manuscript is sent to the publisher, because on that day the people one has loved die; they become what they are—petrified, fossil organisms for others to study and collect. I get asked what I meant by this and by that. But what I wrote is what I meant. If it wasn't clear in the book, it shouldn't be clear now.

I find that Americans, especially the kind people who write and ask questions, have a strangely pragmatic view of what books are. Perhaps because of the miserable heresy that creative writing can be taught ("creative" is here a euphemism for "imitative"), they seem to believe that a writer always knows exactly what he's doing. Obscure books, for them, are a kind of crossword puzzle. Somewhere, they feel, in some number of a paper they missed, all the answers have been given to all the clues.

They believe, in short, that a book is like a machine; that if you have the knack, you can take it to bits.

Ordinary readers can hardly be blamed for thinking like this. Both academic criticism and weekly reviewing have in the last forty years grown dangerously scientific, or pseudo-scientific, in their general tenor. Analysis and categorization are indispensable scientific tools *in the scientific field*; but the novel, like the poem, is only partly a scientific field. No one wants a return to the kind of bellettrist and onanistic accounts of new books that were fashionable in the early years of the century; but we could do with something better than what we have got.

I am an interested party? I confess it. Ever since I began writing *The French Lieutenant's Woman* I've been reading obituaries of the novel; a particularly gloomy one came from Gore Vidal in the December 1967 issue of *Encounter*. And I have been watching novel reviewing in England become this last year increasingly impatient and dismissive. Any moment now I expect one of our fashionable newspapers to decide to drop its "New Novels" column for good and give the released space over to television or pop music. Of course I am interested—but like Mr. Vidal, I can hardly be personally resentful. If the novel is dead, the corpse remains oddly fertile. We are told that no one reads novels anymore; so the authors of *Julian* and *The Collector* must be grateful to the two million or more ghosts who have bought copies of their respective books. But I don't want to be sarcastic. More is at issue here than self-interest.

One has the choice of two views: either that the novel, along with printed-word culture in general, is moribund, or that there is something sadly shallow and blinded in our age. I know which view I hold; and the people who astound me are the ones who are sure that the first view is true. If you want omniscience, you have it there, and it ought to worry you—you the reader who is neither critic nor writer—that this omniscient contempt for print is found so widely among people who make a living out of literary dissection. Surgery is what we want, not dissection. It is not only the extirpation of the mind that kills the body; the heart will do the trick just as well.

October 27, 1967. I finished the first draft, which was begun on January 25. It is about 140,000 words long, and exactly as I imagined it: perfect, flawless, a lovely novel. But that, alas, is indeed only how I imagine it. When I reread it I see 140,000 things that need to be changed; then it will, perhaps, be less imperfect. But I haven't the energy; the dreaded research now, the interminable sentence-picking. I want to get on with another book. I had a strange image last night . . .

FOREWORD TO THE POEMS
(1973)

I, fugi, sed poteras tutior esse domi.[1]

If publication is not the business of poets, then even more surely it is not self-exegesis. But since this collection must, after the fact of my published novels, have something of the air of an autobiographical footnote, I should like to say briefly where poetry sits in my writing life.

The so-called crisis of the modern novel has to do with its self-consciousness. The fault was always inherent in the form, since it is fundamentally a kind of game, an artifice that allows the writer to play hide-and-seek with the reader. In strict terms a novel is a hypothesis more or less ingeniously and persuasively presented—that is, first cousin to a lie. This uneasy consciousness of lying is why in the great majority of novels the novelist apes reality so assiduously; and it is why giving the game away—making the lie, the fictitiousness of the process, explicit in the text—has become such a feature of the contemporary novel. Committed to invention, to people who never existed, to events that never happened, the novelist wants either to sound "true" or to come clean.

Poetry proceeds by a reverse path; its superficial form may be highly artificial and *invraisemblable*, but its content is normally a good deal more revealing of the writer than is that of prose fiction. The poem is saying what you are and feel, the novel is saying what invented characters might be and might feel. Only very naive readers can suppose that a novelist's invented personages and their opinions are reliable guides to his real self—that because Fanny Price represents Jane Austen's idea of the highest moral good,

---

1. The quotation is from Martial and translates as "Go on, run away, but you'd be far safer if you stayed at home."

then meeting Jane Austen herself would have been like meeting Fanny. I have myself got a little tired of being taken for an all-wise millionaire on a remote Greek island.

Of course some poets wear masks (though much more for rhetorical than for seriously deceitful reasons), and of course there is an autobiographical element in all novels. Nonetheless, I think there is a vital distinction. It is rather difficult to put one's private self into a novel; it is rather difficult to keep it out of a poem. A novelist is like an actor or actress onstage, and the private self has to be subjugated to the public master of a novel's ceremonies. The primary audience is other people. A poet's is his or her own self.

This may, I think, partly explain why some writers are poets and others novelists, and why excellence in both forms is such a rare thing. I suspect that most novelists are trying to camouflage a sense of personal inadequacy in the face of real life—a sentiment that is compounded in the act of creating fiction, the fabrication of literary lies, ingenious fantasies, to hide a fundamental psychological or sociological fault of personality. Some novelists—Hemingway is the classic instance—create a real-life as well as a literary persona in answer to this predicament. Most genuine poets have a much happier, or less queasy, relationship with their private self. At least they do not live, like most novelists, in permanent flight from the mirror.

At any rate I have always found the writing of poetry, which I began before I attempted prose, an enormous relief from the constant playacting of fiction. I never pick up a book of poems without thinking that it will have one advantage over most novels: I shall know the writer better at the end of it. I do not have to hope this is true of what follows. I know it is true—and know also how slender a justification mere personal truth is for writing. I mean my line of Martial preceding this foreword.

OF MEMOIRS AND MAGPIES
(1983/1994)[1]

Some years ago I decided to get myself a bookplate. It wasn't quite pure vanity, for part of the pleasure of book collecting lies in the awareness of past ownerships, and I like to think of some browser of the twenty-second century (if books and browsers still then exist) coming on my plate in a volume he or she fancies. There was the question of design: a general emblem for the sort of book I enjoy possessing. Various elegant motifs were proposed by the woodcut artist. But in the end only one, not at all elegant, seemed appropriate, and I now have a plate that shows my name surrounded by magpies. It appears on the title page of this volume.

Everyone knows that writers need understanding agents and editors at the beginning of their career. I suspect they almost equally require understanding booksellers. I was lucky in this respect, since I ran across Mr. Francis Norman and his antiquarian bookshop in Hampstead, London, and learned a great deal more about literature there than I ever did at Oxford.

Let me hazard a definition of what this kind of bookshop should be like. It must be run by a person of humor, learning, and curiosity, to whom nothing in book form is alien, who will show you an Elzevir title page one moment and read you a passage from a sci-fi paperback the next. It should be kept in a permanent state of apparent chaos—always too many books for the shelf space, always piles and boxes of new-bought lots awaiting inspection. Above all, it must be catholic in its offerings, because its

---

1. A somewhat shorter form of this essay originally appeared under the title "Of Memoirs and Magpies" in 1983. The essay as it appears here incorporates material from a later piece, "Ourika" (1994), which makes further reference to its author's magpie book-collecting habits.

prime function for your writers is to help them realize their tastes—even to the extreme of convincing them that they don't like old books at all.

What we learn at university is to appreciate the prescribed master-pieces; we never have time to explore that vast bulk of the iceberg beneath the examination surface. I left Oxford in a state of total confusion as to my real (as opposed to my acquired) tastes in literature. And it wasn't until I began to frequent Mr. Norman's and its presiding spirit—now both dead, alas—that I discovered what I was as a bookman. It was partly the choice, the gamble, the delight of the unexpected; the realization that there were other ways of loving and being erudite about books than the academic. Perhaps it was above all, in those days, never having very much money to spend. The rich may suit their smallest fancies; the poor get to know what they really like.

I regret bitterly the general disappearance of such shops from the Britain (and, I am told, the America) of the 1990s. It is partly, of course, a matter of inflation and scarcity. Not even my friend Mr. Norman could now leave minor seventeenth- and eighteenth-century volumes, coverless and dog-eared, lying about for sale at giveaway prices to whoever might unearth them. The great country-house sources have dried up, while the demands and funds of university librarians the world over seem endless. But I was the other day in one of the largest secondhand bookstores in Britain: a colossal stock, all neatly shelved, catalogued, and unbargainably high-priced, briskly efficient assistants at every turn. Such establishments may be a librarian's, a research scholar's, dream. I could only weep for those two dusty, overcrowded rooms in Hampstead, where nothing could ever be found at once and somehow everything turned up in the end. The one place makes bibliophily seem a coldly calculated science; the other, a love affair.

Every treatise on bibliomania repeats the same excellent advice: stick to one age, one field, one press, one author . . . specialize, or waste your money. All mine has gone down the drain, since I have never bought for editions or bindings or printers, and even less for literary standing. All I have are waifs and strays, a broken-backed detritus from the last four centuries, most of which the rest of the world has quite rightly consigned to oblivion. My lack of decent reading has become increasingly embarrass-ing. I am faced with it every time I meet students, and the vast uncharted spaces in my knowledge of the contemporary—and the classical—novel are revealed. When humiliated beyond endurance, I sometimes pretend that apart from one or two old favorites, like Defoe, Austen, and Peacock, I much prefer bad novels to good ones. In one sense that is true. A bad novel tells you more about the age it was written in than a good one—a proposition so blasphemous to the average classic-stuffed Strasbourg goose, alias academic, that it must be correct.

Unkind; but at least it leads me to a shadow of a first connecting principle in my own reading. Above all I like a book to give me the sharp feel of the age it was written in, which is one reason I prefer early editions, however imperfect, to the best-annotated modern ones. Textual accuracy and apparatus attract me far less than the idea that this is how the book "felt" when the writer was still alive; and this in turn is because I regard the kinds of books I collect as space or time machines: examples of science fiction in reverse, glimpses of an unknown past. Only a few weeks ago I picked up for less than a pound a coverless but otherwise complete descending of hair by the key witness at a French murder trial of 1817. During the trial the lady had broken down and changed her testimony, and got an exceedingly bad name for herself; and the *mémoire* is an attempt on Clarisse Manson's part to explain her behavior to the world before the appeal hearing. To do that she recounts in every detail where she was and what she did on the days surrounding the murder; and suddenly the miracle takes place, one is back in March of 1817, in the remote town of Rodez in the Aveyron, and inside the mind of a neurotically intelligent and self-dramatizing young Frenchwoman. For me such reading experiences are very like landing on another, *and* inhabited, planet.

Or I think of another recent buy: *An Enquiry into, and Detection of the Barbarous Murther of the late Earl of Essex*. Officially the Earl committed suicide at about nine o'clock on the morning of July 13, 1683; but this long pamphlet of 1689 sets out to show that he was in fact murdered by the establishment papists. It was written by "Plotter" Ferguson, a vitriolic polemicist of the Puritan New Left in the late seventeenth century. He recreates that July morning and then analyzes its events with all the sharp eye for conflicting detail and the contemptuous skepticism of a Sherlock Holmes. Once again the reading leaps the imagination back over three centuries—into both the strange and grisly mystery of Essex's death and the oddly proleptic political anger that drove Ferguson and his kind.

Old trial accounts, travel books, and historical memoirs provide this experience far more vividly than any other category. Novels, alas, are very rarely half so convincing or exciting. Yet I believe my predilection for the kind of true history described above does help me in writing my own fiction. The great bulk of such reading must steep the mind in narrative technique—and not the artificial inventions of the novelist, but the real thing. Good memoirists often show an economy of characterization, a swiftness of narrative pace, an ear for the kernel of dialogue, that put the mere fictioneer to shame. I know I have learned a lot from them.

I hate books that can be put down; and if they have no narrative to sustain them, then they had better, so far as I am concerned, be bloody good in other directions. Narrative is my second connective principle in choice of reading. I have an unlimited greed for it, which seriously distorts my literary judgment. An abysmally low boredom threshold has prevented me from ever finishing countless serious and worthy novels by serious and worthy authors. I can admire people like Richardson and George Eliot, but I could never read them for pleasure. All this makes it difficult for me to answer questions about influence.

I would admit it, in a direct and singular sense, of only one of my own books—the first in the writing, though not in the publishing. *The Magus* is a kind of homage to *Le Grand Meaulnes*, but even that flawed masterpiece (whose faults I can see, whose deep emotional hold on me I cannot understand) usurped another, the first book that I ever loved passionately and almost totally lived—and that I think I should have to name, on quasi-archetypal grounds, if I was limited to a unique master-influence. That is Richard Jefferies's *Bevis*. I still consider it the best boys' story in the language; and the fact that not one child in a million today has read it I regard as the others' loss, not as proof of my own faulty judgment.

I have in any case no memory at all for novels, for their ideas, plots, or characters. I could not even reconstitute my own with any accuracy if I was obliged to. I suppose I read as I write. I live the direct and present experience very intensely; but when it is over, it sinks very rapidly out of sight. So all I can honestly offer is a couple of dozen shelves of magpie nonsense, nine tenths forgotten by everyone else and even by myself in every but some very remote and rare-snagging sense. Let me pick down a few at random:

Mémoires de Trenck, 1789, a great prison escape story; *Roswall and Lillian*, the 1822 reprint, Swinburne's copy; *Menagiana*, pirated 1693, full of good anecdotes; *Tell It All*, 1878, an anti-Mormon classic; the *Sporting Magazine* for 1816, splendid on the "fancy"; *The Diaboliad*, 1777, a furious squib by William Combe; *The Wild Party*, privately printed in 1929, a very odd piece of Jazz Age doggerel that I am not alone in admiring; a reprint of the Bedford Eyre Roll for 1227, a real time machine; *On the Height of the Aurora Borealis*, 1828, John Dalton and signed by him; *Account of a Visit to Rome*, 1899, manuscript and hilariously priggish; *Mémoires de Martin du Bellay*, 1573, Joachim's uncle, with an eyewitness account by the old boy of the Field of the Cloth of Gold; *Pidgin English Sing-Song*, 1876 ("Littee Jack Horner/ Makee sit inside corner/ Chow-chow he Clismas pie . . ."); *Candide*, 1761, Geneva, containing the first edition of the spurious second part; *Lost Countess Falka*, 1897, a yellowback by Richard Henry Savage and currently my nomination for the worst novel in the English language; the *Mercure Galant* for September 1685, with a fascinating account of how the Bolognese dwarfed their spaniels (they immersed the puppies daily in eau-de-vie, then bashed their noses in); *Souvenir Programme of the Cornish Gorsedd of the Bards*, 1938; *An Essay on the Art of Ingeniously Tormenting*, 1804 . . .

That seems a fitting title on which to stop, and I will spare you all the other forgotten plays, travels, memoirs, murders, and whatnot I have accumulated over the years. I am afraid this cannot seem serious; and yet it is more so than you may think. A novelist must, I believe, extend *humani nihil alienum* to books as well. A quite literal pair of magpies breed in my garden every year. Wicked creatures though they are, I let them be. One must not harm one's own.

THE FILMING OF *THE FRENCH LIEUTENANT'S WOMAN* (1981)

If the filming, or more accurately the nonfilming, of *The French Lieutenant's Woman* cannot equal that of several other novels—most famously *Under the Volcano*—it nonetheless had some remarkable episodes. I have not forgotten the evening when one famous actress telephoned to say that a quite literally princely friend had offered her the leading role in the picture. She had seen his option agreement, and her call was mere courtesy, to ask if I approved of his choice. I then had, as gently as I could, since I knew where the option really lay, to convince her that someone had just bought himself a very expensive piece of worthless legal paper. To my regret the gentleman concerned preferred to lose his money than to have his gullibility exposed in court. It would have made a very pretty case.

But I should have difficulty now listing all the other more entitled producers and directors who were to a greater or lesser degree, at one point or another, "involved." There were times when my tirelessly active partner in the enterprise, Tom Maschler, and I grew distinctly cynical, as once again an initiative died and yet, by some mysterious perversity, always another candidate sprang from this increasingly worn turf. After eight or nine years of this, and after the failure of the most serious attempt (by Fred Zinnemann) to get a production going, we both began to suspect the venture was perennially doomed. I knew television was prepared to go ahead, and I was on the reluctant brink of giving up any hope of the senior medium. It was only then that whatever fickle gods rule the cinema decided to smile on us.

Before the book was even published, and knowing I was less than happy with two previous films drawn from my other novels, Tom Maschler (who was to prove as gifted an impromptu film agent as he is a publisher) persuaded me that I must this time insist on something that no producer happily grants: not just the usual token say in the choice of who shall direct, but a definite power to veto anyone I did not like. (We insisted on this—more than once at the cost of otherwise attractive offers—in all the dealings that were to come.) We also agreed that we would if possible have no truck with the ridiculous system whereby the finished script goes in search of a director, rather than the other way round. We had no argument over the director we should approach first. It was Karel Reisz. In 1969 we therefore took the book, still only in proof, to him.

Karel was sympathetic—and we had a devoted ally in his wife, the actress Betsy Blair—but it was a singularly bad moment to try to tempt him. He had only recently finished a difficult period picture, *Isadora*, and the thought of yet another (as Karel himself has remarked, the trouble with the genre is that one can find oneself spending as much time on a period as on a picture) was too much. Even if we had not realized it then, the next few years would have taught us just how difficult a project we were landed with. Looking back, I suspect the chief thing that balked and frustrated the directors and writers we talked with was the distinctly mushroom reputation of the book itself. It had been lucky enough to gain not only a huge commercial but a considerable critical success, and its text was in grave danger of becoming sacrosanct. I remember a meeting with Robert Bolt, who had firmly declined the script but wanted to tell us why. By the end of it I felt more than half persuaded by his thesis, that as it stood (or lay printed) the book was, and would always remain, unfilmable. (I recall Bob Bolt, and his friendly honesty, a great deal more kindly than I do another well-known writer who also turned the script down—this time on the grounds that he could not help propagate a story so biased to the female side.)

It was towards the end of this period that we began to feel that what the project needed above all else was a demon barber—in politer terms, someone sufficiently skilled and independent to be able to rethink and recast the thing from the bottom up. Once again we had no argument as to the best man for that difficult task. It was Harold Pinter. Then one day he did by chance form part of a development deal we were offered—but alas, he was the only part of it we truly wanted, and he very naturally declined to rat on his proposed partners. As with Karel, we felt we had forever lost our chance.

In 1978, almost a decade after that first approach, and faced with the imminent collapse of yet another option, Tom went back to Karel; and at last fortune was kind to us. This time he said yes, with the one proviso that he could persuade Harold to tackle the script. Tom and I spent a fortnight on tenterhooks, while the two discussed possible solutions to all the problems. Then the second miracle happened: we found ourselves with the writer and director we most wanted. Further miracles were needed, and largely provided by the faith, tenacity, and patience of Karel—and his leading actress and actor, Meryl Streep and Jeremy Irons—in the face of an unusually grim array of preproduction difficulties. But at last the day we had very nearly ceased to believe in did come to pass. On May 27, 1980, Karel stood beside his camera crew outside a country house near Lyme Regis; Sam the servant waited with a bunch of flowers on his starting mark, and the magic word was said.

I most certainly mean no dispraise of the previous writers who did take the plunge if I say that none had succeeded. The chief stumbling block was in any case one I have already suggested, which no novelist can blame very sincerely—that of trying to remain faithful to the book. But *The French Lieutenant's Woman* was written at a time when I was beginning to develop strong and perhaps idiosyncratic views on the proper domains of the cinema and the novel. There are of course large parts of those domains, since both media are essentially narrative, that overlap; yet there are others that are no-go territory: visual things the word can never capture (think, for instance, of the appalling paucity of vocabulary to define the endless nuances of facial expression), and word things the camera will never photograph nor actors ever speak.

Novels that consciously utilize this area forbidden to the filmmaker (or more anciently, to the illustrator) obviously pose very great problems; and the only likely result of "being faithful" to such a book is a script spilling over with dialogue that is (through no fault of the screenwriter's) really not dramatic dialogue at all, but an attempt to crush into a small valise all those long paragraphs of description, historical digression, character analysis, and the rest that the vast portmanteau of novel form was specifically evolved to contain.

It is not only that language itself first arose to designate and "show" things that could not be physically seen; the evolution of the novel, especially in our own century, and increasingly since the rise of structuralism and semiology (or a more exact knowledge of the nature of language and fictional text), has been more and more concerned with all those aspects of life and modes of feeling that can *never* be represented visually. It was not perhaps entirely by chance that the invention of motion photography, this sudden great leap in our powers of exploring and imitating the outward of perception, coincided so exactly with the journey into inner space initiated by Freud and his compeers. The year 1895 saw not only the very first showing of the very first film, but also the publication of *Studies in Hysteria*—that is, the birth of psychoanalysis.

This business of proper domains is one of the reasons I am no longer in the least interested in scripting my own fiction. To assemble a book with a considerable and deliberate number of elements that you know cannot be filmed, and then to disassemble and reconstruct it out of the elements that can, is surely an occupation best left to masochists or narcissists. Nowhere can there be a clearer case for a fresh and outside mind on the job. The second reason is that I know I am, like most novelists, far too corrupted by and addicted to the solitary freedoms of prose fiction (where the one megalomaniac plays producer, director, all the cast, *and* camera) ever to be any good at a team art—or a team anything, for that matter. The third reason is that true scriptwriters are a race apart in a craft apart. It is only vanity that makes other writers believe that anyone at all can turn a hand to it. I believed so myself once. Then one day I persuaded Sidney Carroll to give me a copy of the superb scenario he wrote, with Robert Rossen, for *The Hustler*; and I recognized (as I do again here) a league I shall never be in.

Another major problem with *The French Lieutenant's Woman* was what one critic called its stereoscopic vision, the fact that it is written from both a mid-Victorian and a modern viewpoint. None of the directors who worked on it ever wanted to dodge that "diachronic" dilemma, though they came up with many different solutions; nor, incidentally, did any of the producers. As one studio head of production put it to me, he was profoundly uninterested in buying a latter-day Victorian romance when there were hundreds of the genuine article—and from the most formidable corpus of writers in English fiction—lying about out of copyright and to be had for nothing.

A popular previous answer proposed an extension of a device used in the book, the creation of a character who was tacitly the author and also had a part in the Victorian story—someone who could both join the action from within and stand back and comment on it, rather as Anton Walbrook does in Max Ophuls's celebrated film *La Ronde*. I never much fancied that, or only once. My path crossed Peter Ustinov's, in the unlikely setting of the Beverly Hills Hotel, and we spent an enjoyable evening discussing the idea. I best recall a wicked and marvelously mimicked series of anecdotes about a far more famous writer than either of us (and for whose work I had expressed too innocent an admiration). The skepticism about novelists' motives in general and the sending-up, through this one instance, of their public masks and private realities sold me lock, stock, and barrel in the great raconteur's cause. He remains the only surrogate I could have borne in that role of author-ringmaster, had it ever survived the discussion stage.

I am convinced now, in retrospect, that the only feasible answer was the one that Harold and Karel hit upon. We had all before been made blind to its existence by the more immediate problem of compressing an already dense and probably overplotted book into two hours' screen time. The idea of adding an entirely new dimension and relationship to it would never have occurred to us—and quite reasonably so—had almost anyone but Harold Pinter been involved.

I do not need to dwell on his universally acknowledged qualities as playwright, as creator of the kind of dialogue that can speak worlds in its smallest phrases, even in its silences, and not least as an issuer of the kind of challenge that every intelligent actor and actress likes to face. In those contexts, this script speaks for itself. But his genius has a further string, and that seems to me to be his truly remarkable gift for reducing the long and complex without distortion. It may to the ignorant seem something of a negative or cutting-scissors skill, yet it is in fact infinitely valuable—and positive—in the cinema. The one practical advantage the novel factory (or novelist) has over his or her cinema equivalent lies in simplicity of production. The actual process of making a narrative film, however few the characters and simple the locations, is hideously complicated, and expensive; and the greatest gift a good screenwriter can give a director is not so much a version "faithful" to the book as a version faithful to the very different production capability (and relation with audience) of the cinema.

I think of the present script not as a mere "version" of my novel, but as the blueprint (since of course this pudding's proof must lie finally in the seeing) of a brilliant metaphor for it. I approve entirely of this approach, and not only because I believe original authors have no right to interfere once they have got the scenarist and director they want, but even more because I am sure that viable transitions from the one medium to the other need just such an imaginative leap. Neither a good film nor a good novel has ever been made on a basis of safety. My same approval, I should add, went to the casting of an American actress in the title role. My liking for that possibility long antedated our good fortune in attracting Meryl Streep to the part, and for the same reason I have just mentioned: the metaphorical leap that such a casting implies. In this particular case it also has for me a historical justice, since the principal freedom the heroine seeks is associated much more in my mind with nineteenth-century America than with Victorian Britain. I suggested as much in the original novel.

If the only thing novelists want is a literally faithful version of their books, they should never in their right (or money-spurning) minds sell to the cinema. The longer the final cut, the more of the original they can hope to see; and if a literal fidelity is to be the criterion, the several hours that a television serial can offer are manifestly superior to the miserable 110 minutes or so that distribution exigencies impose on the motion picture. I have heard filmmakers envy this luxury of time granted their television counterparts; but I suspect that in this they betray their own métier. The arbitrary limits imposed on film length are like those imposed on the dramatist by the physical stage, or on the poet by fixed form and metrical law. This is certainly one principal reason—in my view—that the cinema remains at its best a major art, and television, except in very rare hands (like the late David Mercer's or Dennis Potter's), still dangerously close to a recording device, or mere translating machine.

I am often asked why I sell film rights at all, given the high risk of seeing nothing but a travesty as the end product. It is a question I have invited, since in a later novel, *Daniel Martin*, I did not hide the contempt I feel for many aspects of the commercial cinema—or more exactly, since cost of production and mode of recoupment make all cinema more or less commercial, of the cinema where accounts reign, where profit comes first and everything else a long way after. This vile ethos was neatly exemplified in the main reason given by one studio for turning down a forerunner of the present script. Its chief fault, we were informed, was that there was only one character with whom an American audience could happily identify: my little example of blind Victorian capitalism, the London store owner Mr. Freeman. It was a nice question as to who was most insulted—the author, the director, and the screenwriter, or the studio reader's fellow countrymen. We decided in the end that it was, by several lengths, the last.

But for true cinema, cinema conceived and executed by artists as an art, or at least as a craft by sincere craftsmen, I have always had the greatest liking and respect. I have never had any belief in the notion that the cinema is "killing" the novel (television is another matter, but even that has to do with the ubiquitous availability of reception, not with what is shown). The two ways of telling stories are much nearer sisters than anything else. A good director is always partly a novelist, and vice versa (and from long before the invention of photography). Quite apart from avowedly *auteur* cinema, the shared need to narrate, to create new worlds of character and atmosphere, to play the godgame, brings us incomparably closer together than any other pairs of artists in different arts. It is the techniques that are so different, not the final aims; and if I have to justify (as rather an alarming number of readers have told me I must) the selling of rights, one reason certainly lies in my fascination with that difference of technique. Discovering its exact nature can be a very instructive experience for novelists, even when—perhaps most of all when—the screened result disappoints.

The experience is also valuable in another way, one that may partly explain why some authors crave the literal fidelity I mentioned earlier. Novelists have an almost archetypal fear that illustration will overstamp text, or more precisely that their readers' imaginations (which play a vitally *creative* part in the total experience of the book) will be pinned down and manacled by a set of specific images. This began long before the cinema, of course. The harmony we feel now between Dickens and his two great illustrators, Cruikshank and "Phiz," certainly did not always exist at the time of creation. But it seems to me that this is a test, or challenge, that the author is foolish to refuse—though how much more foolish if, having accepted it, he or she tries to step over into the other art and dictate how things are to be done there. It is particularly absurd to see in novelists, who are notoriously resentful of editorial interference in their own work.

If the text is worth its salt, it will survive being "visualized." If it meets its match, then word and image will marry, as happened with Dickens, and enhance each other. If image does "drown" text, then the latter was never going to survive anyway. I was not amused (everyone else thought it hilariously funny) when a studio publicity man turned up in London during the filming of *The French Lieutenant's Woman* and demanded to know why nothing had been done about the novelization of Harold's script. But I took his general point: there is more than one way of telling a story, even inside the one medium, let alone in others. Risking the possibility that the film or television way may turn out better, or deeply change or color how people respond to the literary way, is also a salutary experience; and one day someone will write a novelization that is better than the film it is based on.

Cynics may think I am sliding over the most important reason for all this: money. I am not so noble-minded that I could deny that the money has its attractions; and I am not so modest that I will not point out that rather more than my own bank balance is involved. I have never seen a contemporary British novelist or playwright congratulated by government or industry for his or her contribution to foreign-currency earnings, job creation, and so on; and I do not expect ever to see it, even though I doubt whether we are, Stakhanovite head for head, to be beaten in that particular race. It is true that we are only the indirect cause of the many millions of dollars that film productions of our work have brought into the postwar series of economies—all of which have failed miserably to support a national film industry. Nonetheless, I think one has to be very sure of one's motives before deciding that one's text is too precious a thing to be risked in the "vulgarity" of a mass medium. What is really in the scales is not personal public image, or even personal financial reward, but work and wages for a lot of other people . . . and well beyond our ailing film industry proper.

But my chief private reason has to do with something else. Novelists are condemned to one of the loneliest professions in terms of actual work, and our wistful envy (the reverse of the coin of our megalomania) of those who work communally in the theater, and now in the cinema, has a long record. I remember standing, that first day of shooting, with Harold and Karel during a break between takes, listening to them discuss some minor problem. I am sure it was the most banal and ordinary experience for them, but for me it was strange—as it has been strange on previous, similar occasions. Words, all those endless rows of algebra on a page, are literally become flesh, have provoked this very actual presence, all this devotion, ingenuity, teamwork, skill with eye and ear. One has an odd sense of having come in for a moment from the cold. The strangeness was also, for me, this time, compounded by an unusual sense of trust. On "first day," with a difficult project in a difficult medium, it could not have been anything to do with a certainty of the final-cut kind; but it had very much to do with a certainty that my two partners had done their best to achieve success.

That good moment at launching is, in my philosophy of life, just as important a thing as an eventually successful voyage. To a degree difficult to convey to the outsider, indeed to anyone who had not lived through those ten years of abortive attempts, the script—the new keel—performed the final miracle: it made possible both the moment and the voyage.

A MODERN WRITER'S FRANCE
(1988)

The notion of the novelist as intellectual and bookman, as universally well read and well informed about what is going on in the contemporary literary world, has been gaining substance all through this century, at least in the academy, if some of the letters I receive are any guide. They assume knowledges in me of the modern novel, of literary theory, all of that, that I lack either totally or as nearly so as makes no difference. All novelists, at least when writing novels, are really to be classed in terms of Lévi-Strauss's *pensée sauvage*; we are not cultivated people. As the great anthropologist pointed out, that does not mean we primitives are not also in pursuit, like scientists and other sternly sane people, of a *mise en ordre*, a fitting of life into a chest of drawers. But the methods and principles of our fitting, and indeed of our chests of drawers themselves, are often remote from reason, tradition, the protocols of scientific analysis, and all that venerable *galère* (in the university context) of desirable qualities.

Some novelists, such as Malcolm Bradbury and David Lodge, are of course also distinguished academics, and others become quasi-academics because they are reviewers; that is, they have to sound expert. I cannot, from my own very limited experience, imagine anyone's reviewing for sheer love of it, for pleasure, indeed for anything much more than the welcome supplement of income it brings to those two Cinderella professions, writing and teaching. Even reluctant reviewers must, willy-nilly, learn quite a lot. I have reviewed very little in my life; and have equally fled (as a fly a spider's web) every kind of literary "world," or circle, that has threatened to enmesh me. I read of such worlds, say in terms of seventeenth- and eighteenth-century *salons*, or of present-day campus society, with a kind of incredulity that anyone taking part in them could ever have enjoyed, or can enjoy, them.

My long-held opinion is also that lack of memory (of the indexing, encyclopedic, good-teacher kind) is of very great benefit to a maker of fiction—is, indeed, one very sufficient reason that highly intelligent academics and scientists so seldom make satisfactory novelists. Knowing everything objective about a highly subjective art is a fearsome handicap; and Monsieur Jourdain's sort of innocence is a better presage for it. A novelist needs a memory of the re-creative sort, the ability to summon up scenes, events, characters, and the rest for his or her readers; but this very seldom requires the accuracy and particularity of recall that so many suppose. When I hear of novelists being sunk in "research," I grow immediately suspicious.

The required virtue is much more akin to a being at ease with the instinctive and the only half conscious, a sort of knowing of one's own junkroom. I have collected old books all my life, sufficient by now to amount to quite a small library. Remembering where everything is has escaped my powers, though not, for some mysterious reason, remembering everything that I somewhere have. I ought to install some rational system that would allow me to move smoothly to the right shelf in the right case; it would certainly spare frequent fruitless and cursing searches. Yet I am a novelist, and the haphazard and disorganized way I keep my books, as I indeed write them, somehow suits me best. It is, in short, very far from the sort of memory that has names, titles, dates, exact details at its fingertips—precisely the memory that every university values so highly and tries to instill in its students.

The prospective nightmare during my own Oxford finals in French concerned a paper on sixteenth-century grammatical theory. The subject had bored me beyond belief in tutorials and reading, and I had done no work on it at all. The night before the examination I borrowed a friend's swotted-up notes, and duly regurgitated them the next morning on paper; the next day again I had forgotten the subject entirely, and have remained in the same wicked state of ignorance ever since. The only alpha mark I received in a not very distinguished second-class degree was, needless to say, awarded for sixteenth-century French grammatical theory.

I say all this by way of warning that though I would happily claim to have been deeply formed by France and its culture, I am as ignorant of postwar contemporary French literature and all its underlying theories as I was long ago of ancient French grammatical theory. All this has had singularly little influence on me. What very skimpy reading I have done of Derrida, Lacan, Barthes, and their fellow *maîtres* has more often left me baffled and frustrated than enlightened, and has led me—in a way I know must seem appallingly old-fashioned—to attribute many twentieth-century French cultural phenomena to a nefarious Germanic influence that crept over the country in the late nineteenth century, and that has blanketed, blurred, betrayed all that lucidity, wit, elegance, etc., associated with an older tradition. I must admit that this attachment to the *eau Perrier* of that old tradition is due in considerable part to sheer lack of comprehension of the muddy clouds that seem to me to spring from too much prose by the gurus mentioned above. I suspect that even if I were French I would not understand; the fact of my not being French merely envelops everything in a kind of double ambiguity. I am not quite sure what they mean, but like the Irishman, I am also not sure that I would understand even if I did understand.

It took me many years to realize the great abyss between the French and English traditions of language use, or rhetoric: the pervasive influence of the metaphorical on the first, and of the literal on the second; life perceived through the intellect, through forms and concepts, and life perceived (more or less) as it appears; words as pure algebra, words as practical and Euclidean; as carefully bred garden pansies and as, in Lévi-Strauss's pun, wild heart's-ease. No doubt expert comparative linguists will cry in outrage at such a crude distinction, and I must, if I am forced, retreat behind the subtitle of this book.[1] Such an abyss, wrong though I may be to suppose it, forms very much a part of my own imagined France.

I may read a French text and feel I have understood it perfectly in every semantic and grammatical sense; but because I am not born French, nor bilingual, a final understanding—indeed, *the* final understanding—is forever beyond me. Like every writer, I read a text in my own language against a kind of absent text, made of all the alternative words and turns of phrase that might have been used; in French, alas, I have no such instinctive thesaurus. In practical terms this does not worry me as perhaps it should. I think of it privately as "the ghost," which haunts every contact I

1. This essay was first published in *Studies in Anglo-French Cultural Relations: Imagining France*, edited by Ceri Crossley and Ian Small (London: MacMillan, 1988). It now incorporates additional material on "Ourika" (see pp. 52–53) that appeared later (1994) in an essay on Claire de Duras's short novel of that name.

have with France; but all old houses have a ghost, and what we shall never quite finally know is, in my philosophy of life, an essential part of any attraction and enjoyment. I should not like France ever to become, in an emotional sense, at its heart, not foreign to me. This ghost of never completely knowing is, I believe, the quintessential part of any true and lasting love, whether between persons or between nations.

I suppose the dark side of the abyss was best demonstrated in the *nouveau roman* episode, that classic case of a wine that does not travel. Its exposition, in the hands of its main theorists, such as Robbe-Grillet and Butor, was fiercely logical; but with a handful of exceptions, its practice, to us backward British, bewilderingly dull. A kind of honorary French part of me by no means thought that of every *nouveau roman* he read; but his quarreling English twin insisted that this was obsessively impractical, by the values and standards of *his* traditions. Novelists may reject the societies they live in morally and politically, but not all normal readers into the bargain.

I was assured on all hands during a visit to Paris in 1981 that the *nouveau roman*, like the structuralist and deconstruction debates, was ancient history, long dismissed by the contemporary French mind. Story now ruled; the Balzac it had once been found pointless to imitate was reinstalled. ("By a small oversight they buried themselves," one literary journalist drily told me, "instead of him.") When I remarked that the theories remained very much on some British and American minds, I was met with dismissive shrugs: typical, that the Anglo-Saxons should be so far behind.

Everyone in 1981 (including M. Mitterand) knew that the greatest living French writer was Julien Gracq. As it happens, I do not disagree with that verdict—and think the general ignorance of his work in Britain a very sad thing indeed—but the point I am trying to make is the folly of our occasional academic *engouement* for movements and theories that require a native soil, their own specific language and culture, even to exist, let alone to be exercised. I might import the vinestocks, the exact methods of Burgundy or the Rhône valley, to England; I am not going to produce their wines. Intellectuals may adore the sophistication, the complexity, the sheer incomprehensibility of much of the Gallic theorizing; but we novelists never took it to our hearts, I am afraid. We never saw it as our duty to bore our readers, just as nowadays I think few of us accept the implications of the more extreme forms of deconstruction, which so cleverly deny us any clear reason for writing in the first place.

I did once plan—and indeed started to write—a publisher's nightmare: a novel to be half in English, and half in French. My written French was in any case nowhere near adequate to the task, but what finally killed the idea for me was the impossibility of feeling truly at home in both cultures, of expressing both methods of viewing, and reacting to, experience. I have in recent years done some translating of plays for the National Theatre, and have found it there too. Superficial meaning flows easily enough from one language into the other, yet deep down they seem to me never to marry, never quite to fit. I can even see this in, so to speak, my own mirror, in having my own work translated into French. Annie Saumont, who has done all my recent books, has excellent English. She is furthermore a gifted writer of fiction herself, with several books in her own language. I know I am very lucky to have her, and was delighted when she won a prestigious translation prize a few years ago for *Daniel Martin*. Yet her solutions to the problems my texts pose quite often set me back at first reading because of what they leave out of the exact nuances of the English meaning, or (more rarely) the circumlocutions she is forced into to express them. Always I have a little private reaction to her work on mine, and it is a humiliating one not for Annie, but for myself: I still don't understand either French or the French.

I was lucky, when I got to Oxford, in 1946, to find myself under Merlin Thomas at New College. As I soon discovered, other students envied his students their good fortune. He was young, quick, friendly, and had a sense of humor that was sometimes Rabelaisian. I went up originally to read French and German, but my German tutors paled beside Merlin, and in my second year I thankfully (though I sometimes regret it now) gave up German. Of course I had other French tutors, but they also tended to pale beside Merlin. One was Dr. Enid Starkie, a famous figure in the faculty at that time, and in *le tout Oxford* also. I was a heretic, and never really took to her. Her French accent was bizarre. I remember smuggling a French friend into one of her lectures. When she began to recite something from Rimbaud, he turned to me in profound puzzlement: "What language is this?" Then there was old Professor Rudler, lecturing on *la passion chez Racine*, a very unpassionate performance indeed. (Later, in France, I was to hear Nadal on Corneille, the very antithesis, rather like some grand ornament of the French bar pleading a case of *crime passionel* before a rapt jury of students). A friend of mine and I watched the audience rapidly diminish as the course of lectures proceeded; when it arrived at precisely two—ourselves—we decided it was our moral duty to stick the course out to the end, which we did.

The time we were obliged to spend on Old French and its literature was then very generally hated, and regarded by most of us as supremely pointless, a torture we (supposedly) owed above all to the fact that Sir Alfred Ewert was head of the faculty. It took me a shameful number of years to realize that for me, at least, it had been one of the most valuable parts of the course, and certainly so with regard to the art of storytelling. If I had been told at the time I should one day introduce a new translation of Marie de France in America (as I did, in the 1970s), I should have laughed. I hope the quotation from *La Chastelaine de Vergi* that is epigraph to my first published novel, *The Collector*, shows my symbolic debt.[2] I still read Marie from time to time; and fall in love with her all over again. She is so far away; then, as close as a physical touch.

Merlin managed to get me into the then newly instituted Maison Française in the Woodstock Road, under Henri Fluchère. Our rooms all had important paintings, and I slept for a year with a Léger on the wall above my head. The food was also distinctly better than was generally found then in Oxford. We had lunch and dinner every day with Fluchère and his attractive French housekeeper. It was the rule that at table we must speak French, something of an ordeal for most of us, given the very low value then put within the faculty (Dr. Starkie was typical of it in this) on speaking French with any fluency or with a decent accent. There were quite often distinguished French guests, such as the composer Darius Milhaud (who was only too happy to drop into English outside the sacred dining room), and then our contributions would virtually cease. On one occasion the guest was an odd little man in scoutmaster's shorts, and the rule about speaking French was waived. We knew he was some professor from "the other place" (Cambridge), but not why; lunch over, he was surrounded on the lawn outside by an excited gaggle of English-faculty students. That was my only living encounter with the famous Dr. Leavis, though his spirit has grown much closer at the several Cambridge seminars I have happily attended since.

We were all a little bit in awe of Fluchère. Very recently I read Courte-

2. *Que fors aus ne le sot riens nee* ("No one knew of it but them").

line's fictionalized memories of life in a nineteenth-century French cavalry barracks, the sarcastically titled *Les Gaîtés de l'escadron*, and felt a strange faint echo of life at the Maison Française. It certainly had nothing to do with Fluchère himself—a kind and humorous man behind the facade—or the comparatively civilized life of the house; much more, I suspect, with finding ourselves pitched into a foreign setting and culture, away from the "home" of England, and embarrassed by our own ineptitudes and naïvetés in it, like so many recruits to an ancient regiment.

Modern students will find it hard to believe how ignorant most of us were in those days of the actual France. The war had banned us from Europe, of course; and also, because of military service, delayed our entry into university, so we were mostly well over normal age. Of course we got to France on vacations, but I think even then most of us went with English friends. It remained a foreign place; going there was still something of an adventure. We had occasional contacts with students, but few with any other kind of French.

By pure chance one summer, I got a job in a French wine factory helping to process the *vendage*, quite the hardest and most unromantic work I have ever done. We were not even allowed sleep, because lorries from the more distant vineyards would come rumbling in at all hours, often in the middle of the night, and we had to be up to receive them. My knowledge of really blue argot leapt during those weeks; and we put things in the vats that have stopped me from drinking that particular kind of apéritif ever since. When I left, I hitched a lift in a Citroën on the nearest road. It was driven by an unusual millionaire from Lyons, a gentle elderly man with heart trouble. He was looking for someone to help crew his yacht at Collioure nearby—a small ten-ton ketch, not millionaire-like at all. With him was his friend, a married but much younger woman from Paris. For several weeks I virtually lived alone with them, in paradise after my bout in hell. M., the friend, was also unusual: fiercely honest as well as very good-looking. She had a very brave record in the Resistance, among other things. Of course I fell in love with her; she was only a few years older than I was myself. The only reward I received was to be allowed to become something of her confidant and her butt: what the Resistance had really been like, why she loved both her Parisian husband and the gentle millionaire (and could never love me—and how ridiculous and sentimental my transparent near calf love for her was); her feelings about life, the impossible naïveté of the English, the monstrous selfishness of her bourgeois compatriots. She was as well read as she was left-wing, and not only in the fashionable authors of the time: Camus, Sartre, Aragon. Her scorching honesty, even about her own faults, her humor, her impulsive moods, her sometimes savage teasing—all these were dazzling. She was like something one had read about in books, but here by some miracle was in the flesh. I have never been able to see countless French heroines, from Joan of Arc on, through Phèdre to Antigone, without the ghost of her face behind. "M" did not stand for Marianne, but so far as I was concerned, it might well have done so. She was, with Merlin, by far the best tutor I ever had on France.

I went from Oxford for a year to the University of Poitiers, where I was appointed to the faculty of English (once again thanks to Merlin Thomas) as *lecteur*; reader I may have been in title, but in all else I was like an *assistant* at a lycée, and a bad one. Above all else Poitiers made me realize how ignorant I was of English literature. Absurdly, most of the reading I did that year was in my own language, not in French. The head of the English faculty I did not get on with, but L., the *professeur-adjoint*, was much more sympathetic, with a *normalien* mind far sharper and more learned than mine was ever to be, far more stringent and severe in its logic, far drier. We used to go on long walks to listen to the plainchant at the neighboring monastery of Ligugé, and I also taught in my spare time in the city's Jesuit college. But the French Catholic mind has always remained closed to me. Claudel, and other impassioned icebergs, I never read with pleasure.

Years later, when I discovered Gracq, I was amazed to hear that he was, or had been, a close friend of Adjoint L. (who indeed features as L in *Lettrines*). The brilliant L.'s story in later years has been sad; but the memory of him has survived.

So too has that of various French students I came to know well. A principal private interest with me all my life has been nature, and it was through these friends that I came to know French nature, in Poitou and the Vendée. My most vivid and happiest memories of Poitiers lie far more in bird-watching expeditions, impromptu shooting trips, and the like than in anything academic; in the naturalists' mecca of the Brenne; in glorious meals, *raie au beurre noir, moules au pineau,* endless oysters beside the bay of Aiguillon; in *beurre blanc*—which remains to this day my favorite sauce—beside the Loire, as also that region's wines, especially from that delectable little area round Savennières, just east of Angers (about to die, I want a glass of Madame Joly's Coulée de Serrant in my hand; you may keep your Montrachets and the rest). I didn't really begin to know rural France until that time. But I will come to that.

I faced something of a crisis at the end of my year at Poitiers. Of all I learned from both Merlin Thomas and L., perhaps the most useful was something negative: I could never be a true teacher, even far below their levels. I had begun a first novel at Poitiers. I knew that it failed, even by my own jejune standards, and that to become a true novelist would take me many years. Teaching *is* a convenient profession for would-be writers, in the time it allows for the other activity; but it becomes a trap, and in proportion to how seriously the teacher takes his or her teaching. I had applied for a job at a bizarre-sounding college in Greece, clearly a dead end in academic terms. Then Merlin wrote to say he had heard a post as French master at Winchester was vacant, and he would be happy to recommend me. It came to a day when I had a choice: go to Winchester, and a sensible and modestly promising future, or to Greece, and exile myself from all that Oxford, and England, stood for.

I chose Greece partly in a mood of deference to the *acte gratuit* of Gide and the existentialism of the time. But that is another story. When I eventually returned to England, I was totally under the Greek spell, and France seemed like a distant episode in the past. What brought me back to it was another chance: an antiquarian bookseller. Francis Norman's shop, just off Heath Street in Hampstead, must, in its flagrant untidiness, its seemingly endless dusty piles of books, have appeared typical to a casual passerby of any other lazy second-dealer's; those of us who went in, however, very soon knew we were in a book lover's paradise. Francis Norman was, behind his shyness, a very distinguished scholar, a delightful man, a prince of booksellers—I might almost say a Maecenas, for his prices were often ludicrously low. At the end of the many years I knew him (and lived for his catalogues, long after I had left Hampstead myself), our conversations often took a distinctly unusual form for the normal antiquarian bookshop. I would hand him some small treasure I had unearthed, say a *mazarinade* from the time of the Fronde, whose price anywhere else in London would have been at least five pounds.

"Honestly, you can't let this go for just a pound."

"Dog-eared. Not worth cataloguing."

"But it's complete, for goodness' sake. Not a tear."

"I really don't want more for it."

"This is ridiculous. You know I'm not an impoverished teacher any longer. I'm jolly well going to give you more."

"Oh well . . . I suppose . . . if you must . . . I don't know . . . would one pound fifty be too much?"

Very occasionally he had not to be beaten up in price, but rather satisfied that you were worthy of the book. I remember once having to argue with him for nearly half an afternoon to prove that I deserved a Commenius; that I knew the great Czech was a genius, the patron saint of European education and all the rest; in short, that I could promise to respect and love the book as much as the seller himself did.

He always carried a large stock of French books, and they, or those I bought, were the road that led me back to France. What I discovered in that shop was the France that no university can teach its students: not in the least that of the famous writers, and the classics, but an endless *galimafrée* of minor poets, minor plays, forgotten memoirs, forgotten theological and political debates, Revolutionary pamphlets, trial reports, eccentricities, collections of anecdotes. Of such trivia I have gained over the years quite a collection, and of a kind that any self-respecting book collector would turn from in horror. Famous "firsts" do not interest me in the least; but countless things that no one has read again since they were first published, yes. One obscure *trouvaille* at Francis Norman's gave me the germ of *The French Lieutenant's Woman*: Claire de Duras's *Ourika* of 1824. There was no indication of author on that text. I had never heard of the book, the copy was badly foxed, and I didn't anticipate much reward for the five shillings I paid for it. If I paid even that it was simply on the strength of a glance at the opening sentence. One of the things I learned in that shop is that I adore narrative, real or imagined. It has become for me the quintessence of the novelist's art—and I liked the feel of the immediate bald plunge into the story of *Ourika*. But I thought that I would be disappointed, that I had lumbered myself with one more insipid *nouvelle* in the Marmontel tradition—some piece of didactic morality tinged with a dilute romanticism, and a wasted buy even to someone with my inveterately magpie attitude to book collecting. I took the little octavo, with its green marbled-paper covers, quarter-bound in worn black calf, home and sat down to prove my fear right. Long before I finished I knew I had stumbled on a minor masterpiece.

I reread it almost at once and have done so a number of times over the years. If anything, my admiration for *Ourika* has grown, and grown more than I realized. I chose the name of the hero in my own novel *The French Lieutenant's Woman* quite freely—or so I thought at the time. It came as a shock, months after my typescript had gone to the printers, to pick up *Ourika* one day and to recall that Charles was the name of the principal male figure there also. That set me thinking. And though I could have sworn I had never had the African figure of Ourika herself in mind during the writing of *The French Lieutenant's Woman*, I am now certain in retrospect that she was very active in my unconscious.

Only in two cases can I confess that classics have consciously influenced me. One French writer I have always deeply liked and been seduced by is Marivaux, while the one novel I have always adored, from schoolboy days, and read countless times, is Alain-Fournier's *Le Grand Meaulnes*. I know it has many faults, yet it has haunted me all my life. Fournier's own life itself has driven me again and again to the Sologne, to stand where he stood—to Yvonne's lost château, before Uncle Raimbault's shop at Nançay, in that tiny attic bedroom above the school at Epineuil. His novel lies somewhere behind all of mine. I have my own professional influence-tracers nowadays, but none seems to me adequately to realize the effect of this one on me.

I was able to go to France very little in the 1950s and early 1960s. That was when Francis Norman's shop was so important for me, its books my only French reality, and indeed much more an imagined one than anything else, and nine parts out of ten a past reality. But since those years I have been to France—or I had better say *my* France—almost every year. My France has no cities (above all, no Paris), no museums, no libraries, no famous châteaux, no autoroutes—and, with one or two exceptions such as Fournier, no literary connections. Through various circumstances I have lost touch with everyone I once knew there, so it also has no French friends, of the human kind, anyway.

What my France consists of is endless obscure countrysides, their tiny towns and lost villages, the more remote the better; some, especially all that lies south of the great curve of the Loire, from Nantes to Nevers—La Vendée, the valleys of the Creuse and the Vienne, down through Auvergne to the Causses and the Cevennes—I am usually revisiting, not seeing for the first time. I know many corners far better than I do many parts of England, indeed think of this France as not foreign in any meaningful sense, so strong is it in my mental landscape, in *pensée sauvage* terms. Friends couldn't understand why my wife and I didn't live in France, or at least have a holiday home there; but the pleasure lies (for me, still does) in the random, drifting, returning nature of this kind of relationship with France, the way it allows me to indulge the many faces of my imagined country.

I was on such a holiday just before Elizabeth died. We revisited some favorite botanical sites on the Causse Noir and the Causse de Larzac, near Millau. It may seem strange for a writer to let a glimpse of a few rare flowers dictate his holiday, but so it is. (As most British naturalists now know, France is a kind of miracle as regards countless species rare in this country; for me, being there is a little like a child's being given the freedom of a sweet-shop.) Then on, the rare orchids remet, to see a bridge in the Cevennes. An *abbé* was brutally murdered on it in 1702: a bleak upland bridge, a very un-Junelike evening. The lady of the drapery and gift shop at one end of the bridge, where the *abbé* had once lived, seems taken aback that this mad Englishman should be interested in this unmarked place and remote event. We discuss Mazel's account of the murder (he was there) for a minute or two; she has read that, but not Marion or Bonbonneau. I buy a pot of the delicious local honey she sells. Such days, in a heaven of flowers in the morning (*Cephalanthera damasonium* growing with *C. longifolia*, unheard of), at the scene of an obscure historical incident (but one that has always fascinated me; it was the spark that started the Protestant Revolt) in the evening—such is my France.

Yet it is not the naturalist or the historical dilettante in me that primarily drives me back to it. Far more, it is a kind of more general aesthetic lack, if I do not souse myself in it every so often. I mentioned my liking for Gracq earlier. That is certainly based on the subtlety of his novels, such as *Le Rivage des Syrtes* and *Un Balcon en forêt* (for my money, the finest—*et le plus fin*—novel of the Second World War), but also on those descriptions of rural France that appear in *Lettrines* and elsewhere. Years before I read him, or even heard his name, I had firmly decided on my own favorite small area of the Loire—that stretch of the south bank that runs to and past

Saint Florent-le-Vieil, past the Ile Batailleuse and the Ile Melet (where Elizabeth and I long ago picked out for ourselves the one place in France where we would happily break our own rules and live—once one of those *fermes épanouies sur leur terre-plein fortifié qui défie la crue*. This farm is in ruins, long uninhabited, now more heron-perch than anything else, but I dream of owning it every time I see it). The chance that this landscape is a favorite of Gracq's also, and has been memorably (in *Les Eaux étroites*) described by him, like his childhood at Saint Florent, is perhaps a poor reason to like him as a writer. But I admire his sharp and sometimes quirky views (the *étrange manque de liant* in Flaubert, yes) of life and literature also; above all the shrewd, rich meditations in the quite recent *En lisant, en écrivant*, essential reading for both practicing novelist and serious student. A *goût de terroir* runs through all I know of his work: a rootedness, a nostalgia, an almost peasant independence, despite all his sophistication and complexity in other ways.

I am trying, through Gracq, to put my finger on what I most love in France, imaginary France; why I may claim it has formed me deeply. At heart it is not the literature, ancient or modern, its wit and elegance, its delicacy and perceptiveness, its variety. It is nothing political or social; it is not its wines and foods, all its subtleties and richnesses in the *art de vivre*. If anything, it is a richness of freedoms, and even there not so much in allowing people to choose from such richness, as in making the choice available. It remains the mother of so many things besides those that du Bellay listed in his famous poem, and not all desirable; yet it is for me the eternal homeland for all those whose personal *mise en ordre* partakes of *pensée sauvage*.

I sometimes imagine what I would be if I did not read French, however less than perfectly, did not know its culture, however erratically, did not know its nature and its landscapes, however partially. I know the answer. I should be half what I am; half in pleasure, half in experience, half in truth.

BEHIND *THE MAGUS*
(1994)

For CIRCE and all the other tomb-robbers

I had spent the 1950–51 academic year as *lecteur d'anglais*, a faintly glorified kind of *assistant*, at the University of Poitiers in France; but was rather firmly told at the end of it that my services would *not* be required during the following year. It was not quite being sacked, but it felt like it; and, moreover, deserved to be it. I had been a truly awful "reader," not least because I then knew a good deal more about French literature than about the English I was supposed to be teaching. I remember vividly describing during my first lecture how Rupert Brooke had died among the poppy fields of Flanders, while my blundering through Eliot's "Four Quartets" must have beaten all records in making the already rather obscure totally incomprehensible. I experience a shiver of horror when I remember how I must have confused and misled all the Poitiers students of English during that year. To worsen the already bad, I fell in love with the faculty professor's favorite student. A true firing had been completely earned, on both personal and academic grounds.

I didn't at all enjoy what I was reduced to after Poitiers, aged twenty-five and still living at my parents' suburban home at Leigh-on-Sea in Essex, and endlessly poring over the gray, gray columns of the *Times Educational Supplement*. Nothing lured me at all, perhaps because I still didn't fully realize that I had absolutely no vocation at all for academic teaching. I had only my second in French from Oxford, and a first-class loathing of suburban England; and on top of that, a near-lethal illusion that I was intended (as if there were a God, and life could show intentions) to be a poet.

Eventually, late in the autumn of 1951, something came unexpectedly to the rescue. The British Council had been appointed the agent of a boarding school in Greece, supposedly based on Eton and enshrining the spirit of Byron. The Anargyrios and Korgialenios College had been built and founded in 1927 and was under royal patronage. I am pretty sure no one there had any real notion of what Eton was like, and quite sure they had no comprehension at all of "Byron's spirit." However, all the other good teaching posts had by then gone, and I was in a field of only two or three other broken-down horses. I duly won the job.

I barely knew Greece or the Greeks at all, and had next to no understanding of their terrible recent history, first under the sadistically cruel Nazi occupation of 1941–44 and then during the multiple horrors of the civil war of 1945–49. Above all I knew nothing of the foul horsemongering that had gone on in the wretched "Percentage Agreement" between Stalin and Churchill. I certainly didn't realize what a dangerous old man the latter had become, driven by his fear of communism and a hopelessly anachronistic vision of a renascent British Empire. I didn't even realize that a distinctly conservative right-wing government had taken over in Greece, aided and abetted by a patronizing and very misguided Anglo-American alliance. Greek women were not to get the vote till 1952, and a king had been reinstated in 1947 (against the wishes of most ordinary people in the country, though not those, officially, of the directors at the school to which I was going). The worst new horror was not to come until 1967, yet the dreaded day of the abominable colonels already lay pent in the air, like so many other latent fascisms in human history.

I had perhaps one small saving grace—though it was far more personal than literary. I had, ever since leaving Oxford, in 1949, been keeping something I then called *Disjoints*, a sort of broken and very personal record of what was happening to me. This journal truly was almost entirely about myself, and in no sense a decent historian's version of matters. Its only worth lay in the clumsy and often distinctly callow account of a young Oxford student born in 1926. That value, it seems to me, must lie largely in its nakedness, by which I don't mean its honesty; "honest novelist" is almost an oxymoron. But perhaps it will one day have some interest as an account of midcentury innocence, if not downright foolishness. At any rate, while I was in 1993 attempting to transcribe its barely legible manuscript pages, I came across the passage that follows. I had totally forgotten it.

I had arrived at the boarding school on the island of Spetsai (in *katharevousa*, the so-called pure form of Modern Greek; it is Spetses in the demotic) at the beginning of January 1952. If Athens, then still some way from its present hideously polluted and overcrowded condition, had impressed me, the six-hour boat voyage from Piraeus to the island, in the armpit of the Peloponnesus, had neighbored Heaven. The five blocks of the school, a mile or two outside the small main village, were very nearly grotesque (actually and architecturally much more so than I made the place in *The Magus*, the novel I was much later to write about the island), yet I found it all both moving and amusing . . . to be only a glance away from the hills above Epidaurus, and those near Mycenae and Tiryns; and above all, to be so miraculously remote from the suburban deserts of Essex.

I have always been deeply interested in, obsessed with, and absorbed by nature, and fell headlong and hopelessly in love with that of Greece, literally at first sight. I remain deeply attached to that difficult, devious, and hospitable, sometimes monstrous yet almost always charming people, the Greeks, and have long said that in fact I have three homelands: my own England (not Britain), France, and Greece. My love for all three of them may seem rather strange since it is above all of their rural, "natural history" aspects and little, or not at all, of their cities and larger towns. I have nicknames of a sort for these aspects of both France and Greece that attract me: *la France sauvage* and *agria Ellada*, the *wild* sides of both countries.

The following passage was written during the very first few days after my arrival on Spetsai. *The Magus* was not even thought of then; yet this last year, when I reread these lines for the first time in decades, I realized that they were the sperm and egg, the very genesis, of the as-yet-unwritten—indeed unconceived—book. That is why I reprint the passage here, almost exactly as it was written. Perhaps it's vain so exactly to detail the moment of conception of an as-yet-unborn child. There are countless little corrections and rewritings I am tempted to make now, but I have avoided all but the very slightest changes. This *was* it, for better or for worse.

The School and the Island: January 1952

The school is in a park by the sea, which one can hear on the shingle. The garden is full of cypresses and olive-trees. There are hibiscus in bloom. A well-equipped gymnasium, a football-pitch, tennis courts, even two fives courts! A school which is a dream, superbly situated and equipped for four hundred boys. But there are only a hundred and fifty, and they are dwindling in numbers. So many things could be done here—an international school, a coeducational one. Sharrocks[1] thinks any change is hopeless.

I met the deputy headmaster—a pleasant man with crinkled eyelids and an honest smile. We ate with some of the boys. I speak no Greek, the other masters speak no English, so I could talk only to Sharrocks.

I have no time to write this in detail. Tant pis. *It needs rewriting from the end of the vista.*

I went for a short walk in the morning. It was very cold with a choppy sea blowing up against the shore. I saw two kingfishers sitting on the strand, least expected of birds. A kestrel, and what looked like choughs; and several other birds. And there were many flowers. Sharrocks says there are no birds here—but there seem to be great possibilities. The variety of natural life excites me—the natural historian has a profound advantage over all other men. When I pass through a new country, the birds and the flowers and insects mean—from the point of view of my own pleasure—as much to me as the humans and their artificial world. They form a kind of ubiquitous sanctuary.

I went down with Sharrocks to the village to buy some utensils. We ate fried cuttlefish—very pleasant—with fat olives and chips, and drank beer in a small restaurant with a moth-eaten stuffed buzzard hanging from the ceiling. The people seem so friendly; amicable—able to be friendly.

Today I met most of the rest of the staff—as yet they possess no characters, but only the nicknames I base on their unpronounceable Greek surnames.

I sat at a table with seven boys for supper—a Cretan on one side of me who was nearly inarticulate, and a Turk on the other who spoke fairly well. But it is going to be difficult to keep up a thriving conversation for a whole term on a vocabulary of a hundred or so words.

The plunge has been taken; the work seems, from the point of view of hours, easy. Four teaching periods a day, total three hours, and two duties a week, total five, which makes twenty-three hours a week. I cannot complain. The boys are ebullient, spontaneous, and eager; more feminine than English boys. I saw a newly arrived (from holidays) boy kiss a friend on the cheek. The older boys show more affection to the juniors than an English boy would dare. Facially, and in other habits, one might almost be in England.

The boys, however, cannot discipline themselves; there are no organized

---

1. The person whom I here call Sharrocks is now my old friend Denys Sharrocks. In 1951 he was the senior English master, whom I'd supposedly come to the island to help.

games; and the day of seven periods followed by two and three-quarter hours'
homework is too much. The teaching methods appear antiquated. The school
needs reorganizing. Partly it is the lack of a university tradition like Oxford
and Cambridge in England, or the Ecole Normale Supérieure in France.
There is no core of cultured masters. Here they seem to know their subjects,
but to have few outside interests, and little gossip in common. Rather like vil-
lage schoolmasters in England.

But the island is a jewel, a paradise. I went for a long walk up into the
hills inland—through the pine trees, up stony goat-tracks in a cold bright si-
lence. It was a perfect cloudless day with a small wind from the central Pelo-
ponnesus; with almost the warmth of a warm March day in England. The
pines are small, shapeless, and loosely scattered, so that the views are rarely
impeded and often superbly framed. A sea of these pines is a sea of round
tops like cork oaks. What is strange in the hills is the silence: no birds (yet
they are everywhere around the school); very few insects; no humans, no an-
imals; only the still silence and the brilliant light and the blue sea below,
with the Argolian plain and its small central mountains opposite. A purity
and simplicity of emotion, a kind of quintessential Mediterranean ecstasy,
pervaded the air, the air infused with pine resin and winter sharpness and the
brine from far below.

I saw no one for a long time; one or two shepherds called in the distance.
Sound carries fantastically. A small boat chugging out to the daily steamer
anchored off the village sounded a few hundred yards away. But it was two
or three miles. I passed an astronomy station, strangely isolated in this hill-
forest. On another hill further east, I could see a monastery looming white
among the black cypress trees which guarded it. The view became more and
more beautiful at each new stage in the climb. Opposite, Argolia, like a re-
lief map, indented, edged by small bays with pink-orange cliffs and, further
inland, dark-green pine woods. But these woods are so open, so airy, that
there is no sense of the somber, the far North. Nothing like the terrible forests
of the Pasvik River in the arctic Norway, where I was three years ago. You
can see these woods for their trees; and they are a relief, like groves, sanctu-
aries from the hot, bare plains. Argolia appears well inhabited—one or two
white rashes of village and a regular speckling of isolated farms and cottages.
Only the central mountains are barren and uninhabited. To the right, the
beautiful islands around Hydra, and Hydra itself blue and pale-green and
pink, floating in the veronica-blue sea. Massy islands, with bluff peaks, and
big cliffs and escarpments, but balanced together in the distance. All the col-

ors are vivid, but soft, pastel without being furry, aquarelle yet solid. To the right, over the bay of Nauplia, the big mountains of the central Peloponnesus—snow-covered, like pink clouds low on the horizon, glittering faintly in the oblique sunlight. Far hills, cliffs, villages, and the vast carpet of the sea.

I climbed up and up and came onto a rough road, and found myself on the central ridge of the island, bathed in sunlight, an undulating sea of pines falling to the southern coast, which is much more deserted than the north, and has only a few cottages and a villa or two to populate it. The sun was over Sparta; the sea between Spetsai and the Peloponnesus glittered brilliantly, variegated by small ruffling breezes. A fire far below, near a cottage, sent a column of smoke straight up into the air; but up where I was, there was a small, cold breeze tempering the warm sunlight. Nearby I saw a man, the first I had seen, cutting faggots. Two more men appeared, riding donkeys. One of them stopped by me and stared at me and smiled, and said something sharply. He wore a stained pale-blue beret and ragged trousers; his face was linseed-oil-brown, like an old cricket bat, and he had a good black mustache. He repeated the same phrase as before. I stammered something. He stared back. "Anglike," I said.

"Ah!" he nodded, half shrugged, kicked at his donkey, and rode on without another look at me. His companion drove the other donkey, minute under a mountain of pine branches, past me, with a friendly "Kal'emera as."

"Kal'emera," I said, and went my way.

I walked along the road for a while. I walked through a small brake, and a woodcock flew off from under my feet. A lizard scuttled away. It was very warm, airy; I struck off the road and came to a cliff facing westwards. I sat on the edge of it, on a rock, and the world was at my feet. I have never had so vividly the sense of standing on the world; the world below me. From the cliff, successive waves of forest fell down to the sea, the sparkling sea. The Peloponnesus was absolutely without depth or detail; just a vast blue shadow in the path of the sun; even with field glasses, no details could be seen, except in the snowy mountaintops. The effect was weird, and for a few minutes I felt incomprehensibly excited, as if I were experiencing something infinitely rare. Certainly I have never seen so beautiful a landscape; a compound of exquisitely blue sky, brilliant sunlight, miles of rock and pine, and the sea. All the elements, and at such a pitch of purity that I was spellbound. I have had almost the same feeling in mountains, but the earth element is missing there—one is exalted and remote. Here the earth was all around one. A sort of supreme level of awareness of existence, an all-embracing euphoria. It can-

not last long. At the time I could not define what I was feeling; the impact and uplifting had made me lose myself. I was suspended in bright air, timeless, motionless, floating on a sublime synthesis of the elements. Then there was the fragrant wind, the knowledge that this was Greece, more than that, the spark which lit ancient Greece; and very strongly, the memory of all those gray streets, those gray towns, that grayness *of England.*

Landscapes like this, on such days, advance men immeasurably. Perhaps ancient Greece was only the effect of a landscape and a light on a sensitive people. It would explain the wisdom, the beauty, and the childishness. Wisdom lies in the higher regions—and Greek landscapes are full of higher regions, mountains over the plains; beauty in nature in every corner, a simplicity *of landscapes, a purity which demanded a similar purity and simplicity. A childishness because such beauty is not human, not practical, not evil—and minds fed on, surrounded by, such a paradise must become its dupes, intensely attached to it, and after the initial offering of worship (i.e., the Golden Age), they must be creatively sapped by it. One creates beauty to supply a lack of it; here there is plenitude. One does not create; one enjoys.*

Such fragments make good shoring.

I walked back towards home, thinking of Treasure Island. The sun fell, gilding the crests; the valleys were green, gloomy. I came to a valley full of the tinkling of goat-bells. There were twenty or thirty of them; the goatherd called regularly "Ahi! Hia!" and gave a fluty, penetrating whistle. I glimpsed him making down through the trees, surrounded by goats, a tall man in dove-gray trousers, patched very pale gray at the knees, and a black coat. I hurried down the path to catch up with him, but then caught sight of a small plant by the side. I fell on my knees, and incredibly, there was an Early Spider Orchid (probably Ophrys fusca*) in bloom before me, a little thing some six inches high, with one large flower, its blotched purple lip insolently outspread, hooded by the pale-green sepals, and the green bud of a second flower. I knelt down and took the details, the goatherd forgotten and his goats tinkling fainter and fainter away. Now it was getting dark; the mountains looked dark blue, the Argolian countryside black. The air was cold. I walked swiftly down the goat tracks, as there was still a good way to go. At last I stood on a bluff from where I could see the school. It was studded with anemones, little plants three or four inches high, pink and mauve, nodding in what slight breeze there was.*

I tumbled down through the olive terraces, past a ruined farm, and onto the road, which led to the school in a few minutes. I think one of the most

*satisfying walks I have ever made. Once one knows the background, I think
the school is best seen as a kind of necessary evil. But such a day—vision—
dwarfs pedagogy and all things pedagogic.*

There is now an excellent history of midcentury Greece, Mark Ma-
zower's *Inside Hitler's Greece* (1993). Andrew Thomas's *Spetsai*[2] has a good
description of the island and its history; and I myself have tried to say
something of the literary background of *The Magus* in the foreword to all
later editions. It was my first novel, and I worked on it for nearly fifteen
years, yet still feel it never quite came off.

There is one other name I should have mentioned among the "influences." He had during my time as a student quite as great a one as
the French Alain-Fournier, but he has recently suffered that fate worse
than death in the English literary world: being judged *vieux jeu*, distinctly
passé. I could never defend the poor dying man's antifeminism and anti-
Semitism, but the older I grow, the more clearly I recognize his genius in
other ways. He is in my view easily our *largest* novelist of the earlier twentieth century, with only one possible rival, James Joyce.

Anyone who has read the preceding extract will guess who I mean:
D. H. Lawrence. My own experience on the island was dense, pregnant
with existingness, an intense, as in a prolonged lightning flash, realizing of
what I was; which was also a shadowing (that I tried to reproduce in another context in *The Magus*) of what I should or must become. Such experiences, which I think most of us artists and perhaps all of us at some
point usually have, come in a very brief space, gone almost as soon as arrived. Often we do not even recognize them. Yet something in them, if we
do, despite their comparative evanescence, *is* forever. A form of that "is-
ness," that present being, runs—however clumsily I expressed it—through
The Magus. And above all else I owe that to Lawrence.

The school is now defunct, I suspect largely unmourned by those of us
who worked there. I was sacked, along with many others on the staff, both
Greek and English, at the end of the 1953 school year. (The romantic side
of the story takes place in England, incidentally, not in Greece, as seems
commonly, though mistakenly, supposed.)

One of the isolated villas on the south coast that I had seen on that first
January walk was Yiasemí ("Jasmine"), then owned by the Botasis family,

---

2. The Lycabettus Press, 1980.

and friends of the more famous Venizelos one. Eleutherios Venizelos was a liberal who died in 1936. He had fought for the liberation of Crete from the Ottoman Turks, and later gained much other territory for Greece, marred only by what the Greeks called, and still call, the Catastrophe—the 1922 disaster or terrible forced exodus of so many Greeks from Smyrna and the rest of Turkey at the hands of Mustafa Kemal (Ataturk). Venizelos became almost a messiah to the new refugees and the people in the lands he had gained; but further south, in an older Greece, he was seen very differently, almost as a devil, and as largely responsible for the Asia Minor Catastrophe. He was also antiroyalist. In effect, he tried in the 1920s to modernize and reconstruct Greece. In 1932 he had to resign; a putsch he attempted in 1935 failed. King George, exiled since 1923, was invited back, and in 1936 gave power to a quasi-dictator, one Metaxas, who was to die in 1941. Now Venizelos was sent into exile. Thus, in the rift between the intelligent Venizelos and the conservative Metaxas, Greece's eternal division between liberal democracy and right-wing monarchy was born. The school's founder, Anargyrios, himself seems to have walked the tightrope between the two sides; at any rate, a tobacco millionaire and himself Spetsai-born in 1849, he had made the great Venizelos president of the trust to run the as-yet-unbuilt school in 1919. It was finally built in 1927. Anargyrios himself was to die a year later. He wasn't much liked on the island, as much Albanian as Greek, though he built its main hotel and most of its few roads. It had a small adjoining island, Spetsopoula, now owned by the shipping magnate Niarchos. He had nothing to do with the magus of my novel; he wasn't even there when it was written. But one thing that certainly did affect it was the old Spetsiot flag from the 1830 War of Independence: an anchor entwined by a snake and with an owl (the scops owl was common on the island), surmounted by the motto *Eleutheria y Thanatos*, "Death or Freedom."

I was later to visit Yiasemí several times, and I kept many of its features in the book, especially its Moorish colonnade. The original name of the headland on which it stood was Sphantzina, according to a map I still have of the island, drawn for John N. Botasis in 1901. It did indeed have its private beach, as in the book, and I well remember that the first time Denys Sharrocks and I visited it, a harmonium was being played, quite the most incongruous sound imaginable in such a divine landscape. The Good Friday beach and the tiny chapel just to the west used to be quite as deserted as they are in the book, but I understand the spot is now a popular tourist haunt, though Yiasemí itself remains private.

To say it is "sacred" would be blasphemous, but I simply cannot bear to see it all changed. I recognize that it must be, but like all novelists, I think of that lonely villa on its beautiful headland far less as it really is, or indeed ever was, than as I invented it. Many people have found it incomprehensible that I've never returned, though I have been back several times to other parts of Greece. Perhaps my account of this walk, which I was to do a number of times again in the following eighteen months, may partly explain a little of why I have never gone back . . . and somehow condemned myself to a kind of exile.

Some thirty years or more later, my translator into Modern Greek, Phaidon Tamvakakis, very kindly gave me a book by Nikos Demou, *The Light of the Greeks* (*Tò Phos ton Ellenon*). It was not until I read the powerful essay and quotations that accompany the photographs there that I began to understand what had happened to me on that then long past January day in 1952. The Greeks see, feel, apprehend light not as others do, and from the beginning of history to its end. It is so infinitely more than the bikini-clad, tanning-oil, bouzouki-dancing experience that so many package tourists (or grockles, as we call them here in the west of England) suppose. Among other things it is all beauty and all truth. It is in every thought of Heracleitus, Socrates, and Plato; it is in every painted vase, in every landscape, in every anemone and orchid, in every line of Seferis and Cavafy, almost in every taverna.

It and its absence are life and death. It reveals everything and spares nothing. It can be both achingly beautiful and consoling; it can be terrifyingly ugly. No other race feels this quite so sharply as the Greeks; so intensely, so all-consumingly.

It was not for nothing that the ancients made the witch-magician Circe the daughter of Sol, Helios the sun, which was also one of Apollo's guises. I fell totally under the spell of Circe during that far-off day in 1952, and unlike Ulysses, with his disinfectant *moly*, I have never really escaped from it. I dedicated the first edition of my book to Astarte, who does in mythological part lie behind Circe. But I wish now I had offered it to something else. On holiday from the school in 1953, I climbed Mount Parnassus alone; when I got to the very top there I remember a ring of violets that someone had rather poetically planted to crown it. The clouds had cleared, all was sun, the view sublime; this was certainly the loveliest moment of my life. Inside the crown of violets, beside the cairn on the very peak, was a word traced in pebbles in Greek.

For all Greeks always, and for all of us who truly love their land, it was the only word: φῶζ.

THE J. R. FOWLES CLUB
(1995)

"The J. R. Fowles" is the name of the club to which I belong, for my sins. A number, indeed most, of its numerous other members consider that they barely do. Indeed, we're generally treated as sheer deadwood—mere ciphers on some wretched mailing list, recipients of obscure requests for charity, badly written annual bulletins (mostly about people we can't even remember), invitations to nauseating reunion dinners (for which we have to pay ourselves, natch) . . . I'm sure you'll all be only too familiar with this sort of horror and its ghastly vacuities. As for the wretched president, Sir John Eye, and the never-available secretary, Mr. Mee, honestly—how the damn thing staggers on at all defeats reality. I certainly never asked to join it, and often wish I hadn't. I suspect my father, attracted by the name, foolishly put me down for it before I was born. Quite a lot of my fellow members will hardly exchange a civil word; others do nothing but whine and whinge. Yet others (talk about egos!) are self-important beyond belief, especially one fathead who fancies himself a novelist. Another pretends to be a feminist. I'd like to see him just once with a duster or and an iron in his hand. Another pair both think they know everything about natural history—one a sort of scientist, the other a sort of poet. You can imagine. They never bump into each other without a bitter slanging match. That's typical, I'm afraid. Nothing that comes before the so-called management committee—aesthetic, moral, political, domestic, you name it—*ever* gets a *nem. con.* vote. We are truly an unspeakably futile shambles. I honestly shall resign if they don't watch out. I've always hated men's clubs, anyway.

GREECE
(1996)

Greece came on me rather suddenly, in 1952. I had never studied Greek, and all I really knew of the classical culture came from its ghosts and echoes in the literature of the other cultures I had been studying, mainly the French and German . . . principally the first. (I gave up the second in my first year at Oxford, when the University regulations were changed and we students were allowed to "do" one language alone). I had run across one Greek I liked, but of so long ago that he seemed almost from another universe, though his ideas did (indeed still do) deeply excite me and lay behind an early book, *The Aristos* of 1964. That was based on Heracleitus; but I arrived in the Aegean only too like Odysseus at one of the darker stages of his voyage, clueless and crewless, near drowned—and, it seemed, fit only for a complete dousing in oblivion.

In fact I came initially to Greece not far from despair. I knew, or rather "sensed," that I wanted like countless others to be a writer, but had already guessed amid the callow mists that though the want might be there, the practical means—patience and willingness to work hard (my parents weren't well off at all)—were not. I had no sort of vocation for the real grind of teaching; indeed, my first taste of the university world, at Poitiers in France, had been discouraging in the extreme. Already I had realized that to teach was to have to pretend, but I failed to realize that "to write" was exactly the same. I had parted with academic Poitiers with very little regret on either side (except for the now dead Professeur-Adjoint Léaud, who had been that remarkable novelist Julien Gracq's friend), but I did at least accept in France that I had been born in the wrong culture, class, and country. All I could do about that was to harbor a deep dislike for my own, especially their more imperialistic side, the swollen myth that still festered under the name of Great Britain: Empire, King and Country, and all the rest. It was partly France but most clearly Greece that would allow me to see the often lethal follies of absolutism, monarchism, and patriotism of the jingoistic kind. If I had a true homeland north of the Channel, it lay a thousand times more in a green island called England than behind the blanketing, claustrophobic Union Jack of Britain and the United (increasingly disunited) Kingdom.

What notions I had of modern Greece were distorted by two gross misconceptions. All my generation had been dazzled by the exploits of a celebrated band of odd men out who had fought beside the brave Greek resistance from 1939 to 1945. The aura of the contemporary Xans and Paddies somehow gilded our dream of those other handsome, dashing, and divine *andarte* and their women friends who had once lived on Mount Olympus. We knew we couldn't rival them; my generation just missed both the fighting in the Nazi war and the bout of world belligerence in Korea, Malaysia, and so on that followed. We read of all those glamorous exploits in Crete rather as the suburbs today read of the flamboyant goings-on in Hollywood. All that was somehow not quite credible, belonging far less to real life—or certainly our own real lives—than to fiction. It allowed us to nibble and float in lotusland, but not to live where we really were. And that, the reality, seriously misled me as to the nature of the school (now defunct) in which fate landed me, the Anargyrios and Korgialenios College on Spetsai. I now realize it was almost entirely corrupt, and to suppose it was a microcosm of the whole country (as I'm afraid for a time I did) was both foolish and very unjust.

I spent a great deal of time to begin with at that Spetsai school despising most things Greek, especially socially and culturally. One half of life on the island just seemed a bad joke. To live almost within sight of Mycenae and Epidaurus and so many of the other peaks of ancient Greek history, yet to be immured in what was apparently an absurd simulacrum of a British private school, was ridiculous, such a head-on clash of opposing values that many of my English colleagues had, as I was to learn, disintegrated under the incongruity. I had once been head boy of my own outwardly not dissimilar school in England (Bedford), but it had taken Oxford, existentialism mingled with the siren voices of Marxism, and several intervening years (they call it growing up) for me at last shamefacedly to reject all the shoddy little triumphs of my personal past. The Spetsai school came to be a sickening emblem of an ancien régime still trying to cling by its fingernails to a sort of power. I didn't realize the extent to which I had dived into the die-hard right wing of Greece. It was almost an honor to be sacked—as I was, with many others of the staff, both Greek and English, at the end of 1953.

We foreigners on Spetsai were aware that we had also entered the not entirely unrelated brothel of a world made up of all sorts of hopeful would-be artists. It seemed at times as if we were frightened northern virgins trembling on the brink of full-time prostitution. I was saved from taking my metaphorical clothes off too soon by falling passionately in love with what I have come to call *agria Ellada*, or "wild Hellas." I was hopelessly, overwhelmingly in love with wild Greece within a day of my arrival in Athens. On Spetsai I soon came to recognize that life at the childishly bureaucratic school and life in the wild island's pine-clad hills and on its ravishingly lonely beaches were two totally different, even mutually exclusive worlds. They belonged almost to separate planets, half a cosmos apart.

Wild Greece was so breathtakingly, heartstoppingly beautiful that it made almost all modern attempts to evoke it in art ludicrous and obscene. I set out to climb Parnassus in June 1952, and did very unexpectedly meet a muse near its peak, Lykeri: a remote descendant of the creature Erato that I much later was to invent for *Mantissa*. She was in fact an intensely shy and suspicious young shepherdess, only too plainly unimpressed by my silly English pride at having climbed a not very difficult mountain. It is simply a long walk, and needs no genuine alpinism. But Parnassus did teach me, as perhaps trying to climb it has always taught, a valuable lesson. This was the real Greece, and the only real light. Until I could resolve to learn—or at least sometimes be able to recall—those divine altitudes, I should never be able honestly to call myself a poet and writer.

I have recently been rereading the diaries I kept in the early 1950s, which I hope may one day be published exactly as written—I fear not much to my credit at all, since they seem largely an account of a man in paradise who had willfully and obstinately blindfolded himself. The real Greece began for me on that day in 1952 when I stood on Lykeri; and very soon afterwards (I had just met the peasant-cool young shepherdess), I put my foot in a wolf trap, a salutary Greek warning against taking too much happiness for granted.

My nearly complete inability to penetrate the smog cast so thickly by the Spetsai college and to see what Greece really was—not only to me but to all who have the luck to go there—now appalls and shames me. I did many times try to convey this wild soul of Greece in poetry, and as regularly failed, especially in the face of many of its native poets, for whom I soon gained considerable respect: Cavafy, Seferis, Ritsos, Elytis, and others . . . I only wish I commanded the demotic well enough to truly savor them. To the poets I would add the little-known (here in always-lagging Britain) work of Stratis Tsirkas. His 1960–65 trilogy *Rudderless Societies* (*Akybernetes Politeies*) must surely rate as one of the most important works of the century about modern Greece, indeed about all remoter Europe.

I suppose, as some are born physically left-handed, so destiny and the wisdom of Heracleitus and Socrates (who are far more appealing to me than Jesus Christ has ever been) incline some of us towards the social, political, and moral left, as perhaps my admiration for Tsirkas will have let you guess. I have the deepest sympathy and pity not only for the general agonies and horrors of the Nazi occupation, but also for the long and dark Ottoman shadow of earlier centuries. Much about contemporary Greece continues (depending on circumstances) to irritate or amuse me; but I long ago resolved not to make the same errors that had trapped me in 1951. Now I remember how much it has suffered, how fatally it remains split; and how much its older self remains the grandmother of us all, and yet how eternally young-beautiful she can still be. Greece is a kind of double miracle, both existential and historical; she not only *is*, but always *is*, like light itself, in every now.

I should like to end this faintly schizophrenic account of what is in effect a love affair with a sort of consummation. In November 1996, I was invited back to Spetsai by Suzie and Lilette Botasis, wife and daughter of the harmonium-playing Askis, whom I had met in the villa there forty-five years before. We were taken to the island in a swift launch by Nikos Demou and met on the beach of Agia Paraskevi below the villa by Lilette and her husband. They took us up to Yiasemí to meet her mother, Suzie—"us" being my by stepdaughter Anna (who first came to the island as a little girl and has stayed closer to it than I), Eileen Warburton from America, who is writing my biography, and last but not least my Athens friend Kirki Kephalea, who's already written a book in Greek about my experiences there, *E Ellenike Empeiria* ("The Greek Experience").[1] When Kirki first wrote to me many years ago, I told her rather dismissively that I really

---

1. Olkos, Athens, 1996.

didn't have time to spare for just another foreign student; but with a name like Kirki (Circe), how could any lover of Homer and Joyce quite ignore her? In the end we met, and I immediately found another reason to fall in love with Greece. I could find no *moly* to resist her. There was no one with whom I'd rather have shared this deeply moving return than these three.

I can't really describe it, but its deepest sense was of a kind of almost unexpected sanction—that I hadn't been wrong to have lived for so many years dreaming both *of* and imaginatively *in* that exquisite landscape. So many returns are disappointing; but never this one. The Botasis family played a not unimportant part in the 1821 revolution—the one Byron died for—and the house (like the island itself) is full of old relics and memories of that struggle to cast off the Ottoman tyranny. It reeked of freedom . . . and the cyclamen, the pines, the sea, the silence, the ineffable view. Some returns and the kindness of the people who make them possible make one weep. Good fortune is always rare; its reality, beyond words.

THE JOHN FOWLES SYMPOSIUM, LYME REGIS, JULY 1996 (1997)

Those of you who were interested enough to come to the meeting at Lyme last July can't, poor devils, have avoided seeing me. I had some sympathy with the speaker who said he felt for the poor French infantry storming Wellington's grimly massed British cannon at Waterloo . . . though quite who was trying to face out whom, in our battle, I'm not sure. On my side, I tried to keep one rule: I would seldom argue the toss . . . seldom, since like all true Englishmen, I know laws and rules are made only to be transgressed. They are always implicitly redundant; if they weren't, no Milton, no Shakespeare, no Keats, no Austen, no Brontës; elsewhere, no Newton, no Turner, no Samuel Palmer (it hurt me a little that that last was, I think, never mentioned in July). But I mustn't sink into one of those silly pothers where the subject blames his followers for not having spotted his peculiar secret tastes and quirks. Perhaps some of you will have noticed a certain rather bright young student from the Sorbonne at our meeting. Since she is French (and I'm one of those peculiar Englishmen who like France) and since she is also rather pretty (I begin to reveal embarrassing predilections) and since I've just been in California staying with Dianne Vipond and not least because I'm only too aware that my contribution to James Aubrey—the symposiarch's distillation, his Calvados from the scrumpy of our session—is hideously overdue, I hope you'll forgive me if I appear to address just one of you: Dominique from Dieppe . . . but only appear. This is intended for all.

Chère Mlle. Lagrou, dear Dominique, bless you for your recent letter, which managed in one charming (not foul at all!) swoop to convince me that I am not wrong to have put my money on two outsiders: "Europe" and "woman." In short, that like all decent Socialists I am sure the destiny of this green iceberg lies with the continent from which it recently (a mere few thousand years ago) calved. We must learn to be European again, or dissolve into the dirty water whence we stemmed. Rather similarly but much more importantly, we men, our whole gender, must come clean and confess that our macho attitude to your sex has been grossly and barbarously wrong for at least three millennia . . . and please, we'd like to be allowed back into the marriage. (There may seem to be "cultural" reasons; but I don't think true humanism, except when brainwashed by "political correctness," ever admits them.) A sensitive and thinking male can't have felt innocent since the time of the Hittites.

As I say, Dominique, I've just been in Los Angeles staying with Dianne Vipond, and meeting your friend Lisa Colletta. I came back via New York, where, while having a first drink in the Algonquin with Katherine Tarbox and Eileen Warburton (who, brave woman, is coming here very soon to embark on my biography), I saw a not totally unknown face, who seemed also vaguely to remember mine. This was Billie Whitelaw, Samuel Beckett's friend and muse and his great interpreter on stage. So the next day I am, thanks to her, in the Y, hearing her marvelous voice and dryness recreate him and his work—no nicer transmigration back across the Atlantic. The problem for me is this: how can one bear the wretched stiffness and inflexibility of men, how can one not prefer the sinuosity of women? The United States is not just the world's leading democracy; I hope it becomes its first gynocracy. Dominique, Dianne, Lisa, Katherine, Eileen, Billie, Kirki in Athens, so many others, I pray you shall all one day rule the world.

Being under the spell of something is not me, is very un-English; I've always rejected the idea. So I now feel a bit like the ancient Circe's most famous victim: foolish, *niais*—soft in the bad sense. *Et très jeune*, though sort of proud that what I term my "sense of being" (Virginia Woolf had another phrase for it) is still alive and keeps sweeping me off my feet. I can't be what convention or "correct behavior" or "the suburbs" or "academia" imagines I ought to be.

Academia: I like the sound of what you're proposing to do at the Sorbonne, and will try to answer your questions when you come tomorrow. I'm not just blockishly against deconstruction—please believe me. I see there is something there; but for me it is both enough (certainly with Barthes and much of Kristeva) and yet not enough. I bought two books in

Claremont, Dianne's charming and book-proud Los Angeles "village." Understand Lacan in half an hour, Baudrillard (rated almost as high as Foucault in the U.S.) ditto. Oh dear. If only these gods had a sense of humor. Dianne has one, so does Lisa; and so does Katherine, though you should see her bookshelves . . . not a deconstructionist classic missing. I sat beside her last summer on the banks of her lovely little Maine river, ferruginous and gently idyllic, so lovely. America is more than just the Atlantic away. Those who come to America and think they can snap-judge it don't realize how physically *vast* it is; and how that explains its rampant excesses, its being very often so wildly toppling on the brink, and (incidentally) the way we Anglo-Saxons are so unable to communicate with each other humanly and emotionally. The French "expert" on America still to beat or be bettered remains de Tocqueville.

I used to blame various defects I saw in myself squarely on Oxford, I now think rather unfairly. Like most such barbed-wire fences erected between the ego and the world, they come mainly from personal temperament; in other words, from something far beyond simple remedies and solutions. I like *not* knowing, not being sure, the feeling that there is always room for change. The easy catholicity of taste and opinion in Oxford, even in 1945, that seeming license to follow one's nose and pursue private interests, made it seem almost a legitimate duty to do so. It was later to seem both oddly un-American and un-Victorian, freedom-obsessed, almost Rabelaisian (*Fais ce que vouldras*). The war and a spell of compulsory duty in the Royal Marines didn't help me at all. But being able to read what one wanted and when one wanted . . . that was a sudden intoxicating bliss, devoted mostly in my case to discovering the existentialists (Camus much more than Sartre). The most useful thing I learned at New College, and for which it used to have a reputation, was a sort of Socratic skepticism. Some people take this for a twisted pessimism, a constant love of carping. But it isn't; at best it is a sincere belief in the virtues of doubt, and I have never unlearned it.

All this has left me in a familiar predicament for all those who have tasted, or tried to taste, as I suppose I have, too much of life. In one way we are cramped like Joan of Arc into an oubliette, constantly squeezed between different periods, ages, times, schools, and fashions, and thus condemned to live in any actual present in only a very minor way. Chronology, the actual time, *now*, only very rarely seems real and important. Speaking for myself, I generally feel hopelessly scattered, disseminated, in absurdly too many places at once.

I wish happiness to all of those who came to the symposium, and thank them for all that they individually contributed to it. With my endless doubts about literature (that skepticism again!) and the constant neuroses of writing, I know I must seem difficult and uncertain. I rarely even know where I am myself, nor where I am going; but in that I am in part acting out what I sense my antediluvian existentialism has become, or becomes: a need both to feel and to be continually free, always (though this sounds a pleonasm) to be being, both *still* and *in the now*. As I wandered last month around the two absurdly Roman Getty museums in California, through the dazzling Joshua Tree and Anza-Borrego deserts, as I stood beside Dianne, pursuing John Fante both on lovely Point Dume and macabre Terminal Island, or gawping at the superbly displayed archosaurs and pterodactyls (symposiast Kevin Padian's "field" at Berkeley) in the Manhattan Natural History Museum, I may seem to have hardly been there at all. But I was, I was just happily *being*; as indeed I was through the symposium. For years I have passed on a Zulu wish, *Go well*. Go well, and forgive me!

II

CULTURE AND SOCIETY

ON BEING ENGLISH
BUT NOT BRITISH
(1964)

Look how imaginative English poetry is. But who ever heard an English-
man say, "How imaginative the English are!"?
MICHAEL MACLIAMMOIR

For a decade now I have been haunted by the difficulty of defining the essence of what I am but did not choose to be: English.

It must be said at once that "being English" is a vague sort of being. Few of us can claim a purely English ancestry, and yet Englishness is something more than having spent most of one's life in England. Arbitrarily, I will define it as follows: it is having at least two grandparents out of four be English; having lived at least half one's life in England; having been educated there; and of course having English as a mother tongue. But above all I believe it means recognizing and accepting, at every class level, the vices and virtues of the specific forms of Englishness discussed in these notes.

Increasingly I see my Britishness as a superficial conversion of my fundamental Englishness, a recent facade clapped on a much older building. "Britain" is an organizational convenience, a political advisability, a passport word. In all the personal situations that are important to me, I am English, not British; and "Britain" now seems in retrospect a slogan word that was most useful when we had a historical duty to be a powerful military nation, for which patriotism was an essential emotional force. The heyday Briton believed that Britain was and should be stronger than any other country in the world; but the true Englishman has never willingly believed this. His subversive ideal has always been a demiplatonic one: to live in the justest country in the world. Not the strongest.

This subversive ideal also lies, for obvious historical reasons, at the core of American life. The war of 1775–1781 was between an English desire for justice and a British demand for obedience, and indeed the greatest modern formulation of this English desire for justice is the Declaration of Independence. But the preoccupation of Georgian and then Victorian Britain, and now twentieth-century America, with military, imperialist (or crypto-imperialist) strength can be at least partly justified by the fact that the Anglo-Saxon tradition is notoriously practical and pragmatic; we have always believed that a would-be just country in a world of largely would-be unjust countries will survive only for as long as it is strong enough to keep the dragons down. It is not for nothing that Saint George is our patron saint.

Jingoism, natural aggressiveness, and a delight in bullying no doubt play some part in our love of power; but the best English and American political thought has always recognized that this longing for power is fundamentally a longing for the only means, in this imperfect world, to a just end; and at their best the idea and the historical reality of "Britain" have been manifestations of that longing.

The failure to recognize this further motive is one of the great faults of Marxism. If we all believed only in power—power as an end in itself—then Anglo-Saxon capitalism would indeed contain the seeds of its own destruction. But because it is really justice that we are trying to get at *through* power, our capitalism is in fact transformable and remediable. It contains its own self-correcting dialectic, its own formidable antitheses, such as freedom of speech and all those safeguards of the individual that characterize our law, and the proof of its ability to transpose to better keys is clearly to be seen in such recent achievements as the welfare state and the New Deal. In short, the grossnesses of English *means* always finally stand a good chance of being purged, from inside, by the virtues of their *ends*.

This purging and often puritanical obsession with justice is to me the quintessence of Englishness. It explains why we are admired in general and disliked in person by most other races. We stand, willy-nilly, for something good, but like all people who stand for something good, we don't stand easily among the rest of humankind. Moreover, in a kind of excess of fair play, we have allowed the rest of the world to have its revenge on us for being so frightfully, frigidly just and Minervalike.

Other nations spend a great deal of time defining themselves and one another; but the general view has always been that the English need less defining than redesigning. One of the first foreign gentlemen to report on us sneeringly noted that we are *non Angli sed angeli*—prigs to a man, in other words, and only exiguously fit for decent non-English company. But I think our chief crime in foreign eyes is that we as a race are not only superciliously just but also fundamentally indefinable—the least definable, rather than the most perfidious, Europeans. This indefinability, or contra- dictoriness, is partly caused by the Great English Dilemma, and partly by the basic English mental mechanism.

The Great English Dilemma is the split in the English mind between the Green England and the Red-White-and-Blue Britain. I am going to use the rest of these notes to attempt to define these two poles.

For centuries the English have had to put up with the aggressive national- ism of the other three quarters that make up the United Kingdom. The reason, of course, that the other three countries have never forgiven the English for "conquering" them is that the moment they do so they will have to stop having revenge. They are never happier than when belabor- ing; and the English, as all flagellologists know, are in their turn never hap- pier than when being belabored. Britain subsists internally on a sort of symbiosis of dislike and willingness to be disliked.

However justified the "Celts" may be in disliking us, their dislike has always been lucrative to them. Every Scot who wants to govern, every Irishman who wants to satirize, every Welshman who wants to sing—in short, every fame-and-fortune hunter—descends on London and if he is any good at his job gets handsomely rewarded. He may also get hand- somely contaminated by English ideals, but that seems a risk most are will- ing to take. This centuries-old usurpation by the non-English of the active functions in the running, criticizing, and entertaining of *England* is a result of another distinctively English trait, the love of umpiring—that is, of stating principles and then watching other people act on them. Britain might be (tentatively) defined as Celtic genius and love of action displayed on the field of English high principle.

I am emphatically not a Little-Englander. It is quite clear that man is a federal being, and that states' rights are the most lost cause in evolution. The familification of individual countries, the merging into blocs, is well under way, and in the United Kingdom only a handful of lunatics in the Celtic twilight still caterwaul for home rule. The time has come when there is no other but administrative and political necessity to talk about being British, and the agonizing reappraisal we English-Britons have had to make of our status as a world power since 1945 in fact permits us to be much more English again. The other three countries have always kicked against the idea of being British, and since we had the original responsibility *for* it, we have long retained an earnest sense of responsibility *towards* it. We have always felt that we had to show the others how to be British; and this has exacerbated our now unnecessary schizophrenia.

The Scots, Welsh, and Irish are no more (or no less) English than the Australians and the Americans. There are in the United Kingdom the additional factors of geographical proximity and shared institution; but that is all.

We have to be British and we want to be English. The reason our emotional attitudes towards matters such as the dissolution of the Empire and our engagement in Europe cut across both party and class lines is that our Englishness is still battling our Britishness. The same ambivalence has for long been apparent in our literature.

What is the Red-White-and-Blue Britain? The Britain of the Hanoverian dynasty and the Victorian and Edwardian ages; of the Empire; of the Wooden Walls, and the Thin Red line; of "Rule Britannia" and Elgar's marches; of John Bull; of Poona and the Somme; of the old flog-and-fag public-school system; of Newbolt, Kipling, and Rupert Brooke; of clubs, codes, and conformity; of an unchangeable status quo; of jingoism at home and arrogance abroad; of the paterfamilias; of caste, cant, and hypocrisy. In neither of the great political parties do the moderate majorities any longer defend this antiquated concept of an Imperial Britain-on-Which-the-Sun-Never-Sets, a concept now at least twenty years stranded in the past. But it creates a kind of afterglow, it pervades many of our moods with a nostalgia, it hampers our present, and, worst of all, it still obscures the Green England.

There seem to me to be two primary constituents of the Green England, both explanatory of our mania for justice. One is shared by the other members of the United Kingdom: the fact that England is virtually an island. We have always been a people who watch across water from the north; from the nonstriker's end of the wicket. As many writers since Montesquieu have noted, our mooring on the globe allows us to be, and often makes us, observers rather than experiencers. It has also largely permitted us to be pioneers in law and democracy, and it explains at least one important element in our famous—and infamous—hypocrisy. We are not holier than the others; only geographically luckier.

This hazard of geography married to this mania for justice also accounts for our love and need of emigration in all its forms: as pioneers; as colonists, as sailors, as proconsuls, as liberators (rejecting the role of voyeur), as lovers of the south, like Norman Douglas and Robert Graves, as refugees from the double-talk of the homeland, like Byron, D. H. Lawrence, and Durrell. The *reason* for the emigration has often been nationalistic ("British") or individualistic (selfish), but the *quality* of the emigration has depended and still depends much more on its Englishness (that is, on the spreading and maintaining of our concept of justice) than on its Britishness (the desire to spread and maintain imperialistic and master-race ideals) or its individualism (the desire merely to live abroad).

The other and much more specific constituent of the Green England is the survival in the English mind of that very primitive yet potent archetypal concept, the Just Outlaw. The Just Outlaw is the ancestor of the Good Umpire. He is the man too empirical, too independent, too able to compare, to live with injustice and stomach it. What John Bull is to the Red-White-and-Blue Britain, Robin Hood is to the Green England.

It is symptomatic of the stranglehold that Britain has on the English imagination that Robin Hood has now degenerated into a subject for children's-hour television serials and comic strips, instead of being the first idea that true English genius (a Britten, an Osborne, a Nolan) might be expected to turn to. But this failure to see what the Robin Hood legend ought to be to us in fact began much earlier. Already, at the hands of Ritson and Percy in the intensely *British* eighteenth century, Robin Hood had become a quaint ballad figure, castrato first cousin to the present cutout figure on the sides of breakfast-cereal packets. Yet this legend is the only national one of which it can be said that it has been known to every English man and woman since at least the year 1400. There is indeed only one other so ubiquitously well known: the Christ story; and I believe that robinhoodism is a practicalization of Nazarene Christianity, a belief that life is too short, and too unjust, for that battered other cheek to bear alone.

What Robin Hood was or who he was, in the dim underwoods of history, is unimportant. It is what folk history has made him that matters. He is the man who always, when faced with either taking to the forest or accepting injustice, runs for the trees.

Robinhoodism is essentially *critical opposition that is not content not to act.*

Robin Hood ceases to be Robin Hood as soon as he comes out from the
trees either as an acquiescer or as a conqueror (like Fidel Castro). *The
essence of Hood is that he is in revolt, not in power.* He is an activity *against*, not
a passive statement *of*.

The trees and forests have steadily disappeared since 1600; all we have
left is here and there the ghost of the old reality of the forest of the land
where the squirrel could jump from the Severn to the Wash and never
once touch ground. What we have done is to transfer the England of the
trees to our minds. Our life routines, our faces, our social codes and conventions—almost all that is outward in us—are hostage now to the eternal
enemy, the Sheriff of Nottingham (the power that is); but still our minds
look to the forest and keep us, in our fashion, at our most English, Just
Outlaws.

This process can be, and is, abused. Long-hostile foreigners such as the
French and the Scots will detect another source of our hypocrisy in this
habitual disappearance into the metaphorical greenwoods, this retreat behind the mask of our ability to simulate agreement when we disagree, to
smile when we hate, to say the exact opposite of what we secretly mean.

But it is the same ingrained habit of withdrawal, our basic mental
mechanism, that allows us to be the most self-critical people in the world,
and the most self-conscious, and one of the most tolerant. Part of what we
are withdrawing from is always that aspect of ourselves, our compromising
public face, that we have surrendered, partly through personal laziness,
partly through force of historical and social circumstance, to the Sheriff of
Nottingham. We English are first of all Just (or Justified) Outlaws against a
part of ourselves; and only then against the others.

A characteristic case here is that of the hyper-English *(malgré le nom)*
Max Beerbohm, a tireless debunker and deflater of the royal family, of
Kipling, of Shaw, of Wells—all forms, to a true Green Englishman, of
British vulgarity. Yet through all the long years at Rapallo, Max never lost
his intense love of England and of being English; he never, for instance,
caricatured an Italian. Max had the dandy's faults, but he belonged to a line
that goes back through Rowlandson and Gillray to Swift (the most English
Irishman there ever was) and that is continued today most clearly in Kingsley Amis. The thing is to keep England and English justice in judgment
pure; that is, unaffected, unpretentious, unbigoted, unimperial—in a word,
un-British. In both Max and Kingsley Amis (and in countless other greater
and smaller English artists and writers) we see the same preoccupation,

productive of both their triumphs and their failures: that is, the problem of how to be censorious without being pretentious. How to judge, in other words, without inviting judgment in return. The problem is insoluble, of course; but its specific insolubility is perhaps the most characteristic tension at the heart of all our best art.

Of course, withdrawal is a kind of movement, but not necessarily a kind of morality; and many of our least endearing characteristics spring from the facility with which we can play the Cheshire cat, Lucky Jim of the thousand faces. Ideally, a robinhoodist withdrawal is made in order to gather force to remedy the injustice—*pour mieux sauter*. Practically, it may be simply the observation of injustice from the safe cover of the trees. Thus every year we hear of crimes that passersby or lookers-on could have prevented. Ten persons watch another drown; not one acts. And not out of cowardice, but out of being English.

English consciences are too often too easily satisfied by the interior act of disapproval; our national fallacy is that such an act means something. We suffer from a sort of ethical sluggishness, a moral constipation. A lot is made of our love of tradition, our hatred of innovation, but a great part of our attitude towards events that do not closely affect us is in fact sheer indifference—the belief that when we have judged them privately, there is very little to be said for making that judgment public, for acting. Our gorgeously mockable love of discussing the weather with strangers is a love of not discussing more serious things with strangers, mainly because such a discussion would reveal our own particular hiding place in the forest. One does not get to Robin Hood's headquarters until the most unimpeachable credentials of friendship—or of hostility—have been presented.

A characteristic manifestation of this determination to withdraw can be seen in the Wykehamist view of life—"manners maketh man"—carried to excess. The "Wykehamist" (to be found in every class) exhibits a very typical sort of sheepish petulance when forced into the emotional declarations that would seem quite normal to any other race; he idolizes (not simply worships) common sense and noninterference; he will always see a good side in bad things ("If people want to take drugs, why shouldn't they?"); and any emotional statement of opinion, however just, will immediately arouse his intense suspicion and probable hostility.

Most Englishmen (once again, at all class levels, though the middle and upper subspecies are most guilty) get the keenest pleasure from being English, or withdrawal-adept. Nothing is nicer, to us, than not saying what we really think. We play this stranger-baiting game in several ways. We advance opinions we do not believe in. We deny those that we really support. We listen in silence when begged for opinion. We are noncommittal when goaded. We make deliberately obscure, oblique remarks (our "genius" for compromise). And all the time we watch our interlocuters getting hopelessly lost in the trees, as they stumble after echoes, shoot at shadows, and nine times out of ten end up with yet another sharp attack of anglophobia. (The tenth time, they take out naturalization papers and become even more skilled at the game than we are—as Conrad, Henry James, and T. S. Eliot prove.) Occasionally one of them stumbles on us as we really are, and the virulence of our hatred of royalty, or of the working classes, or foxhunting, or antifoxhunting, or whatever it may be, and the passion of our loves and enthusiasms, shock deeply, and generally offend. This is because the implications of all our deviousness *and* this secret other life are not difficult to discover. We play games with strangers because we have an innate mistrust both of the ordinary social situation, such as the dinner or cocktail party, as a field of serious communication and (far worse) of the capacity of other people for serious discussion.

Our protestantism, our nonconformism, is of course a function of our concept of the Just Outlaw; and to the extent that socialism is a product of dissent's expressing itself through reform, chartism, bradlaughism, trade unionism, and the rest, it is obvious that the Whig-Labour-Democrat movement is (or has been) more characteristic of the Green England than the Tory-Conservative-Republican, which is (or has been) characteristically hostile to changes in the status quo. (We are plainly at a point in history where it becomes difficult to know whether we are not evolving too fast *in some ways*; in short, progress may not necessarily be progress.) But as soon as dissent of whatever kind comes to power, it is Robin Hood out of the trees; and somewhere the new Robin Hoods it creates will be going into them.

Nothing I have said so far makes the English (beyond whatever incidental justice they create) seem anything but the cold, priggish, deceitful race some foreigners like to see in us. It does not explain our achievements in the arts, especially in poetry; nor does it explain many features of the real English in private—in the trees—that no serious observer can ignore, though many superficial ones do. I mean such good and bad things as our imaginativeness, our humor, our melancholia, our choleric temper, our bitterness, our sentimentality, our possessiveness, our frankness, our obsessive and complicated sexuality, our plunges into deep private emotion—all characteristic features, it may be noted, of one of the most revealingly English of all documents, Shakespeare's sonnets.

The truth is, of course, that the Green England is far more an emotional than an intellectual concept. Deep, deep in those trees of the mind the mysteries still take place; the green men dance, hunt, and run. In contemporary psychological fact this Green-Englishness shows itself in our preoccupation with seclusion, with practicing the emotions, the desires, the lusts, the excesses, the ecstasies, in private, behind walls, behind locked doors, behind the current code or codes of "correct" public behavior. In all our causes célèbres and scandals it is not the facts of the case that shock us worst, but the fact that there is a case at all. What a Palmerston is privately known to do is nothing; but what a Profumo is publicly caught doing is everything. In the light, the clearing, the nonforest, we conform, are stilted, are cold, talk in clichés; in darkness and privacy we are fantastic, romantic, and word-inventive.

Although the evidence of this other world is everywhere in our arts and entertainments, very few foreigners ever really understand that more than all other races, we live two emotional lives: one under the Sheriff of Nottingham's eyes, and the other with Robin under the greenwood tree. No other race can realize (or perhaps wants to realize) the complementary joys of the two modes of existence, or of our addictive need for this tension, this keeping up of the two opposing worlds, the gray and the green.

In art the Green England is in different ways in Hogarth and the great caricaturists, in Blake, Constable, Bewick, Palmer, Turner, Sutherland, the Nashes, Bacon; in our folk music, in the Fitzwilliam Virginal Book, in Elgar (split between "Britain" and "England"), and very purely in Britten; very literally in *England's Helicon*, Clare, Jefferies, Hardy, Hudson; metaphorically in Fielding, Smollett, Jane Austen, the Brontës, Lawrence, Forster; brilliantly and deeply in that strange Pole's *Heart of Darkness*, more English than any mere Englishman could manage.

In philosophy it is in our empiricism, our impatience with metaphysics, our taste for logical positivism rather than for castles in Spain. In law, in our elaborate system of safeguards to protect the individual against state injustice.

There is an obvious Green-English ancestry in many New England attitudes: in Thoreau and Hawthorne, in Emily Dickinson, in *Billy Budd*.

Mark Twain, too, has the characteristic hatred of pretension, of arrogance, of excess. Even the Wild Western hero, the man who one high noon has to take the law into his own hands, is a direct descendant of Robin Hood.

The Green England is green literally, in our landscapes. This greenness is not very fashionable at the moment; it is the burned rock of the south that we long for, and more than that for the burned, black, cynical experience of mainland Europe. But we have no choice: England is green, is water, is fertility, is inexperience, is spring more than summer. We are neither historically nor psychologically suited to be cynics, Spenglerians, quietists, or martyrs; no race that has made such an art of meiosis could sincerely believe that this is the worst of all possible worlds. It is not absolutely the best, of course; but it will do. And our job in it is to reform justly, or at least to ensure that just reform is always a possibility.

The Green-Englishman is then distinguished above all by emotional naïveté and moral perceptiveness. Because of this, every Englishman who travels abroad must at times feel like an adolescent among adults. It is all very well to wink at political corruption, totalitarianism, tax evasion, demagogy, and all the other sins that foreign flesh is heir to; but behind the wink, the attempt at a hard-boiled mask, the Robin Hood in us is always making for the trees. We despise this nausea at what the Romans do in Rome; we hate it, this weak stomach of ours, this poor head for the heights of iniquity. But there it is; our one great virtue and our vulnerability.

We are natural spreaders of justice; to the Sheriffs of Nottingham we represent a kind of creeping dry rot in the fine healthy house of established injustice. We can be as irritating to the foreigner as Socrates, with his peculiar humor, his long nose for cant, his incessant quibbling, his frequent refusal to sound like a real Herr Doktor of philosophy ought to sound, must have been to the Athenians who wanted only to get on with the business of living life as life had always been lived. It is precisely this one thing in which we can claim to be fully adult (moral judgment) that the world does not require of us; but that we must continue to require of the world. We *are* prigs. But a world of closed and closing societies desperately needs its prigs.

We see through law. We know that justice is always greater than the law and further than the law, further in definition, further in application, and further in our history. This is the greenness at the heart of our growth. We are condemned to be green; and in all ways green.

GATHER YE STARLETS

(1965)

I had better confess at once that I am writing about a subject with which I have never slept; and nothing, as Genet has five or six hundred times reminded us, is quite so immoral as total innocence. To make matters worse, I can't claim that my professional knowledge is any greater than my carnal, though I did recently spend some time at an important European film festival. Of course, starlets are a sine qua non of such gatherings—pleasanter to look at than, but as typical a feature of the landscape as, the kites round a dead elephant—and so at least I have watched them a little at what I suppose one must call their work. I think I would just as soon watch the kites at theirs. But I am not interested in what starlets are; only in *why* they are. And I am going to use them simply as caryatids for my quarrel.

At the festival, tirelessly, shamelessly, with smiles as natural as those cut in a Halloween pumpkin, Scandinavians, French, Germans, English, they exhibited their poses (and almost everything else) on the various *plages*, to the greater glory of their agents and the delectation of the cosmopolitan bird-watchers—for like music, the body is an international language—assembled on the promenade. I am sure some went away as intact as they came; others had propositions and refused; and a few, rediscovering or remembering a celebrated bit of Californian female folklore ("If you wanna get on, get laid"), no doubt chose, at the pricking of their ambition, to buy a kind of stardom with a kind of whoredom.

Well, life may reek on what the snobs now call the Côte de Sewer, but again and again I caught myself wondering what it was that drove, or required, all these good-looking but in the main dramatically untalented young women to hawk their golden curves along the beaches and hotel corridors of Cannes. Not many of them are conspicuously innocent, however virginally their fair hair streams, Primavera-like, in the breeze from the passing cameramen. They all know that in the world of the entertainment industry, which is half a cosmos away from that of the art cinema, they can expect nothing but ruthless exploitation and an absolute subordination of all other considerations to the economic. Few of them go like captured medieval princesses, their eyelids sewn with silk, to the lecherous pasha-producer's bed, or studio; and yet they are not, even at their worst, what Hollywood cynics sometimes maintain they are: *simply* prostitutes.

If they were (and charged money for their services), I think they would be treated with less contempt than they privately but generally are inside the industry. However, it needs only a very short acquaintance with the movie world to see that there is something anomalous about this contempt. Any given starlet may be sneered at, but starletry *as an institution* is far from despised. Indeed, it is essential, one of the most important elements in the walling myth of power-and-glory that international moviedom erects to keep reality at bay. Individual starlets are as common and gettable as individual bricks; but the wall they together make is something other. And as these callipygous and cone-breasted bricks lie on their beach mattresses, or simper imbecilely under the flashlights on some demicelebrity's arm, or sit in silent loveliness (until they open their mouths) around a producer's dinner table, they exert a subtle hegemony over the whole; just as do, in Watteau's pastoral paintings, those ghostly flocks of silly-pretty girls sitting on the grass or strolling down the *allées* in their pink and gray sateens and ribbons.

While I was watching the shepherdesses at Cannes I was aware of a constant nagging echo, from something much further back in history than Watteau. Then one day I overheard someone use the word *mogul.* I had it. I remembered those swarms of houris that infest every Moslem picture of paradise. The houris too were not simply prostitutes, but indispensable creators of ambience—and shutters-out of reality. Naturally they offered glimpses of free sexual bliss, they suggested that it was not only the gates of Heaven that opened gratis to the brave; but their primary function was to constitute the visual-tactile decor in a best of all possible male worlds. At the same time it is surely significant that we speak of movie moguls but not, for example, of movie samurai or movie aristocrats. The real samurai and aristocrats liked culture and intelligence in their geishas and demi-mondaines, as the ancient Greeks liked them in their hetaerae. Women such as Thaïs and Aspasia, Ninon de Lenclos and Harriette Wilson, had fascinating minds first and fascinating bodies second; their lovers sought from them an intellectual as well as a merely copulatory relationship. So here we begin to see two quite different roles demanded of the woman as mistress. In one she is the hetaera-geisha, prized as an individual and judged as much for her other accomplishments, her full humanity, as for her value as a bed partner. In the other she is the houri-starlet, and it is this role that I want to explore.

The Old Persian *huri* is derived from an Arabic verb meaning "to be black-eyed like a gazelle"—that is, the etymology springs from appearance rather than function, from the world of dreams and wish fulfillment rather than from that of practical reality. Now it is plain that a profusion of beautiful but will-less (therefore tongueless and mindless) girls is an essential of any decently run male paradise, just as it is equally plain that monogamy, with its filthy doctrines of responsibility and fidelity, is the nastiest subversive activity of them all. It accordingly may not seem remarkable that a congregation of insecurity-prone men such as movie executives should enjoy having coveys of houris surrounding them; indeed, it is not remarkable. But before I say what I do find remarkable, I should like to widen my field and point out some allied contemporary phenomena.

First there are the bunny girls, who offer a vicarious substitute for the true Paradise (from the Old Persian *pairidaeza*, meaning "park of pleasure," or open-air bunny club). Then there are the front-office girls who can barely write longhand, let alone shorthand. There are the expense-account secretaries, the company hostesses, the executive escorts—a whole monstrous regiment of peculiar euphemisms for the old houri. Next there is the meteoric midcentury rise in the social cachet of what twenty years ago was known as the mannequin—now, by another significant linguistic change, the model. That is, the perfect type, the one to be imitated.

There is the weird and now universal fashion of referring to women decades past thirty as "girls"; and a corollary down-stretch at the other end of the time scale to include in full girlhood, or hourihood, what once were known as schoolgirls. One sees this yearning of all womankind for girlhood in cosmetics publicity, which is more and more orientated towards rejuvenation ("Smooth away the years with . . ."); and unmistakably in their clothes fashions, which are now all based on those of the generation in its late teens and early twenties. Once daughters dressed up to their mothers; now mothers dress down to their daughters. The same theme runs through the reports of the 1965 Paris collections: the "in" look is the young look. Yves St. Laurent makes his models wear "little-girl hairstyles"; and perhaps for once Paris is only copying the trends set by the "Chelsea" designers in London: Mary Quant, Caroline Charles, and the rest of the (of course) girls.

Then consider the nature of the six great female stars (and therefore the sociological fashion setters) in the world cinema since the war. Lollobrigida and Loren are on the whole honorable exceptions to my thesis, no doubt because they come from a country where mothers have never given in to daughters—or to silence. But Monroe, perhaps to counteract the visual effect of her copious figure, cultivated a marked little-girl voice and mannerisms. Audrey Hepburn (compare her with her older, and much greater, namesake on the screen) is beautiful, but even more beautiful because she never looks a day over twenty-four. Bardot, who in her heyday probably had the greatest impact of the six, was never presented as anything but an inarticulate bundle of pouting nineteen-year-old sensuality—one hundred percent houri. And the current darling, Moreau, admirable actress though she is, undoubtedly owes a large part of her popularity to her chameleon-like ability to change in a second from a bag-eyed old wreck of forty to a ravishingly pretty girl of half that age. Bardot set the pace, so to speak; but Moreau suggests that an older woman can keep up with it. The one, in this context, was inimitable; but every woman in her thirties can today put her hopes into Moreau.

And then each age has a favorite member of the family. A hundred years ago it was the father; today it is beyond any doubt the daughter. We see this in the now-characteristic desire of many prospective parents to have daughters rather than sons, a desire that might have been predicted from Professor Galbraith's forecast that in an affluent society children must partly become status symbols, or luxuries. The factors we apply to other domestic luxury acquisitions (visual decorative value, voguishness, cost and ease of maintenance, and so on) must weight the dice against boys. We see it also in the increasingly common pattern (promulgated in fiction by Sagan) in the marriage age gap: the man old enough to be the father marries the girl young enough to be the daughter. It is true that on the father-husband's side, such marriages are very often second marriages, and that they seem most popular among the most successful. But it is precisely this group that has always been the least inhibited about surrendering, if no ostracism from their peers is risked, to new general sexual drives and infantilisms.

Equally revealing is the Beatle cult. The best-known visual emblem of the Beatles is the wig—the girlish hairstyle. Whoever they may appeal to now, they began by exciting predominantly girl audiences, and it was because they excited girls that other young men began copying their appearance: the long hair, the androgynous dress styles, and all the rest. Nor should one overlook the use made by many of these male singing groups of soprano voice techniques, unfashionable since the days of the castrato and the countertenor—the High Renaissance, another woman-dominated age. Crosby, Sinatra, and the other great crooners never quit the safely virile corral of the male octaves. Similarly, the tough male image made familiar by countless Hollywood stars, such as Bogart and Wayne, is as "square" as can be—and every anthropologist knows, incidentally, that the square is a male symbol, and the circle a female. I listened the other day to an intelligent young woman defining what she found attractive about the New Young Man. She said, "Older people think they're effeminate, but for us they're sexy"; and she followed up this interestingly narcissistic statement by saying, "Muscles and virility are out. It's things like the way they dress and the way they walk." The New Young Man is still, I am sure, fundamentally a male man; but he wants to look like a she-man, not a he-man.

Now it may seem that the other great pop cult of the day, that of the idiotic and ithyphallic James Bond, proves the contrary of all this. But Bond is notoriously more enshrined among the over-thirties than among their juniors; and I see in his following a very thinly concealed nostalgia for a world where men controlled girls, not girls, men. In fact, under the contemporary veneer, Bond is once again the mogul. Several critics have remarked on Ian Fleming's considerable skill as an evoker of visually erotic scenes and on his apparent inability to write anything but the most cursory and stereotyped love dialogue. Bond and his houri of the hour may act very sexily, but they talk (as one expects of a mogul and his moll) in a most painfully stilted way. Agent 007 was always a victim of that most dreadful secret organization of them all: his own century. And if you doubt this sacrilegious view, you must account for the fact that there are at the moment (I write in September 1965) no less than *five* films in production featuring *female* James Bonds. No clearer (and since one of these Jane Bonds is in real life none other than Mrs. Sean Connery herself, no more ironic) proof could be given that we are facing an insidious revolt of the houris.

This girlification of the boy has also been encouraged by the huge boom in two special types of magazine in recent years: the girlie magazine and the girl's magazine. The first spreads the idea that the high peak of human bliss is to be surrounded and sensually dominated by seminaked girls, and the second is devoted largely to showing its gazelle-eyed readers how to effect the surrounding and dominating in practical fact. But perhaps this tyranny of the girl is seen most patently in the advertising techniques of the sixties. We have become so used to seeing the girl selling everything from Cadillacs to coffins that we have hardly noticed the disappearance of the older woman as a selling image. The family, too, has lost much of its old sales appeal. Characteristically, where men appeal in publicity material, they are cast (by positioning or camera angle) as disguised worshipers of the girl. And even in those masculine products that need to suggest they are aids to seduction, the seduced one more and more assumes the appearance of a propitiable goddess rather than a helpless victim.

Well, by now my quarrel has emerged. I am saying that Western, or at any rate Anglo-American, society has become girl-besotted, girl-drunk, girl-distorted. Our artificial world sprouts girls as Cadmus' teeth once sprouted armed warriors, and regardless of gender we all worship this plague. It has become one of the ubiquitous follies of our time. It so happens that there is a word that expresses this condition: nympholepsy. The dictionary defines it as "a state of rapture inspired by nymphs, hence an ecstasy or frenzy caused by desire of the unattainable," and that is more or less what is infecting us today.

I am very far from being a misogynist, and I immediately acquit the girls themselves of any intention to subvert the progress of the human republic. They are not consciously befuddling us, or at any rate no more than Eve first befuddled that egregious dimwit Adam; it is we, the men, who are befuddling ourselves with girls. We can assume that men will always be more or less fascinated by them; and all I am complaining of is the current intensity of that fascination. There is, in connection with this, an interesting passage in a famous essay of George Orwell's.[1] "The impulse," wrote

---

1. "The Art of Donald McGill."

Orwell in 1941, "to cling to youth at all costs, to attempt to preserve your sexual attraction, to see even in middle age a future for yourself and not merely for your children, is a thing of recent growth and has only precariously established itself." To bring that sentence up to date, one needs to make a change: "only precariously" should be "now fully."

Man's adoration of woman has taken many forms. In primitive societies it was generally the mother (as fertility goddess) who was chosen as the ideal, a tendency that has survived in the various cults of the Virgin Mary and—until recently—in many Socialist (and totalitarian) theories of woman's place in society. In the classical age it was the virgin who symbolized the more mystical and noble of man's feelings about the female sex. Pallas Athene, the Roman Minerva, stood for wisdom and reason; though often got up as a sort of tough female Marine, she was for arbitration in war rather than for war itself. Her emblem was the olive branch. Artemis (Diana), goddess of the moon, of chastity, of lust controlled, reaches back into the furthest recesses of human civilization, and we can perceive in her perhaps the earliest of all man's attempts to turn himself into a moral being.

But it is difficult to detect much mother- or virgin-worship (unless in the one aspect I mention later) in our present adulation. The urgent need to reduce the population of the world, about the only matter both East and West can agree on, has tarnished the image of the mother beyond redemption. And as for virginity, it has surely become with us much more a temporal than a physical matter—something to do with age, an asset a woman loses at twenty-five rather than at first sexual intercourse. Time is the great violator now, not man; and virginity is a cosmetic, an extra titillation, rather than a source of mystery. But if we reject woman as fertile mother and as mystic virgin, then we are (or appear to be) left only with woman as a source of pleasure, as an instrument, as a substitute for masturbation—in short, as a houri. And it is not man who is imposing this role; woman herself is accepting it.

We do not have to go very far to find *social* reasons for this. There is the revolution in sexual self-understanding—and sexual mores—initiated by the discoveries of Freud. And there is the universal collapse of religious belief. However gallant a rearguard action the churches of the world are fighting, however intrinsically just their causes, it is as obvious as the dome of Saint Peter's that twentieth-century man is not a religious animal. It is the here and now that obsess him, not the there and then of an afterlife, which comes more and more to seem simply a charming medieval hypothesis. Heaven knows, or apparently doesn't know, that life on earth is precarious enough, since Hiroshima. So gather ye starlets while ye may; and if the almighty powers of commerce, public relations, art, and show business all invite us to the gathering, to the consumption of as many pleasures as the already lax conventions of society will allow, we need wonder no more why we have all turned Moslem—that is, into would-be houris and moguls.

We live in a typical *entre-deux-guerres* period, one that is history-bound to be rococo and frivolous in its pursuits and loves; and what the painted and carved cherubs and cupids and putti were to the age of Boucher and Fragonard, the omnipresent image of the starlet–model–cover girl is to ours. There have been various explanations of the Baroque and Rococo ages' mania for combating the horror of empty spaces with hordes of plump little pink male children. The Marxist explanation is that the putti served, like the heavy perfumes of Versailles, to cover a stink—the metaphorical stink, in this case, of grossly unjust economic conditions—and it is certainly easy to find in such great and period-revealing pictures as Watteau's *Embarcation pour Cythère* a grim retreat from reality as well as a poetic entry into fantasy. The putto was very much a member of the ancien régime; and his head fell, along with many others, soon after 1789. Another theory is that the cherubs were, in an age of atrociously high infant mortality, wishful symbols of fertility. In Boucher, for example, emblems of death and old age are surprisingly frequent in the shadows. They are never spotlit, but they are there. In general, though, the skies, or at any rate the ceilings, of the eighteenth century rained showers of deathless babies, just as our pages and screens now rain immortally ageless girls.

It cannot be a coincidence that the reign of the fat pink baby was also an epoch of insecurity, of turmoil in the province of ideas, as was that of the theory of perfectibility (humankind marching into an ever happier future); and the dawn of industrial technology, barred—or so it seemed—from glorious fulfillment only by a shortage of manpower. What the age was saying with its cherub mania was something like, Give us the real babies, and we'll create a perfect world. In a way the putti were symbols of man's sense of injustice, both at the failings of his self-created social system, as the Marxists maintain, and at the far less comprehensible cruelty of the human condition itself.

I am not maintaining, of course, that our contemporary turning of women into houris represents a desire for higher fertility. The one thing no one wants from a starlet is a baby. What we *do* want is more pleasure. That is why both Lolita and her grandmother have got to be girls. It is tempting to see in this a partial revenge of man on female emancipation. Woman's old dependence, her need to cling, was an attractive condition to many men; and it is not a long step from having economically enslaved women to creating sociologically enslaved ones. Tempting it may be, but not, I think, convincing, especially since women themselves are conspiring to bring about the present situation. I see a greater, darker, and sexless shadow behind; and it is fundamentally the same as the one behind the eighteenth-century cherubs.

For above all, the houri-girl is ageless. Like a true goddess she never grows older. And nowadays it is not only women who fear menopause. Like virginity, menopause has become as much a temporal as a physical thing. It is sexless; it is that moment when we know (or think we know) that we shall never be young again; and carried to its ultimate horror it is simply what begins the moment virginity (that is, being fashionably young) ends. Against this black delusion the girl stands like a charm, an amulet, a proof of agelessness, as the rococo putti stood, or tumbled, as proofs of fecundity.

Death is, in terms of life, the passing of time. The houri appears to make time stand still; and if we manage to make love to her, then it will not matter that time never stands still, so she is both amulet to the blind and consolation to the clear-sighted. This is why for an older man happiness so often comes to mean the *affaire* or the marriage with a girl young enough to be his daughter. And here I must point out that another important function of the virgin in mythology and religion has always been that of patroness and protectress. It may seem absurd, before the exiguous bikinis and flesh-peddling poses of the starlets at Cannes, to talk of the virginal and the protective. Yet in a sense what these girls offer—the mythical sexual happiness in their arms, the myth-youth to be milked from their unmaterial bodies—is the only protection against old age that modern man can understand, because he knows now that death, his total extinction, cannot be averted; it can only be made anodyne. And the only palliative of death, he is led like an ancient mogul to believe, is a life full of onanistic pleasure.

This is what we are saying with *our* mania: give us the houris, and we'll never grow old.

Just as I am certainly not a misogynist, I am certainly not a hater of pleasure. Progress can mean only that more pleasure is brought *to more people*; and it is because I believe this, and especially in the importance of those last three words, that I am against the houri. She may bring pleasure, but never to more people. Earlier I compared the starlets to a defensive wall; but walls have two sides. One defends, the other imprisons, and both obscure the real world outside. A mogul may appear, from outside, to be encapsulated in Paradise; from inside he may well, and in my view he does, live locked in Hell.

But the real victim in this sick situation, and the one for whom I feel most pity, is the older woman. She is torn between trying to keep up with the houris and wishing them all death and disfigurement. Thus three important groups in our society live permanently on the verge of a situation like that found in the early Mormon households[2]: an intolerable triangle of strain between husband, older wife, and younger wife; between man growing old, woman growing old, and girl (or girls) still young.

The irony of all this is that most of us know damned well—and I mean damned—that we shall never be twenty again. We also know, unless we are stupefied by our nympholepsy, that the notion that a woman's attractiveness and her ability to find and give sexual satisfaction diminish abruptly after the age of twenty-five is ridiculous. If anything, the opposite is true. And the human mind, thank goodness, has a built-in system of contrasuggestibility. Tell a man that the surface of the world is flat, and he will one day begin to suspect it is round. Monks may dream of orgies, but orgiasts dream of monasteries; and this age's quirk is not likely to be the next's. But meanwhile we aged relics who were born before 1935 are besieged on all sides. It is as if we were a shadowy ring of gray failures who could only stare, mesmerized and envious, at a bright little green-golden ring of film starlets, fashionable models, and their attendant parasites. And this I find inhuman and outrageous.

---

2. The parallels between Mohammedanism and Mormonism are obvious, right down to the special use of the word *prophet* and Brigham Young's Victorian nickname, "American Mahomet."

I have, over my desk, a putto hanging on the wall. He was carved in limewood and painted in the early eighteenth century, and given a small glistening smile essentially the same, in all but subtlety, as the smile on every starlet's fixed public lips—and the smile, it seems to me, that haunts the maxillae of every skull. The trouble and the truth are that death rarely uses that particular old-bone cliché of a mask. Once it was the done thing for writers to have a skull on their desks. But I prefer my limewood boy, who, given that he spent the first two hundred fifty years of his life in Rome, may have smirked down on that celebrated nympholept Casanova, and seen John Keats ("What mad pursuit? What struggle to escape?") die. For I need nothing to remind me of death; but always something to remind me of death's cunning.

Starlets, putti, the inexorable passage of the years . . . easy to know what we desire, but wiser to learn to know what we fear. The next time you see a pretty girl, look at her; and then, I beg you, look beyond her.

THE FALKLANDS
AND A DEATH FORETOLD
(1982)

Just after the Falklands war started, I read a proof copy of a richly sardonic new novel by Gabriel García Márquez. Set in a torpid estuary town of his native Colombia, *Chronicle of a Death Foretold*[1] narrates the quasi-ritual murder, by two brothers, of a man falsely accused of having seduced their sister. Although outwardly the theme recalls the Donna Elvira episode in the Don Juan legend, García Márquez gives it a very different moral. Here the brothers try desperately to avoid their debt of honor. They tell the whole town of their intention, even the chief of police—who promptly decides (shades of the British Foreign Office) that it is empty boasting. Again and again their victim might be warned. Even when he finally is, he cannot believe that the brothers won't see he is innocent. In any rational world the violence would be avoided a hundred times over; but this being South America, all is to no avail. In the end, poor Santiago Nasar is duly—indeed literally—butchered.

It is a pity this powerful Buñuelian fable did not appear last year, instead of this. One could not find a more vivid caricature of that lethal blend of machismo, braggadocio, and hypertrophic sense of honor that sullies South American society—and that has also, in its Spanish form, soiled Europe through the centuries. Although for García Márquez the ultimate Franco of existence is evidently the inescapably perverse nature of things, I should be inclined to blame also some especially fatal capacity in the

---

1. Published in the United States by Alfred A. Knopf, Inc., in February 1983. García Márquez, most famous as the author of *One Hundred Years of Solitude*, was the 1982 winner of the Nobel Prize in literature.

Spanish language to put its speakers under its spell, so that they cannot think for themselves, but only react (or kill, or die) to the resonances of certain words. When I recently translated Molière's *Dom Juan* for the National Theatre, the scene that defeated me on all counts was the one in which Elvira's two Spanish brothers debate their senses of honor in front of Don Juan (one is for killing him on the spot, the other for a few days' delay). Molière manages to convey both the massive gravity and the total absurdity of this black Iberian faith that offence to personal honor excuses every crime and lunacy under the sun. I failed to master the paradox. But an even greater one lies, I think, in the way the same general culture can produce a Cervantes, a Borges, now a García Márquez . . . and I mentioned Buñuel. His splendidly pungent autobiography has not, at the time of this writing, come out in English; but it too is as full of dry and often self-mocking humor as it is of underlying humanity.

At any rate I suspect no more pertinent book will be written about the Falklands war than this by García Márquez, and I should like to add a few thoughts to its general thesis, which is that humanity is a willing victim of its own tradition-besotted stupidity, and thus self-cast as both the dumb steer and the slaughterman.

I have no doubt about the chief sign of that stupidity, in global terms, and that is our ubiquitous refusal to face up to what is infinitely our major problem, overpopulation. All international and most civil conflict is at root caused by this terrible bane, with its totally unneeded pandemic of hands to employ, wages to find, mouths to feed. Meanwhile, the individual expectation of "happiness" (scilicet money) keeps in firmly rising step with the birth rate—and in inverse proportion to the ability of governments and natural resources to satisfy it. Any baby must be innocent; it is parents who are the new bubonic plague.

The ostrichlike response of the world's politicians to this horror is, I believe, due largely to the professionalization of their once-amateur trade; in other words, to the substitution for conviction of calculation (not what I believe, but what the electorate will bear), and for principle of personal ambition. Just as the Catholic Church in the past often proceeded on the maxim that there was no evangelist so effective as poverty, so do our would-be statesmen now. They may weep public tears over world instability; they have also, like the crocodile and the arms manufacturer, learned to thrive on it. Overpopulation, with all the discontents it brings in its wake, creates excellent excuses and levers for any power elite, left or right. At extremes it justifies both terrorism and martial law. "Give me a prejudice," says the investigating magistrate in *Chronicle of a Death Foretold*, "and I will move the world."

Cynics may argue that I am being far too generous to the politicians of the past; but even they, I hope, would admit that the stakes now—the potential international consequences of self-seeking and blinkered leadership—are hugely greater. Politics, we are too often told, is the art of the possible. That slithery adage has now become the tyranny of expediency over principle. Glib selling replaces product quality, in politicians as in kitchens. The main cause, if not the culprit, is of course the huge extension of the mass media. I also place a very black mark against the ubiquitous commentator-pundit who sees all in terms of short-term tactics and calculation, or the strategy of the football match. This reduces politics to public entertainment, or the bread-and-circus view of what the people need.

In overcrowded societies, political independence becomes not only suspect, but increasingly difficult. The real victors of the Falklands war were the opinion manipulators, in both Britain and Argentina. It also hideously demonstrated that the organ stop of nationalism remains the most effective, mainly because that particular pipe, once in full voice, drowns every other. The junta and Mrs. Thatcher might almost have colluded, so bare were their political cupboards just before the attack. They equally faced growing unpopularity, equally craved a diversion, and equally knew that with the Heaven-sent scapegoat in the southern Atlantic, their initial guilt (the flash-fisted aggression, the decades of British *dolce far niente* that provoked it) would be quickly forgiven by their respective nations and their allies . . . provided they won, of course.

But what distressed me far more than the sight of a jingoistic prime minister and a sword-kissing clique leaping gratefully into a self-serving war was that such large majorities of both their peoples should support it. The real villains in García Márquez's story are not the reluctant avengers, but the townspeople in whose midst the easily preventable murder takes place. They do not, or cannot, stop it because they are hog-tied by false assumptions, by apathy, by tradition, by social myth and convention, by an inability to think before speaking words such as *honor, duty, pride,* and the rest.

We lack a word for what García Márquez so subtly describes: all that nexus of instincts and feelings that we inherit quite as much from our pre-historic past as from our historical one, the antique lumber room of the species mind, choked with totems and fetishes, ignorance and fear, selfishness and unreason. In a world already overfilled with dissatisfied human beings, this "ancient psyche" is as menacing as the nuclear missile (which can be seen as a mere product of it, a logical extension of the first weapon Cain picked up to kill his brother). Its public effect is always regressive—a return to past barbarism, to the animal in man, to the child in the adult, whether it be the bully-boyism of the Iron Lady or the flagrant fibbing of the junta when caught with jam (or rather, young men's blood) on its greedy fingers.

I am not saying that the ancient psyche is all maleficent. It plays a considerable part in the creation and appreciation of the arts, in our enjoyment of many private pleasures of life and countless other innocent things. It is a vital constituent in our sense of the richness, the depth, the echoingness, like a Bach fugue, of human history; so vital indeed that I suspect this is the major reason we have such difficulty separating its good (and mainly aesthetic) effects from its morally bad ones. These latter lie for me on the tribal side of the ancient psyche, in all those socially institutionalized elements derived from the primitive survival needs of early man. When this side dominates public feeling or, even worse, is deliberately invoked by government in order to dictate public response, Armageddon moves visibly closer.

The Falklands affair showed us how quickly and simply this mothballed tribal past and its emotions can still be reactivated. A few images, a few phrases and slogans, a largely servile press, an apparent conspiracy of silence among those reluctant to declare themselves until they have seen which way the electoral cat will spring: the ease with which the monster can be resurrected (even in the world's supposedly oldest and wisest democracy) leads me to believe that its main cause, and its breeding ground, are the equally archaic worship of rank and power in society, and especially when that is based on semimystical and traditional grounds.

I found Pope John Paul's visit to Britain during the war particularly revealing. I don't doubt his sincere intentions as regards peace, and most certainly not his personal probity and courage; but I profoundly doubt the theology he brought with him. When a man speaks of the sanctity of human life and in the same breath inveighs against abortion and birth control,

I smell the ancient psyche again, a mind trapped in the past, as I do in all religions that offer a better afterlife, that age-old invitation to do nothing about the faults of this one.

Kinder atheists may dismiss John Paul as a well-meaning old man on a worn-out Rosinante (an image I take from another new novel I have just read, Graham Greene's *Father Quixote*). I see him, given his undoubted "charisma," as something far more ominous, a perpetuator of an outmoded and damaging worldview, deep rooted in precisely those obsolete communal attitudes and myths that bring about the murder in García Márquez's fable (in which a bishop sails past the town on a steamer, making signs of the cross "without malice or inspiration" from the bridge); and that also brought about the most famous murder in all history, the one on Calvary.

But again, what distressed me far more than John Paul was the respect accorded him not only (and naturally enough) by Roman Catholics, but by the nation at large. Public Britain suddenly became like nothing so much as an awed Stone Age sept faced with a famous shaman; the Reformation, the whole seventeenth-century debate (the greatest this country has ever held with itself), might never have taken place.

Our century has given abundant evidence that the Stone Age component in our psyches still often rules our actions: faith in ritual tradition (and its symbols), lust for power and territory at others' expense, sadistic revenge on dissenters and enemies, terror of the unknown (why, in science fiction, is almost everything in outer space hostile and evil?), mindless acceptance of self-appointed oligarchies and "chieftains," xenophobia . . . the list could be extended. This sinister complex of morally and rationally long-disproved (not least by Jesus) responses to social and international life must to a novelist seem very like the always partly unconscious symbolic or metonymic structure he or she imposes on characters when writing a book.

Characters have a curious habit, very often, of trying to elude this, an escape many of us are happy to aid and abet. What is so powerful, almost Zolaesque, in García Márquez's parable is that the structure is made inescapable. All that is human and individual in it is predestined, ended before it begins, precisely because of this surrounding world ruled by the evil, tribal half of the species mind. Foretold and told become the same thing. In such a world, tragedy is not a risk, or even probable, but inevitable. Its hero-victim has no choice—as some pessimists say of all humanity and its eventual nuclear suicide.

The three most foolishly conjoined words in history were surely *Liberty, Equality, Fraternity*. As well put a hungry tiger and two lambs in a cage and expect a happy future for the lambs to result. Liberty is individual, and the deadly enemy of the two social virtues. Even the most partial institution of equality in society requires a high degree of state control. Untrammeled liberty of the kind extolled by so many British and American backwoods conservatives can justify itself only in the context of the belief that we are all equally able to succeed if we want to; and that if we don't, the fault must lie in us. That this poisonous child of the Puritan ethos was ever maintained is surprising enough; that many in power still maintain it (or policies tacitly based on it), and after a century of major discoveries in genetics and psychology, defies belief. Nowhere does the ancient psyche, always terrified by the specter of pure hazard (the idea of no one in ultimate charge), remain more potent.

It is the ancient psyche that prevents us from seeing that liberty in itself is not an automatic good. As abstract concept it is amoral; as political one, as slogan, it is nowadays as often used to justify autocracy or cultural hegemony as it is to liberate. The one thing the overcrowded raft of this planet does *not* need is the liberty that regards all social and economic control of its highly successful minority as "Communistic." The "Free World" cries out for more restraint, not more liberty; and that must mean a severe encroachment on the sort of freedom preached by so much of the official West, whose real attachment is to the maintenance of the system by which they themselves hold power and make money. In my view, the necessity for such control is no longer debatable in political terms. It has become a biological, or ecological, imperative.

All this is one strong reason I am a republican. Unlike Mr. Hamilton[2] and most of my fellow antimonarchists, I do not object to the personal failings, real or reputed, of the present royal family. On the contrary: it seems to be

---

2. The best-known of the "antiroyals" in the House of Commons at this time.

something of a miracle that they have, given the puppetlike public roles demanded of them, so few. No, what I dislike is the nefarious *symbolic* nature of the institution; not its representatives, but what others make them stand for. And again, that seems to me difficult to distinguish from a Neolithic clan-totem. Tories support the monarchy so fervently for this very reason. A totem is also a useful mooring post for any ship of state trying to stem the tide of progress—and especially that of those two second terms in the French Revolutional triad. I should perhaps here, this October 1997, so soon after the death of Princess Di, say I had some sympathy with her position. Neither her ex-husband nor her son should have to bear the Stone Age cross of kingship.

Unquestioning reverence for kingship, for hereditary peers, for titles and ranks, for caste and class, for all artificial hierarchy, provides the inflexible social structure needed by any nation intending to play the war game. We like to think that we have in Britain achieved a much more classless, open, "realistic" society since 1945 and the loss of empire. If there was any substantial truth in that, a Falklands situation would never have arisen, let alone an expedition been sent; and one may doubt whether a Thatcher-style government could ever have been elected in the first place.

The trouble with a constitutionally tame monarchy is that it must, in the hands of those with real power, become when required the leader of the chauvinist band, the drum-major for the nation as *miles gloriosus*, or bullshitting soldier. The system of the elected "titular" president may have its drawbacks, but one it does not have is that of constantly referring the national back to a medieval concept of a separate class of pseudo-divine beings (and eternal Conservatives) chosen by the chance of their blood alone. Nor does it suggest that the nation's life is emblematically led by inalienable tradition, and is therefore unchangeable. This is what the Americans who so ironically call themselves Republicans really admire about British royalty and its ceremonial occasions.

"Cross and Sword" has been the age-old curse of Spain; and ours is the prostitution of "Queen and Country," its increasing use as a bulwark of the chauvinistic side of nationalism, together with its constant companion, racism. I know that republicanism is not a popular cause in this country, and that there are some practical political arguments (not least the savoir faire of the present incumbent) for the actual system; but nothing will persuade me that the symbolic arguments against are not far stronger. We cannot forever go backwards into the future; it is too high a price to pay for the pageantry.

I long ago decided that I did not want to be British. I am English, as a Welshman is Welsh, or a Scotsman Scottish. "Red, white, and blue" imperial Britain is a matter of history, a perhaps once necessary fiction, but most of all it is a mirror for larks, and as obsolete as that metaphor. I cannot respect such a superseded, jealous, exclusive notion, and above all when it serves as clothes to a naked emperor.

Humanity is one now, or nothing; and the only taste our dearly bought "British victory" in the Falklands left in my mouth was one of bitterness at the quantity of futile human suffering it caused, and of outrage at the hypocrisy and lying by omission spewed out by its promulgators on both sides. We did not need this additional proof—or that in Lebanon and the Persian Gulf—that the majority of the human race remains in essentially the same state it was in five thousand years ago: ignorant, self-blind, and barbarically addicted to violence when thwarted.

I also know that "evolutionary socialist" ideas like mine, with their suspicion of all traditional institutions, can be dismissed as intellectual nonsense, especially in a country still "proud to be British" and even more generally addicted nowadays to sitting back and enjoying the human comedy—or treating it like the World Cup, as amusing (even when brutal) patterns on a distant field. But I am a novelist; and whatever our other failings, the one thing we all learn from our profession (and share with the politicians) is the frightening capacity of the image and the word to trigger buried things, and to drown sober reason. A second thing most of us have to learn is that we too can fall under that spell—and then usually fall ourselves, as artists. But bad and self-indulgent art hurts few; bad and self-indulgent politics hurts millions.

Right-wing or centrist philosophies dominate the mass media the world over, and the last thing such chained voices will ever advocate is electoral skepticism, the demotion of idols and fixed ideas, the clearing-out and demystification of that unlit mental lumber room. Whatever their aims, all bidders for power seem trapped in their need of the ancient tribal psyche and its easily conditioned responses. A caustic vein in *Chronicle of a Death Foretold* deals with the endless regrets and sometimes hilariously irrelevant excuses of all those who might have prevented the murder, but somehow didn't; and perhaps the saddest thing about the Falklands affair was its revelation of how trapped by the monster even our opposition parties remain, and how great is our need of a genuine radical party, as free from the yesterday's cabbage of the Tories and the Social Democrats as from the equally stale recipes of much of our older socialism.

The two brothers wait with their whetted pig knives. Santiago Nasar, become Christ by accident, walks home to meet them and his death, while his town watches, as remote from intervening as a movie audience, or readers of a novel. Nothing has changed, nothing can change, it is all as foretold. Mrs. Thatcher may speak for Britain, but García Márquez speaks for me.

III

LITERATURE AND
LITERARY CRITICISM

MY RECOLLECTIONS
OF KAFKA
(1970)

I am in one way well equipped to write this essay, as I read most of Kafka when I was a student at Oxford over twenty years ago—and haven't read a word of him since. I am absolutely confident that I should now fail even the simplest high-school paper on his work. Fools rush in, you must be thinking. Later I hope, in my crabwise fashion, to show that there may be something to be said about an average ignorance of great writers. Plainly I can offer no new views on Kafka; all I can try to do is describe, rather in the manner of a field naturalist, the reality of his presence in my own cultural landscape. With that I want to combine some reflections on a central dilemma for the practicing novelist—not a new dilemma in itself, but one about which we are all becoming very self-conscious these days and to which the posthumous influence and "standing" of Kafka are very relevant.

My method may serve to emphasize that it is a practicing novelist, and not an academic, who is writing this essay; and a novelist, moreover, not too happy about the present relationship between the teaching and the literary professions. I am not at all convinced that the university aegis is one that any writer of fiction—or poet, for that matter—ought to put himself or herself under. One doesn't apprentice a would-be celebrator of life to a college of morticians, however necessary and excellent that institution may be in fulfilling its function; nor, in an art that places such a high premium on individuality, freedom, and open-mindedness, can a young novelist safely enter an environment preoccupied with past "ritual" and the codification and dissection of literary aim and method.

There is perhaps a lesson for literature teachers in the science of biology. There, over the last two decades, a vital dissatisfaction has grown with the limitations of laboratory observation as a reliable account of how birds and beasts actually behave in the wild; we know now that caged animals acquire a host of atypical behavior traits—a complex cage neurosis—in captivity. I suspect literary criticism too ought to devote more time to its subjects' ethology: how living writers (off the campus) actually feel and behave. Too often we are credited with quasi-academic views on other writers of the past, and with a much too conscious and deliberate incorporation of such views into our own work. I intend later, in the interests of just such an ethological study of *homo scriptor*, to write down exactly what I recall (without, of course, going to the texts or the reference books) of Kafka's life and work. It will not impress the scholars.

As even the most frivolous novelist must, I have had to think an increasing amount about the problems of style, both in my own work and in general. One discovers fairly soon that the difficulties tend to come more and more from this quarter; which is to say that they come less, as one grows older, from doubts about what one wants to say or uncertainty about the right general metaphor (using that word in its largest sense) to carry the message. I certainly don't mean that problems of narrative and character development, of symbolisms, can now be wafted away with a flick of the wand of creative experience; it's rather that one knows one can probably, in time, solve most of the problems in these areas, since one has solved them in one's fashion before.

Once I was always writing first chapters of novels. I have some facility with narrative, and I used to think nothing was easier than the first chapters of a new book . . . just as very often nothing seems easier than the first slopes of a mountain to be climbed. But nowadays first chapters have become distinctly nightmarish for me. I find I can't get on until I have hit the right angle to shoot from; exactly the right tone or voice; and most important and complicated of all, exactly the right attitude *in myself* towards the theme of the book. Curiously, getting the right attitude *in the characters* is not so hard; but that does not solve the real problem between the potter and his or her clay, since one dangerously easy way out is to allow the clay to dictate the shape. Characters are generally only too happy to write the book, if they are given their heads and hearts; in less anthropomorphic terms, a writer can overindulge his or her own lesser skills with serious unbalancing effect on the deeper structures and intentions. It is, for instance, the characteristic fault of Dickens—characteristic indeed.

What I propose to do here is think a little about this "right voice" aspect of the craft. You will by now, I hope, have guessed the relevance to Kafka, since no modern writer of fiction has achieved a more distinctive style and voice, a clearer flavor in the literary cuisine. We see it in all the common (common at least still among educated people) usages in ordinary conversation that invoke Kafka's world. Let me list a few I have noted recently.

"It might have been something out of Kafka." "It was like a madhouse. Pure Kafka." "You know who'd have been happy there? Kafka." (Descriptions of various personal events and habits.)

"Somewhere between Lewis Carroll and Kafka." (From a report on the Chicago trials.)

"Kafka lives!" (On a student placard in a demo against university red tape.)

"Watered-down Kafka." (From a review of a new film.)

What can be said about all these familiar reductions of Kafka to the role of a useful descriptive tool? First of all, this application evidently filled a gap in existing equipment; it encapsulated in one word (and a phonetically rather pleasantly evocative one . . . *Kafkaesque*, hard-soft-hard-soft-hard, like a shuffled slipper on an empty staircase) what had previously required at least adjective plus modifier: "stiflingly bureaucratic," "inexplicably sinister," "frustratingly mysterious," and so on. Second, all these common usages are really extrapolations from a surface appearance rather than from the deeper side of Kafka's writing. The metaphysical aspect is disregarded; what is remembered most is the sense of meaningless process and frustration, and especially in connection with personal failure to get some simple service or answer from some large, impersonal institution—a ministry department, a hotel, a big business firm. Third, it is not at all necessary actually to have read Kafka to use him like this. In fact it almost requires a lower-case setting: *kafkaesque*.

Finally, this extrapolated use (or abuse) of a writer is not very common. It has not happened to many equally or more important writers. Most adjectival forms that are quite often seen or heard are really no more than historical or critical labels and have not entered general usage in nonliterary contexts: *Shakespearean, Voltairean, Shavian, Dickensian*, and the rest. Perhaps *Dickensian* did once have a more general use. I suppose it meant something like "amusingly grotesque," "redolent of older and jollier times"—but the very fact that this use is now obsolescent suggests that it was tied closely to the particular grotesqueries and Pickwickian older times that Dickens created. Then there is the category of writers whose "adjectival value" is limited strictly to discussion of their work. There seems no reason on grounds of insufficient popularity, excellence, influence, distinctiveness, or the rest that (to take only the nineteenth-century English novel) we find no extramural usages derived from Austen, Scott, Peacock, the Brontës (though *Heathcliffian* crops up), Thackeray, George Eliot. Only *Trollopean*, *Hardyesque*, and *Jamesian* seem to have some sort of external life; but none of these begins to compare with *Kafkaesque*.

It seems, in short, that *Kafkaesque* belongs to a rare category. Another obvious candidate is *Rabelaisian*[1]; and another, at any rate in Britain, is *Chekhovian*. Can we see any common factor? Well, one thing is obvious. Their work is centered rather narrowly (which does not of course mean shallowly) on limited areas of human experience or feeling about it. In Rabelais it is the exaltation of physical experience; in Chekhov, the sense of waste and futility; in Kafka, the feeling of frustration and victimization. Now all these are ubiquitous experiences, but evidently inadequately defined—or labeled—before their geniuses arrived to celebrate them. In Kafka we may see a special appositeness, a focus of interest that links the ultimate consequences of the Industrial Revolution with the terrors of the Brave New World.

This type of use is really much closer to that of *Galilean*, *Newtonian*, *Darwinian*, *Freudian*, *Einsteinian*, and so on. My own guess is that the passport for literary men (some irony that Kafka gained his so easily!) must be sought for in this scientific direction. Specific literary genius has very little to do with it. The three men I have cited all analyzed and explored "dark" areas of general human experience. In this perspective Rabelais was a pioneer in ethics and the permissive society; Chekhov in the psychology of failure; Kafka in existential sociology—in being and nothingness. But the oddest conclusion is that all three must have based their work on a fundamental reality of more significance than that of many more overtly realist writers. This paradox is best seen in a fourth writer one might add to the trio: Lewis Carroll. Although he lacks the distinction of an adjective, his

---

1. With similar extrapolation from surface appearance, "healthily bawdy," and so on.

work is frequently applied to certain common situations. We know there was an important if deep-buried stratum of mathematical logic in the Alice books; and we can certainly see in Dodgson a scientific pioneer in both humor and psychology, if not in mathematics itself—though the new physicists' mirror universe and antimatter would surely have appealed to him very greatly. But evidently his symbolic world is a little too abstract and nebulous for *Carrollian* or *Alicesque* to have slipped into our vocabulary. Which seems a pity; I can't think of better words to summarize, for example, the conduct of United States foreign policy over these last few years.

But let me now hop back to that red rag for the academic bull that I hung out in my first paragraph. Of course it is essential that the teacher of literature should be closely familiar with his or her texts; and very understandable that he or she should be outraged by anyone boasting, more or less, of ignorance of them. Yet the hard (and perhaps fortunate, in many cases) truth of most practicing writers' situation is that what we produce is going to go the way of myself with Kafka—is going to be a dim memory at most, and often enough a totally erased one, in the great bulk of our readers' lives. We are, in short, writing not for intense "laboratory" scrutiny but for a highly inattentive general mind; to be not the subject of some expert's study, but a lightning-brief experience in some nonexpert's multifarious life.

This is not to suggest, needless to say, that we don't wish to be remembered. In an age where the greatest intellectual crime has become pretension, very little is said of the old literary preoccupation with *aere perennius*. I think the general assumption is that no decent modern writer would let such a vulgar and hubristic thought ever come near his or her typewriter. In any case, it has become almost axiomatic now that good writers must have poor sales. I believe this whole question—the effect on a writer of how he or she sees his or her own success-duration graph—is another badly in need of an ethological approach. I can't believe that any but the most basely commercial novelists are not powerfully influenced by their future reputation when they write. Economic considerations may force a writer *for a time* to see the big advance and the high sale as the greatest literary good; and immediate success is no doubt addictive . . . like every other drug, one way of compensating for failure in the real race. For all that, I can understand a girl's temporarily whoring for the freedom not to whore; but not for the hell of being a lifetime prostitute.

One solution to this desire for duration of name is to write not for the generalist, but for the specialist; from there one may leap to the notion that since the academic literary establishment is the chief arbiter of lasting worth, one may as well address oneself straight to it. The figures at the writer's shoulder then become the highbrow journal reviewer and the professor of literature. If I can please their refined and perceptive tastes, why should I worry about that casual, dim-memoried crowd out there beyond the ivied walls?

One good reason to worry, I think, is that the criterion invoked is less that of some (semimythical) literary establishment than that of the past and present writers who happen to be in intellectual vogue at any given time. One can get fatally too close to jealous gods—and their votaries—such as these. But I reject this solution mainly because it seems a contempt of due process, and rather similar to that old evasion of justice whereby aristocrats could elect to be judged only by their peers; and also because it is a denial of the duty of all art, which is in some way (if only in terms of pure entertainment) to improve society at large. I regard this particular shortcut between Parnassus and the Groves of Academe with the greatest suspicion: it may be that the academy has been the first on occasion to reveal the real merits of a disregarded writer, but that does not excuse us writers from going on public trial. It is where we must begin, and where we must end. There is no other honest destination.

The academic attention all writers hope one day to receive is really rather a special abstraction from audience reality as the writer *ought* to consider it. The real task is that of registering something durable on that much harder surface of the general reader; and I want to use the rest of this essay to think about that, and in particular about the role that the acquisition of a distinctive voice plays in the enregistration.

But first I will write down what I remember of Kafka. I hope it will be clear by now why it is convenient, if disgraceful, that I haven't read him for twenty years. I want to convey the general ordinary nature of reading memory in an ordinarily forgetful person: what remains, in short.

I cannot remember a single scene from Kafka except one, in which a man is turned into a cockroach as he lies in bed. I think it is in a story called *Metamorphosis*. I can't recall anything else beyond that one image. I don't know what Kafka was trying to say in the story. I am pretty sure *The Castle* was about a man trying to speak to someone in a castle. He stayed in an inn nearby? I wouldn't swear to that. I can't remember if he ever got into the castle, or what he wanted to ask—neither the peripatetic nor the conclusion. *The Trial* started with an arrest without motive, and was all about a man hopelessly trying to find out why he had been arrested and what he was accused of. Again, all detail has disappeared. *America* I have never read. I have read other shorter pieces, but have no recall of them at all. I am almost sure I also read the biography by Max Brod at Oxford (since I remember that there is such a book), but I haven't retained a single fact from it. I think Kafka lived from about 1870 to 1930, but I could be decades wrong either way. I don't know if he married or not, how he earned his living or where . . . I associate him with Vienna, but I may have got him mixed up with Freud or Schubert—or someone.

An appalling confession of ignorance, as you see. And I must seem to add insult to injury when I go on to say that I feel I know Kafka well, precisely so well (*unforgettably* is hardly the word) that I haven't needed to reread him. What I think I know well is his spirit, his tone of voice, his coloration (or lack of it), his drift, his one brilliant metaphor. In memory the two great novels have become one and indeed seem almost two variations on the same theme—very possibly a quite unjustifiable lumping-together. I don't remember Kafka as being very enjoyable to read; I have only an impression, in my student mind, of a specific new flavor and of a striking new formulation of a question (or complaint) about human existence. Perhaps because I am English and was educated a long way from central Europe, I found little emotional appeal in his work—none of that tender attachment I have to Chekhov, for instance. No doubt something in Kafka grated with my racial quantum of empiricism in one direction, and of Romanticism in another. He took his fantasies too seriously. Not in the whimsical or satirical Anglo-Saxon style at all.

But having unkindly said all that, I am conscious that I have been influenced by Kafka. Several German reviewers have told me so. Two alternative titles to *The Magus* were "The Maze" and "The Godgame"; and the first draft of that book attempted a much more Kafkaesque style and "climate." I don't think there is anything very significant about this, since it is almost impossible to think of any novel with a strong element of obsession that does not borrow something from the master; one could as easily think of a well-stocked kitchen cupboard without black pepper.

So Kafka registered a strong "image" on my not completely sympathetic and far from perfect cultural memory. Can I say how that has been done? I think myself that it is mainly through a tone of voice, a style perfectly suited to the content, rather than anything in the content itself. He remains permanently distinct here. Nobody else has "spoken" quite like that. It is as if he cleared a space round himself in literary history; and this makes him a kind of landmark, a reference point for all novelists who come after. But more than that, a landmark that it is dangerous to approach—to imitate, in other words. It has a fatal magnetism, a cannibal aspect. Here, trespassers *will* be prosecuted—of plagiarism.

I am returned now to the dilemma of today's writer in pursuit of his own *Ars longa, vita brevis*; or in more practical terms, in search of the method that will cut into that cold granite of public indifference and forgetfulness. Kafka will stand very well as a supreme example of one method. It involves limiting oneself to one field (which may have universal relevance) and elaborating a unique "methodology" to analyze and describe the nature, "laws," and problems of that field. It is clear that the method is as important as the choice of field. The insoluble mysteries of existence, the futility of society, the paranoiac sense of victimization—a realization of all this existed, and was articulated, at least as far back as the pre-Socratic philosophers, indeed right back to that very first and most underrated of all underrated literary masterpieces, *The Epic of Gilgamesh*. It was implicit or explicit in many earlier novelists' work—in Dostoyevski, in Zola, in Dickens, even—and in every great tragic playwright's. *With Kafka it is the articulation, not the articulated, that fundamentally matters.*

The failure to see this is why so many who have tried to climb by Kafka's route have failed. It is a route made all the more dangerous by one of his most characteristic techniques: the negative treatment of character. I don't think it is altogether mere bad memory that makes me unable to recall concrete scenes from his work. It is of course part of his intention that what should stay in the reader's mind is the general process, not its details, nor those who inflict or suffer it; and of course the technique is essential and excellent for the ends in view. You cannot make discoveries about anemia with normal-blood-count patients; or about anxiety neurosis with the bovinely contented. Nevertheless, if not a dead end in itself, this has, I believe, led many writers into impossible situations.

The most notorious of these "impossible situations" is the French *nouveau roman*. Here Kafka has played the role of the piper of Hamelin. Even when we discount the great barrier for English readers that is constituted by differences in rhetorical traditions (*langue écrite* and *langue parlée*) and by the much higher value placed by the French, all through their cultural history, on pure style, I think it is now accepted, even in France itself, that the *nouveau roman* experiment has failed to prove its thesis. Its first successes were really *tours de force* of technique and proved quite the opposite of Robbe-Grillet's claim that a greater "truth" could be got at by jettisoning all the old methods of conveying character and narrative. All that was really proved was that though you *can* get from Winnipeg to Montreal by heading westwards, the more obvious direction still makes for a better journey for your fellow travelers—that is, your readers.

One might state it as an axiom: the anticharacter requires not only a nonrealistic setting, but a nonrealistic (or fabulous) purpose and philosophy of life in the author. Kafka himself admirably fulfilled this axiom. Not even his most fervent admirers would maintain (at least I hope they wouldn't) that his assumptions about the human condition, and far less normal human reactions to it (even if we did accept his premises), are a realistic portrayal of what is the case. We have to say something like this: he conveys how things sometimes *feel* when we are depressed or frustrated. In all those common extrapolated usages I mentioned earlier, there is a sense of the ludicrous. Real life suddenly became like "something out of a book"—it seemed unreal. Kafka erects a model of a hypothetical universe that is much worse than the actuality. And this is a technique more characteristic of tragedy than of the novel. No one has ever blamed *Oedipus Rex* or *Lear* for lacking realism, since we have all been trained to make the necessary metaphorical leap, to suspend what constitutes our ordinary standards of reality.

But there is a paradox here. Something in the novel form strains after realism in the ordinary sense of the word, just as in poetry and the drama something strains away from it. In the sense that all literature is an attempt to escape, an effort to transcend iron reality, one might say that prose fiction, the last to evolve of the major literary forms, is the least noble in its endeavor. It escapes less; it stays in its cell and tries to live with reality.

Every novelist has been through this experience, or perhaps *tension* is a better word: the struggle between the desire to be exact to life as it is and the wish to be exact to one's "artificial" theories about its nature, its purposes, and the rest. One must concede a good deal of courage to the *nouveaux romanciers* precisely on this count; and that their attack has turned out to have been a defeat is perhaps no more futile a result than the demise of the Light Brigade in its ill-chosen valley. It had, so to speak, to be done once.

One may come at this from another angle, by comparing the tragic novels of, say, Thomas Hardy with those of Kafka. Hardy clearly belongs inside the "cell" I mentioned above. Although the machinery and the cathartic effect may, in a book like *Tess*, seem analogous to that of classical tragedy, the aura and texture of the story are realistic. This is even more marked in Zola's work. It is symptomatic that the several attempts to dramatize Hardy's work have all failed miserably. I don't know whether Kafka's novels have in fact been so transmogrified, but I would expect them to survive the sea change much better. Kafka has always seemed to me closer to Beckett than to any other novelist of this century, just as he is, oddly enough, so far from that archcreator of positive character (and Beckett's master) James Joyce. I suspect our current system of literary classification badly needs its Linnaeus, and I think he would see in Kafka more of a tragic playwright than a novelist proper. He swam in our sea, but that makes him no more a fish than Moby Dick was.

But I plunged away this time in pursuit of the question of whether it is advisable to imitate him and his "method." It is not quite beside the point that we may be dealing with a tragedian in disguise; and it is very much to the point that his achievement of "voice" depended on a very complex set of accompanying requirements, especially when those seem more likely to be met by a central European mentality and cultural framework than by an Anglo-Saxon one. I can't think of a single convincing tribute to Kafka in English. Our own best fabulist, George Orwell, stems much more from the English satirical tradition. Some of the new Czech and Polish writers—Havel, Hrabal, and Mrozek spring to mind—have been a good deal more successful, though two of them, incidentally, are playwrights.

I had better put my cards on the table now and admit that I am questioning not just the advisability of imitating Kafka's method of attaining a memorable "voice," but too great a contemporary preoccupation with the thing in general. It still carries altogether too much weight among many academics and reviewers (and creative-writing schools)—that is, too much emphasis is put on getting a distinctive style, or flavor for the critical kitchen. Since so much of literary criticism is devoted to influence tracing and textual analysis, there has arisen an unreasonable demand for instant recognizability, whether in terms of sentence-by-sentence style or of treatment and theme. This can trap some writers in a prison of their own idiosyncrasies. A great deal of tyro writing in the United States (that is, in the country most addicted to pragmatic and rational solutions) suffers from an obsession with technique as a means to this end. I am certainly not advocating a new *sans-style* anonymity. But I think one can get too involved, like certain actors, in voice production, and this tends to serve as a closing device on what ought to be the most open of literary forms.

An image that came to me recently to define these voice-ridden writers was of traveling abroad. They always go in effect by the same means to the same country. Naturally they become experts on that country and its language; and their work will have a coherence, a built-in set of structural interrelationships that will in turn afford plenty of opportunity for neat and no doubt technically satisfying work by the literary surveyors. Nuance hunting may become almost an industry in itself.

The method I myself prefer can be illustrated by the opposite image: of travelers who go to different foreign countries. The opportunity here is to write in different styles and voices, and different forms of the novel. The disadvantages are obvious. We do not create a recognizable personal style. Our work may seem bewilderingly diffuse and unconnected—searching, but in quite the reverse of the complimentary sense. Nor can we escape comparisons with the grasshopper and the ant. I have heard it said that the inability to command an instantly recognizable style (that is, to be parodiable) is equivalent to a kind of moral cowardice, a failure in literary seriousness. That may be so; but I don't think there is really much cowardice (though overleaping ambition is another matter) in the attempt to command different styles. And it is most definitely not easier work.

This issue is one of the most basic for the embattled novelist today; and perhaps the key factor in determining which path a writer will take is the degree to which he or she is an obsessive and the form that his or her obsession takes. I believe myself that all writers are obsessives, so it is really the form that matters—whether the priority is the act of writing or the expression of some feeling or insight about life. For myself, I enjoy the actual process of writing very much and can think of nothing more pleasurable than exploring it in all its varieties. This may tend to make what I write seem like a series of travel books about my own pursuit of this enjoyment. My obsession is with new (to me) writing worlds, not with the consolidation of one chosen old one. I am not, I hasten to add, sustaining my own objection to the reverse fix to the point that I ban it except for geniuses such as Kafka. I really want to do no more than suggest that if I am right in my belief that the novel is more closely committed to describing experience realistically than are other forms of literature, then there is no obligation to attack always the same point with the same weapons; and something can be said for adopting a more varied armory and strategy—or to put it another way, for not remembering Kafka and his like too well.

All I want, indeed, is to keep the choices open and not see would-be writers self-driven into some sort of creative (more accurately, imitative) process whereby they feel they must stake their little claim and then defend it for the rest of their days. Increasingly human freedom lives in human art, and we cannot tolerate—it is the one and only thing we must never tolerate—any outer-imposed restriction on artistic methods and aims. That, after all, remains very possibly the deepest and most paradoxical moral in Kafka's haunting darknesses.

CONAN DOYLE
(1974)

The Hound of the Baskervilles is, I suppose, the most widely remembered of all Conan Doyle's accounts of Holmes and Watson at work. What most of us have forgotten is that it was also, for reasons that had very little to do with the story itself, among the most rapturously received when it first saw the serialized light of day in August 1901. The reason for the rapture was simple. Holmes had disappeared on May 4, 1891, locked in a literal cliff-hanger at the Reichenbach Falls with his archenemy Moriarty. In *The Final Problem* (1893), Watson had told the story of Holmes's end: "the last that I was ever destined to see of him in this world." The real murderer had, of course, been Conan Doyle himself. He was through with frivolous yarn-spinning, and for eight long years he resisted all blandishments; he was a much more serious man than that, as he had proved by his courage as a field doctor and by his outspokenness as a man of letters with a public conscience during the Boer War. But in 1901, while he was recovering from his South African experiences in Norfolk with a journalist friend and golfing partner, it one day rained too hard for the course. Fletcher Robinson amused the writer by telling him some Dartmoor legends, including one about a spectral hound. A month later Conan Doyle was striding over the moor himself, cultivating the seed of a new novel. Holmes was still firmly dead in his mind, and the first conception was presumably of doing something in the historical line. But when it came to the writing . . . the hound demanded Holmes, and Holmes it got, though Conan Doyle insisted adamantly that the story dated from the pre-1891 past. No one was really deceived. The serialization ended in April 1902. In October 1903 there appeared the most eagerly awaited case of the whole series: *The*

Empty House. It announced that Holmes had survived the Reichenbach incident; in other words, Conan Doyle had recrucified himself. The news was greeted like that announcing one of the great Boer War beliefs, with universal joy.

This book was therefore a kind of test case, both of the depth of public demand after the eight years of silence and of the author's ability to satisfy it. His frequently expressed boredom with the two great incubi of his imagination has always to be taken with a large pinch of salt, and I think nowhere more than in this first step towards a full resurrection. The way to kill off characters (or to keep them dead) is to show them in some banal repeat of a previous situation, not to put them in a highly romantic setting and face-to-fang with one of the great archetypal monsters of human folklore.

The dog of death has the most ancient pedigree of any canine species, well recorded at least as far back as Anubis, the sinister jackal-headed undertaker-god of ancient Egypt, who must in turn derive from a much older fear. The northern European Mesolithic peoples had begun breeding the hostility out of wolves by 7500 B.C.—dog bones of that age have been found at Star Carr in Yorkshire—but the terror of that ancestry has persisted the world over. In Britain this lycophobia[1] has lingered longest in the Black Dog group of legends. Not a mile from where I live in Dorset there is a lonely lane. You walk there one night, and you see a little black dog following you. As it comes closer, it grows larger and larger. However fast you run, it is not fast enough. The little black dog is as big as a bull when it finally slavers over you for the kill. All very picturesque and harmless—yet recently the Borough Council decided that Black Dog Lane had better have a new name, and the pub at its corner had a new sign painted . . . showing an amiable black retriever. Some folk memories apparently still require castration.

There are countless variations of the Uplyme Black Dog all over the country. There is another famous one at Hatfield Peverel in Essex, and others in Suffolk and Norfolk with the name Black Shuck. On August 4, 1557, Black Shuck entered the church at Bungay "with fearful flashes of fire" and killed two of the congregation, then raced twelve miles south to

---

1. The wolf was the most recent of our large native mammals to disappear. It was not totally extinct until about 1750.

Blythburgh and killed a man and a boy in the church there.[2] The Isle of Man had the Mauthe Doog, a demonic spaniel. One of the many Dartmoor spectral hounds showed huge glassy eyes and steaming sulfurous breath, and killed every man it met at the place where its former master had been mysteriously murdered—by way of encouraging the others, one must presume, to call in Baker Street as soon as possible.

Dartmoor is most famous for its Wisht (a West Country dialect word meaning "sad and uncanny") Hounds, which were led by the Black Huntsman—Satan—and could hunt the sky as well as the ground. They were more often heard than seen. An ordinary dog died on the spot if it heard their baying, and an imminent human death was certain. One moorlander met the Black Huntsman one night near Widecombe and foolishly asked him for game. He was thrown a bundle. When he got home and could see what it contained, he found himself staring at his own small son, who was away on a visit. The vision disappeared when a servant ran in to tell him that the child had truly just died. The Wisht Hounds were also called the Yeth Hounds, *yeth* being Devonshire dialect for "heathen." These were inhabited by the tormented spirits of unbaptized children, hunting for their souls or those of their negligent parents; the early Church knew all about the value of shock publicity in encouraging wider use of the eschatological safety belt. But the most terrible of these phantom packs came from the North of England: the Gabriel Hounds, which had human heads on canine bodies.

All this may seem a long way from 1901, and even further from 1973. Yet strangely enough, there are senses in which it is not. I once lived very near the moor; and I even worked on it for a year, training young Marines. I have seen Hound Tor and others in the kind of light (unlike fighter pilots, the Wisht Hounds preferred low cloud cover for their operations) and from the distant angle that still require surprisingly little effort of the imagination to turn a long granite outcrop into a gigantic pack in full cry. But there is another sense in which the hound is associated with Dartmoor. I have also been taken for an escaped convict (as well as having myself

---

2. And also made the steeple collapse. It was the day of a great storm, and the real visitation was almost certainly an instance of that rare phenomenon, ball lightning.

helped hunt for escapees) and had Alsatians set on me from several hundred yards away—not an experience I wish to repeat. And I've even seen the Hound itself.

I went on Dartmoor alone one winter dusk in 1946, with a mist coming down, to search for a section of recruits lost on an orientation exercise. I was climbing a slope up to a tor. The light had gone, and I could just make out the massive boulders against the coming night. Then suddenly and silently a formidable black shape moved and stood in a breach of the rocks above me. I haven't forgotten the few moments of pure atavistic terror that possessed me before I had the sense to pull out the Very pistol I was carrying . . . and plainly, I lived to tell the tale. And yes, of course, it must have been a wild pony; but what I *saw*, like many a lonely and bemisted moorman before me, was the Hound. They, after all, did not carry Very pistols; nor had they read Jung and Freud.

So two kinds of rather curiously related fear—both used by Conan Doyle—haunt the moor. The first is a very primitive one caused by its isolation and the still-potent sense of menace it can evoke when visibility turns bad. Even in this year of disbelief, one's revealing instinct, if one is alone there in a mist or at night, is to turn constantly to see if one is being followed—the loom of the unimaginable. One experiences the more rational (if statistically hardly more probable) fear when a convict is out and on the run. But both experiences draw on ancient memories of hunting and being hunted, of man versus dog . . . or, originally, wolf.

Needless to say, the real black hound is the moor itself—that is, untamed nature, the inhuman hostility at the heart of such landscapes. That is a universal terror; and one thing Conan Doyle must have seen at once, during that wet day by the fire at his Norfolk hotel, was that he had at last found an "enemy" far more profound and horrifying than any mere human criminal. The Hound is the primeval force behind Moriarty; not just one form that evil takes, but the very soul of the thing.

There are those who think that making any criticism of the Holmes *épopée* is like taking a sledgehammer to a butterfly—or, more accurately, to a kind of delightful Gothick folly that is now also a national monument. The fact that it was erected at all seems far more important than discussion about whether it could have been better designed or built. This is above all the view of that amiably eccentric band of enthusiasts who like to pretend that

Holmes and Watson were real people, and therefore quite beyond the scope of literary judgment. To point out faults is to be guilty of humorlessness, as bad as blaming *Alice in Wonderland* for lack of surface realism. Yet this kind of credulous, and very English, adulation seems to me finally to devalue both Conan Doyle and his profession. He was a fallible writer of fiction, not an infallible recorder of reality; like all novelists, he was a dealer in plausible hypotheses, a confidence trickster—though out for your belief and attention rather than your money. That his recipe worked brilliantly at the popular level we all know; but I should like to give another con man's view of his technique—both where it worked and where it didn't. In any case, the way we exempt writers such as Conan Doyle (Ian Fleming is a later example) from serious criticism is by no means as generous a proceeding as it may seem. A good deal of condescension is involved as well. But let's start on the credit side.

Conan Doyle's stroke of genius was in solving a problem that all novelists are familiar with: the natural incompatibility of dialogue and narrative. In essence this is a kind of conflict between what the reader wants and what the writer wants. At the very heart of the novel form is the story, that hard lump of pure narrative to be summarized on a single page, but which in the final product has, by means of description, analysis of motive, conversation, and all the rest, to be spun out over two hundred pages or more. Conversation and narrative are generally antipathetic, since continuously moving narrative displeases the writer's sense of realism; but if he or she concentrates on realistic conversation, which like the Wisht Hounds loves running round in circles, the narrative goes out of the window. That is why so many children skip the "talk bits" when they read; they want the lovely chocolate taste of pure story, not the dull old cabbage of he-said-she-said.

Yet one has only to flick through the pages of *The Hound of the Baskervilles* to see that the book is quite astoundingly full of dialogue for a story of such exciting action. Conan Doyle gets away with this by three principal means. The first is that he rigorously excludes almost everything from conversation that has not directly to do with the forward movement of the story, or those aspects of character that fuel such movement. He is even very sparing with that second vital (for most novelists) characterizing function of dialogue. What use he makes of it is confined mainly to the early scenes or the mere first page on which a new character appears. Thus Dr. Mortimer is allowed a dotty little speech about Holmes's dolichocephalic skull in the first chapter. With typical economy, it kills two birds with one stone: it stamps Mortimer for good and tells us that Holmes is a remarkable fellow even in his anatomy. But such luxuries largely disappear as the action warms up. Everything is fined down to the one end: move the story.

Conan Doyle's second insight was to perceive that if you are going to rely heavily on conversation as your narrative medium, then you will do much better with two vividly characterized and temperamentally opposed mouthpieces than with one central "I"—or eye. The same rules apply as in the music-hall routine or the TV comedy show. One of the roles of a feed is to be a surrogate for the audience: the punch line is delivered not only against the punching bag on stage, but against everyone else in the audience who failed to see it coming. The butt is arguably more important than the marksman, in fact—and certainly the most effective way for Conan Doyle to kill off Holmes would have been to kill off Watson instead. It is only in a very superficial sense that he is less "important" and less intelligent than the master detective; technically and symbiotically, he is completely his equal—indeed, in my judgment a much cleverer creation on the author's part.

It is not simply that Watson is the obvious foil for Holmes's brilliance and that his ineffable capacity for not understanding what is really going on allows Conan Doyle to provide explanations for the slow-minded reader as well; by being the principal narrator, imbued with an unfailing talent for following the false trail, he is also cast as the main manufacturer of the suspense-and-mystery side of each case. In *The Hound of the Baskervilles* Sherlock Holmes grasps the essential nature of the problem very early indeed—by the time of the theft of the new and old boots. A hound is involved, and it must be a real hound, since supernatural hounds don't have to bother with scent. Ergo, some human means to offer Sir Henry up to a four-footed fiend. Ergo, he must live near Baskerville Hall. It cannot be Dr. Mortimer, and it is not likely to be an old-established resident such as Mr. Frankland, which leaves . . . one senses that Conan Doyle knew he was on thin ice here—and not for the first time—in making Holmes so cryptically unforthcoming (and very nearly, dare one say it, foolishly slow). Immediately following the scene about the old boot, Watson says, "We had a pleasant lunch in which little was said of the business which had brought us together." This is blatant murder done on credibility. Yet we accept it: Watson (your and my man at Baker Street) is such a dimwit—and so clever at leading us on by the nose.

Nor is it that Holmes and Watson are always set to work against each other in order to spin out the story. They form a very useful alliance in another direction for the author. As a bald narrative basis (as Dr. Mortimer presents it in the beginning) for a case, the notion of an ancient family cursed with the attentions of a supernatural hound is dangerously near a piece of macabre kitsch. But if it is apparently found plausible by both a brilliant skeptic and a staidly unimaginative doctor, who are we to doubt its possible truth? Two such different buyers are much more convincing than one.

But I think it is Conan Doyle's third reason for using conversation so much that is by far the most important. It is this: dialogue is intensely *immediate*. It might seem that the descriptive passages in a novel would be the only properly visual ones; but conversation is much closer to the immediacy of the actual image than we generally realize. Take the most conventionally descriptive chapter in the book, where the landscape and ambience of Baskerville Hall are dealt with; and take the very first chapter, which is almost all conversation. The former is like reading a set of stage directions (and rather crudely done, at that); but the latter is like being in a darkened theater: true, one can't quite see the actors onstage, but one is very close indeed to their voices . . . much closer to their fictive reality, I would suggest, than one is to that of that countryside and manor house in Devon. The latter are already dated; but Holmes and Watson and their visitor are timeless.

That Conan Doyle was a great deal better at narrative-moving dialogue than at straightforward description (that is, at drama rather than prose) prompts me to believe that we ought to see him as a forerunner of the strip cartoon—as also of radio- and television-script techniques. In his time he was not alone in this: one thinks of *The Dolly Dialogues*[3] and their like, and, much more important, of the tremendous increase in illustrative content in all writing, from advertising to poetry, throughout the second half of the nineteenth century. Hardly a popular novel, between 1880 and 1914, whose most melodramatic moments were not also drawn. What Conan Doyle seized on—as did the *Strand* magazine (founded to foster "popular literature")—was this universal new public desire to have the visual as well as the verbal faculties entertained. The spread of literacy, the renascence of the theater, improvements in print technology—all these played their part. His *coup de maître* was to see that this thirst could be bet-

---

3. *The Dolly Dialogues* (1894) were by Sir Anthony Hope Hawkins (1863–1933), generally referred to as "Anthony Hope."

ter quenched by conversation than by the more obvious answer: lengthy bastard-visual description. The eye is a lightning-fast absorber of real images, whereas the written description of such images is painfully slow. Good dialogue dances you forward, whereas even the best descriptive passages put the brakes on; and the strip cartoon is simply an attempt to get the best of both worlds.

In communications-theory terms, then, Conan Doyle devised a very successful method of accelerating information output—just how good a method is shown by the fact that even in our own intensely visual age, his fragments of the Gutenberg Galaxy remain very difficult to put down. No English writer knew more about sinking that mysterious hook into the reader. In *The Hound of the Baskervilles*, he "strikes" at the very last sentence of chapter 2:

"Mr. Holmes, they were the footprints of a gigantic hound!"

The trout is done for. My guess is that the least-read chapter title in all literature is the one that heads chapter 3.

But now I should like to look at the debit side. I referred advisedly just now to the strip cartoon. The danger[4] of Conan Doyle's method is caricature, which is properly a weapon of humor or satire. That is why Holmes and Watson have been endlessly parodied, have been sent up in both senses—into the pantheon of national archetypes as well as by countless teams of professional comedians. Watson was clearly conceived as a partly comic figure from the beginning; but Holmes has acquired a ludicrous aura that cannot have been intended. It is not just that he is too clever to be true, but also that he is too true to pure caricature to be "clever" by the highest literary standards. This is not to say that great characters or novels cannot be based on caricature; *Gulliver's Travels*, *Don Quixote*, and many others prove the contrary. But where Conan Doyle failed (as his cartoon-

---

4. Almost a genetic one, in Conan Doyle's case. His grandfather John Doyle was the most famous political cartoonist of the 1830–1850 period. One of John Doyle's sons, Richard Doyle, was the pride of *Punch* during the 1840s; another was director of the National Gallery of Ireland. Conan Doyle's own father, Charles, was an architect by profession and an artist "in the Fuseli manner" by inclination, while his great-uncle (and the godfather who gave him his second name) was Michael Conan, the Paris art critic. A formidable predisposing array.

ist forebears failed beside Rowlandson, Gillray, and Cruikshank) was in matching ends to means. In the Sherlock Holmes stories caricature becomes the end; it is not related to any significant truth or human folly. Of course, this lack of any deeper content, never a deprivation that ordinary man has conspicuously wept for, makes for easier entertainment; but it raises other problems when it comes to an honest literary appraisal.

All this was very shrewdly discussed a year or two ago by Jacques Barzun in an essay called "The Novel Turns Tale,"[5] in which he suggested that the appalling snobbism of the average literary critic towards crime and detective fiction was founded on a grave confusion of two different forms. The novel proper is a "narrative that professes to illuminate life by pretending to be history"; the tale "is a narrative too, but comic; not in the sense of laughter-provoking, but in the sense of high make-believe, indifferent to direct portraiture." He went on, "The tale, much older than the novel, appeals to curiosity, wonder and the love of ingenuity. If it 'studies' anything, it is the calculating mind rather than the spontaneous emotions, physical predicaments rather than spiritual." Very clearly, if this classification is correct, Conan Doyle belongs to the tale-tellers, in the long modern line from Poe to Ross Macdonald, and not with the novelists. To say that he lacks the stature of a Hardy or a Conrad is like saying a long jumper lacks the height of a pole-vaulter. What is really meant is that the novel is a much more important form than the tale.

Although I should be prepared to argue that the latter statement is generally true (even in the novel's present sickly condition), I think the futility of judging long jumpers by pole-vault standards is obvious. Professor Barzun finished his essay with an interesting specification: "One goes to a tale because it is a marvellous invention, because it is ingenious, full of suspense and concentrated wisdom, because it flatters the eye and the mind by its circumstantiality, liberates the spirit by its 'disdain of realism,' and appeases the heart by its love of reason." Does *The Hound of the Baskervilles* pass that test (framed, one suspects, with *Candide* in mind as exemplary model) of the form?

In my view it fails in three particulars: in concentrated wisdom (or love of reason); in ingenuity; and in circumstantiality. Barzun has pointed out that this last quality and "disdain of realism" are not contradictory, and especially in the detective tale. Raymond Chandler's brilliant thrillers are

5. In *Mosaic* 4, no. 3 (University of Manitoba Press, 1971).

not—any more than are works of the corpse-in-the-library school—realistic portrayals of men and women and their societies; but they are, at their best, highly accurate in page-by-page detail. They are convincingly "real," in other words, as we read. It is only when we stand back and compare the whole to actual life that we see we are knee-deep in fantasy—a simplistic socialist one in the case of writers such as Chandler and Hammett, where all rich people are baddies, and the private eye, behind his peccadilloes over whiskey and women (as Holmes over cocaine), is ethical first cousin to Sir Galahad and Robin Hood.

Sherlock Holmes had been on Dartmoor before—in "Silver Blaze," published in 1892—and his creator had already in that instance had trouble over just this matter of circumstantiality. His horsey admirers complained that he had got his training and racing world very wrong indeed. "I have never been nervous about details," riposted Conan Doyle, "and one must be masterful sometimes." An even more bizarre mistake in this story was his putting Tavistock, "like the boss of a shield, in the middle of the huge circle of Dartmoor"; and I am afraid he does not do much better by the moor (if Baskerville Hall is "fourteen miles" from Princetown, it is not on Dartmoor at all) and its natural life in *The Hound of the Baskervilles*. The whole description of Grimpen Mire, for instance, is Romantic-Urban nonsense. I have been in and out of a lot of such bogs and mires. One might just drown in a few of them by taking a really long leap from the edge, but I doubt it. They are far more an irritating than a lethal hazard at night; by day you mistake their livid green for grass once only. Then, too, very few wild orchids grow at all on Dartmoor, and none flower anywhere in Britain in mid-October; hart's-tongue ferns do not have "fleshy" leaves; bitterns bloom only in spring. Such very minor details may not be of importance in themselves, but signs of ignorance in the creator sort ill with the omniscience granted the created; too "masterful" an attitude here brings Conan Doyle closer to Watson than to Holmes. There is an analogous weakness in the Baskerville "statement" of 1742. Its pastiche fustian will do for the page-gobbling ignoramus, but not for anyone who has the least real knowledge of the cadences and vocabulary of eighteenth-century English; nor do I think a paleographer would be very convinced by Holmes's one clue as to his dating method for the same document.

Another way of betraying circumstantiality is by fudging it over with too much impasto. For two pages, as Watson drives to and arrives at Baskerville Hall, the lines are so clotted with *darks* and *gloomys* and *blacks*

(Dartmoor granite isn't black, by the way) and their synonyms that one feels very nearly back with Mrs. Radcliffe and "Monk" Lewis. A more serious lapse still affects the credibility of the two female characters in the book. Conan Doyle was never very happy with his fictional women—especially where he was so strong with the men, in dialogue—and neither Laura Lyons nor Mrs. Stapleton manages to rise above the late-Victorian stereotype of the compromised "lady." The former's scene with Dr. Watson is handsomely the most tritely and stagily artificial (even allowing for the reporter) in the whole book.

The least successful character of all seems to me to be the villain. Stapleton is far too much of a "prim-faced" pale shadow beside his outlandish murder weapon, and his straw-hatted mania for British entomology goes neither with his past nor with his present. That circumstance was added, one must suppose, on the old detective-tale principle of keeping your real criminal hidden well up your sleeve. I pointed out earlier that hiding was desperately necessary in this particular case. The smoke screen laid down here just about works at that level (though it is very thin compared with the brilliant cover-up in *The Valley of Fear*), but at the cost of credible psychological motivation. I think I know why Conan Doyle sends Stapleton to a silent death in the Grimpen Mire: he is not a man who otherwise could have explained himself convincingly. Indeed, outside Holmes and Watson, the book makes a poor showing on character throughout; one wryly recalls the almost Dickensian richness and charm of *The Sign of Four* in this respect.

The book must also be criticized on the side of ingenuity. There is a marked shortage of pure detection and a great deal too much of Watson's stupidity and trailing of the red herring; too much is engineered (and sacrificed) to the end of a spine-chilling denouement. The hound must run; and more likely courses of events are all sent begging. Conan Doyle was a fanatical, and very good, player of real games all his life, and in all his work there is, so to speak, a conflict between the intellectual and the cricketer (as there was, in all his family, between "serious" and cartoon art). He was a bowler of near–county standard[6] and a very useful bat—and not the man, I imagine, to hang about at the crease. In *The Hound of the Baskervilles*

---

6. If the most important event for him in August 1901 was the new "Holmes," in August of the previous year it may well have been that he took the most treasured scalp in cricket, W. G. Grace's . . . caught at the wicket, moreover.

there is very much the feel of a batsman chancing his arm on a lively wicket, getting in some cracking cuts and off-drives . . . but missing a fair few as well. Of course we owe his tremendous narrative brio very much to this love of attacking sports such as cricket and boxing, of set rules for the brisk exercise of physical and mental energy. But we are not seeing here one of his more thoughtful innings.

It may seem harsh to demand wisdom and reason of a book of entertainment, and of course we do not expect the "wisdom and reason" of a *Candide*. But I think we can ask for a little more than we receive. The irony is that many other Holmes cases are much more satisfactory in this respect, though with far less potentially fertile material. Perhaps we can grasp the failure best by comparing *The Hound of the Baskervilles* with *Dr. Jekyll and Mr. Hyde*, in the way in which one remains an exotic murder story and the other rises to a much higher symbolic level—as do the best Poe stories.

This failure to exploit a little more richly the chances offered, the sense of a missed opportunity, is undoubtedly the price of that virtue I cited on the credit side: the splendid gift for fast narrative, and in particular for narrative told through dialogue. Even the most intimate conversation is a quasi-public thing; few of us think as frankly and profoundly in our mouths as we do in our minds. And then the one person in the Baker Street world who does sometimes reflect on the wider implications, who is given the luxury of generalizing, is Sherlock Holmes himself; but he is absent from very nearly half the book, and we have to make do much more than usual with Watson's literal and plodding view of things. Far more, for instance, could have been made of the hound symbolism—for Holmes also is houndlike in his cunning, his pertinacity, his secretive patience, his ability to dog, his ferocious concentration once the scent is warm. Baker Street is his kennel, and his snapping boredom there between hunts is very canine indeed. We are glutted with story; and starved of pause for atmosphere, for darker shadows and depths to congregate, darker confrontations between man and nature, man and evil, man and his past. Things happen too fast, too vividly and eventfully, almost like the film of the book rather than the book itself.

Such velocity matters less in a short case, where compression is of the essence; but the technique brings dwindling returns with a long one, which may well be why Conan Doyle wrote so few of them. It is significant that he fell back upon another device with his two other—and artistically much more convincing—long-case mechanisms. Over half of

The Valley of Fear is taken up by the McMurdo "flashback," while even Jonathan Small's makes up nearly a quarter of *The Sign of Four*.

But when all is said and complained of, the real criminal here is very possibly less Conan Doyle himself than an innate flaw in the detective-tale genre. However fantastic and far-reaching the first half of a detective "mystery," the second half is bound to drop (and only too often flop) towards a neat and plausible everyday solution. The determination is the negation of everything inherent in the theme except the identity of the murderer. A degree of bathos is inevitable as soon as the mundane processes of the law take over. This is one good reason that the thriller evolved from the detective story proper. There a Chandler can criticize right-wing America, a Le Carré can explore the psychology of deception, in a way that the cramping demands of the old crime-solution formula do not allow.

In Conan Doyle's case we are left finally with superb caricatures and an unsurpassed narrative technique; and a sympathetic regret. He never really understood his greatest talent. But that makes him the normal artist, not the exception.

I do not want to end on what may seem an unduly theoretical and puritanical note. The incisiveness of the caricature remains remarkable, and the lasting appeal (and indeed the increasing appeal of period charm—is anything more redolent of their era than the three sentences that close the novel?) of the Holmes-Watson saga is too universally well proved to allow a case for major failure, as opposed to minor faults, any real ground. On paper we can all adapt animals better for survival than evolution itself has seen fit to do, give eyes to the blind and ears to the deaf—only to find that the old lady knew rather better what she was doing in the first and only real place than we had imagined. One can invent a more subtle, more significant Conan Doyle; but I think it is revealing that it is very difficult indeed to imagine a more popular and healthily enduring one. To be no more than fun to read could be a sin only in a world where everyone was fun to read. It is not a sin that most of the writers of this world are ever going to permit a man such as Conan Doyle to commit. They try too hard. His secret was that he tried enough.

HARDY AND THE HAG
(1977)

—Then meseemed it the guise of the ranker Venus.
Named of some Astarte, of some Cotytto.
Down I knelt before it and kissed the panel,
Drunk with the lure of love's inhibited dreamings.

Till the dawn I rubbed, when there leered up at me
A hag, that had slowly emerged from under my hands there,
Pointing the slanted finger towards a bosom
Eaten away of a rot from the lusts of a lifetime . . .
—I could have ended myself in heart-shook horror.

THOMAS HARDY, "THE COLLECTOR CLEANS HIS
PICTURE," *LATE LYRICS AND EARLIER, 1922*

"I am under a doom Somers. Yes, I am under a doom."
THOMAS HARDY, *THE WELL-BELOVED*

Most English novelists, however happy to indulge in literary gossip, are fanatically shy of talking of the realities of their private imaginative lives, just as they entertain an ancient preference for a narrating persona that is above all unpretentious and clubbable—a predilection that extends well beyond the strict arctic (where all is Snow) of the middle-class novel. I believe this proceeds far more from the cunning puritan in our makeup (our fear that investigation of the unconscious may lessen the pleasure we derive from being its playground) than from some fatuous association between amateurishness and gentlemanliness. The simple truth is that novel writing is an onanistic and taboo-laden pursuit, and therefore socially shameful to the more conforming, and morally dubious to the more fastidious. Hemingway's is only an extreme case of the kind of public mask that knowledge of this truth forces most novelists to assume.

Yet we English have been so successful at the novel—and at poetry—very much because of this tension between private reality and public pretense. If the glory of the French is to be naked and lucid about what they really feel and make, ours is to be veiled and oblique. I do not see this as evidence of our finer taste and greater seemliness. I think we just enjoy it more that way, in bed as in books; for the second simple truth is that creating another world, however imperfectly, is a haunting, isolating, and guilt-ridden experience, very similar indeed to the creating of a "real" perspective on the actual world that every child must undertake. As with the child, this experience is heavy with loss—of all the discarded illusions and countermyths as well as of the desires and sensibilities that inexorable adulthood (or artistic good form) has no time for.

The cost of it is a constant grumbling ground-bass in the Hardy novel I wish to consider, *The Well-Beloved*. Pierston-Hardy feels cursed by his "inability to ossify," to mature like other men. He feels himself arrested in eternal youth; yet he also knows (the empty maturity of his contemporaries, such as Somers, gets savagely short shrift elsewhere) that the artist who does not keep a profound part of himself not just open to his past, but *of* his past, is like an electrical system without a current. When Pierston finally elects to be "mature," he is dead as an artist.

A seriously attempted novel is also deeply exhausting of the writer's psyche, since the new world created must be torn from the world in his head. In a highly territorial species such as the human, such repeated loss of secret self must in the end have a quasi-traumatic effect. This may be why, like many other novelists, I cannot think very critically of Hardy; there is too strong a sense of a shared trap, a shared predicament. In any case I have long felt that the academic world spends far too much time on the written text and far too little on the benign psychosis of the writing experience—on particular product rather than general process. Equivalents of the now-dominant ethological approach (the living behavior) in zoology are sadly lacking in the world of letters. This is what I should like to try here with the Hardy of *The Well-Beloved*, not least because with this approach the artistically less excellent may often be the "behaviorally" more revealing. If space had allowed I should have liked also to examine his two earliest fictions, *An Indiscretion in the Life of an Heiress* and *Desperate*

Remedies, which already unconsciously bare much that was to be deliberately exposed in his last novel.

I should add, first, that my main private interest in life has always been nature, not literature—understanding function rather than making value judgments—and second, that if I seem to cite personal experience too frequently, my aim is emphatically not to suggest invidious comparisons, but to try to explain a little the view from the inside, some of the natural, and unnatural, history of my peculiar subspecies.

By supposing the ubiquitous scamping of technique and the almost algebraic impatience with anything but the basic formulae of his fiction to have been intentional on Hardy's part, I have over the years tried to see *The Well-Beloved* as a black farce. But even if that was the original premise (as the very last lines of the 1892 version hint), its execution was badly botched. Taken straight, the book cannot be judged as anything but a disastrous failure by Hardy's standards elsewhere. Indeed I think its closest cousin in modern English writing is that last spew of bile from H. G. Wells, *Mind at the End of Its Tether*—which, the reader may recall, dispatched rather more than mind to eternal oblivion ("The end of everything we call life is close at hand and cannot be evaded"). Despite the avuncular preface from 1912, *The Well-Beloved*, seething as it is with the suppressed rage of the self-duped, is fiction at the end of its tether. It is also the closest conducted tour we shall ever have of the psychic process behind Hardy's written product. No biography will ever take us so deep.

One thinks of Hoffmann, of the maker whose automata become so lifelike that they enslave him. But here it is a stage worse: the case of a god whose supposedly living Adams and Eves are now seen to be a tatter of trompe l'oeil, a creak of cogs and levers, and who can only abscond in horror from the realization that he himself is the archautomaton. There is evidence that this grim revelation, accompanied by Hardy's equally grim disillusion with his marriage, was dawning long before the 1892 version of the story. However, two failures in his own self-destructive logic in that version (to be mentioned later) suggest that he had not yet fully seen his "sickness." There is also the striking enigma that the two versions of this technically worst novel span the writing of one of the finest, *Jude the Obscure*. That, too, I hope to explain in part.

Hardy's nightmare is painfully familiar to most contemporary novelists.

The question of whether fiction is at the end of its tether is now universally in the air. It comes to us, far more consciously, as a nausea at the fictionality of fiction (less of a tautology than it may seem), or as a dread of once more entering an always ultimately defeating labyrinth. No further explanation is needed of the marked drop in fertility that has beset novelists during the last fifty years. The more you are aware of a hopeless obsession, the less you are driven by it. This is why *The Well-Beloved* is infinitely the most important of all Hardy's books for a practicing or intending writer of fiction to establish an attitude towards. The others, his far greater novels in ordinary terms, are now Victorian monuments, safe prey for the literary surveyors. *The Well-Beloved* still waits, potent, like a coiled adder on the Portland cliffs that brood distantly on where I sit, across Lyme Bay.

I had the interesting experience, a few years ago, of being psychoanalyzed by proxy—through one of my own novels, *The French Lieutenant's Woman*. Professor Gilbert J. Rose, who teaches clinical psychiatry at Yale, wrote a good paper on the book, but I was rather more interested in his general theory of what produces the artistically creative mind, since it largely confirmed—and greatly clarified—intuitive conclusions of my own.

In simple terms, his proposition was that some children retain a particularly rich memory of the passage from extreme infancy, when the identity of the baby is merged with that of the mother, to the arrival of the first awareness of separate identity and the simultaneous first dawn of what will become the adult sense of reality—that is, they are deeply marked by the passage from a unified magical world to a discrete "realist" one. What seemingly stamps itself indelibly on this kind of infant psyche is a pleasure in the fluid, polymorphic nature of the sensuous impressions, visual, tactile, auditory, and the rest, that he receives; and so profoundly that he cannot, even when the detail of this intensely autoerotic experience has retreated into the unconscious, refrain from tampering with reality—from trying to recover, in other words, the early oneness with his mother that granted this ability to make the world mysteriously and deliciously change meaning and appearance. He was once a magician with a wand; and given the right other predisposing and environmental factors, he will one day devote his life to trying to regain the unity and the power by re-creating adult versions of the experience: he will be an artist. Moreover, since every child goes through some variation of the same experience, this also explains one major attraction of art for the audience. The artist is simply someone who does the journey back on behalf of the less conditioned and less technically endowed.[1]

I do not know on how much empirical evidence Professor Rose's theory is based, but I find it a plausible and valuable model. One enigma about all artists, however successful they may be in worldly or critical terms, is the markedly repetitive nature of their endeavor, the inability not to return again and again on the same impossible journey. One must posit here an unconscious drive towards an unattainable. The theory also accounts for the sense of irrecoverable loss (or predestined defeat) that is so characteristic of many major novelists, and not least of Thomas Hardy in particular.[2] Associated with this is a permanent—and symptomatically childlike—dissatisfaction with reality as it is, with the "adult" world that is the case. Here too one must posit a deep memory of ready entry into alternative worlds, a dominant nostalgia for what Hardy himself called metempsychosis.

Beyond the specific myth of each novel, the novelist longs to be possessed by the continuous underlying myth he entertains of himself—a state not to be attained by method, logic, self-analysis, intelligent judgment, or any other of the qualities that make a good teacher, executive, or scientist. I should find it very hard to define what constitutes this being possessed, yet I know when I am and when I am not; know, too, that there are markedly different degrees of the state; that it functions as much by exclusion as by awareness; and above all, that it remains childlike in its fertility of lateral inconsequence, its setting of adultly ordered ideas in flux. Indeed, the work-

---

1. Sensitive female readers may not be too happy about the pronoun used in this paragraph and below, but the theory helps to explain why all through more recent human history, men have seemed better adapted—or more driven—to individual artistic expression than women. Professor Rose points out that the chances of being conditioned by this primal erotic experience are (if one accepts Freudian theory) massively loaded towards the son. The novel is, of course, something of an exception to the general rule, but even there the characteristic male preoccupation with loss, nonfulfillment, nonconsummation, is usually lacking in women writers. I can think of only two, among the great, who seem clearly to have been "fixed" in the normal male way: Emily Brontë and Virginia Woolf. Perhaps the masculine component in their psyches was stronger.

2. This sense of loss does not, however, give automatic birth to the tragic novelist. It may generate irony and comedy in the writer, and indeed has preponderantly done so in the English novel, perhaps because the comic is, given our national penchant for the veiled and oblique, a better public mask over the basic situation. Waugh and Nabokov exhibit interesting alternations of reaction—"tragic-naked" and "comic-concealed"—in this context. Hardy evidently attempted the latter in *The Well-Beloved*. But the true comic novelist dulls the loss by mocking it.

bench cost of this possession is revision—the elimination of the childish from the childlike, both in the language and in the conception. Like Venus with Cupid, each muse has her accompanying imp. It is also a state that withdraws (like the Well-Beloved) as the text nears consummation; and its disappearance, however pleased one may be with the final cast, is always deeply distressing: one other sense of loss, or reluctant return to normality, that every novelist-child has to contend with.

This obsessive need to find Pierston's "conduit into space"—to transcend present reality—opens a Pandora's box of associated problems in more ordinary life. One that I wish to discuss, partly because it is so generally ignored, and partly because I believe it very important with Hardy, is that of marital guilt. No one who spends most of his life in pursuit of a chimera can live comfortably with his everyday self or with that of the person closest to him. At one level he must know that for as long as he is on his voyage, the central emotional truth of his life is not where it should be; at another, that he is constantly, if only imaginatively, betraying his wife in other ports. It is easy to dismiss the first Mrs. Hardy; but I have no doubt that she underwent many years of feeling herself shuffled off—in some cases, flagrantly travestied—by the man she had married. I am equally sure that, "drunk with the lure of love's inhibited dreamings," her husband knew it.

One may view the wife's predicament in terms of an important subtheme of *The Well-Beloved*: the conflict between the pagan and the Christian on Portland—Portland as the combined arena, peninsula-womb and *domaine perdu* of Hardy's imagination. If the pagan there stands for permitted incest, premarital relations, the unchecked id, it also stands for consummation; and if the Christian stands for current social convention (as in the first Avice's "modern feelings" about staying chaste), the superego, and "mainland" reality in general, it also forbids consummation . . . in other words, it forbids what Hardy as a writer needs to have forbidden. The role of a wife in this conflict (and some such polarized tension between creative "desire" and social "duty" will exist in every novelist's mind) is complex. The one trait she possesses of the permissive pagan, available presence, is the very one the writer does not need; and in all else she stands against the cherished dream: she is the Marcia without makeup of the final chapter of *The Well-Beloved*, the "real" reality, armed with the sanctity of the conventional institution and so on. Her function and value are therefore certain to be oxymoronic to her husband's creative self: if she is potentially the strongest ally of his conscious, outward self, she can equally seem the greatest threat to his inward, unconscious one.

There is a further complicating factor. An essential part of the novelist's mental equipment is an iconogenic faculty that is crystalloid (repetitive of structure) in process—and that certainly, like the crystal, needs a stable nurturing culture. Although the wife is the mortal enemy of the mother as Ashtoreth-Aphrodite, she is also required to assume a rather more practical aspect of maternity, to be protective Jocasta against the cruel Laius of the review columns.

This relationship is in my experience a far more important consideration in the writing and shaping of a novel than most critics and biographers seem prepared to allow. We must also remember that the voyage undertaken is back to an indulged primal self and all its pleasures, and that the main source of those pleasures was that eternal other woman, the mother. The vanished young mother of infancy is quite as elusive as the Well-Beloved; indeed she *is* the Well-Beloved, though the adult writer transmogrifies her according to the pleasures and fancies that have in the older man superseded the nameless ones of the child—most commonly into a young female sexual ideal of some kind, to be attained or pursued (or denied) by himself hiding behind some male character. In one extraordinary and very revealing early case, Hardy hid behind a female stalking horse, Miss Aldclyffe in *Desperate Remedies*. The transmogrification can also, of course, be vindictive, as in so much of *The Well-Beloved*, or in any novel where Eve is treated as the betrayer of Adam. Both transmogrifications, into the idolized love-object and into the unforgiven "whore," may very often be seen side by side in the same novel.

Against this constant emotional fugue must be set the real presence of the woman the novelist shares his life with. She is bound willy-nilly to take on the face of the moral (in Hardy's case, the "Christian") censor; and this can seriously alter both the shape of a particular text and the general tenor of the novelist's career. I am convinced that this was the case with Hardy, who had the additional problem of a childless marriage to contend with. There is his lifelong need, self-parodied in *The Well-Beloved*, to avoid consummation. I cannot believe his reasons were solely artistic, or some effect of "natural reticence"; a much closer reality had to be placated.

For me this plays an important part in explaining the extraordinary difference in the quality of his last two novels. I can see the two attempts at

The Well-Beloved only as an admission of sin,[3] and *Jude the Obscure* as a "recklessly pleasant"[4] relapse into the enduring obsession—almost a case of a burglar's so relishing his penitential memoirs that he is driven back to the old game. I do not know how Mrs. Hardy could not have seen more of herself in Arabella than in Sue Bridehead; or, even in the intended mea culpa itself—since the obsession remained far stronger than the will to repent—more of herself in Marcia and in Nicola Pine-Avon (both "corpses" as soon as they become amenable) than in the three Avices, even if she did not know they stood for the three Sparks sisters. In short, *The Well-Beloved* was written less for a public audience than to assuage a private guilt. This also explains a great deal of its cursory impatience with realism, and its obfuscating classification under "Romances and Fantasies." Essentially the damage was long done, and the would-be "Christian" husband must have known his cause was hopeless. The only proof of real contrition would have lain in silence; and even the genuineness of that proof would be suspect, since self-exposure to his public in such matters must become more and more painful to a writer who was far from regardless of his conventional reputation and social status.

I hasten to add that I am not suggesting Hardy would have been a finer writer if he had been less trammeled, more frank. In practical terms this form of marital censorship is far more generally a valuable check on excess—the real woman in one's life symbolizing both social consensus and artistic common sense—than an unhappy stifling. But what must often remain, alas, is a reciprocal accusation: on the wife's side—with far more justice—of imaginative infidelity and *mauvaise foi*, of being unfairly condemned as inadequate in a situation in which the desired adequacy (erotic elusiveness, unattainability) is plainly impossible; and on the husband's side—much less reasonably—of lack of pity (plentifully demonstrated in Pierston for himself) over his "disease." Fair-copying wives know far better than anyone else the extent to which texts are lived in the writer's

---

3. Not least because the self-flagellation is so overdone. When Pierston terms the experience of the Well-Beloved as "anything but pleasure," "a racking spectacle," "a ghost story," I must reach for the saltcellar. It is also noticeable that the flagellant's loudest (and least convincing) cries are usually given a "Christian" coloring: "I have lost a faculty, for which loss Heaven be praised!"

4. Pierston feels the Well-Beloved shift from Nicola to the second Avice: "A gigantic satire upon the mutations of his nymph during the last twenty years seemed looming, . . . but it was recklessly pleasant to leave the suspicion unrecognised as yet, and follow the lead."

mind; and a final aggravating factor is the very specific and detailed way in which the novelist, given the length and dominance of realism in the form, is obliged to body forth his infidelity—"the carnate dwelling-place of the haunting minion of his imagination," in a stiffly embarrassed phrasing from *The Well-Beloved* itself. I suspect that one strong reason Hardy reserved himself to poetry after 1896 is precisely because verse is, in this context, a less "naked" medium than prose: not an exposed field, but a shady copse.

Since it is in the nature of pleasure to wish to prolong itself, the writer will always invent obstacles (such as Hardy's favorite hurdles, malign coincidence and class difference) to his hunt of the Well-Beloved—one further cruel-vital function for the wife, it may be noted. But because the real goal is eternally doomed to failure, its attainment no more feasible than that the words on the page can become the scene they describe, the fundamental nature of the hunt is tragic. The happy ending, the symbolic marriage between hero-author and heroine-mother, is in this light mere wish fulfillment, childish longing of the kind reflected in the traditional last sentence of all fairy stories. This is another major psychological dilemma (in his myth of himself) for the novelist, and one in which Hardy, by so often choosing the unhappy solution, foreshadowed our own century.

However, his choosing of the "reality" as against the "dream" cannot be explained simply in terms of a pessimistic temperament and a deterministic philosophy, of some put-upon Atreid cursing the unkind gods. To a psyche such as Hardy's, both highly devious and highly erotic, it is not at all axiomatic that the happy consummation is more pleasurable. The cathartic effect of tragedy bears a resemblance to the unresolved note on which some folk music ends, whereas there is something in the happy ending that resolves not only the story, but the need to embark on further stories. If the writer's secret and deepest joy is to search for an irrecoverable experience, the ending that announces that the attempt has once again failed may well seem the more satisfying. Like the phoenix, Tess in ashes is Tess, under another name, released and reborn. In the deeper continuum of an artist's life, where the doomed and illicit hunt is still far more attractive than no hunt at all, the "sad" ending may therefore be much happier than the "happy" ending. It will be both releasing and therapeutic.

If this seems paradoxical, I can call only on personal experience. I wrote and printed two endings to *The French Lieutenant's Woman* entirely because from early in the first draft I was torn intolerably between wishing to reward the male protagonist (my surrogate) with the woman he loved and wishing to deprive him of her—that is, I wanted to pander to both the adult and the child in myself. I had experienced a very similar predicament in my two previous novels. Yet I am now very clear that I am happier, where I gave two, with the unhappy ending, and not in any way for objective critical reasons, but simply because it has seemed more fertile and onward to my whole being as a writer.

From the very beginning, from the schoolroom of *An Indiscretion*, there can be seen in Hardy a violent distaste for resolution, or consummation. The chance of happiness is almost always put in jeopardy by physical contact, the first hint of possession. His two earliest heroines, Geraldine and Cytherea, both behave absurdly like startled roe deer when they are first kissed; and their continuing capacity for not fulfilling their respective lovers', and the reader's, expectations exhibits a striking lack of psychological realism in a young writer who already showed ample command of it with less emotive characters. Even here it is clear that Hardy finds his deepest pleasure in the period when consummation remains a distant threat, a bridge whose crossing—or collapse—can be put off for another chapter.

I think it must be said that this endlessly repeated luring-denying nature of his heroines is not too far removed from what our more vulgar age calls the cock-tease. It is a very characteristic movement—advancing, retreating, unveiling, reveiling—of the meetings in *The Well-Beloved*, and like so much else, this is done with the angry disregard of a man forced to lampoon himself. The actual sexual consummations in both versions are totally without erotic quality, indeed are merely recorded by implication; and they bring nothing but disillusion to both partners.

This leads me to that most Hardyesque of all narrative devices: the tryst. The isolated meeting of a man and a woman, preferably by chance, preferably in "pagan" nature and away from the "Christian" restraint of town and house, preferably trap-set with various minor circumstances (whose introduction often shows Hardy at his the weakest, as if emotional pressure choked invention) that oblige a greater closeness and eventual bodily contact—all this was transparently a more exciting concept than the "all-embracing indifference"[5] of marriage.

---

5. The phrase is used of the second Avice's marriage to Ike: "having as its chief ingredient neither love nor hate, but an all-embracing indifference."

Significantly, Hardy always gives the trysting Well-Beloved the same physiological reaction, the rush of blood to the cheeks. This tumescent sexual metaphor is once again used to the point of self-satire in the present novel: Marcia is "inflamed to peony hues," and so on. One may see a disguised death wish where the first bodily contact is so perversely made the secret trigger (not *post*, but *ante, coitum tristitia*) of the frustration and misery to come. But I suspect this predilection for the first faint erection of love, and the distaste for the thereafter of it, is one of Hardy's most enduring attractions. He had his finger on a very common death wish, if such it is.

The importance of the tryst becomes clear when we realize that the Well-Beloved is never a face, but rather the congeries of affective circumstances in which it is met; as soon as it inhabits one face, its erotic energy (that is, the author's imaginative energy) begins to drain away. Since it cannot be the face of the only true, and original, Well-Beloved, it becomes a lie, is marked for death. In other words, the tryst is not the embodiment of a transient hope in the outward narrative so much as it is a straight desire for transience, since gaining briefly to lose eternally is the chief fuel of the imagination in Hardy himself. In *The Well-Beloved* this is shown in the highly voyeuristic treatment of the early relationship with the second Avice, and in the corollary masochistic—or "Christian"—misery of their life in Pierston's London flat, where the girl is put, with a ghastly irony, to "dust all my Venus failures."

Plainly the tryst is also a scarcely concealed simulacrum of the primary relationship of the child with the vanished mother. In *The Well-Beloved*, when Marcia and Pierston retreat from the storm under the tarred and upturned lerret, fetally crouched since they cannot stand, the model is particularly clear. He could "feel her furs against him"; he thinks of himself as playing Romeo to her Juliet, implicitly breaking a taboo far greater than that dividing two rival families. As they walk on to Weymouth, he goes on thinking "how soft and warm the lady was in her fur covering, as he held her so tightly; the only dry spots in the clothing of either being her left side and his right, where they excluded the rain by their mutual pressure"; and then finally there is the strange near-fetishist scene, the most overtly erotic in the book, when Pierston dries Marcia's wet clothes at the inn, manipulating the veils while the baggageless dancer stands naked in his imagination, if not his sight, upstairs.

Nor can it be a coincidence that incest plays so large a part in the novel, not only in its triple-goddess central theme but also in the Portland setting.

There are constant references to shared blood relationships; the second and third Avices live in Pierston's natal house, even in his former room there. The kimberlin, or non-Portlander, is unmistakably associated with the Oedipal father, the frustrator of the dream, the intruder in the primal unity. In the 1892 version Hardy followed the lerret scene with the marriage of Pierston and Marcia instead of the more casual hotel liaison of the final revision. He also had Pierston marry the third Avice in the earlier text. These were both, it seems to me, errors of his unconscious, results of a lingering desire to give himself, behind his hero, some reward—characteristically enough, in the form of a sanction on the pagan by a "Christian" institution. But on reflection he must have seen that this was the last novel—last novel indeed—in which he could indulge such conditioned wish fulfillment.[6] When all is to reveal the tyranny, it is absurd to behave at its behest. One cannot exorcise witches—least of all the ultimate witch—by symbolically marrying them.

This *abnormally* close juxtaposition, or isolating, of a male and a female character is so constant a feature of the male novel that I think it adds further support to Professor Rose's theory. I know myself how excitement mounts—if there was a Creator, how much he must have looked forward to the chapter on Eden—as such situations approach, and how considerably their contrivance can alter the preceding narrative. Although I gained the outward theme of *The Collector* from a bizarre real-life incident in the 1950s, similar fantasies had haunted my adolescence—not, let me quickly say, with the cruelties and criminalities of the book, but very much more along the lines of the Hardy tryst. That is, I dreamed isolating situations with girls whom reality did not permit me isolation with—the desert island, the air crash with two survivors, the stopped lift, the rescue from a fate worse than death . . . all the desperate remedies of the romantic novelette—but also, more valuably, countless variations of the chance meeting in more realistic contexts. A common feature of such fantasies was some kind of close confinement, as in Hardy's lerret, where the Well-Beloved was obliged to notice me; and I realize, in retrospect, that my own book was a working-out of the futility, in reality, of expecting well of such metaphors for the irrecoverable relationship. I had the very greatest diffi-

6. Although there is an interesting relic of what one might call the sultan syndrome of male novelists in the final paragraph of chapter 8 in part 2, where Pierston thinks of "packing" the second Avice off to school—finishing her in all senses!—and then marrying her and "taking his chance."

culty in killing off my own heroine; and I have only quite recently, in a manner I trust readers will now guess, understood the real meaning of my ending, of the way in which the monstrous and pitiable Clegg (the man who acts out his own fantasies) prepares for a new "guest" in the Blue-beard's cell beneath his lonely house. It is a very grave fallacy that novelists understand the personal application of their own novels. I suspect in fact that it is generally the last face of them that they decipher. Just as the Well-Beloved passes from glimpsed woman to woman in our private lives, so it is with our characters. This is one other principal reason we can, as we grow older, kill them off with so little real pain. Creating an embodiment of the Well-Beloved is like marrying her; and she would never stand for that.

In his biography *Young Thomas Hardy* (London, 1974) I was taken to task by Dr. Robert Gittings for having swallowed whole the Tryphena "myth." Although I would, accepting both the biographical and the auto-biographical evidence in *The Well-Beloved* itself, concede at once that the likelihood of there having been only one Tryphena in Hardy's life is nonexistent, I remain a total apostate when it comes to dismissing this type of experience as unimportant. The reference to Tryphena's death (in 1890) in the preface to *Jude the Obscure* cannot be ignored; nor can I think what else, or who else, could have delayed the smashing of the psychic generator, apparently already decided on by 1889, to enable that last great output of fictional power. There is reinforcing evidence of her potency in the present book, in the scene (part 2, chapter 3) where the London high society in which Pierston finds himself fades to nothingness before the "lily-white corpse of an obscure country-girl"; he refers to the "almost ra-diant purity of this new-sprung affection for a flown spirit." The very ti-tle of the chapter—stylistically one of the best-written and emotionally one of the most deeply felt in the book—is "She Becomes an Inaccessible Ghost."

If the Well-Beloved ever took a quasi-perennial "carnate" form in Hardy's life, I believe it was in the "charm idealised by lack of substance" of the Tryphena of the Weymouth summer of 1869.[7] The outward of the

---

7. Lack of substance was already inherent in the affair long before the final separator, Emma Gifford, appeared, in March 1870. Tryphena's hopes of going to Stockwell Normal College, and the strict pro-priety of conduct expected of candidates, must have borne a "Christian" connotation for Hardy. Al-ready loss offered itself, and the frustration of the pagan-permissive.

Well-Beloved may flit from shape to shape, but she is also a spirit, and spirit inheres much more tenaciously in its most powerful original manifestation. Pierston says of the second Avice that "he could not help seeing in her all that he knew of another, and veiling in her all that did not harmonise with his sense of metempsychosis." And when the second Avice later plays tacit procuress, at Pierston's command, to her own daughter, we are surely to see that the Well-Beloved, if discontinuous in the epiphany, is one in the genesis. After all, it is not only novelists who cherish and recall first loves most dearly and deeply.

We know of the very practical and vital role played in Hardy's creative life by his mother, Jemima Hand; of his long tryst with her at Bockhampton during the writing of his first indisputable masterpiece, *Far from the Madding Crowd*. We know that, in Dr. Gittings's words, "he was attracted again and again by the same type of woman, a replica of his own mother, with the striking features shared by all women of the Hand family"—of which one was the eyebrows like musical slurs reflected in the "glide upon glide" Hardy used to describe the heroine of the novel he was writing during the 1869 summer. We know of his previous attraction to Tryphena's sister Martha; know how closely a dry shrewdness in each of the Avices echoes a similar quality in the three sisters of real life and in Jemima herself; how exactly the social differences between the second and third Avices parallel the "peasant" and "educated" sides of Tryphena. We also know how resolutely Hardy ostracized his "pagan" relations after the mid-1870s—thus making his continuing use of them in his fiction and his imagination doubly illicit. Hardy may have seen the emotional tug-of-war between Emma Gifford and Tryphena in the early 1870s only in terms of pain and suffering; but it seems clear that this is where the Well-Beloved first *consciously* manifested herself in his life, never to leave it again. Marriage simply meant that her lasting dominance was assured, and that his wife from then on was condemned to the punishment foreshadowed in the poem "Near Lanivet 1872": "In the running of Time's far glass, / Her crucified. . . ."

Of course it would be absurd to suppose that Hardy ever realized who truly lay behind Tryphena and all the other incarnations of the Well-Beloved, and indeed I suspect that the power—and frequency—of a novelist's output is very much bound up with his failing to realize it; and that we later novelists have yet to come to terms with that knowledge. If ignorance here can hardly be termed bliss, it is certainly more fertile.[8] The difficult reality is that if in every human and daily way ("In one I can atone for all"), the actual woman in a novelist's life is of indispensable importance to him, imaginatively it is the lost ones who count, first because they stand so perfectly for the original lost woman, and second (but perhaps no less importantly) because they are a prime source of fantasy and of guidance, like Ariadne with her thread, in the labyrinth of his other worlds.

Because they were never truly possessed, they remain eternally malleable and acquiescent, like the sculptor's clay model. The repeated use to which they can be put may even finally suggest a fuller possession of them than any mere real or carnal knowledge could ever have allowed. And this above all is why, to the extent that a creator of fiction needs such a figure behind his principal heroines, he is unlikely to want to grant her even imaginary happiness at the end of the narrative; and must therefore deny it to himself in the male character who is his surrogate. Hardy seems to have grasped this indispensable corollary under the shock of the suicide of Horace Moule in 1873, since it is first clearly enunciated in the fate allotted Farmer Boldwood. From then on, the doomed and thwarted child sits firm inside all his major male characters. They too become phoenixes, sacrificed so that their sacrificer may once again summon up the Well-Beloved and her further victim. Lost, denying and denied, she lives and remains his; given away, consummated, she dies.

This is the redeeming secret behind all the self-disgust in *The Well-Beloved*. If superficially the three Avices may be seen (by the reader) as sadistic sirens, luring the poor sailor to his death in the Race, or (by Pierston-Hardy) as the trumpery puppets of his own morbid and narcissistic imagination, more deeply I view them as something quite contrary: the maternal muses who grant the power to comprehend and palliate the universal condition of humankind, which is, given the ability of the human mind to choose and imagine other than the chosen or the actual course of events, a permanent state of loss. I spoke earlier of the book's lying like a coiled adder on the cliffs of the Isle of Slingers, but I think finally that it

---

8. Thus, in my view, the characteristic abundance of the Victorian novel—and novelist—can be partly attributed to the taboo on sexual frankness, which in turn prevented the potentially inhibiting awareness of underlying psychic process. In short, outward sexual "honesty" in the novel may be creatively far more limiting (or lethal, if *The Well-Beloved* is to be believed) than we generally imagine.

contains its own antidote; it remains a grave warning, but against the sailor, not the voyage.

And then surely, in the last account, one has to smile. Who, faced with the hell of being a true and deeply loved artist ("How incomparably the immaterial dream dwarfed the grandest of substantial things") and the paradise of being Mr. Alfred Somers, that "middle-aged family man with spectacles," painting for the "furnishing householder through the middling critic," would not still rush to tryst with the hag, and book a seat on the first broomstick down to Bockhampton?

"ELIDUC" AND THE *LAIS* OF
MARIE DE FRANCE
(1974/78)[1]

De un mut ancïen lai bretun
Le cunte e tute la reisun
Vus dirai . . .[2]

As a student of French at Oxford, I read omnivorously, though much more out of ignorance than out of intelligence. I had very little notion of my real tastes, having swallowed the then-prevalent myth that only one's teachers had a right to personal preferences. This is not an approach I could attempt to sell to any student today, but it did have one advantage. Likes and dislikes were eventually formed on a strictly pragmatic basis; I learned to value what I couldn't, over the years, forget. One such obstinate survivor was Alain-Fournier's *Le Grand Meaulnes*. A number of young thesis writers have now told me they can see no significant parallels between *Le Grand Meaulnes* and my own novel *The Magus*. I must have severed the umbilical cord—the real connection requires such a metaphor—much more neatly than I supposed at the time; or perhaps modern academic criticism is blind to relationships that are far more emotional than structural.

I felt Alain-Fournier's appeal from the beginning. That wasn't the case with another part of the student syllabus. Old French, with its latinities, its

---

1. This essay revises and combines two original essays on Marie de France. The first, "A Personal Note to 'Eliduc,'" appeared in the collection of stories entitled *The Ebony Tower* (1974) as a preface to the story "Eliduc," a reworking of one of Marie's lais. The second, "Marie de France," was written as an introduction to *The Lais of Marie de France* (1978), translated by Robert Hanning and Joan Ferrante.

2. "I'll tell you the story and all the meaning of a very ancient Breton *lai*."

baffling orthographies, its wealth of dialect forms, may be fascinating to the linguist; but to someone who wants to read meaning and story, its difficulty is just plain irritating. Nevertheless, I was to discover later that one field of Old French literature refused to subside into the oblivion I wished on the whole period once I had taken finals. This field—"forest" would be more appropriate—was that of the Celtic romance.

The extraordinary change in European culture that took place under the influence of the British (in the original Celtic sense of that word) imagination has never, I suspect, been fully traced or acknowledged. The mania for chivalry, courtly love, mystic and crusading Christianity, the Camelot syndrome, all these we are aware of—a good deal too aware, perhaps, in the case of some recent travesties of that last center of the lore. But I believe that we also owe—emotionally and imaginatively, at least—the very essence of what we have meant ever since by the fictional, the novel and all its children, to this strange northern invasion of the early medieval mind. One may smile condescendingly at the naïvetés and primitive technique of stories such as "Eliduc," but I do not think any writer of fiction can do so with decency, and for a very simple reason: he is watching his own birth.

The attendant midwife at this event is Marie de France, the first woman novelist of our era. If I cannot quite simply call her the first woman novelist, that is only because I believe the writer of the *Odyssey* was also a woman. The great Greek story, woven as it is of questing, of false ambition and hostile fate, of selfish and unselfish love, of the relationships between men and women, stands grandparent to all subsequent fiction—and not least, through the intervening generation of the *Aeneid*, to Marie de France herself. Indeed, I regard Marie's work as a strong retrospective argument for assuming a female mind behind the *Odyssey*. This is not the place to discuss the parallels in moral attitude, in sensibility and angle of vision, in the sophisticated embroidering of folk theme, even in certain social problems common to twelfth-century northern Europe and the Greece of two thousand years earlier . . . though I recommend a reading of the two texts side by side to the curious. We shall never know who Homer, or the Homer of the *Odyssey*, was; but Marie was undeniably a woman. Hers is the first indisputably feminine view of the human comedy expressed through art.

The more fastidious may complain that I am abusing the term "novel" and extending it intolerably backwards, especially since Marie, like Homer, wrote in verse. But to class writers by a mere historical hazard of outward form has long seemed to me an appallingly old-fashioned view of literature, as false as the pre-Linnaean classification of the natural world by fortuitous external correspondences—calling whales fish because they live in the sea, and so on. Virtually all Marie's importance, to say nothing of her charm, lies in her storytelling, her psychology, her morality, her highly individual use of her material—that is, it lies in her fictional powers, not in her versifying ones. The latter are, I suspect, no more than competent in purely poetic terms. She is generally crisp and neat, but little more; and at times, at least to my ear, she can descend dangerously near to doggerel.

However, on that score it must be added at once that we know miserably little of a vital factor in the understanding of any writer: how he or she conceives the medium of transmission to the contemporary outside world. We must read Marie in cold print and silence, but it is almost certain that she would have seen herself, at least during the original composition, as providing matter for oral performance. We know that the Celtic *lais* she based her stories on were, in Bédier's phrase, "half sung, half spoken"; and Marie's verse is far less easy to dismiss if one includes a deliberately intended spoken function in the valuation. It works almost uniformly well, sometimes brilliantly, at a quasi-dramatic level; and we should also not forget the primordial other functions of verse both as a concentrator of wisdom and as a rudimentary mnemonic system.

In the original, the *Lais* are in rhyming octosyllabic couplets, and they were to be performed, sung and mimed, probably to a loose melody, or to a variety of them, and perhaps in places spoken almost conversationally against chords and arpeggios. The instrument would have been the harp, no doubt in its Breton form, the *rote*. The Romantics turned minstrelsy into an irredeemably silly word; but what little evidence we have suggests a very great art, one we have now lost beyond recall. In the case of writers such as Marie de France, to see only the printed text is rather like having to judge a film by the script alone. The long evolution of fiction has been very much bound up with finding means to express the writer's "voice"—his or her humors, private opinions, nature—by means of word manipulation and print alone, but before Gutenberg we are lost. Twice in "Eliduc" Marie is very formal about the way her hero visits the wayward princess he is in love with; he does not crash into her rooms, but has himself properly announced. One may take it as a piece of padding, a conventional show of courtly etiquette. But I think it much more probable that it was instead a dry aside, and directed at her first listeners. Indeed, if what we know of Henry II is true, and Marie was related to him, I could hazard a guess as to whom the little gibe was directed toward.

Modern readers need therefore to bear in mind the possibility that what they are reading is, so to speak, only the libretto. The art of the *diseuse* derives from early-medieval public story recitation, and gives us a good clue to the now largely vanished skills of the professional oral narrator. One thing from which such skills tacitly excused the writer was the insertion of all those implicit stage directions about physical details and emotional reactions (adjectives and adverbs) that novelists have been increasingly obliged to employ since the invention of print and the consequent tyranny of an atomized, single-reader audience. This is perhaps the hardest leap of the imagination that we have to make to appreciate Marie today—in simple, to read between her lines.

Fortunately, things are much easier when it comes to the content behind the form and the style. Here we are unmistakably in the presence of a born and engagingly shrewd storyteller. Marie's method must, for the reason I have suggested, seem naive to anyone coming fresh from the complex and elaborately realistic techniques of our own print-conditioned culture; but her actual themes are far less naive than they are archetypal. The great majority of them are antique only in their outward setting and detail, while her characteristic obsession with the problems of sexuality and fidelity (identical bees—long-suffering Penelopes and marriage-wrecking Circes—buzzed in that old Greek bonnet, it may be noted) is nothing if not contemporary.

The Freudian and Jungian undertones of almost all her stories are obvious. One that has always particularly pleased me that way is the erotic "Lanval." It would be hard to imagine a more exact premonition of what Thomas Hardy, much later in European literary history, termed the "Well-Beloved"—the unattainable muse-figure that haunts every male novelist. "Eliduc" is a beautiful reworking of one of the oldest themes (and aging wives' nightmares) in all literature. The strange "Bisclavret" is about far more than a werewolf. Even the tiny and subtly ambitious "Laüstic" might serve as label to a familiar-enough syndrome, still today. Never mind the medieval image; we have all known of the not-very-daring *affaire* between two overromantic egos that ends up as a dead bird in a precious casket, more treasured for its failure than lamented for its lack of courage.

I should in any case like to suggest that Marie's surface naïveté—I would much rather call it economy—is misleading. The pen has one great advantage over the camera. It can leave out—in movie jargon, "lose"—far more easily, and leaving out is a key trick in all good prose fiction. A camera cannot photograph a voice; it has to show the face as well. And you can tell novelists quite as much by what they do not describe as by what they do—that is, by how well they use their art's exceptional facility for exclusion.

It is true that in Marie's age writers had infinitely less choice in terms of form and technique; but to assume that we have nothing to learn from them or to admire in what they did achieve with very limited means, and that they can therefore be dismissed as mere primitives, childish at worst and childlike at best, seems to me foolish—as foolish as calling the ancient Greek architects primitive because they made no provision for heating ducts and elevator shafts. Personally I would award Marie, along with her contemporaries Chrétien de Troyes and Béroul, high praise for the elegance of some of their solutions to basic and in no way outdated problems of narrative technique, and especially in this matter of what they choose to leave out. One of the oldest human chauvinisms has to do with time—the notion that our own must be wiser than the rest. This may be true of science; but it is very seldom true of art.

Marie also possesses an exquisite eye for the precise, poetic, and colorful detail when it is needed. The editors of her *Lais* justly praise her very marked gift for hitting on symbolic correlatives of action and personality. The same flair is seen in the characterizing touches, the moods and humors, the fragments of dialogue, that she gives her men and women. The result is that her stories remain both universal and particular—they are as formal as tapestries at one moment, as natural as life the next. It is a gift, like her frequent dryness, that she shares with that other laborer on two inches of ivory, Jane Austen. Marie works very small, is very deft and concise, and the miracle is that she so often reaches far beyond her historically and formally restricted setting. Her greatest attraction, for me, is her extraordinary ability suddenly to reach out across eight centuries, to be present again. I know of no other medieval writer, except perhaps Langland, who has ever had quite that effect on me, of being at certain moments nearer my own livingness than actual daily life itself. This is not a test that any academic critic would or could allow, yet I think most readers will know what I mean, and agree that there is no surer hallmark of genius in fiction. It is the one gift that all its greatest exponents share: the imagined present, however past, drowns the real present. The notion that time is linear and irreversible becomes the ultimate fiction; and the long-dead writer lives, not a hand's touch from your side.

Biographically, next to nothing is known of Marie de France. Even the name is only a deduction, made long after her death, from a line in one of her fables—*Marie ai nun, si suis de France*, "My name is Marie and I come from. . . ." But it isn't even certain that she intended what we today think of as France. The region around Paris, the Ile de France, is more probable. There are faint linguistic and other grounds for supposing that she may have come from the part of Normandy called the Vexin, which borders on the Paris basin.

At some time she went to England, perhaps in or with the court of Eleanor of Aquitaine. The king to whom she dedicated her *Lais*, or love stories, may have been Eleanor's husband, Henry II, Becket's cross; and there is even a plausible possibility that Marie was Henry's illegitimate sister. His father, Geoffrey Plantagenet, had a natural daughter of that name, who became the abbess of Shaftesbury Abbey in about 1189. Not all medieval abbesses led solemn and devout lives; and in any case, the romances were almost certainly composed in the previous decade. The fact that the other two works by Marie that have survived are religious and certainly date from after 1180 reinforces this identification. If "Marie de France" was indeed the Marie from the wrong side of the Angevin blanket who became abbess of Shaftesbury, she must have been born before 1150, and we know that the abbess survived until about 1216.

It is very difficult to imagine the *Lais'* being written by other than a finely educated (therefore, in that age, finely born) young woman. That she was romantic and high-spirited is easily deduced; and that her work was a tremendous and rapid literary success, a wealth of contemporary manuscripts and translations bear witness . . . and one might even proceed to see her as an early victim of male chauvinism, sent to Shaftesbury to mend her wicked ways. There is certainly evidence that her stories were not approved of by the Church. Very soon after the *Lais* came into the world, a gentleman named Denis Piramus—a monk in fact, but evidently a born reviewer by nature—wrote a sourly sarcastic account of her popularity. He knew why the stories gave their aristocratic audiences such dubious pleasure: they were hearing what they wanted to happen to themselves.

Overtly Marie set out in the *Lais* to save some Celtic tales from oblivion: stories from the diffuse folk corpus that scholars call the *matière de Bretagne*, and of which the Arthurian cycle and the story of Tristram and Isolde are now the best-remembered. Whether she first heard them from French or from English sources is unknown, since her own description of their provenance, *bretun*, was a term then used racially of the Brythonic Celts, and not geographically—that is, it included the Welsh and the Cornish as well as the Bretons proper. There are records of how far the Celtic minstrels wandered long before Marie's time, and she could have heard their performances at any major court.

But far more important than this quasi-archaeological service was the transmutation that took place when Marie grafted her own knowledge of the world onto the old material. Effectively she introduced a totally new element into European literature. It was composed not least of sexual honesty and a very feminine awareness of how people really behave—and how behavior and moral problems can be expressed through things such as dialogue and action. She did for her posterity something of what Jane Austen did for hers—that is, she set a new standard for accuracy regarding human emotions and their absurdities. One may bring the two even closer, since the common ground of all Marie's stories (what she herself would have termed *desmesure*, or passionate excess) is remarkably akin to the later novelist's view of sense and sensibility. Another similarity is much harder for us to detect today, and that is a shared sense of humor. Because her stories are so distant from us, we tend to forget that much of their matter was equally distant from her own twelfth century; and we grossly underestimate both her and her contemporary audience's sophistication if we imagine those auditors listening with totally straight faces and credulity. That was no more expected than that we should take our own thrillers, Wild Westerns, and sci-fi epics without a pinch of salt. Marie's irony is all the harder to sense now for the historical reasons already stated: her *Lais* were not meant to be read in silence, or in prose.

It also needs to be remembered that "Eliduc" and the other stories in the *Lais* are told against an anachronistic background based on three real-life systems. The first is the feudal system, which laid a vital importance on promises sworn between vassal and lord. It was not only the power structure that depended on a man's being as good as his word; all civilized life depended on it. Today we can go to law over a broken contract; in those days you could only take to arms. The second context is the Christian, which is responsible for the ending of "Eliduc," but not much else. Marie is patently more interested in the human heart than in the immortal soul. The third system is that of courtly love, where the same stress on keeping faith was applied to sexual relations. It is hardly a fashionable idea in the twentieth century, but *amour courtois* was a desperately needed attempt to bring more civilization (more female intelligence) into a brutal society; and all civilization is based on agreed codes and symbols of mutual trust. An age in which the *desmesure* of Watergate—in my view far more a cultural than a political tragedy—can happen should not find this too difficult to understand.

I have always associated Marie's memory with one of Mallarmé's most famous lines, *Le vierge, le vivace, le bel aujourd'hui* . . . —with that freshness, greenness, immediacy that have from the beginning distinguished the less coldly classical side of her country's art. Marie cannot be known in a day or in a single reading; but once known, like a spring day in the Anjou of the royal family to which she may have belonged, she will not be forgotten.

MOLIÈRE'S *DOM JUAN*
(1981)

Dom Juan is the most political of Molière's plays, and I'd like to begin by briefly recapitulating something of its historical background.

Molière had already been accused of atheism and impiety after *L'Ecole des Femmes* in 1663. This culminated in the successful campaign to have *Tartuffe* banned in May 1664. Molière rankled over the injustice until January of the following year. His company had by then grown short of material—and money—and they may have pointed out to their author-director the success that two other versions of the Dom Juan story (themselves based on Italian versions of Tirso de Molina's *El Burlador de Sevilla* of fifty years earlier) were currently enjoying in Paris. Molière had therefore a double reason to take up the theme: to make some quick profit for his troupe, and once more to throw down the gauntlet before the Cabale des Dévots, or Bigots' Cabal, on which he quite correctly blamed the suppression of his beloved *Tartuffe*. The new play was written very quickly, and in anger; and with the added need to ensure a public success, one major explanation of the famous "schizophrenia" of the end product.

But schizophrenia was already in the air. From the beginning of the century there had been a rising tension between religious conservatism and free thought. On the left hand were the *libertins*, with their belief in individual conscience and their sympathy for the growing empiricism in science; on the right, the dévots, with their faith in immutable divine, royal, and social traditions. Molière had been a frequenter of the free-thinking salons, and admired the epicurean Gassendi, a chief exponent in France of the new philosophy. There is little doubt that he was sympathetic to *libertinage* intellectually.

However, by midcentury the free-thinking movement was in increasing trouble, from both without and within. An obvious social reason was that a number of noblemen had notoriously slipped from doubting ecclesiastical authority to rejecting all normal morality, to the horror of the more sincere free thinkers. The very word *libertin*, once a mere label, was fast becoming an accusation. There were many recent real-life models Molière might have used for his own Dom Juan. He is said mainly to have based him on the Prince de Conti, but there are elements too from other rakes of the time—Henri de Lorraine, de Vardes, Bussy, the Chevalier de Roquelaure (the source for the pauper scene). By 1653—in a society rapidly closing after the Fronde—prison, exile, even the stake had made this life-style dangerous, and the shrewder false *libertins* began to drop the philosophical justification for their selfishness and to hide behind the hypocritical mask of religion. It was a program explicitly set for himself by another candidate for a prototype Dom Juan, the Cardinal de Retz ("to sin cunningly, which is the most criminal before God, but wisest before society").

This, then, is another of Molière's schizophrenias: that of someone who admired the principles of free thought, but disapproved (no doubt on bitter personal grounds as well, in view of his marriage) of their abuse in practice.

His split mind was shared by his protector, the king. The driving force in the reactionary camp was the Compagnie du Très Saint-Sacrament de l'Autel, a society founded secretly in 1629 and kept clandestine for another two decades. This society, the (so to speak) CIA behind the Bigots' Cabal, harked back to the spirit of the Council of Trent. It wanted the Inquisition restored in France, and the Vatican placed in charge of the royal and national destiny. Under a thin cover of charitable works, the Company (which already had powerful support at court from the queen mother, Anne of Austria) intrigued furiously against the policies of Mazarin and Louis XIV. Among its aims was the institution of a Spanish-style Catholicism, with an important role reserved for the lay director of conscience (Tartuffe's part) in every well-to-do family. In international matters this politico-religious right wing was for alliance with Spain and war with England—exactly the reverse of the king's intentions during that period. He was in any case, especially after a row with the pope over protocol in 1662, less and less inclined to brook ultramontane interference in French affairs.

As a matter of policy he therefore tolerated some elements of the free-thinking movement—and not least its great dramatist. But his protection was far from disinterested, and equally far from comprehensive. He was on weak ground in other directions, even in his own mind, since he had always blamed the Fronde partly on *libertinage*. Louis was, in short, very vulnerable to criticism from the right, and he himself is believed to have told Molière to cut the pauper scene after the second performance of *Dom Juan*. Although he did allow (after his mother died, in 1666) *Tartuffe* to be staged again in 1669, *Dom Juan* was never pardoned.

The Company of the Most Blessed Sacrament had met a month before *Tartuffe* was first mounted to discuss a tactic for having it banned, and they launched an even more violent attack against *Dom Juan* when it opened on February 15, 1665. Although it was enormously successful (receipts for the first ten performances averaged £1,600 a night), and despite undergoing many cuts, it was withdrawn on March 20. A bowdlerized printed text appeared in Paris in 1682, but the play remained on the shelf until the 1840s. In 1947 the Comédie-Française could still list only a hundred performances of it against two and a half thousand for *Tartuffe*. Even today it is not hard to detect—in the most popular French student's edition, for example—a lingering air of shocked disapproval.

It is probable that Molière himself did not fully comprehend the contemporary political situation, in terms of either the king's delicate position or the highly organized lobby that lay behind the Bigots' Cabal. The play was certainly much too extreme to be of any use to the moderates as a propaganda weapon. But even if he had been more aware, one may argue that under the dual influence of the seventeenth-century notion of *caractère* and the free-thinking view of the active power of the individual conscience, Molière was much more concerned with attacking the bigotry and hypocrisy he saw "on the ground" in the Parisian society about him—and above all in its most obvious manifestation, the abuse of language.

In effect, with this aim and theme, he placed himself in front of an insoluble dilemma, and one can view *Dom Juan* as a kind of explosive solution, which makes clear why both the libertines and the bigots are finally demolished in it. Dom Juan himself has to provide the damnation both of the conscious rake and of the hypocrite—that is, he is a two-edged knife, both scourge and criminal, angel and demon, accusing and accused. In Freudian terms, both id and superego. He serves Molière's moral and social purposes admirably, two birds with one stone, but at the cost of audience identification. This largely explains why so many logic-besotted French critics have had such perennial trouble with the play; and incidentally why I think it may be much more easily approached by the British. We are rather more familiar with paradox and loose ends in our arts.

At any rate, no play of Molière's is more open to differing interpretations, and accordingly I had better explain the one I tried to pursue in my translation. It is based on the idea that just as he was made to serve two very different purposes for Molière, Dom Juan is fundamentally two very different men. One is the callous rake of the legend and the plot; but the other is an amateur philosopher, and above all a student of language, especially of what modern linguists call "registers of discourse," or characteristic patterns of vocabulary and rhetoric. In this he is a dark cousin to Hamlet. If his calculated immorality puts him ethically below everyone else in the play—even Sganarelle—his keenness of ear, his smell for the empty phrase, for the dissonance between what is said and what is meant, set him well above them. In this aspect he is like a man returned out of the future, a would-be Wittgenstein (or Roland Barthes) let loose, or imprisoned, among people who are not fully conscious of the consequences of the language they use.

The internal evidence for this lies in a number of things: in his own skill at imitating other registers of discourse; in his pleasure in Sganarelle's company (which in any honest production, despite overt dialogue, he must betray) and the constant word games between them; in his notably laconic answers when he is faced with long, traditional tirades, and in his ubiquitous refusal to be moved by them; above all, in his own moments of self-honesty. The famous "two and two makes four" applies to language as well as to religion and philosophy. Perhaps his one enduring marriage is with his own scathing skepticism; and his tragedy is certainly that his is a linguistic or stylistic intelligence, not (rather implausibly) a moral one.

We know from the famous barber-shop story that Molière himself was an equally sharp observer of registers of discourse in real life, and not only because they were the basics of his trade in terms of characterization, but because they are of the very essence of comedy itself—and of hypocrisy also. In one of the placets concerning *Tartuffe* that he wrote to the king at the time of *Dom Juan*, Molière put it thus: "Most comic situations come from a failure of reciprocal understanding and from using the same word to express contrary things." The aim of all his more serious masterpieces is the same: *dévoiler l'imposture*, to unmask the phony. Their moral is equally clear. The good lies in learning to mistrust the surfaces of language, both in oneself and in others.

It follows from this that the four characters in the play (Elvira, Dom Carlos, Dom Alonso, Dom Louis) who habitually go in for the long tirade in the *style noble* derived from tragedy are Dom Juan's victims in more than the plot sense: they are also laboratory rats under a professor's eye. This does not—with one complicated exception—mean they are necessarily hypocrites, but rather more, in Dom Juan's book, victims of an outmoded or conditional vocabulary and cultural style. One may even extend the proposition and say that Dom Juan's greatest fault is his excessive belief in Pascal's famous dictum about the style's being the thought: the *gravitas* (or pomposity) of Dom Carlos and his father blinds him to the moral justice of what they are saying.

There is not a single textual indication of how Dom Juan behaves when he is listening, but plainly he needs to do an enormous amount of it in this play; and I should like to suggest that his reactions make it quite clear that he observes high rhetoric—in both speech and gesture—with something of the keen enjoyment of the ornithologist before a rare bird.

Which leads me to the complicated exception: Elvira. She seems to me a far more confused (or, once again, schizophrenic) character than most commentators have allowed for. I have treated her as something of a halfway house between the outright—and gullible—*style noble* characters and Dom Juan himself. I won't cite chapter and verse, but it is to my mind clear that Molière intended a strikingly similar development in her two scenes. In the first, in act 1, she begins like someone out of Corneille, then abruptly descends to a rather shrewish sarcasm, and then, at the end, sufficiently jibed by Dom Juan, bursts out with real emotion.

In the second, in act 4, she declaims two enormous speeches that are choked full of the stock euphemisms and catch phrases of high rhetoric. Dom Juan is profoundly untouched; and for me the turning point of the scene is Sganarelle's "Poor woman!" . . . and Elvira's realization that Dom Juan is thinking much more along the lines of "Absurd ham actress." Once again, at this point (and I should be happy to argue from the French text), Elvira descends from her tragic and religious high horse, and the true emotion comes through. I have tried to mark this in the descent to a much simpler, more broken language in her final appeal—which does move Dom Juan, even though only sexually (or at least he covers himself, under Sganarelle's famous sentimentality, by pretending so).

I realize that all this presents problems for the actress, but I am convinced it would be quite wrong for Elvira to be played throughout as "pure and innocent." She is really a young woman who tries to hide from her own sensuality behind a screen of idealism and its conventional rhetoric, as Dom Juan is perfectly well aware—witness his savage parody of her "style" in the first act. She cannot break through to her more natural self until she is truly angry or moved—and this is precisely when Dom Juan is most vulnerable to her.

I should add that for me this end of her final scene and the immediately following dialogue between Dom Juan and Sganarelle form the emotional and moral climax of the play. I think it would be to sell Dom Juan very short not to show between the lines that he himself knows it. This is the point where he finally damns himself beyond hope of redemption; the assumption of hypocrisy in the last act is merely the consequence of this rejection. Indeed, he has nowhere else to go, since Elvira's proving that she can escape from the bonds of language is at the same time a declaration of the reality and possibility of love. Perhaps the crux lies in Sganarelle's little aside ("He hasn't understood a word she's said") at the end of this passage. In my strong opinion, this is his one such aside that is said not for comic effect, but out of a genuine sadness—perhaps even a despair.

One less fraught instance of how Dom Juan might react to the *style noble* is found in the cliché-ridden debate between Elvira's two brothers on the nature of honor in act 3. Here one could well see him progress, as the two Spanish noblemen clatter and clash, from being the potential victim of the argument to being something not too far removed from an amused spectator at a tennis match—or Alice before Tweedledum and Tweedledee.

If all this may seem to be a torturing or anachronizing of Molière's intention, I must point out that his contempt for preciosity of language has a long record elsewhere, as does his linking of preciosity with at least potential hypocrisy. It is not, I think, for nothing that as an actor he was a very mediocre performer in tragedy, yet without equal as an intelligent buffoon. Only a few months after *Dom Juan* made its brief appearance, an angry young tyro playwright withdrew his own first tragedy from Molière's company, evidently because the troupe lacked conviction in its performance. His name was Racine. There is a moral there.

EBENEZER LE PAGE
(1981)

There may have been stranger recent literary events than the book I am about to discuss, but I rather doubt it. It is first of all posthumous, since the author, born a year older than the century, died in 1976. Then it is an only novel, seemingly not begun until he was in his late sixties. Even without those oddities, its voice and method are so unusual that it belongs nowhere on our conventional literary maps. Such a writer might at least have enjoyed the thought of a little personal publicity beyond the grave? Not at all: he made very sure before he died that any future biographer would have an exceedingly hard time of it. Mr. Edward Chaney has kindly let me see a series of letters Gerald Edwards wrote to him in his last years. They tell us a good deal about the psychology and character of the man, and even something about his family background; but about his own history, next to nothing.

So far as we know it was not until 1974 that Edwards made (through Mr. Chaney, to whom he gave the copyright) any attempt to have *The Book of Ebenezer Le Page* published. He bore the rejections it then received with an at least outwardly patient obstinacy. He more than once likened his stubbornness to that of a donkey; but this was a wise and well-read donkey, a very long way from being the innocent that a surface view of his book might suggest. He knew very well that it no more fitted contemporary literary taste (what in one of his letters he called "helicopter thinking," judging everything "from a superior height") than a furze bush does a greenhouse. If I cannot think much of the judgment of the various eminent London publishers who turned the typescript down in the mid-1970s, at least I can understand why they all seem to have had trouble explaining their rejection. What had landed in their nets was a very strange fish, and one, I suspect, that on a quick reading it was only too easy to place in a wrong literary species, that of the provincial novel.

I think myself that it is no more properly so classifiable than Flora Thompson's famous trilogy, *Lark Rise to Candleford*. Of course any book whose ground is the close observation of a small community risks this damning label of "provincial." Yet even if Edwards's account of the life and times of one Channel Islander had to be thus valued, it would still seem to me a remarkable achievement. If Guernsey feels that it has, since Victor Hugo's famous fifteen years of exile there, been rather left out in the literary cold, it need worry no more. It now has a portrait and memorial that must surely become a classic of the island.

But what Edwards does, as those who read his novel will soon realize, is to extend the empire of the book well beyond the confines of one particular island. All small islands conform their inhabitants in markedly similar ways, both socially and psychologically. On the credit side there is the fierce independence, the toughness of spirit, the patience and courage, the ability to cope and make do; on the debit, the dourness, the incest, the backwardness, the suspicion of nonislanders . . . all that we mean by "insularity." None of these qualities and defects is special to islands. One might argue that the "island syndrome" occurs with increasing frequency in many of our embattled inner cities, and very much in the context of what finally becomes the major theme of this book—that is, the impact of new values on old ones, of ineluctable social evolution on the individual human being.

Edwards's own view is made very clear through his fictional alter ego. For him the new values—in local terms, all that has turned Guernsey into a tourist resort and international tax haven—are anathema. They have destroyed nearly everything on the island (and by implication everywhere else) that he cherished and celebrates so well and elegiacally, beneath the plain language, in the first half of his novel. Whether Edwards was right or wrong to see more ashes than hope in progress is not, I think, what matters. What does is to have such a richly human account of what it felt like to live through the period of the book, from about 1890 to 1970.

We are still too close to it to realize what an astounding and unprecedented change—unprecedented both in its extent and in its speed—took place in the psyche of Western humankind during those eighty years. In very many ways, and certainly for the working-class majority, the late nineteenth century remained closer to the seventeenth than to our own. It is only the very old now who can fully understand this: what it means to have known, in the one life span, both a time when city streets were full of horses, the car not yet invented, and a time when man stood on the Moon; or, even more incomprehensibly, both a time when even the most terrible weapons could kill a few hundred at most and a time when their power risks entire cities—and their aftermath, whole countries.

It is almost as if in those same eighty years we had left the old planet and found a new; and we are all, however brashly contemporary we may be, however much we may take modern technology for granted, still victims of that profound cultural shock. One symptom of it is the recurrent recrudescence of conservatism (and in far more than politics) in the second half of this century. We have at least realized that we made a very clumsy landing on our new planet, and also left a number of things behind on the old that we might have done better to bring with us—qualities very close to that list of traditional island virtues I mentioned just now.

This inability to forget the old, this querulousness over the new, are what make Ebenezer Le Page such a convincing portrayal of a much more universal mentality than the matter of the book might at first suggest. Edwards himself recognized this when he wrote that Ebenezer "expresses from the inside out the effects of world events." His novel is really far more about the impress of recent human history on one fallible but always honest individual than it is about Guernsey and its traditional manners and mores, fascinating and amusing though those often are to read.

The very general contempt for England and the English (and outsiders in general, even the sister Channel Island of Jersey) must similarly be taken in a metaphorical way. The encroachment is of infinitely more than ugly holiday bungalows and tourist dross, of greedy entrepreneurs and tax evaders; and it is essentially upon the individual mind, and therefore upon individual freedom. To those who want a homogenized world (because such worlds are easier to manipulate), Ebenezer is an eternal thorn in the side. He may seem an exceedingly unfashionable reactionary in regard to a number of things, including women. But his saving grace is that he is equally reactionary about anything that tries to occupy, as the Nazis did Guernsey in the last war, the island of the self. He is much more against than he is ever for, and that kind of againstness, or bloody-mindedness, however irritating it may be in some circumstances, is a very precious human (and evolutionary) commodity. Provincialism is not merely the lack of city taste in arts and manners; it is also an increasingly vital antidote to all would-be centralizing tyrannies. To give such a convincing illustration of this very common contradiction, this eternal suspicion lying at the less articulate base of society, is one of Edwards's major achievements.

Another seems to me a technical one, and that is the creation of such an intensely colloquial speech, with its piquant French undertones, for his hero. Even more remarkable is the author's almost total reliance on it, the way he manages, despite the general absence of normal linear narrative, despite the way characters meander almost haphazardly into and out of his pages, despite the minute stitch of social detail, to carry us through with him, at times to the point where we no longer care how inconsequential or digressive the story becomes, so long as that voice is still speaking. I can think of very few novels in which this extremely difficult device, of the prolonged reminiscence, has worked so well.

Edwards's choice of it was quite deliberate. He spoke several times of the "circular form" of the book, of its "indirection." On another occasion he said, "Writing has for me, I think, always to be done obliquely . . . it feels to me phony when I'm not allowing an incubus to speak in a circumstantial context." He also revealed that the "beginning and the end were conceived simultaneously . . . the book grew out of the pivotal image of the gold under the apple-tree." That may have been true thematically; but the literary gold was buried in the voice of the incubus. We may note too that Edwards always thought of the patois as his native language. His deep regard for Joseph Conrad was not purely literary: here was another exile forced to write in an "acquired" English.

Two other things must be said. One is that Edwards never received expert editorial advice. This is most noticeable at the very end of the book, where one senses that he began to identify too closely with Ebenezer, and surrendered to a common impulse among novelists: the wish to reward his surrogate, or hero, with a distinctly sentimental ending. This was pointed out to him, but he refused to change his text. He wrote that the aged Ebenezer "sees in a romantic glow. I don't; and the reader should not." Perhaps here the "Guernsey donkey" was sticking his heels in a shade too firmly; but even a professional editor might have had some difficulty in persuading him to wear less final a heart on his sleeve. Mr. Chaney once sent Edwards a copy of Wyndham Lewis's *The Lion and the Fox*, and the judgment received in return showed no mercy. After condemning Lewis for his slipshod scholarship and "his rasping, harsh, abusive manner," Edwards went on, "It all adds up to no more than a chaos of logical positivist deductions, heartless and intellectual . . . 'romantic' is not a dirty word, you know."

The second thing to be said is that *Ebenezer Le Page* was to form the first part of a trilogy. The second and third parts were to be called *Le Boud'lo: The Book of Philip le Moigne* and *La Gran'mère du Chimquière: The Book of Jean le Féniant*.[1] Edwards left enough hints in his letters to make it plain that he saw the first part as something of a humorous contrast to the other two. Readers may be interested to know that Neville Falla, the cause of much of the final sentimentality in this first novel, was in fact earmarked for an early death in the second part, and that the tone of that work was to have been much more tragic than comic. Edwards himself remarked wrily of it, "I will certainly thereby graduate out of the charm school."

But the main virtues of *Ebenezer Le Page* sit to a rare extent in each page, each episode, each character, in the waywardness of memory, in the accuracy and strength of evocation within the strictly imposed linguistic means. What Edwards was aiming for is expressed in a passage of the same letter in which he damned Wyndham Lewis. He praised Conrad by contrast for remaining "within a human and material continuum; but masterfully with controlled passion and exquisite tenderness." It was clearly this sort of quality that he found so lacking in an age of helicopter thinking, and that also helped explain for him why his own book found so little sympathy among publishers' readers. Elsewhere he defined its purpose as "humanizing"; and to that end, he realized that it had to risk things that no trend-conscious novelist today would care to risk his reputation on, just as in some ways it had to stay resolutely old-fashioned and simple-tongued. But that is precisely what I like most about it. It seems to me, beyond its occasional lapses into cantankerousness and sentimentality, an act of courage; and of a kind that can never be old-fashioned if the novel, and the free society of which it is still the deepest artistic expression, are to survive.

---

1. Literally, "The Puppet: The Book of Philip the Amputated" and "The Grandmother of the Cemetery: The Book of John the Sluggard." Edwards's full title for the first book was *Sarnia Chèrie: The Book of Ebenezer Le Page*, in symmetry with the other two. The first phrase has been dropped in the edition I am discussing because of the unfortunate connotations of *chèrie* to English ears and the general ignorance of Sarnia, the Latin name for Guernsey. The phrase was not of Edwards's invention: "Sarnia Chèrie," or "Beloved Guernsey," is the island's private anthem.

. . .

"The mere thought of having a public image appalls me"; "I would not willingly supply the public with any autobiographical data whatever"; "I'd rather be a hermit-crab than live *en famille*"; "By the way I've got rid of all fragments, correspondence and records (except for those essential for my official survival)." So Gerald Edwards wrote in various letters to Edward Chaney; the last quotation comes from one written six months before he died. Mrs. Joan Snell, with whom Edwards stayed in the final five years of his life and who has kindly relented a little over one of his last instructions to her (that she should stand "like a dragon" in the path of any future re-searcher), tells me that the holocaust was total: only his birth certificate and—touchingly, as will shortly be seen—a photograph of his mother were spared. Nor was this an isolated act of self-destruction.

Gerald Basil Edwards was born on July 8, 1899. He gave an account of his family past in a letter to Edward Chaney, and it is worth citing at some length. Dalwood, a small village near Axminster in East Devon, was long blessed or notorious locally (depending on one's religious viewpoint) for being a breeding ground of dissenters.

The earliest ancestor I know of on my father's side was Zackariah Edwards of Dalwood, Devon, who married a gipsy and begat a brood of stalwart sons, who migrated to every quarter of the globe. He was my great-grandfather. My grandfather, Tom, married one Mary Organ of Honiton and migrated to Guernsey at the age of nineteen for the "stone-rush," when the quarries of the north were opened. It was a hard life. My father, the eldest son, also Tom, was born on Guernsey, but at twelve ran away from his strap-wielding father and his mother, who had a bosom of iron, to the softer usages of sailing ships. He sailed and "saw the world" until he came home and married at the age of twenty-six. He wouldn't have come home then, except that he never over-came his tendency to sea-sickness. He worked for his father, who was by now a quarry-owner, and in due course inherited the quarry and the house, Sous les Houghues, where I was born. I was the only child of his second mar-riage . . . my mother died in 1924. A couple of years later he married the housekeeper and sold up to disinherit me, buying another property which he could legally leave her. Hence my exile. (It won't make sense to you; but it's Guernsey law.) He was a very tough man, my father: with a very tender core. He was passionately attached to Guernsey and refused to leave before the Occupation. He lived for more than a year after the Liberation and must have been well over ninety when he died. I have to be vague on this, for it was not considered decent for a Guernsey child to know the precise age of its parents. I was only truly in touch with him on one occasion; and that was in 1938, the year of the Munich Crisis, when I visited him at Les Rosiers, where he ran a small growing concern, the quarry being worked out. He was rather humiliated, though over eighty, by being reduced to so effete an occupation. He regarded quarrying granite as the only work fit for a man.

My mother was a Mauger. I cannot claim she was pure Guernsey, for the purest Guernsey are Neolithic. . . .

My boyhood, adolescence and young manhood was an increasingly intense fight to the death against my mother; and indeed all my relationships with women have been a fight to the death. I survive, but in grief; for I have sympathy with what I fight against, and sorrow at the necessity. That should make clear to you my disorientation from Lawrence, with whom in other ways I have much in common . . . underneath I am steel against the female will. I do not mean the feminine nature. D. H. submitted. To my mind, his is the saddest story. The White Peacock becomes the flaming uterus of Lady C. They are the same. The Phoenix is swamped.

I should add that in fact very few names could be purer Guernsey than Mauger; it goes back to Norman times. Edwards must have savored the possibility of descent from the first member of the clan, who is said to have been banished to the island by William the Conqueror for having the temerity to suggest that no good would come of his adding the perfidious English to his subject peoples.

In 1909 Edwards won a scholarship from the Hautes Capelles primary to the States Intermediate School, now the boys' grammar school of the island. In 1914 he was made a pupil-teacher at Vauvert School, Saint Peter Port. A contemporary remembers Edwards as "a real loner, an odd sort of character who never had any friends." In 1917 he joined the Royal Guernsey Light Infantry. He never saw active service, but ended in Portsmouth as a sergeant instructor of gunnery. Between 1919 and 1923 he was at Bristol University, but neither subject nor degree can be traced. It seems from the above letter that he placed himself in permanent exile from Guernsey in about 1926. In this period he worked for the university settlement of Toynbee Hall in London and also joined the Workers' Educational Association as a lecturer in English literature and drama. He apparently also had a spell with the Bolton Repertory Company, and wrote plays for it. At some point he got to know Middleton Murry, and through him met Frieda Lawrence. That manifestation of the "female will" he recalled frequently to Edward Chaney, with a predictable blend of fascination and repulsion. He told Mrs. Snell that he had also known Tagore and Annie Besant quite well.

By 1930 he was married. A surviving document of that year reveals that he was living in Hornsey; and he gave his profession as "author." The marriage was not a success, and he seems to have gone abroad to Holland and Switzerland in the early 1930s to try to earn his living by his pen, writing articles and poetry as well as plays. He told Mrs. Snell that he had destroyed much of his best work, including a "very good play." Like many (perhaps all) writers, he would remain a manic depressive about his work throughout his life.

His marriage finally broke down in about 1933. One of its four children tells me that her father disappeared entirely from her life between that date and 1967, and that the gap had become too great by the time the relationship was renewed to be very successfully bridged. Even to her, very little was ever said of the past. Where or how Edwards spent the next years (the Toynbee Hall records were severely war-damaged) is not known; but during the Second World War he worked in an employment exchange, and he seemingly remained a civil servant (in 1955 he was living in Balham) until his retirement, in 1960.

The storm petrel then went to "live rough" in Wales for a year. From 1961 he spent three years in Penzance; from 1964, three years in Plymouth; and in 1967 he moved on to Weymouth. In that last year he told his daughter that the first draft of this book was completed, and the second part, *Le Boud'lo*, half done. He also spoke of returning to Guernsey "to die," but one may guess that the high cost of living—and property—on the island made that impossible for a man of his limited means, and perhaps added a bitterness to both his book and his exile. That his sense of the latter remained very real can be deduced from the move to Weymouth—the nearest place one can be to Guernsey on the English mainland.

In 1970 he became Mrs. Snell's lodger in "the small room of a large house" at Upwey, just outside Weymouth. Mrs. Cynthia Mooney, a Guernsey woman herself, remembers the room as being "like that of a monk": it was "very tidy, terribly tidy." Edwards himself wrote in 1972 that "I live from day to day, at the edge of living." But the general impression given in his letters to Mr. Chaney is one not of crabbed misery, but of a kind of tart serenity of soul, an acceptance of ascetic outsiderdom. On the one hand the tartness—"My dislike of Heath, like my aversion to television, is almost pathological"—did not spare anything or anyone surrendered to what Edwards saw as false values; yet his affection, when it was given, was unmistakably sincere and unstinting. One can assume that the very similar combination of traits in Ebenezer is closely autobiographical.

The vital new encounter for him in this last period was undoubtedly with Edward Chaney and his wife. Their sympathetic encouragement made him entirely rewrite *Ebenezer Le Page*, a task he undertook in 1973 and 1974. He continued revising it until the end. Mr. Chaney thinks there were never more than brief drafts for the rest of the intended trilogy; and most of those, Edwards seems to have destroyed before he died. Once or twice he showed a restlessness, a need to escape Weymouth (and a truly remarkable willingness in a man of his age to travel light); but these fugues to the Scillies and the Orkneys ended back in Upwey. The letters show an impressive blend of honesty and self-humor, besides a frequent Orwellian excellence of plain English prose. They would do very well as a contemporary appendix to the Grub Street side of Dr. Johnson's *Lives of the English Poets*, and I hope that one day Mr. Chaney will consider publishing parts of them.

Joan Snell sums up her recollections of Edwards thus: "He was a man of dynamic character, yet full of feeling and sympathy. Proud but humble, he had a superb memory. He could remember conversations of fifty or sixty years before, word for word. He hated machines, modern technology, he thought they had brought so many bad things into the world. He needed nothing and lived on a small pension. All he possessed could be packed in a small suitcase. He was charming and endearing; he was despairing and moody. A man of heights, and of deepest, blackest depths. I cannot do him justice in a short comment. All I can say is that it was a great privilege to have known him."

Gerald Edwards died after a heart attack, in his small room near Weymouth, on December 26, 1976. His ashes were scattered at sea. I should like to think that some at least were washed up among the *vraic*[2] and granite of his long-lost native shore.

---

2. Guernsey patois: wrack, seaweed.

JOHN AUBREY AND
THE GENESIS OF THE
MONUMENTA BRITANNICA[1]
(1982)

To net John Aubrey in a brief essay is no easy task. How does one describe a genius who never completed anything? Who left not only all his work, but all his posterity, in enduring confusion? Who constantly apologized for his lack of literary skill, yet whom we now see as one of the most attractively natural prose writers of his age? Who was hopelessly improvident in all personal matters, yet a brilliantly intuitive hoarder of otherwise lost facts, an enduring gold mine for all students of seventeenth-century life? Who never managed to command even one science well, yet whose place in the history of science is assured? Who did more than anyone to point the way towards modern archaeology, yet until very recently was generally regarded as little better than an amusing minor tattler?

We can today realize that Aubrey's prime fault, what we would term his disorganizedness, was in a way his prime virtue. A more concentrated and orderly mind (or one less paradoxically structured) would have edited, censored, standardized, improved the chaos of drafts and notes that constitute the manuscript *Lives*; and at the same time would almost certainly have lost for us their incomparable freshness and anecdotal vividness. Countless men of his age, both major and minor, from John Milton ("He would be cheerful even in his gout-fits and sing") to that mercenary civil-war rogue Carlo Fantom ("Said he"—about to be hanged for rape by Charles I—"'I care not for your cause: I come to fight for your half-crown,

---

1. Written in 1981 to introduce American readers to this work, and reprinted here in response to British requests for an essay on John Aubrey's part in the development of learning.

and your handsome women'"), cannot be fully known until seen through Aubrey's eyes. Nor can we fully understand the complexity of the seventeenth-century mind until we have read, through the endless scatter of his autobiographical notes, Aubrey on himself. I think not even with Pepys are we closer to an existential awareness of what it was like to be alive then: the anxieties, the delusions, the hopes, the joys, the melancholies and poetries.

Generations of scholars, as they have stumbled and groped their way through the three decades' worth of notes, erasures, incomprehensible cross references, repetitions, classical quotations, insertions in other hands, blanks where Aubrey's memory failed him, illegible additions, and all the rest of it, have cursed the wild undergrowth of the *Monumenta Britannica* manuscripts. Yet I doubt if we shall ever have a more revealing view from the inside of what it was like to be finding one's way, though often enough down cul-de-sacs and wrong turnings, towards a new vision of the past and a new scientific discipline of the future. Any first edition of such a book must have detailed exegesis and easier reference as its main reasons for being. But I hope American readers will also see it, in spite of the geographical and temporal remoteness of many of its items and topics, as a voyage through an ancestral Anglo-Saxon mind, as revealing and remarkable in its individual way as that other coming-to-terms with a both ancient and new world that was going on across the seventeenth-century Atlantic.

John Aubrey was born on March 12, 1626 ("about sun-rising, being very weak and like to die"—he was to worry about his health all his life), at Easton Piercy, near Malmesbury in Wiltshire. His parents belonged to the minor but ancient gentry, with many connections by marriage and remote cousinry—*cousin* in this text is not to be taken in strict modern terms—in the West Country and Wales. There were some modestly distinguished forebears, the most famous being Dr. William Aubrey, a favorite lawyer of Queen Elizabeth. These relations reached "down" to John Whitson, a merchant lord mayor of Bristol (also at one time the owner of the *Mayflower*), and "up" to aristocrats such as the Earl of Abingdon. The one financial good fortune Aubrey had, during an otherwise conspicuously luckless life in that way, was his unquestioned rank of gentleman; this was to serve him in good stead when he was near penniless in later life. A lonely, sensitive, and morbid child, "bred up in a kind of park, far from neighbours and no child to converse with" (his next two brothers and a sister all died in infancy, and his other two brothers were not born till 1643 and 1645), he seems to have been a fair scholar, and his love of the past declared itself very early on. Even at the tender age of eight, he was later to recall, he grieved at the then-common custom of binding schoolbooks in ancient parchment documents.

This was to be a marked, if not the dominant, feature of his life. He was one of the first clear and declared conservationists—as opposed to mere collectors—in modern history. Even his own collecting was essentially conservationist and public-spirited. It was not for nothing that he was inscribed among the founding donors of the famous Oxford museum that still bears his friend Elias Ashmole's name; and laments for lost or vandalized material recur again and again in all his work.

He was still at a village school when he came under another enduring influence, that of a celebrated former pupil of his schoolmaster, the philosopher Thomas Hobbes (1588–1679). Hobbes was to become a friend in later years, and Aubrey would write an invaluable life of him. From Leigh Delamere he went to a famous school at Blandford Forum in Dorset. He wrote a little report on himself at the end of those years: "Mild of spirit; mightily susceptible of fascination. My idea very clear; fancy like a mirror, pure crystal water which the least wind does disorder and unsmooth. Never riotous or prodigal; but . . . sloth and carelessness are equivalent to all other vices."

From Blandford he went to Oxford, at the age of sixteen, in 1642. But he never completed his studies there, because of the disruptions of the civil war, which began that year; nor did he complete those at the Middle Temple in London, where he went in 1646 to study law. But he had by this time graduated in a subject and from a faculty for which universities have never managed to find a place, and that in many cases (still today, alas) they seem especially designed to suppress: universal curiosity. Even as a young undergraduate of eighteen, Aubrey had drawings made of Osney Abbey near Oxford, knowing it was soon to be destroyed. Hollar's later engraving of one of these drawings is now our only visual record of the lost building.

It is a little as if he realized he could never rival his more orthodox contemporaries in any one field, and therefore instituted himself magpie, with privilege to raid from all of them. All his life he was to remain diffident and humble before what he deemed to be real scholarship. Although the eventual value of this go-between role was appreciated by the huge network of learned friends and acquaintances he accumulated thereby, it was unfortunate in the sense that Aubrey was often relegated by it to becoming a kind of research assistant, or what we might think of as a "useful contact." Few of the men who used him thus can have appreciated his real originality, precisely because it was so unorthodox. They may too have been blinded by something more personal: his very unscientific genius for friendship. He was indisputably one of the nicest, and most amicable, human beings of his century.

Perhaps his agreeable and unusually tolerant nature was in part inherited. His famous ancestor Dr. Aubrey was one of the commissioners at the trial of Mary Queen of Scots who tried to save her from the scaffold; even more remarkably, he kept Elizabeth's regard despite his unwanted quality of mercy. His great-grandson was first and foremost what the French then called an *honnête homme*—that is, civilized and conformable, with reason and common sense, wherever he was. *Honnêteté*, in this special sense, is most nearly synonymous with decency and sanity. In art it is supremely enshrined in Molière (whose philosophical master, Gassendi, had close relations with Aubrey's, Thomas Hobbes). Whatever their own specific religious or political beliefs, all these French and English "liberals" were (unconsciously at least) united in their hatred of rabid extremes—of the horrors of the civil war and the Fronde in the 1640s, and the sometimes equally unbalanced reactions they provoked in the succeeding decades.

Just as with drinking friends he drank, and with thinking friends he thought, so Aubrey seems to have felt and behaved in political and religious matters. Although his family and milieu in Wiltshire were generally royalist in their sympathies, he was as nearly apolitical as it was possible to be in that highly politicized century. His dislike of the Puritan Commonwealth was much more a hatred of destructive philistines and antityrants turned tyrants in their turn than anything more abstract or philosophical; and in his admiration for Hobbes, in his frequenting of the Rota Club—the London coterie formed round James Harrington, with its republican and "democratic" theorizing—he was, as the 1660 Restoration made very plain, on dangerous ground. Like so many others he quickly trimmed his sails, and indeed wrote to Hobbes, advising and warning him to do the same. He once summed up his own political views in a way many a twentieth-century mind might echo: "A pox on parties."

His religious views (here his friend Sir Thomas Browne's *Religio Medici* must have impressed him) were similarly formed much more negatively than positively: he simply suspected excess, either way. He more than once mourned the dissolution of the English monasteries, but only because he envied the comfortable shelter they had once provided for men like himself. He thought of taking orders in the Church of England (purely for the income; a curate would have had to do the work), and at one point even dallied with the idea of becoming a Jesuit—about as wise a speculation then as it would be now for some Washington official to think of spending the rest of his life with Russian friends in East Germany. He was suspected at Oxford of being a papist, as was his friend Anthony Wood. But we can be sure that this was an effect—at least in Aubrey's case—of tolerance, not a real inclination. He had faith in God, but very little in doctrine. "I am no Puritan," he once wrote, "nor an enemy to the Old Gentleman on the other side of the Alps." One aspect of contemporary English Protestantism that he detested was its suspicion of natural science. He said that before 1650 " 'twas held a sin to make a scrutiny into the ways of nature; whereas it is certainly a profound part of religion to glorify God in his works, and to take no notice at all of what is daily offered before our eyes is gross stupidity."

These dreams of becoming a priest had one simple cause: lack of money. So did a series of rather Micawberish plans, put forward by various of his friends, for his emigrating to America. First it was to be New York, then Maryland ("I could, I believe, be able to carry a colony of rogues; another of ingenious artificers"). Bermuda and Jamaica were also considered. Later in life, in 1687, Aubrey was in fact offered land free in the New World: a thousand acres in Tobago, and six hundred in Pennsylvania, the latter by William Penn himself ("He adviseth me to plant it with French Protestants for seven years gratis"). This was not Penn's first attempt to woo Aubrey across the Atlantic; a letter of 1683 survives, presenting the future state as being next door to Paradise. But such powerful sales talk fell on incurably timid and indolent ears. "For why should I at this time of day, and being of a monastic humour, make myself a slave and roast myself for wealth?" American Clio may regret that Aubrey never made the voyage (I think he would very probably have forestalled the recent realization of the parallels between American and European Neolithic cultures); but one cannot help suspecting he would have been the most incompetent plantation owner in colonial history. He only twice left his native shores. He spent a month in Ireland in 1660, and four months in France in 1664.

Aubrey was not left a pauper when his father died, in 1652. But he somehow managed, in the course of the next two decades—partly as a result of his own fecklessness, partly because of a long-drawn-out and bitter lawsuit with Joan Sumner, a woman he had offered to marry, to say nothing of further differences with his own "tiger" of a younger brother (who even menaced Aubrey with prison at one stage) over their joint inheritance—to end up a near-bankrupt, and more than once on the run from "crocodiles," or bailiffs. From the 1670s on, his life was to be lived perpetually under this evil star. Aubrey believed very literally in the evil star, since like many of his time (including some far finer scientific minds) he had a firm faith in astrology.

Modern believers in that supreme foolishness may care to hear what a celebrated astral interpreter, Henry Coley, had to say when he cast Aubrey's horoscope in 1671: "The nativity is a most remarkable opposition, and 'tis much pity the stars were not more favourable to the native." It soon emerges why, for they "threaten ruin to land and estate; give superlative vexations in matters relating to marriage, and wondrous contests in lawsuits: of all of which vexations I suppose the native hath had a greater portion than was ever desired." Coley knew Aubrey, and evidently used rather more than heavenly knowledge in his casting. A rival astrologer (who did not know Aubrey) pronounced the horoscope no more like its subject "than an apple is like an oyster." But Aubrey was only too happy to blame his endless financial and wife-finding problems (a number of ladies were sought and lost, and he never married) on the stars and planets.

He fell back on the traditional seventeenth-century insurance against penury, if one had birth and brains, and for much of the rest of his life lived by what might appear to us to be sponging off friends. But to see it thus would be to misunderstand polite society then. Such hospitality, or tacit patronage, was regarded as a duty by the rich and well landed, largely because it was also a source of pleasure, a means of entertainment, of keeping in touch. A closer parallel might be with the medieval minstrel, even if the notion of singing for one's supper is not appropriate. One noble friend, Lord Thanet, did once (unintentionally) imply that the relationship was salaried, between master and servant. The armigerous gentleman in Aubrey was evidently deeply offended, for an immediate and complete apology was made. His appearance at one's door must in fact have been like the arrival of some human intellectual-magazine-plus-lively-gossip-column, hot from the coffeehouses of London and Oxford. Then too he loved books, music, painting; wit and women; he was never a grave doctor.

Aubrey began his habit of jotting down "philosophical and antiquarian remarks" in notebooks in 1654. Neither adjective, of course, meant then quite what it does today. The first covered anything to do with human knowledge, the second anything to do with the past, from Aubrey's own boyhood memories to remotest antiquity, the domain we now call archaeology. We must always remember this before we start complaining about the lack of order, the mishmash of subjects, the way he will jump without warning between fields that are for us totally distinct and without modern scientific connection at all. His view is holistic; he thinks far less of different subjects, all neatly frontiered and separated, than of different angles of approach to the central problem: what was the past, what was it like?

His truly archaeological (before the invention of the term) side was given a sharp new spur by the publication in 1655 of the very first book to be devoted entirely to England's most famous ancient monument, Inigo Jones's *Stonehenge Restored*, "which I read with great delight." Part of this delight was of a kind agelessly familiar to scholars, that to be had in shooting down someone else's theory. Aubrey, who knew Stonehenge, not far from his birthplace, saw at once that Jones and his son-in-law and editor, John Webb, had allowed preconceived theory (that Stonehenge must be Roman) to override the evidence on the ground. "This gave me an edge to make more researches," he said. One of the results of these was the discovery of the famous ring of holes, just inside the surrounding ditch, that now bears Aubrey's name, and whose exact function remains a major bone of contention between contemporary archaeologists and astronomers. Of equal importance with this first empirical approach to the enigmas of Stonehenge was a discovery Aubrey had made even earlier: that of the great "sister-monument" of Avebury, a few miles north across Salisbury Plain. He first saw this in January 1649, in his twenty-third year. Of course, it had been there for anyone to see for four thousand years or more, but it had to wait until John Aubrey came to be recognized for what it was: a document—though wordless—as vital for British prehistory as Stonehenge itself.

It is typical of the man, of his focal—one might almost say public-relations—role that by 1663 he had lured King Charles II and his brother, the future James II, to visit the site under his guidance. They had first heard of it by a characteristically striking simile he had coined, to the effect that Stonehenge could no more be compared to Avebury than a church to a cathedral; this pricked their royal ears. Their visit made, they commanded that he write upon the subject, and this was the origin of the *Monumenta Britannica*.

It was not the origin of his desire to be published. Seven years earlier, in 1656, he had decided to embark upon a *Natural History of Wiltshire*. The spur here had been provided by the immensely learned antiquarian Sir William Dugdale, whose *Monasticon Anglicon* (1655) and *Antiquities of Warwickshire* (1656) were universally admired and set new standards for historical erudition. This first literary essay was not to be published until long after Aubrey's death, but already in it his originality is apparent. There is the unusual feel of someone who works on the ground quite as much as from documents in a study or library. Its attempted comprehensiveness is equally striking. Quite apart from natural history proper, it covers a huge range of subjects, from histories of local cloth manufacturing and of fairs and markets to witchcraft and phantoms. Another chapter heading is "Men and Women." In other words, it stretches from geology through local history to anthropology and folklore. It was the latter material that shocked so many earlier students of Aubrey, the plunges into (by eighteenth-century rationalistic and nineteenth-century scientific standards) superstition and blind credulity. We are wiser now, and can see that whether Aubrey himself believed in these things or not is far less important than that they were recorded for posterity.

We must be very careful over the word *superstition*, or what it really meant to Aubrey. He could never resist recording supernatural occurrences, inexplicable events; but the great bulk of this material covers what a modern social historian would regard as folk tradition and folk custom. Aubrey was always intensely conscious, having lived through it, of the appalling blow the Puritan Revolution ("modern zeal," as he sarcastically baptized it) had dealt to this side of English life—as viciously doctrinaire an iconoclasm as the endless window smashing and image defacing that had gone on in the churches themselves. He was determined to save what he could, and we must see this as an aspect of his conservationism, and a far more original side of it than the one preoccupied with old documents and Roman remains and the rest. In his concern for the latter, he was not alone in his already museum-minded age. In having a similar interest in folklore and oral tradition, however, he was virtually unique, far more of our century than of his own. When he wrote that "wars do not only extinguish religion and laws, but superstition," he was talking far less about ghosts and weird prodigies than about the archaeology of the rural mind, in his own phrase the "ancient natural philosophy of the vulgar."

Nor was it because he was a conservative. He had a strong belief in progress, both in knowledge and in many social matters. In one well-known passage he describes the stiff-necked tyranny Jacobean parents once exercised over their children, even when the latter were "men of thirty or forty years" or "grown women." We may guess that Aubrey's palpable disgust for that came from the heart, since his relations with his sternly practical and authoritarian father had never been good. He said himself that he had been forbidden to waste time on his newfangled learning at home, and had to keep his studying for horseback and time spent on a stool not usually associated with reading.

Certainly Aubrey seems to have believed in superstitions, in recipes and spells, that we know are absurd. But in those days the "praeternatural"—as Aubrey called it—was rather more than a matter of sheer unreason. Those who studied it were not always merely credulous. Their age had a desperate thirst for explanation of the ways of the world, both natural and human, and their manias for astrology, alchemy, mystic ciphers, and the like were also a part of this. It may surprise (or horrify) us to think of Newton's wasting so much time on decoding the Book of Revelation, of Kepler's believing quite literally in a music of the spheres, but in another way they were allowing for every possibility, leaving no avenue unexplored. The area was also fraught with dangers of a quite practical kind: the Puritan spirit was very far from dead in Restoration England.

The anonymous diatribist of *The Doctrine of Devils* (1675), a tract designed "to rectify those undue notions . . . men have about demons and evil spirits," pours anathema on those apostates who take

> old wives' tales, and profane fables, seconded by romantic inventions, and poetical fictions to be the original of all. Some old, crazy-brained, doting, melancholical, hypochondriac dreamers in the paroxysm of their distempers,

seem to see strange sights, creatures, goblins, devils, as they think; this they
report, with confidence; the rabble is credulous, and believes straight; the
diurnallers are willing to swell up their pamphlets, unto volumes; philoso-
phers (to show their wit) undertake to prove all credible, yea necessary. . . .

And before you know it, says the raging author, showing all the paranoia of the witch-hunters he hunts, you have the Papistical Inquisition on your hands, extorting what "mad confessions" it pleases. Superstition and the Whore of Babylon, alias Rome, were never too far apart in the seventeenth-century mind; and the string of adjectives prefixed to "dreamers" in the above passage might nearly enough describe one aspect of Aubrey, who loved nothing better than old wives' tales, even as he mocked them. The most celebrated, and unkind, remark ever made about him says more or less the same thing.

Even many kinder friends, such as the naturalist John Ray, felt that Aubrey based himself too much on idle hearsay; and this is a justifiable complaint when he is dealing with natural phenomena, or here in the *Monumenta*. But in folklore (and anthropology) there is no idle hearsay; it is all evidence of some kind. The endless past scorn poured on this side of his work also overlooks the fact that more often than not he is either downright disbelieving or openly skeptical, or else simply recording what he has heard. He says of ghosts, for example, "Where one is true, a hundred are figments. There is a lechery in lying." And here is Aubrey recording, as well as any modern anthropologist, at the end of his life:

On the day of St. John the Baptist, 1694, I accidentally was walking in the
pasture behind Montague House [where the British Museum now stands]. It
was twelve o'clock. I saw there about two or three and twenty young women,
most of them well habited, on their knees very busy, as if they had been
weeding. I could not presently learn what the matter was. At last a young
man told me that they were looking for a coal under the root of a plantain,
to put under their head that night, and they should dream who should be
their husbands. It was to be sought for that day and hour.

We know now where this strange idea came from—a book published in 1613—but without Aubrey, we would never have known it was put into practice. (The girls were wrong, incidentally: it should be Saint John's *Eve*, not the day itself.)

"Fancy like a mirror" was to remain true of him all his life. He was an ideas man, a lateral thinker. Possibilities and hypotheses cascaded from him, even in matters as mundane—in a little work called *Faber Fortune*, or "How to Make a Fortune"—as his own perennial lack of the ready. Many of his ideas and theories are farfetched, or flagrantly based on too little evidence or wrong deductions (not least some of his archaeological conclusions), but others show great predictive insight. Aubrey had at least one feature of scientific genius: a nose for what was missing. He wished, in *The Natural History*, for a geological map "coloured according to the colours of the earth, with marks of the fossils and the minerals," a desideratum that would have to wait more than a century, and for the pioneer geologist William Smith, to see fulfillment. He demanded a history of the weather, and thus foretold the paleoclimatology of our own century. He thought the world "much older than is commonly supposed," on the hard evidence of the depth at which fossils had sometimes been found. He even touched Darwin with a fingertip when he wrote that "fishes are of the elder house"—that is, have older origins than man and mammals. His whole approach to history was in fact markedly "evolutionary." Others of his writings concern histories of costume and of architecture, changes of style through the ages. Nothing more commonplace, we may think. But no one before Aubrey had thought of studying clothes and buildings in this chronological way, or for that matter, studied them in any way at all, except in the Greek and Roman context.

In 1662 came the best possible testimony to the position Aubrey had already achieved in English scientific life. In the late 1640s a Philosophical Club had been started at Oxford. In 1658 it moved to London; and four years later it became the Royal Society. Aubrey was nominated as one of the Original Fellows. Although he was far from being the most learned of that distinguished band, he matched, perhaps better than any, the most important practical function of the new institution, which was to act as a collecting, discussion, and disseminating center for knowledge. He was fast on his way to becoming such a center in miniature; and even if his work was unpublished, and was to remain so, it was quite widely circulated among his friends and Royal Society colleagues. They make up a formidable list: Hobbes, Locke, Newton, Halley, Boyle, Christopher Wren, Sir Thomas Browne, and many others. An especially close friend (who passed the greatest test of friendship, as a source of loans, besides acting as postbox when Aubrey was dodging the bailiffs and creditors) was the brilliant experimental physicist Robert Hooke. His dazzling fecundity of idea and invention must have deeply appealed to Aubrey, who would remain convinced, in the controversy over Newton's debt to Hooke, that his friend's part had never been fully acknowledged.

But the most famous friendship in Aubrey's later life was of a much less happy nature. This was with the Oxford antiquarian and biographer Anthony à Wood, or Wood. Wood was a difficult, jealous, not to say paranoiac man in private life, however grateful posterity may be to him for his history of Oxford University (1674) and the *Athenae Oxoniensis* (1691–1692). They first met on August 31, 1667, at Oxford. Inevitably it was the open, always curious Aubrey who initiated the meeting, and went to find Wood at his lodgings. A quarter century later, Wood was to write down his memories of that first meeting, referring to himself in the third person and using bile quite as much as ink: "Mr. Aubrey was then [in 1667] in a sparkish garb, came to town with his man and two horses, spent high and flung out [i.e., cheated] A.W. at all reckonings." After describing Aubrey's financial folly, Wood went on to say that he "at length made shift to rub out by hanging on" to richer friends and relations. He then framed the famous damnation mentioned earlier: "He was a shiftless person, roving and maggoty-headed, and sometimes little better than crazed. And being exceedingly credulous, would stuff his many letters to A.W. with fooleries, and misinformations, which sometimes would guide him [Wood] into paths of error."

"Maggoty-headed," it should be added, does not quite mean what it may seem to our eyes. *Maggot* at that time denoted a whim, a crotchet, and the adjective here conveys something like "fantastical." But that hardly redeems what must count as one of the nastiest stabs in the back in English intellectual history. What provoked, after so many years of close friendship and collaboration, such a blow? Nothing else but Aubrey's generosity as a scholar. For years he had acted as what was in effect an unpaid researcher in London for his sour and unpopular Oxford friend. As so often, Aubrey played second fiddle. It was true that he felt he owed the idea for his own *Lives* to Wood, and he could not publish them until the *Athenae Oxoniensis* was completed. In 1680, on top of all the searching and inquiring he had done, he sent all his notes for his own biographies to Oxford, for Wood to make free use of and write up (with a heaviness and moralistic one-sidedness Aubrey himself could never have managed) for his book.

Aubrey, with his hatred of losing the smallest scrap of information, however private or scandalous, was well aware that his notes had to be used with discretion. He said as much to Wood: "I must desire you to make castration . . . and to sew on some fig-leaves." But when the first volume of the *Athenae* appeared in 1691 (the second came a year later), it was immediately clear that Wood, never averse to finding fault in others, had ignored this advice. A number of people felt that skeletons in family cupboards had been shamelessly betrayed, and some were out for blood. One in particular, the second Earl of Clarendon, was outraged by a story Aubrey had sent Wood concerning the corruption of his father, Lord Chancellor Hyde, the first earl. The story was true, and Hyde was long dead, but that did not stop Clarendon from issuing a writ for libel against Wood. The latter was fined and expelled from the university, and the offending parts of the *Athenae* were publicly burned.

He had only his own folly to blame; but all his rage fell on poor Aubrey, hence the reference to "fooleries and misinformations." But that was not the worst injustice he committed. When Aubrey at last received his notes back, he found that Wood had severely mutilated them and removed the index. A dozen lives or more had been lost, including those of James I and Monmouth, perhaps because Wood considered them "dangerous," or perhaps because he simply appropriated them to paste into his own rough copy. Aubrey was cut to the very quick of his conserving soul, yet a year or so later he tried to mend the old friendship. The attempt was without success, and Wood died in 1695, though even then Aubrey still had the heart to mourn his loss. All that can be said in Wood's favor in this sad affair is that he did not accuse Aubrey in court; but that may well have been because he knew Aubrey had an excellent defense.

Wood's authority as a biographer meant that his cruel judgment was to stick for a very long time, once it was publicly known. One may set it against what Aubrey wrote of himself: "My head was always working, never idle, and even travelling (which from 1649 till 1670 was never off horseback) did glean some observations . . . some whereof are to be valued." Where "shiftless" and "roving" (another friend once referred to his "wonted trapishness") may have had some justice was in regard to his almost comic, were it not so sad, inability ever to get his manuscripts into a fit state to print. It is obvious, in the various dedications, the hopeful directions to the printer, in letters to friends, that the wish was there; what was always lacking was the practical will—and no doubt the permanent state of flux of much of his material, as new information came in, made completion especially difficult.

Aubrey was finally to see only one of his works in print, the *Miscellanies* (subtitled *A Collection of Hermetic Philosophy*). That appeared in 1696, the year before he died, and must also be held in part responsible for the butterfly-brained and credulous image of him that has taken so long to correct. It is enough to read some of the subject headings: "Blows Invisible," "Transportations in Air," "Visions in the Beryl or Glass," "Converse with Angels and Spirits," "Second-sighted Men," "The Discovery of Two Murders by Apparition," and so on. A truer picture may be gained if I now list his more important works, both surviving and lost.

The Natural History of Wiltshire, not in print until 1847.

An Essay towards the Description of the North Division of Wiltshire. This was contained in two notebooks, called by Aubrey *Hypomnemata Antiquaria* ("Antiquarian Memoranda") *A* and *B*. The essay was originally mooted as part of a collaborative county history in 1659, but it ended, said Aubrey, in tobacco smoke; and he continued to collect material on his own. The two notebooks were given to the Ashmolean Museum, but Aubrey's brother William borrowed Liber B in 1703 and never returned it. It has not been seen since the 1830s, and is probably the greatest single loss among the vanished work. Liber A was not properly published until 1862.

A Perambulation in the County of Surrey, written in 1673, printed in 1718.

An Interpretation of Villare Anglicanum. This was never finished, even by Aubrey's standards, but was to deal with place-name etymology and British (Celtic) elements in English. Aubrey was also something of a pioneer in using place-names as an archaeological tool, a use frequently seen in the *Monumenta*.

The *Lives*, now usually known as *Brief Lives*. Fairly entirely in print, 1813. Its importance was first realized by the Shakespeare scholar Edmund Malone.

An Idea of the Education of a Young Gentleman. This was one of Aubrey's own favorite books. It is a predictably humane and enlightened attempt to improve seventeenth-century schooling, in his usual diffuse and personal manner. It has the well-known anecdote about Thomas Hobbes's vainly trying to teach the Duke of Marlborough geometry, only to discover that the young gentleman was otherwise absorbed—in creating a leviathan of his own inside his codpiece. Not in print until 1972.

Monumenta Britannica. Eventually brought to publication in 1980–1982, in the volumes originally containing this essay.

Miscellanies, 1696.

The Remains of Gentilism and Judaism. This was to trace the customs and superstitions of England back to ancient times. Like the *Miscellanies*, it would be classed today as folklore; once again it shows Aubrey's interest in history as evolution. Not completely in print until 1881.

Adversaria Physica. A natural-science notebook, to which there are references in the *Monumenta*, marked by the Greek letter phi (ϕ). It has vanished in the original, but fragments survive in copies. Another serious loss.

Hypothesis Ethicorum et Scala Religionis ("The Foundation of Ethics and the Ladder of Religion"). Lost.

Various lesser manuscripts (including sketches and notes for a bawdy satirical comedy called *The Country Revel*) survive, and others are known from a list Aubrey himself made in 1692 of twenty-two "books written"—a phrase, needless to say, that has to be taken to mean "sketched and projected," rather than literally completed.

To return to Aubrey's life: an important and sad private milestone for him was the year 1686 (he was then sixty years old himself), when his mother died, an event that affected him deeply. It was from this time that anxiety over the safekeeping and future of his manuscripts became a constant preoccupation. Perhaps at long last he began to realize that the unstinting help he had given to other scholars had hurt his own career, a feeling that the wretched treatment he was soon to receive from Wood must have intensified. In the end he accepted Elias Ashmole's suggestion and deposited his works with the new museum at Oxford. But he went in fear for some he had kept, including his favorite, *The Idea of the Education of a Young Gentleman.* "If I should die here," he wrote to Wood (this was before their quarrel), "they will be lost or seized by [his landlord] Mr. Kent's son; if I send them to the [Ashmolean] Museum, the tutors would burn it [*The Idea*], for it crosses their interest exceedingly; if in your hands when you die, your nephew will stop guns with them." The little boy who had hated the way his schoolbooks were bound in pages of ancient charters now found the iron biting much closer to home.

Under the pressure of this age-old author's terror—feeling himself near death and still without a book to his name—Aubrey did make some last attempts, mainly by adding to already quite sufficient confusion, to prepare for the press. He did much recopying, though he found it exhausting. For a brief moment, in 1693, it seemed possible the *Monumenta* might be printed at Oxford by subscription; but it came to nothing, mainly because Edmund Gibson and Edward Lhwyd's eagerly awaited edition of Camden's *Britannia* (1695) was also subscribing at the time. This latter did include passages from the *Monumenta*, though Lhwyd had to assure Aubrey that he would be given full acknowledgment. He was clearly afraid that once again his own work would be "stolen" and he would have no credit. In the end he had to make do with the *Miscellanies*.

By an irony, we know nothing of the circumstances of Aubrey's death, a sad fate for one who so loved to record such details about others. But we know he had been suffering from gout and apoplexy for several years. He had written, "My candle grows low," in the summer of 1694. The year before he had fallen prey, on March 20, to a modern social disease: he was mugged by thieves in London, and received fifteen wounds in the head. A century and half had to pass before even the briefest details of his death were discovered in the parish register of the church of Saint Mary Magdalene, Oxford: "1697. John Aubrey, a stranger [i.e., not of the parish], was buryed June 7th." He had left instructions for a marble epitaph-tablet, but it was never erected. Earlier in his life he had dreamed of being buried beside the urn in a barrow he had discovered on his farm at Broad Chalke in Wiltshire. He knew ecclesiastical law forbade it, but true to his reverence for the past, he at the same time noted that "our bones in consecrated ground never lie quiet; in London once in ten years (or thereabout) the earth is carried to the dung-wharf." Whether his bones have lain as quiet as he would have wished, we cannot tell. His grave is unknown.

I must now turn to the *Monumenta Britannica*, otherwise known as *A Miscellany of British Antiquities*. It was designed to be in four parts,[2] the last of which comprises a medley of subjects, including the studies of costume and architecture mentioned above, and also one on paleography, remote from archaeology proper.

The desirability of publishing the manuscript was recognized early. Even in the 1670s, both Sir Thomas Browne and John Locke had urged Aubrey to get the *Templa Druidum* section into print. On August 11, 1690, the notebooks, by then of course much richer in content, were left with Robert Hooke. In 1692 they were tried on various London bookseller-publishers, without success. By 1693 Aubrey was hoping for publication by subscription at Oxford, where he had found a new young (he was only twenty) scholar friend, Thomas Tanner, later to be Bishop of Saint Asaph. Tanner was sympathetic over the iniquity of such a valuable collection's not being published, and Aubrey seemingly placed great hopes on the young man as a supervising editor. A "Proposal for Printing" was even issued, and 112 subscriptions were taken, but these were not sufficient to proceed. As already mentioned, Aubrey's subscription conflicted with that for the new edition of Camden's *Britannia*, and was the loser. The "Proposal" said the *Monumenta* was "to be printed in folio with abundance of cuts [engravings]," total price eighteen shillings, with nine due on subscription, nine on delivery, which was promised before "Candlemas next," or February 1694. The blurb declared that ancient British history had been drowned and perverted in the "deluge" of the Saxon invasion (Aubrey seems to have thought as little of the Saxons as he did of the Puritans), which "I do here endeavour (for want of written record) to work out and

---

2. Written in two notebooks, Bodleian Library T.G.c.24 and 25.

restore after a kind of algebraical method, by comparing those that I have seen one with another and reducing them to a kind of equation: to (being but an ill orator myself) to make the stones give evidence for themselves."

In other words, he means to proceed by comparing known to less known, and from field evidence—a very new approach to antiquities. In 1695, the Oxford venture having failed, Aubrey found an interested London bookseller, Awnsham Churchill, and even entered into an agreement with him. But Churchill never honored his side of it, and the notebooks were still with him at Aubrey's death. They eventually came into the hands of a descendant, Colonel Sir William Greville, who in 1836 sold them to the Bodleian Library.

However, they had by no means been entirely lost to view before they finally returned to Oxford. Copies existed of parts of the manuscript, which had moreover already been used by Gibson and Lhwyd in *Britannia*. Above all it was seen by the next major British antiquarian, William Stukeley, and gave him (though he never acknowledged it) the central idea of his life; for it was Stukeley who took Aubrey's quite cautiously stated belief that Avebury and Stonehenge were Druid temples and succeeded in converting it, during the first half of the eighteenth century, into the most notorious false trail in British archaeology, one that was to mislead the science well into our own century, and that has its benighted followers even today.

Aubrey himself had been quite sure that the monuments predated the Romans and the Danes, in itself a step forward; but he lived at a time without any notion at all of the prehistorical—that is, of the existence of cultures not only without written record, but unreported-on by any other that was literate. The only known culture before the Romans came was the one they subdued (and their historians described), the Celtic or British, and we can hardly blame Aubrey for suggesting it, or its Druid priesthood, as the most likely architects and builders. Above all he cannot be blamed for the absurdly religious element that Stukeley introduced. Stukeley's mind truly was crazed in parts. I was recently shown one of his unpublished notebooks, entitled *Religious Antiquity* and dated 1731. Much of its content can be described only as very peculiar indeed, even by eighteenth-century standards of mystical eccentricity. His obsession was the need to show the purity and nobility of primitive Christianity, as personified in the Druids, who (he supposed) had first come to Britain from the Middle East, a wandering tribe of Israel. All his theory is bent, as Inigo Jones had earlier bent reality to suit his own Roman hypothesis, to implement this.

Nonetheless, there are some parallels between Aubrey and Stukeley of a more fortunate kind. The latter was also, when off his hobby horse, a sharp observer and an invaluable recorder. He too spent years of his life traveling England, sketching and noting, a true field archaeologist. In both men one senses that the irrational side is somehow the price of the saner and more scientific one. Both existed, of course, before the atomization of modern man, before science was severed from all personal feeling, before the strict protocol of empirical method invented a mode of discourse for itself.

On one simple but very important count the value of the *Monumenta* is unassailable, and represents something for which we can only be grateful. Perhaps the most characteristic note in the entire work is scribbled as an afterthought above another entry, on page 473 of volume 1: "Force in this here," writes Aubrey, "though it be foreign [i.e., misplaced] as to the county, to preserve it from being lost and forgotten." Not for the first time he found himself caught between method and instinct. His answer was always the same: when in doubt, include. The sorting and pigeonholing and censoring could come later. We see this deliciously in the draft of his life of Hobbes, who had an uncle who was a mere glover. Having mentioned that fact, Aubrey is assailed by doubt and adds a parenthesis to himself: "(Shall I express or conceal this *glover*?)" In archaeology as in biography, the "glover" is always finally allowed to creep in. In this alone the *Monumenta* is beyond price. Countless of his sites no longer exist, and many have changed beyond recognition; but some that have disappeared may one day be rediscovered from his clues. Nor does this take any account of the information left us therein on the early history of known sites, to say nothing of all we can gather of how his fellow antiquarians felt and thought, what they collected, and so on.

But his book has greater claims on our admiration, though they are less easy to grasp from our modern viewpoint. One might argue that Aubrey himself never quite consciously saw the shape and the ultimate meaning of the wood he was planting, in the confusion of the individual trees. The outward conception was not entirely his own; schematic models for it can be found among earlier antiquarian works and county histories, such as Dugdale's. Like many of his contemporaries he greatly admired the works of the Danish scholar Wormius, or Ole Worm, *Monumenta Danica* (1643) and *Museum Wormianum sea Historia Rerum Rariorum* ("History of Unusual Things") of 1655. It was under Worm's influence that he changed his original title, *Monumenta Druidum*, to the present one.

Aubrey's originality lies much more in the accent—one might almost say the flavor—he gave his work: in the stress on direct observation and field knowledge, as opposed to that from books and traditional authority; in the attention paid, for the first time, to whole new classes of monuments, such as hill-forts and barrows (in effect, to nonverbal evidence); in the attempt to reconstitute the past, to imagine it, to reconstruct its changes and cultural flow; in showing that one must look "behind" the Romans, a brave leap of the imagination in a period deeply imbued with unquestioning respect for ancient Rome. It was not things, but rather books and documents, that dominated the writing of history in the seventeenth century. But even when Aubrey fell back on this usual method, he was often imaginative in his use of quotation. Long before Schliemann, he took an archaeological look at Homer. No one reading his Homeric extracts on Greek burial customs will need reminding of the astonishing recent discoveries at Vergina and elsewhere in Macedonia.

It is this general spirit that surely matters most. Of course, Aubrey suffered from countless misconceptions, he made mistakes (two obvious ones are his trying to separate "Roman" and "Danish" camps and forts by shape—an error still being made by antiquaries in the nineteenth century—and the assumption that barrow groups must indicate the site of some ancient battle), and he still leaned far too much on secondhand evidence and tradition. He was undoubtedly split between the old and the new science of his age, perhaps partly because historiography then lagged behind the natural sciences. By the end of the century, enormous advances were being made in natural history by botanists such as Ray. It was not that this did not filter through to Aubrey, in whom natural history was always a major interest; indeed, a leading authority on Aubrey, Dr. Michael Hunger, argues convincingly that it was his view and philosophy of natural history that structured, and lent much of the originality to, his antiquarianism. That is, at his best he was trying to do for the past what the better naturalists were then doing in terms of ordering and refining the study of nature; and this is why he may be distinguished from more orthodox—and pedestrian—antiquarians.

Another facet of his spirit was its moderation. Aubrey was someone much more cautiously feeling his way than dogmatically asserting it, as Stukeley and so many later archaeologists were to do. He had none of the savage *parti pris* and lack of tolerance that tarnished much of the other 'science' of his age. His approach seems but an extension of his approach to life in general—that is, its major key is of civilized curiosity, of disinterested concern to explain and to preserve. If we think of him today as the father of British archaeology, it would be as well to do it as much for this as for his more specific achievements. Science does now begin to recognize that the *blind* pursuit of objective truth has dangers for its practitioners— that there is a price for forgetting that a scientist is also a human being. This price must be greatest in a science that is always poised between the history of human culture and anthropology, that is always essentially about other human beings. Aubrey never forgets that. It is one reason his work is always so full of personal and extraneous material. This may be irritating to the category-obsessed pedant, but it is far from irrelevant, either to the general tone or, I think, to the institution of a free spirit of inquiry.

There are, in this second volume, some superficially rather ghoulish passages about the ancient corpses revealed during the rebuilding of Saint Paul's after the Great Fire of London in 1666. We are obviously close here to Aubrey's more morbid and "supernatural" side; but it is worth noting that he also quite scientifically records their appearance (even their taste, in one passage), and also mentions that he himself saw to it that some remains were decently reburied. What is really being recorded here is his humanity, his deep sense that respect for the past, or conservation, is the rock on which all historical investigation must be founded. Our modern tendency to reify the past, to turn it into so many objects for museum laboratory dating and analysis, might have impressed him technically; but quite certainly it would have distressed him humanly. Of course such coldly objective study is legitimate, in context; the danger arises when it becomes the *only* context in which we are allowed to view these things and accept them into our lives.

We can safely guess that Aubrey was first drawn to the past for emotional rather than intellectual reasons. Solitude, melancholy, anxiety, an abiding fear of death haunt his private soul. From this dark humor spring all the complex strands of his adult life, from the man obsessed by astrology and the supernatural to the one who depended so deeply on friends. The dependence was very far from merely financial. All his life he was to need them as the shorn lamb needs the fold. It is this, quite as much as a conscious belief in decency and the virtues of the golden mean, that made him such an agreeable companion. He said it himself, in remembering his first years at Blandford School, Dorset, where he first met the hostile outside world: "The boys mocked me, and abused me, they were stronger than myself; so I was fain to make friendship as a strong line to protections." His own theory of education was to prove almost modern in its gentleness, its hatred of corporal punishment, its condemnation of any method that tried to bully the child into instant adulthood.

Above all this tenderness of mind explains the antiquarianism, the obsession with conserving and preserving, whether it be Bronze Age barrows or the minutest details of the lives of his century, from the famous to the humble. Every fact retrieved from oblivion, every morsel of the past explained or brought back to life, was a little victory against the real enemy. It is in this *timor mortis* that the main clue to his achievement resides. He had many rivals far more learned in their fields than he ever became himself, and in comparison with whom he can really be called only a dabbler or dilettante. Others, such as Sir Thomas Browne, wrote in a style equally beyond him. Very few can read *Urn-Burial* today for archaeological reasons; but it will be read for its magnificent baroque cadences as long as the language survives. Nothing could have been further from the elaborate taste of the day than Aubrey's highly idiosyncratic, fastidious-careless style, as he well knew. It was much too near to spoken English, the tone of the private letter, as if he were always half talking to himself; not nearly artificial or latinizing enough for serious consideration. His modesty here is scarcely credible to us now, who see him as one of the great masters of unforced, naturally poetic English prose. He once wrote this: "I did see Mr. Christopher Love beheaded on Tower Hill in a delicate clear day." All his genius lies in that unexpected *delicate*. I have long held it the most pleasing short sentence in the language.

But if in his time Aubrey could not pretend to vie with these dignified and sober professionals, the sort of men who would today occupy university chairs, yet somehow he slipped through (as he does also in the *Lives*, which manage to break every proper rule of sound biography, though at their best touch essences a thousand staider men would never find) to matters and philosophies, and feelings, beyond their reach. He is the great amateur of archaeology, but in all senses of that word, and most of all in its radical: *amo*, "I love."

GOLDING AND "GOLDING"
(1986)

I met William Golding only once, at a pleasant, small, private occasion in the autumn of 1983, just three weeks before the announcement that he had won the Nobel Prize, a coming honor he must have known of but breathed not a word of at our lunch. We were both outshone by David Cecil, who was also there. It is rather difficult to be anything else before someone with amusing memories of being snubbed by Virginia Woolf in her own drawing room and the like; but I think our being outshone by a skilled conversationalist and raconteur was fairly typical of most novelists in such situations. Our talent seldom lies in the spoken, or in the leaving, after such informal encounters, of an indelible impression. I hasten to add that I was not disappointed in my famous fellow author; much more, slightly dislocated. Somehow Golding the man, the presence that day, did not quite fit how I had supposed he might be either from his books or from what small gossip I had heard of him—did not fit what I need really to put in inverted commas, an entity made purely of punctuation, "Golding."

This must seem naive and foolish of me, since I have long had to realize that I share my own life with just such an entity as "Golding." In an extremely unfair kind of way something called "Fowles" has become my representative in the public world, a kind of vulgar waxwork figure with (it seems to me) only a crude caricature resemblance to the original. I believe the Japanese set up stuffed hate figures in their factory gymnasiums, for the workers to take out their resentments on. That is "Fowles." Occasionally this monstrously insufficient surrogate provokes something rather different, a kind of foolish idolatry, like some sort of obscure local saint in

Catholic countries . . . but both simulacra remain equally remote from recognizable life.

The real Golding: an affable, gentle man in all outward respects, though not without the bluff asperity or disagreement now and then. Had I not known who he was, I might have guessed a spry retired admiral, as indeed he appears (with clearly comic intent) in one of the crew photographs in the very recent *An Egyptian Journal*. In the flesh he shows a mixture of authority and reserve, with a distinct dry humor, a tiny hint of buried demon; a man still with a touch of the ancient schoolmaster, and also of what years ago in the Marines we used to call the *matelot* . . . as anyone who has read the potted biography on the back of one of his books could foresee. He looked older than I expected. I had always thought of him as being of my own age, not a decade and a half my senior, white-bearded, as he is in reality.

For some reason he reminded me that day—it must seem absurdly—on the one hand of an Elizabethan bishop-scholar of the more tolerant humanist kind, a sort of quietist Sarum that never was; on the other, of a Slocum, someone who had done long voyages single-handed, metaphorically at least, but preferred now not to talk of them. We managed one or two compliments, when attention was elsewhere. He told me that his new novel (*The Paper Men*, not then published) was to be about a novelist persecuted by a literary researcher, and we discussed briefly that aspect of both our lives: the letters, the academic visitors, the thesis writers. We chatted about his interest in small boats and sailing (which I understood) and his lesser one in horses and riding (which I did not, my dislike for that animal being exceeded only by my suspicion of its human admirers). It would have been a very flat occasion for anyone present who had swallowed the old myth, that novelist must equal brilliant talker—wit, outrageous gossip, profound intellectual discourse, all the rest of it. I am (temperamentally, and now upon something like principle) a complete failure in that line, and I sensed that Golding felt no need to excel in it either. But what that meeting most brought home to me was how little I knew of Golding, this agreeable elderly man beside me, and how much more of "Golding"—that is, a semimythical, semifictional figure. In plain English, of him not as he is, but as I imagined him.

I know that the friends who hospitably brought us and our wives, and Lord David, together did so with the kindest intentions. But I must confess that I have a long distaste for literary meetings of any kind, however congenial and well meant in other ways, and however fascinating to spectators. In my admittedly very limited experience there is an essential precondition if they are to succeed. It is that the two writers are alone . . . no wives or husbands, no third parties, above all no other literary person, no bookish audience. Perhaps some writers do meet each other for the first time with pleasure and enjoyment, something beyond idle or cautious curiosity; but I must beg leave to doubt it.

Both parties know too much, for a start, of the very special nature of their joint pursuit. They may know very little of each other's private triumphs and disasters, of their dark nights and sunlit days, their fair winds and foul, of their experience on the voyage; but at least they know they are with someone who has also been at sea. They know what havoc their solitary profession performs on the private psyche; know of its guilts and anxieties, its vices and egocentricities, its secret pleasures, its sloughs of despond, its often appalling personal costs; know what they are in reality, and what they have become, in quotes. I remember meeting a young American writer years ago (a would-be Hemingway, needless to say) who demanded to know how many times a day I pulled myself off. He meant, how many hours I spent writing. His metaphor, as every writers knows, has a certain truth, whatever it lacks elsewhere. One can no more think of making fiction without onanism, or selfishness, than of the sea without waves.

Nor usually can we writers ever meet each other without a sense, however subdued, of rivalry. The absurd model of the beauty contest or the athletics race haunts such occasions; or perhaps I should liken the ghost to that of a sinister and irrational football league, where the place, even the division, of one's own club is never fixed, and the standards of judgment are never clear, and in any case always fluctuating in themselves. Most older writers are, I think, wise enough not to lose sleep over this; they know they will be asleep forever, well out of the stadium, by the time the final match is decided. It is when they are only face-to-face with each other that the question of comparative status threatens to raise its ugly head.

Both Golding and I have, in our different ways, been through an experience denied the majority of writers—that is, a degree of both critical and financial, and international, success. We have both been best-sellers in America, and seen our status in Britain suffer for it. We have both seen our work endlessly discussed, analyzed, dissected, been overpraised and overfaulted, victims of that characteristic twentieth-century mania for treating living artists as if they were dead—a process that may please teacher and student on campus, but that (speaking at least for myself) does something rather different to the still-breathing subject on the anatomy table, especially when he is expected gratefully to welcome the dissection and happily to play corpse. I think Golding himself once described how absurd he found it when he realized that more books had been written about him than he had actually written himself. The contempt in *The Paper Men* for both persecuted and persecutor speaks for itself.

I have till now been speaking objectively about "Golding," but that is misleading. Despite the ordinariness of our meeting, it is not how I feel about him. I do that in ways that I suspect neither ordinary readers nor academics generally suppose writers feel about other writers. I am quite often asked that question beloved of interviewers, Which other living writers in English have most influenced you? To this I usually, and wickedly, answer Defoe; but driven from my quibbling over what "dead" or "living" really means in the context of literature, and forced to answer the question, I have for many years named William Golding, with the paradoxical (for the interviewer) proviso that "influence" is not the word, that I should have to use something like "exemplar" or "tutelar" to come near it, but even they are not accurate.

It is simply that I have always had a warm feeling, a quasi-fraternal, quasi-nepotal affection for "Golding." I was delighted, in almost a family sense, when he won the Booker Prize, and even more so when he was awarded the Nobel; not, I am afraid, a very frequent reaction on my part to the winners of either honor. Far more usually it is nine parts sheer indifference. I was appalled, when the Nobel was announced, to hear from one well-known Fleet Street literary editor, who telephoned for my reaction, that he was having difficulty getting anything suitably warm (Doris Lessing was an exception) from various other English novelists he had approached. Again, I felt it almost as a personal slight. Such lack of generosity mystified me (and the editor) then, and mystifies me still.

The cynic will say it is childish, or disingenuous, to be surprised by lack of generosity in other writers. Perhaps; but I could interpret it only as a sort of parochial blindness, an incomprehensible inability to see the role Golding has played in the contemporary novel by remaining (I put it very simply) so conspicuously sui generis, his own writer, his own school of one. I could take this coldness only as one more proof of the English fixation on schools and traditions—so close, beneath the surface, to our wretchedly enduring love of social class—our suspicion of anyone not immediately placeable within that system. So close also, in the tone of so much reviewing and even in how we usually talk about books in ordinary conversation, to the literal middle-class school, in which the writer is cast as an eternally backward pupil and the critic—amateur or professional—only too often as a sarcastically reporting or sadistically caning prep-school master. In my experience even the most hostile and damning reviews in non-English cultures are at least from adult to adult, not from schoolmaster (or schoolmistress), in the implicit context of the classroom, with the whole weight and power of a supposedly unquestionable senior institution behind him, *de haut en bas* upon the head of some contemptible and irritating young dunce. *De gustibus* . . . of course one may dislike, even hate, a book; it is the gratuitous invocation of a disapproving establishment beyond such personal judgment that is the national malady.

I can see that "Golding" has faults and weaknesses as a writer, beside his outstanding virtues. (So does any writer read any other, I would not let the greatest—among *my* greatest, at any rate—off blameless there: not Defoe, not Austen, not Austen-drowned Peacock, not Hardy, not even Flaubert.) I suspect I don't share some of his views of life, or the priority he puts on those I do have sympathy with; and as I explained above, I can't claim to have paid him the traditional greatest compliment—that is, I don't feel influenced by him in any textual sense. Yet all this is, for me, next to nothing. I do not write like him; yet he remains generically, if not specifically, the kind of writer I most try to be. We shook hands when we met, like conventional middle-class Englishmen, as part of each of us is; but something in me wished that I could have found, or that circumstances allowed, something a little more Latin and demonstrative: a *cher maître*, a Gallic embrace perhaps. In England, alas, one must play such cards close, or be counted peculiar.

Another of my *bêtes noires* is the confusion of writers with pop stars, sporting "personalities," film actors; all that presumes that the very act of writing for a public must be synonymous with craving constant limelight, always more publicity. That we write to be read, no novelist, no writer of any kind, would deny. It is the assumption of our thirst for *any* sort of glory that I would like sent to China (like the too-clever Greek inventor Phanocles in that dry little fable *Envoy Extraordinary*).

Of course there are novelists who do encourage this popular delusion; whose belief in themselves, in their talent, their "genius" (or their sales and the size of their advances), in the face of the icy wind of reality, deserves immediate entry into any *sottisier* of literary folly. I suspect this is why some do indeed become actors in a sense, half-aware schizophrenics, expert at projecting whatever public persona they have elected, or let themselves be forced, to wear. In advanced states of the disease they can grow much closer to the mask than they are to their real minds and selves. Little discourages this process of self-inflation; certainly not publishers or agents or the literary world in general, for whom the writer and his public ego, his robbinsisms and rowseries, are always the choicest fodder, not his texts.

This refusal to be a personality in the above sense, to allow Golding and "Golding" to drift apart, is one of the first reasons I have always liked Golding's work: the feeling that here, by some miracle, is a writer content to be himself, to rest his case simply on what he writes, not on how grandiosely, or bizarrely, or publicity-consciously his persona makes him behave. In this he is for me the quintessential amateur writer, not the professional.

Expectability is both the great defect and the great virtue of the English novel. Defect in its sometimes too eager and complaisant willingness to obey the conventions of the genre (as in life, those of society), and even to obey those self-established by an author in his own earlier work, whereby he or she sometimes founders on his or her own forte (self-parody is every writer's dreaded reef). Virtue in the richness it can derive from an outwardly narrow range and restricted palette. If the novel must be written on a few inches of ivory, we are not to be beaten in England. This palladium still lies in a sacred triangle, among hatred of excess, respect for the past, and good taste. Its devotees sprang, from the time when the waters began to divide, from Richardson, achieved a silvery climax in Jane Austen, and continue today in such gifted women novelists as Elizabeth Taylor and Barbara Pym. The other side first declared itself in Defoe and Sterne and reached an apotheosis in this century with Joyce and D. H. Lawrence.

All these latter writers have been dissenters from the received traditions of their various times. Some gently, some as bulls in a china shop, but they have always in some way *broken*, whether it be in language, character portrayal, narrative technique, emotional or sexual frankness, or a thousand other things. This distinction between breakers and conformers is very rough, and provides singularly little guide to quality, since a good conformer will always beat a bad breaker, and vice versa. Nevertheless, another thing I have always liked about "Golding" is the lack of expectability (so closely allied with respectability) I have always found in his themes, indeed even in his line-by-line style. At heart it derives, I am sure, from an honesty and an independence, a will to follow his own imagination, wherever it may lead. Publishers' readers may groan here, and certainly the one who once described to me the ubiquitous fault of the many typescripts she had in her time rejected: "Too much imagination, not enough technique." This too-much-imagination, or refusal to write what is safe and expected, may sometimes have led Golding astray. But I think this not a fault of tyros. It is endemic in the novel, even at the highest level; and almost its main source of energy. Imagination is always ahead of the technique to express it; and one of the greatest pleasures of writing is trying to make the laggard catch up—just as how well or how variously the novelist attempts this is certainly one of the greatest pleasures of reading. This also I like in "Golding": how he seems to attack the problems afresh in each book, and by no means always on the lines of past successes. No one disputes that he is a master fabulist, and a brilliantly creative interpreter of remote history (as in *The Inheritors*) when he wants; but he has never rested on one given approach, one given power.

Being possessed of one's own imagination, having the courage to let it dictate technique, rather than the reverse, is to my mind one of the most enviable gifts or states a novelist can have or be in, for all its obvious dangers and penalties. It must, in the nature of things, attract enemies. One battalion must come from the publishing trade itself, which dotes on repetition in the extreme form in the so-called recipe novel, written as much by the commissioning editor as by the writer. To all that sick tendency in modern publishing to let carefully calculated commercial considerations rule over any natural artistic ones, "Golding" remains a peremptory denial; and equally to those other enemies, the unreasoning worshipers of received tradition, whose fixed ideal of the novel is held rather as an orthodox churchman holds his faith, and who tend to regard any infringement of that ideal, any lapse of observance towards it, as the equivalent (at any rate in the venom with which it is commonly prosecuted against the offender) of blasphemy. This is why I think of "Golding" as tutelary and exemplary. Look, he has come through; it can be done, and on one's own.

I don't suppose that my own idiosyncratic view of other writers, both dead and alive, which thinks of them primarily in a natural-history way (that is, far less morally and evaluatively than on the principle that all species are equal—or at any rate, to misapply Orwell, more equal than we usually like to think), makes much sense to anyone else; but nor, I think, does an unhappily prevalent opposite view, one I associate with a question I have here in Dorset had asked of me on more than one occasion: Why can't you modern people write like Thomas Hardy? I did once, goaded beyond bearing, answer that I was profoundly glad I couldn't write like Hardy—and was promptly damned beyond redemption for unspeakable vanity and lèse-majesté. Readers, alas, the world over, ignore the etymology of *novel*; for them it was always better in the past. There also "Golding" has always stood for me like some ancient menhir or monolith, enduring proof that there are other beliefs, other religions.

Perhaps neither Golding nor "Golding" will like this presenting of him as something of an iconoclast in the Holy Chapel of Eng. Lit.; yet part of the unspoken meaning of that lunch did lie for me in David Cecil's presence. A Martian present would, I think, have assumed Lord David the well-known novelist, and the rest of us his votaries, which I must confess I am not—or once was not. When I was an undergraduate (in French) at New College in the 1940s, we were fiercely divided over him, and far beyond the English faculty. To some (the puritans) he was an intolerable lightweight, a dancing damsel-fly on the river of life; to others the very personification of the literary life, knowing everyone, knowing everything; above all, in the drab austerity of that immediately postwar Oxford, he was *different*. One might see him, leaning gracefully and aesthetically in the evening against a wall beneath a wisteria overlooking the college gardens, reading some slim volume and seemingly oblivious to us noisy undergraduates playing bowls on the lawn; or hear him, at the right angle in New College Lane, a weirdly disembodied voice, as he recited Tennyson aloud to himself before walking into sight. Apocryphal anecdotes about him, in that easily parodiable, pouncing-gabbling voice, were legion, as they were of another don, Sir Isaiah Berlin, also by chance my "moral" tutor ("Don't for goodness' sake come to me with any problems, my dear fellow. I know positively nothing about young men's morals").

I remember seeing one of them, I forget which, entering the front quad with an exotically dressed Dame Edith Sitwell on his arm, a far more impressive (I nearly wrote "empressive") sight than that of the present queen, who had visited us shortly before. This was Literature herself; and her companion infinitely more honored by her presence than by any rank or title—or indeed scholarly reputation—given by society at large. That vision was symbolic of the image I had of living literature at Oxford: it was a profession for immensely exalted beings alone, almost as remote from ordinary life as that terrible café-society crew on Olympus. All lay in "famous" names, and in knowing them, being seen with them. I did not really reject that fame-besotted view of literature until I became a writer myself, and learned at first hand what an illusion the popular notion of a "successful" literary life is—its pleasures very seldom those the public supposes, and most of its pains to be found in what it imagines we must welcome with open arms. To be sure, one may pick up a certain savoir faire, or *savoir-écrire,* at Oxbridge (though even those two can be mixed blessings, elegant bracelets that—in terms of the novel—grow into iron manacles). But university is, I think, no guide to the realities of the writing life.

I am afraid this meretricious and dream-inducing side of a past literary Oxford had become rather linked in my mind with the figure, no, the aura of Lord David (as also with the most envied undergraduate of my vintage, Ken Tynan). That aura was resurrected only a few years ago, when I was sternly threatened with a libel action by the secretary of the Thomas Hardy Society. A magazine had published a remark in which I compared some of the more idolatrous members of the Society to pop groupies. The secretary had taken it upon himself to inform me that the comparison was outrageous and would give grave offense to "members like Lord David Cecil." Such pomposity was not Lord David's fault, of course; I am sure his opinion had not been asked, nor had I in the least meant his sort of scholarly member. Any irrational resentment I might still have felt towards what I had chosen to make him stand for at Oxford very soon disappeared before the reality again at our lunch, nearly forty years later. And yet . . .

The source of what I felt was, I think, no more than that Golding and I chanced to be seated together in an inglenook bench on one side of the table, and that Lord David was opposite us, on the other. Clearly he and Golding held each other in friendship and respect. Yet there drifted into my mind, as we all sat there, the presentiment of an ancient polarity, that between distinguished literary-establishment figures and self-made (all novelists are self-made) writers; just the very faintest whisper of a confrontation, purely symbolic, between the discriminating professor, with all the memory of his celebrated family hovering imperceptibly behind him, and the fallible living novelist, that heretic humanist I mentioned at the beginning. All this was purely in my mind, not theirs; I describe something that was in no way present in anything that was said. Such a polarity was, of course, between what I alone had made of them both, two figments of my imagination, a "Golding" and a "Lord David Cecil"; between someone who has a knowledge of literature from reading, teaching, thinking, and writing about it, and someone who is willy-nilly literature, because he makes and constitutes it. Perhaps I should more decently say that for a moment I felt the unbridgeable abyss that lies between even the most sensitive and knowledgeable critic and exegetist and the creator. Their lives may seem intertwined, and in many ways they are. Only in their essence are they eternally separate.

I wish now to say only that in that self-made confrontation, I felt myself, metaphorically as literally, very firmly at Golding's side. There are a number of other living English novelists I admire for various reasons, but none whom, like him, I feel almost emotionally, certainly imaginatively and empathetically, attached to; inalienably of his party. Perhaps, who knows, if we knew each other properly as ordinary beings, we should not get on at all. Golding might turn out a much more difficult proposition than "Golding." We both have formidable quirks. He would never get me into jodhpurs, or into anything less than a "floating Hilton" on the Nile. But after all, I don't think it matters that I do not know him, outside those quotes. Golding will die (though I hope not for many years yet); "Golding" will not. I know him as the future must.[1]

The spry admiral, the Joshua Slocum . . . I fancy he may not like all this

---

1. Since this essay first appeared, in 1986, William Golding has, alas, died. The book of which it formed a part, *William Golding: The Man and His Books* (New York: Farrar, Straus & Giroux, 1986), was a tribute on his seventy-fifth birthday. Incidentally, the original of this essay was sold to the "villain" of *The Paper Men*.

nautical imagery, and I dare not add "the privateer." Yet he has done his own free voyage, which makes him a precursor; has by his example helped carry me, and I am sure other writers, through many of our own storms and doldrums; has shown us the vital importance of trusting our own noses (or imaginations), of letting them steer, even into error; and of remaining oneself in the face of convention, fashion, critical ups and downs, commercial "wisdom," all the rest. Such is my debt, at any rate. And now to hell with embarrassment, either his or mine . . . once he called me in print "young Fowles," which mortally offended me. In revenge I call him *cher maître*, and most warmly embrace him.

THE *LOST DOMAINE*
OF ALAIN-FOURNIER
(1986)

I like the marvelous only when it is strictly enveloped in reality; not when
it upsets or exceeds it.

ALAIN-FOURNIER, IN A LETTER OF 1911

The Lost Domaine (Le Grand Meaulnes) is, I suspect, one of the rare books
that a reader may well feel happier not to have analyzed.[1] I remember feeling this myself when I first read it as a schoolboy, many years ago. It had
been an experience of such strange force, touching so many secret places
in my own nature, that I really did not want anyone to tell me what it
meant. It certainly wasn't that I then understood it, or its effect; but to treat
it objectively, as just another book, seemed a sort of sacrilege, the vulgar
throwing-open of a very special place.

Later in life I wrote my own first novel, *The Magus*, very much under
its influence. Since then I have read almost all else of what Fournier wrote,
and several books about him; and have been a pilgrim to most of the main
places of both the book and its author's life. I am, in short, a besotted fan,
and still feel closer to Fournier than to any other novelist, living or dead.
This kind of self-elected "special relationship" with him is not rare. Indeed
it is typical of one side of *The Lost Domaine*'s fate over the years; all those
of us who were from the beginning literally set in a trance by the book

---

1. By good fortune, for those who do like their texts explained, an excellent such analysis is now available: Robert Gibson's *Le Grand Meaulnes* in the series Critical Guides to French Texts (London: Grant
and Cutler, 1986). The same author's *The Land without a Name* (London: Paul Elek, 1975) is by far the
best account in English of Alain-Fournier himself.

have never, whatever the colder and sterner judgments of adulthood, lost our intense love for it. But I must confess that this is only one side of the picture, though it remains the majority one. Ever since it appeared, in 1913, there have been others (in France and elsewhere) who have found it sentimental, even mawkish; unbalanced, ill-planned in its development; and much too redolent of German Romanticism and devoid of the qualities we most commonly (or classically) attribute to French literature.

One obvious reason for this is not literary. It concerns what we ourselves feel about adolescence. For what Fournier pinned down is the one truly acute perception of the young, which is the awareness of loss as a function of passing time. It is at that age that we first know we shall never do everything we dream, that tears are in the nature of things. It is above all when we first grasp the black paradox at the heart of the human condition, that the satisfaction of the desire is also the death of the desire. We may rationalize or anesthetize this tragic insight as we grow older; we may understand it better; but we never feel it so sharply and directly. The intransigent refusal to rationalize this intensity of adolescent feeling is the tragedy of both Meaulnes and Frantz de Galais. They strive to maintain a constant state of yearning, they want eternally the mysterious house rising from among the distant trees, eternally the footsteps through the secret gate, eternally the ravishingly beautiful and unknown girl beside the silent lake.

The Lost Domaine is, then, about the deepest agony and mystery of adolescence. But adolescence is in every way a condition not much admired in the artistic world. Wisdom, maturity, and command of the medium are the qualities we look for, both in eminent artists and in eminent critics, as Thomas Hardy pointed out in his last novel, *The Well-Beloved*. Childhood proper, very well, its condition cannot be helped; but adolescence may seem a very imperfect adulthood. It is idealistic and mutinous, violent and vague, thoroughly green and unripe—"romantic" in all the bad senses. Now here is the greatest novel of adolescence in European literature; and I suspect that what many of its critics cannot face is that it is so essentially and crucially about qualities and emotions they have tried to eradicate from their own lives. In short, they cannot embrace what they once and now ashamedly were themselves, but must instead recoil in distaste.

This is not the place to defend the book against its enemies, nor to recite all its virtues. Literary attraction is rather like the sexual kind, the factors governing it are far too complex for words: either one is smitten, or one is not. But what I will try to do is convey the remarkable—and finally tragic—story of Fournier's life and how *The Lost Domaine* came to be written. This in itself is almost another novel, and accounts in no small part for the fascination many of us continue to feel for his figure.

Henri Fournier (Alain-Fournier was a part pseudonym) was born in 1886 of schoolteacher parents, in a small town in the Sologne region, an isolated area of forests and lonely meres (and now a favored shooting area for rich Parisians) in central France; but most of his impressionable childhood in the 1890s was spent where career sent his father, the village of Epineuil, some forty miles south of the city of Bourges. Epineuil and its school became the school and village of Sainte Agathe in the book, and feel very close to it even today. Fournier was always to remain very attached, physically and emotionally, to the landscapes of his childhood, and to their life. He was really of peasant stock himself, despite (confusingly to us English) his becoming a Parisian "intellectual" in later years.

Like every imaginative inland boy, he was fascinated by the sea, and spent a year at a naval college in Brest in his early teens. But he changed his mind over a maritime career, and went finally to a high school in Paris to prepare for university. There he proved a rebel against the strict system, like the Meaulnes he was still to create; but he also formed, in practical if not romantic terms, the most important relationship of his life. This was with a far more analytical, rational, and conventional boy of his own age, called Jacques Rivière. Rivière was to become a very distinguished critic, as well as Fournier's brother-in-law. As his close confidant, yet something of a temperamental opposite, he was able to help greatly in the writing of the novel; and their lengthy correspondence together is prime evidence of how Fournier developed during his late adolescence and after.

Both boys were at first heavily under the influence of the "perpetual autumn" of the Symbolist poets and their followers, such as Henri de Régnier. Rivière said that they hardly listened to the sense of the lines, but only to the echoes of their images, in a kind of impressionist dreamworld. The great names of the past, whom they were meant to study, did not speak to them at all. Yet they were far from identical in their tastes. Fournier, for instance, fell heavily for the post-Symbolist poet Jules Laforgue, whose influence (the distant piano, the sad clown) remains marked on the strange fête in the lost domain. (It was marked also on

T. S. Eliot, who later took private French lessons with Fournier in Paris.)
Fournier proceeded much more by personal feeling than by accepted
judgment. Rivière found his constant sensibility, his reliance on private
emotion, excessive at times; and Fournier as frequently took offense. "I
understand many things that escaped him," said Rivière much later, "but
it was he who flew, I who stayed where I was."

Like Laforgue, Fournier was always very sensitive to women, but he
treated them in a paradoxical manner. He loathed the way his sensual needs
put him at their mercy, for what his idealistic side sought was a purity and
candor few could reasonably offer. This pattern, of tender love alternating
with cruelty and cynicism, repeated itself again and again in his *affaires*,
from that with a girl called Yvonne in 1903 to the last love of his life,
Pauline, actress and sister of the writer Jules Benda. His first literary stir-
rings also emerged in these early years of the century. Here he followed the
earthy simplicity of another poet of the time, Jammes; and developed
(partly in opposition to Rivière) a hatred for dry theory, for fixed formulae for writing. "I shan't be truly myself so long as I have a single bookish
phrase in my head"; "I have a horror of being pigeonholed"; "All art and
truth lie in the particular and individual": these are typical pronounce-
ments of this period.

What he wanted above all to express was his own nature and his burning obsession with recapturing his own childhood, his own past, in (as he
put it in 1906) "brief, light words." The actual first attempts, in a series of
free-verse poems, were not impressive. The cause was largely Fournier's
then contempt for the "coarse theory" of realism. However, one poem,
"A travers les étés" ("Through the Summers"), did unmistakably pre-echo
the world of *The Lost Domaine*, and in retrospect convincingly demonstrated that the writer was at heart not a poet, but a storyteller. This was
something he very soon acknowledged himself.

In fact, "A travers les étés" was a first response to the single most important event in Fournier's life, something that affected it to its very core,
and to find a parallel for which, one has almost to go back to Dante and
Beatrice. On the first day of June 1905, he saw at a Paris art exhibition a
tall girl with blond hair, in a chestnut cloak. She was very beautiful, and
chaperoned by an elderly lady in black, an aunt in reality. The gauche
young student followed them onto a river-bus, and then to their home,
without saying a word. As soon as he could, he went back to their house
and waited in vain outside. The next day he returned. This time the girl

came out alone. He followed her, and eventually plucked up the courage to speak. He first used the same phrase as in the book, "You are beautiful"—not quite so naive as it sounds, since it was a celebrated quotation from Maeterlinck, then at the height of his fame. By some miracle his frantically scribbled notes on what happened next have survived. The young couple walked and talked for an hour. The girl's name was Yvonne (again) de Quièvrecourt, of a distinguished French naval family, and she did not live in Paris. She seems to have treated the lightning-struck young man sympathetically, but said in effect that there was no hope, that they were "behaving like children."

No doubt this was intended as a gentle discouragement, but "behaving like children" was ominously close to Fournier's own view of why he wanted to write: to convey the vivid and magical innocence of the child's perception of life, to arrest the past. What he had in effect found in this second Yvonne of his life was his *princesse lointaine*, the pure and unattainable symbol of feminine perfection. She was only too well cast for the role, being remote from him both by social class and by physical circumstance. He had no chance of knowing her better, of discovering the blemishes that his fastidious eyes found in every other woman he was ever close to; and like some knight of medieval chivalry, he craved sacrifice to just such an immaculate ideal and its hopeless quest. As Rivière said, he loved her because she was impossible. Fournier had long taken a sentence of Benjamin Constant's to his heart: "Perhaps I am not altogether a real being." In Yvonne he had found someone also "not altogether a real being."

He was not to meet her again for many years (and revealingly, made little attempt to do so), by which time she had married a Captain Brochet and had children. Nor was he physically faithful to her, for he afterwards had several love affairs with other women (one, a young dressmaker from Bourges living in Paris, was the model for Valentine in the novel). Nevertheless, this outwardly banal encounter and seemingly rather ridiculous example of calf-love was to haunt, torment, and dominate the rest of his life. For him its constituents became *Elle* and *la Rencontre*—"She" and "the Meeting." Other women stood to it as candles to the sun; and the novel is very essentially a prolonged metaphor of both it and its inherent "impossibility." It is why Meaulnes cannot discover the road back to the lost domain; why he leaves after his wedding night; why Yvonne de Galais dies. To attain ideals is to kill them.

But the writing of the novel still had to wait several years. Fournier had begun to know, by the time of the Meeting, what he had to do: "My task is to tell my own stories, only my own, with my own memories, to write nothing but poetic autobiography; to create a world, to interest people in very personal memories—for all that, the memories that make my deepest being what it is." He held to this task with an almost peasant obstinacy through the vicissitudes of the coming years: his academic failure, his increasing involvement in the Parisian literary world, his military service, two religious crises (expectedly enough, it was the humble circumstances in which the supernatural so often arises in Christianity that attracted him) . . . and behind all, the intensely living memory of the Meeting. This last undoubtedly caused him untold suffering, but it was equally self-imposed, almost a masochistic necessity before he could create. As Rivière remarked, he felt to the fullest when he was most deprived; when he was empty of everything he desired, his strength rose.

By 1910 he told Rivière that he was "working on the imaginary, fantastic part of my book and on the simply human one. Each gives me strength for the other." By September he had evidently found his road. The story was coming "naturally, directly, like one of my letters." At long last he was near where he had prophesied, or hoped, in perhaps the most famous of all his declarations about himself, made as long before as August 1906: "Childhood is my creed in both art and literature; and to render it and its mysterious depths without childishness. Perhaps my future book will be an endless and imperceptible moving to and fro between dream and reality. By 'dream' I mean the vast, vague world of childhood hovering over the adult world, and forever perturbed by its echoes."

What had slowly changed was his ideas of how to write the book, called at various times *The Land without a Name*, *The Wedding Day*, and *The End of Youth* (as Frank Davison explains, the final French title, *Le Grand Meaulnes*, has set translators insuperable problems ever since). To this end there were a number of more ordinary literary influences to take into account. From his eminent contemporaries came a brutal rejection by Gide ("This isn't the age for prose poems anymore") that eventually proved fruitful, as did an enthusiasm for Claudel; and a close friendship with the peasant polemicist and poet Péguy, both ardent Catholic and convinced Socialist, who, with his detestation of myth, taught Fournier to humanize his passion for the marvelous, to make it familiar and real. In 1911 there appeared a novel by a woman who had been a shepherdess in the Sologne: Marguerite Audoux's *Marie-Claire* (a book enthusiastically introduced by

Arnold Bennett in its English translation).[2] It ravished Fournier, and helped him greatly to achieve his own final style, that extraordinary blend of very concrete reality (who else would have introduced "cotton-wool soaked in phenol"—against decomposition—in the sacred Yvonne's death scene?) and a deliberately blurred poetic vagueness, the latter an echo of his early free verse.

There were also some cross-Channel influences. Fournier visited London very soon after the Meeting of 1905 (as a temporary clerk to Sanderson's, the wallpaper firm), and English was one of his best subjects academically. As a small boy, and teacher's son, he had been allowed to read all the prize books before they were awarded, and his love of Defoe stayed with him all his life. He admired Hardy, characteristically praising *Tess* "for the three farm-girls in love, so simply unreal in spite of a thousand deliciously precise details." He was deeply struck by the paintings of Watts and Rossetti, and of the Pre-Raphaelites in general. The greatest influence was probably that of Robert Louis Stevenson, whose novels Fournier adored for their "poetry of action," their movement. But I should add that some experts think this influence is most marked in the character of Frantz de Galais, in many ways the least effective in the book.

The origin of Yvonne de Galais is evident. But for me the masterstroke is the division of her male counterpart (or of his own psyche by the author) into three very different characters. The aloof, stubborn, and "difficult" Meaulnes is closest to his outward self, while the Byronic, hyperromantic Frantz is quite certainly the remotest from it—and the most difficult for the earthbound reader to feel sympathy for. Again and again he comes formidably close to being a spoiled and selfish child; and the apparent charm he has for both his sister and Meaulnes takes a good deal of swallowing. Undoubtedly for Fournier he represented that headlong passion for adventure that filled his own childhood, though only through books. He was in fact the last major character introduced into the story, and we may see him in part as a last cry of despair on Fournier's part over the loss of dreams, of the childhood world where all is possible. Robert Gibson, in his shrewd new study (mentioned above) points out that Frantz is also the great organizer and practical "impresario" of the book, the converter of the fantastic into reality—that is, successful in an area in which Fournier often saw himself as the eternal failure.

---

2. *Marie Claire*, Marguerite Audoux (London: Chapman and Hall, 1911).

But the true hero, and surely the true impresario, of the book is François Seurel, something one may not fully realize on a first or superficial reading. We learn virtually everything through his eyes and sensibilities, and his narration, with (to the literal-minded) its many inconsistencies, improbabilities, and flagrant omissions, is conducted far more by his will—or the writer's intuitive imagination—than by any supposedly objective witness. In a way all the other characters are his puppets, while his endless references to "childhood" and "adventure" are the great keys to his function and, through that, to the book itself: to create the world in which they can exist, and to exalt and celebrate them.

His "innocence" must, I think, be regarded as very suspect, outside the literal terms of the text. Many have remarked on the strong hint of femininity behind his overt timidity, purity, and modesty, a psychological equivalent to the fact that his crippled leg was drawn in reality from Fournier's sister Isabelle. Some have even suggested that a latent homosexuality lies behind his hero-worship of Meaulnes (and his seeming blindness to his own feelings for Yvonne), though there is absolutely no evidence for this either in the text or in Fournier's own life. I would rather simply say that he is by far the most complex and subtle of the three characters, in one way a master of apparent self-effacement and humility, in another very much the controller of the final "feeling" of the book, and of how its story of paradise lost is told; in yet another, a very astutely calculated and almost hypnotically plausible guide, or spellbinder, for the reader. The school at Sainte Agathe and its daily life are made so precisely real that the fantastic world Meaulnes discovers on his fugue must seem real also.

One final complaint of the critics has to do with the morbidity of the whole. Death, loss by passage of time, haunts its pages. Fournier took the real name of the lost domaine, Les Sablonnières, from his birthplace; yet it is also highly symbolic, since in French it means "the sand-pits." All is sand, nothing lasts, not the paradise of childhood, nor the dreams of adolescence, nor the lost domaine, nor the body of the well-beloved. In *Colombe Blanchet*, the novel Fournier was planning to write next, it is again the pure, eponymous heroine (her name strongly suggests "the white dove" in French) who is destined to die, not the fallible hero, avatar of Meaulnes, her lover. But this was not merely a fate, or mood, that Fournier imposed arbitrarily on his literary characters. He wrote himself as early as 1909 that he was "haunted by the fear of seeing youth end," and that before the world he felt "like someone about to leave it," that he believed himself fu-

tureless. When the Great War threatened, he declared that it was inevitable
and that he would not return from it.

The novel at last appeared in 1913, first as a serial. It was a success,
coming very close to winning the prestigious Prix Goncourt, and went
through several more editions in 1914. The last few months of his life were
not unhappy for Fournier, by then finally convinced that Yvonne was
effectively dead for him, and deeply in love with Pauline Benda, or
"Simone," as she was known publicly. But his darker presentiments were
fulfilled, and with tragic speed. He was called up at once, as a military re-
servist and infantry lieutenant. On September 22, 1914, before trench
warfare had set in, his company was involved in an obscure skirmish with
the Germans in the high beech woods between Verdun and Metz. No one
saw him killed, no body was ever found; but he was never seen again.[3]

Several invaluable collections of his letters have by now appeared. Some
earlier poems, stories, and prose pieces were published in 1924, under the
title *Miracles*. This volume also contained a long appreciation by Jacques
Rivière, one of the first and still one of the best accounts of Fournier and
his masterpiece of alchemized personal memory.

An immense amount has been written on both author and novel since
then, and it is now a safely established classic, while the concepts of the lost
domaine and the land without a name have become stock expressions,
with an almost Jungian status, in literary discussion and psychology. Yet
something elusive remains after all the learned analysis, after all that has
been discovered since Fournier's death about his own declared intentions,
his countless sources and influences, both literary and autobiographical . . .
some mysterious magic, some secret knowledge of how far a poetic imagination can outfly gross reality, some miraculous flair for saying the impossible.

A few years ago, on my way to the far south, I chanced to pass Nançay in
the Sologne, and stopped to see once more the shop of his uncle Florent
Raimbault (the Uncle Florentin of the novel). This shop was the paradise
found of Fournier's youth, and of course it is where he set the rediscovery

---

3. Part of this statement must now be revised. Only in this last decade, the skeletons of the French soldiers killed and buried in this place by the Germans were found; insignia proved that one of them was
that of Lieutenant Fournier.

of Yvonne de Galais. Now a private house, it was being redecorated, and the windows were open. The room was empty, and a painter's ladder stood at the back. On it was perched, of all things, a resting swallow. It was there, a very real being; yet not quite altogether a real being, like the ghost of the long-dead writer who stood in the shadows behind. For a moment or two there was only one time, and it was not the present, but that of the *domaine perdu*, so impossible to find; yet once found, so impossible to forget.

THOMAS HARDY'S ENGLAND
(1984)

Our house stood quite alone, and those tall firs
And beeches were not planted. Snakes and efts
Swarmed in the summer days, and nightly bats
Would fly about our bedrooms. Heathcroppers
Lived on the hills, and were our only friends;
So wild it was when first we settled here.

THOMAS HARDY, "DOMICILIUM,"

FROM *THE LIFE OF THOMAS HARDY 1840–1928,*

BY FLORENCE EMILY HARDY

A purist might perhaps complain that the title of this book of photographs[1] is not strictly accurate. In many respects, not least in popular imagination, Thomas Hardy's England was the England of his young-manhood (he was born in 1840), well before the period when most of these pictures were taken. One might also say it was even earlier still, since he never forgot, and often used, many of the stories his mother and grandmother had told him. By the middle of his life he himself was sadly aware that the ancient and immemorial Dorset of his early years was changing deeply in countless social and economic ways. Quite apart from the evidence in his novels and poems, he wrote one of the shrewdest sociological accounts of its passing. The figures and ways of life we see here were often, at the time of being photographed, already becoming picturesque relics rather than the living or common reality. Nor of course are we truly dealing with England, but rather

---

1. The text that follows originally appeared as an introduction to a volume of text and photographs, produced by Jo Draper and entitled *Thomas Hardy's England* (Boston: Little, Brown, 1984), documenting the vanishing rural world of nineteenth-century Wessex.

with that fluid-boundaried part of it, as much imaginative as geographical, that Hardy called after the Dark Age kingdom of the West Saxons: Wessex.

If Hardy's Wessex is to include every geographical scene in his works, we have to cover a considerable area. To the east it reaches at least to a line drawn south from Oxford to Winchester, and to London beyond; to the west, to the Scilly Isles in Cornwall; it must include the modern counties of Berkshire, Wiltshire, and Hampshire, as well as the true southwest of Somerset, Dorset, Devon, and Cornwall. But any map of this diffuse "theatre" (as Hardy called it) soon shows, by the frequency of the thinly disguised fictional names he gave to real places, where its core lies. It is much smaller: not even all of Dorset, but overwhelmingly the east and north of it, and above all the area close to where he was born, and grew up. Bockhampton lies only three miles from the center of Dorchester, the county town. Between 1862 and 1881 he was often living away from this heartland. But then he spent all the last half of his life, from 1885 to 1928, at Max Gate (so called from a turnpike gatekeeper named Mack), which is even closer to Dorchester, and still only just over two miles from his birthplace. An extraordinary number of places famous in both his work and his biography—Puddletown, Stinsford, Kingston Maurwood, "Egdon Heath"—lie within a radius of a few miles.

We tend, naturally enough before the size and breadth of his work in literary and human terms, to think rather too largely of Hardy in biographical ones. That jealously preserved and frequently concealed Dorset peasant self that lies somewhere near the heart of so much of his creation springs essentially from a very small landscape. It is easy enough now to denigrate the sometimes rather snobbish doublings he displayed in his later years to escape the hounds of his own humble past; just as it is to sneer at his self-designed house at Max Gate. There is, I think, no greater shock in English literary biography than to go round that far-from-distinguished villa just outside Dorchester, set on its rather bleak upland. It matches neither that environment, which he made so vivid in words, nor any conception of Hardy himself gained from his books; and can conform rather painfully to almost every prejudice we may have against late-Victorian taste and the middle-class ethos behind it.

Standing inside Max Gate, and remembering what came out of it—*Tess of the D'Urbervilles*, *Jude the Obscure*, *The Dynasts*, the countless poems—that is when most of us feel we should give up trying to understand great writers. We come expecting the palace of a maker of a fabulous kingdom;

and are faced with a brick mediocrity, more suitable to a successful local merchant of his time than anything else. But to put it so ignores the huge distance that Hardy had come, both economically and socially, from his beginnings. He may well have felt Max Gate was leap enough in a world where everyone knew his real past. Harold Voss, the professional chauffeur who used to drive Hardy on his tours in later years, recalled that Hardy's father and his own grandfather were both small builders, and sometimes worked together. As a small boy Hardy had often had to take messages between the two (six miles to Dorchester and back), and would get three-penny tips. It was the great writer himself who told Voss this one day; his snobbish side was never simple. I suspect we may think of Max Gate as the kind of neutral matrix where his masterly power of close and particular recall functioned best, a much more fertile environment for the writer than any of the romantic and history-drenched old Dorset houses that the more conventional of his readers might expect him to have settled on, and in, for the latter and "famous" half of his life.

Hardy has long been regarded as a valuable source for local history. In this he is rivaled only by his older contemporary the poet-philologist William Barnes (1801–1886). Dorset remained, all through Barnes's life and so well into Hardy's, something of a national byword for its backwardness and the infamous conditions in which a large part of its agricultural poor lived. The fact that one of the key events in British trade-union history, the Tolpuddle Martyrdom of 1834, took place in Dorset (and only five miles from Hardy's birthplace) was no coincidence. The county has been fortunate in terms of orthodox history, since John Hutchins's *History and Antiquities of the County of Dorset*, first published in 1774, is one of the best—if not the best—of that kind ever written in Britain. But it has very little to say, even in later editions, about the indigenous poor and their culture. Barnes worked particularly on their rich native dialect, in a version of which he wrote most of his poems; while Hardy not only wove into his fiction a great deal of native custom and folklore, but also (obeying that important function of his art that records society) gave us many pictures of what rural Dorset was like in his youth, and even earlier. Hardy himself was fully aware of this historical function. He wrote in the general introduction of 1912 to the Wessex edition of the novels, "I have instituted inquiries to correct tricks of memory and striven against temptations to exaggerate, in order to preserve for my own satisfaction a fairly true record of a vanishing life."

Hardy knew the old Dorset for the very simple reason that he was of it, and very much *not* as most of us must be today, quasi-tourist, visitor from outer space, however sympathetic and nostalgic we may feel before his writing. He did rather pretend as he grew older that he took a more or less scholarly, antiquarian view of it himself; but a private emotion keeps slipping through, and is quite naked in much of his poetry and fiction. History chose to begin to destroy the old rural world very soon after he was born into it, and part of his general pessimism and determinism must be closely associated with that process.

When Edmund Gosse asked his celebrated question—"What has Providence done to Mr. Hardy that he should rise up in the arable land of Wessex and shake his fist at his Creator?"—at least one answer Hardy could have given was that the culture he was born into at the Bockhampton cottage, that of his mason father and servant mother, had been destroyed. Never mind that his acute shyness, his increasing fame, the need to placate his unmistakably (but normally, for the time) snobbish first wife, and other intellectual and artistic factors all led him to dissociate himself outwardly from his real past and family circumstances; public dissociation is not suppression. The child remains father to the man. The photographer Hermann Lea's[2] niece, Joyce Scudamore, made some shrewd comments about Hardy after she came, as a friend of his second wife during the First World War, to know the forbidding old man. She said he was "wrapped in himself and his writing." She did not like his novels, finding them morbid and immoral, and believed them to be attributable to "some terrible early experiences." And she wrote this: "For an imaginative writer, he showed little imagination in life for some of the living. His relationships did not appear to me to be like those of other men. It was as if there hung a veil between him and the present."

Most serious writers would, I think, recognize this syndrome and its underlying cause: an inability to bury the past, and not least because it seems more the present than the present itself. Hardy's dilemma was that his literary and social success—in the context of the rigid Victorian class system—inexorably turned him into an outward or seeming denier of his own past; yet inwardly he remained vitally dependent on it. If he had remained only an architect (his first profession), he might have severed all connection, and taken Max Gate and all it stood for as reasonable ambition

---

2. Many of the photographs reproduced in *Thomas Hardy's England* were taken by Hermann Lea.

reasonably fulfilled. But writers cannot cut the umbilical cord so easily; they have to lead split lives—authentic and inauthentic ones, in the later vocabulary of existentialism. Yet the deep sense of loss this self-exile engenders, the guilt, the sense of the wasteful futility of human history, are a very valuable thing for a writer, since they are also a deep source of energy in creation. All novelists are in a sense undertakers or morticians, concerned to give the past a decent, or at least a thorough, burial. We are all reporters at a wake of that kind.

I think myself that Hardy's astounding and continuing popularity all over the world, even compared with that of other great novelists, can be at least partly explained by the fact this his central loss, or wake, was of an ancestral culture. It is not just the woman Tess who dies, but a whole manner of life; and it is not enough to say (remembering its hardness, its flagrant exploitations and injustices) good riddance. Something of its poetries and moods, its humor and simplicity, its courage and innocence, always remains to be mourned . . . and even envied. At first sight it may seem bizarre that Hardy should be so respected in Japan, for instance; but only at first sight. He matches perfectly a trait in the Japanese soul, a travail and loss that people too has passed through, and on whose debit-and-credit balance they cannot decide.

Much depends, in this latter, on whether we think of the past in moral or in aesthetic terms. Like Barnes a little earlier, Hardy has left us a rich and unforgettable image of a lost world. He judged himself that a new one was determined to come, must come, and that it was best for most that it should. But whether that old utilitarian standard truly repaid the loss elsewhere for him, we may doubt. An equally perceptive writer across the Atlantic, Thoreau, complained two decades before Hardy of one of the great practical causes of the loss: the railway. He spoke of the increased obsession with money, the greed it had brought to the New England countryside: "This is one of the taxes which we pay for having a railroad. All our improvements, so called, tend to convert the country into the town. But I do not see clearly that these successive losses are ever quite made up to us."

Rather oddly, the historians have not settled on any name for the huge metamorphosis that took place in British rural society during the second half of the nineteenth century. Perhaps this is because its manifestations were too vast, its causes likewise, and its progress too long-drawn-out to be easily comprehended as a single event; nor of course was it, except spasmodically and indirectly, ever a political revolution, with a clear climax. It was never planned, it merely happened. But the bare statistics of rural depopulation reveal the hugeness. Four fifths of the nation dwelled in villages or very small towns in 1801; by 1851 half the nation had moved to the cities and large towns, and three-quarters by 1901. The nearly one million agricultural laborers in 1851 were cut by a third fifty years later; and today, I am told, there are more hairdressers in Britain than there are farm workers.

To a striking degree it was a predominantly cultural upheaval, a profound change, over a century long (though most intense between 1870 and 1914), in the way the countryside lived. It has sometimes been described as a technical and agricultural revolution—the transition from the old labor-intensive system (which in many ways had altered very little from that of medieval and manorial England) to the final and grim destination of the mechanized and monoculture farming, or agribusiness, of our own times—but that seems to me to limit its real effect far too much. It is not so much that a hundred old agricultural and rural everyday crafts, from hedge-laying and coppicing to haymaking and cart-horse handling, were slowly extinguished, or survive now only as rare special skills. A complete tradition of surviving in rural conditions—not only a whole manner of life, but an unconscious philosophy of it—also disappeared.

The victims here were less human beings than their ways of working and behaving, of seeing and being. Nothing withstood the Great Change—not folk song (though the last of the Dorset kind were mercifully recorded by the Hammond brothers in 1905–1907) or folk speech; not clothes, domestic habits, or superstitions; neither family nor community relationships. To be sure, many aspects of the old country life have been artificially resurrected, in matters as far apart as fabric design and thatching; while a very bastard image of its supposed virtues (ludicrously ignoring the contemporary reality of the factory farm and the universal need of farmers nowadays to pursue high production rather than quality) remains in constant use, or misuse, in advertising. But all these siren calls of the "country-fresh" and the "traditional" are transparently commercial, and largely repeat the Victorian urban myth of rural England, that comfortable vision maintained in art by sentimentalists such as Birket Foster; even when old-fashioned methods and recipes and "natural" products are used in the home, one may usually safely guess that it is a middle-class one, and the use driven at least in part by a mixture of chic and nostalgia.

It is very difficult to present the old rural past without creating this nostalgia, precisely because nowadays we have the bastard versions of it thrown so continually at us—that is, the implication that the old countryside must have been more beautiful, more peaceful, more worthy, more stable and reliable . . . all that our present world is not. But Hardy was right: very few of the victims of the Great Change can have finally regretted it. They may sometimes have hated it where it hurt most directly—in the loss of jobs caused by first the steam and then the internal-combustion engine, the new labor-saving machinery, and so on—but behind many of the picturesque photographs there lies a very unpicturesque and generally bitter, Judelike story. The rural masses were undoubtedly culturally impoverished by the Great Change; but if that had to be the price of escaping from the more literal and far more terrible impoverishment of most laboring and living conditions, who is to deny it—and who, seeing the price we still pay, not to regret it also?

Hardy wrote one of his finest nonfiction pieces for the July number of *Longman's* magazine in 1883. It was called "The Dorsetshire Labourer," and is a very valuable corrective to our stock notions of the farm laborer, or at least to our notion of his existence as one of monotonous misery. In it Hardy suggests with a convincing sarcasm that "Dick the carter, Bob the shepherd, and Sam the ploughman are, it is true, alike in the narrowness of their means," but they emphatically cannot be rolled together into one uniform type, the "Hodge" of middle-class mythology. He adds that "drudgery in the fields results at worst in a mood of painless passivity"; while at least the field laborer has a "pure atmosphere and pastoral environment" by birthright. He is equally skeptical about dirt as a chief proof, to the well-educated (and very often socially—rather than genuinely— pious) Victorian outsider, of ingrained misery and low morale: "Melancholy among the rural poor arises primarily from a sense of incertitude and precariousness of the position."

The precariousness arose very largely from the annual hiring-fair system, whereby the farmer bought his labor for each next year. In 1883 Hardy recalled that it was much changed even in his lifetime: now the hiring was based on a written agreement (as opposed to the old handshake and shilling handsel), and already there was a significant change in clothes—the old smock had begun to disappear, along with the traditional symbols of particular trades. Many laborers now wore their Sunday best to such fairs. The great day was the old Lady Day (April 6), for that was when the agreements had to be honored, and the roads were crowded with laborers and their families moving to new cottages on fresh farms. Only a generation before, Hardy tells us, not one cottage on a farm changed hands yearly; but "Dorset laborers now look upon an annual removal as the most natural thing in the world."

This restlessness meant that laborers had by the 1880s become a good deal less simple than before: "They are losing their peculiarities as a class." Being constantly shuffled, like a pack of cards, also meant that they had become far less locally attached in their feelings. "They vent less often the result of their own observations than what they have heard to be the current ideas of smart chaps in towns," and Hardy says the women had often gained the "rollicking air" of factory hands. This was Thoreau's "railroad tax." Not only was the country being magnetized to the towns and to foreign countries such as America and Australia, from both of which attractive reports must frequently have percolated back; but the spirit of the town was invading the countryside. Hardy comes to the nub of it in the following passage:

> *That seclusion and immutability, which was so bad for their pockets, was an unrivalled fosterer of their personal charm in the eyes of those whose experiences had been less limited. But the artistic merit of their old condition is scarcely a reason why they should have continued in it when other communities were marching on so vigorously towards uniformity and mental equality. It is only the old story that progress and picturesqueness do not harmonise. They are losing their individuality, but they are widening the range of their ideas, and gaining in freedom. It is too much to expect them to remain stagnant and old-fashioned for the pleasure of romantic spectators.*

The result was of course a painful (and ever-growing) dissociation of humanity from the land, and also of the farmer from his men, now that they were valued strictly according to their labor-worth, rather than for their past knowledge of "fields . . . ploughed and known since boyhood." The children were not the least to suffer in this breaking of the old ties with familiar lifetime place and master. Hardy reports, of one village school he knew in that same year of 1883, that well over a third of the previous year's pupils had disappeared on Lady Day, forced to follow their parents to new work and new places.

Wages in 1883 had risen in general to some eleven or twelve shillings a week (fifty-five or sixty pence in modern currency, though inflation makes comparisons misleading) from the seven or eight of earlier in that century.

There were generally extra sums for special work, called tut-work, such as harvesting and haymaking, besides various customary perquisites, such as cheap rent (two pounds per annum at Corfe in the 1840s) for cottage and garden, right down to a quarter acre of potato ground and some wood for burning. Extra sums could also be earned by the laborer's wife and children—for turnip hoeing, like Tess, stone picking, or bird scaring—but these jobs were occasional and even more miserably paid than the men's. Every such family hoped for sons rather than daughters.

Pregnancy before marriage was a very common occurrence, indeed almost universal in remoter communities; and was widely interpreted as wicked immorality by the more respectable. There were several cases of this in Hardy's own family, and he himself, an eldest child, was conceived three months "before the altar." A report in 1846 mentions the especially unfair position of unmarried men, who were paid even less, at five or six shillings a week, yet expected to work as hard as their married counterparts. Their crime lay in not providing more hands for the future, and this was why ensuring that the future bride was fertile was much less a wickedness than a wise precaution. The state of farm cottages was often atrocious, a matter aggravated by this economic pressure to overbreed; add to that the general penury, and it is no wonder that child mortality was high.

Many girls had to go away into service, and thus became—if we may believe that other great witness to Victorian rural England, Flora Thompson, in *Lark Rise to Candleford*—important if unconscious agents in the Great Change. They returned back home with a host of new ideas absorbed from their jobs and mistresses, very often in the latter's cast-off clothes; and for the first time let their more sedentary parents and brothers know the meaning of culture shock. Flora Thompson tells a story that epitomizes it. One such young bride, returned home from service to marry and faced with a first visit from her new in-laws, puts a vase of sweet peas on the meal-table. Her laboring father-in-law regards them with extreme puzzlement. "Danged if I ever heard of eatin' they before," he says.

Hardy ends "The Dorsetshire Labourer" by saying that all these changes by no means came uniquely from "agricultural unrest." Another important rural class—the one he had himself been born into, that of the small tradesman or craftsman, and shopkeeper, who effectively owned his own small house or cottage on a lifehold lease (these were called "liviers")—was being driven away to the towns, not least because the all-powerful local landowners wanted all available property for their farm laborers, and had no time for this "unattached" element in their villages. This was before mechanization bit; but of course even when it did, the reduced workforce simply meant fewer customers.

The immensity and final destination of the Great Change are still not easy for us to grasp today, and it must have been far more difficult to do so at the time. Hardy himself, only four years after "The Dorsetshire Labourer," was sounding a less humane and sympathetic note. He wrote that he was "equally opposed to aristocratic privilege and democratic privilege. (By the latter I mean the arrogant assumption that the only labour is hand-labour—a worse arrogance than that of the aristocrat. . . .)" He was even more positive in 1891: "Democratic government may be justice to man, but it will probably merge in proletarian, and when these people are our masters it will lead to more of this contempt (for non-manual work) and possibly be the utter ruin of art and literature." This is clearly the new middle-class owner of Max Gate speaking, as also the writer now taken up by the aristocracy (and finding it much more conversable than he had in some of his earlier novels). Hardy was never really a political person; yet he remained to the end of his days a Liberal in practical terms, and a liberal in the more modern sense.

One final irony will be well known to anyone who has, as I have, tape-recorded stories of old people born in the 1880s and 1890s: the immense difficulty of persuading them, even on their own often abundant evidence, that they were not happier then. That they somehow were seems an almost universal feeling among those who recall the lost world of before 1900, or even 1914. I have just been reading a collection of such memories recorded in Appalachia, in the United States. Childhood after childhood of appalling deprivation and poverty; yet hardly a person who does not recall it with a warmth, love, and affection very seldom shown for the outward improvements in life since. One may subtract as much as one likes for the notorious golden distortion of memory; yet there is still something, a secret, that none of our politicians or sociologists seems quite to have penetrated. Perhaps it is made of those losses Thoreau spoke of, that are never quite made up to us.[3]

---

3. *Spring 1997*: I can't resist adding here that the further losses that have taken place since Hardy left us in 1926 are barely comprehensible; and not only would they have been so to Hardy himself, but they are to all of us who keep a dim memory of the old rural England. I doubt if even Hardy at his gloomiest and most pessimistic could have imagined the kind of bleak horrors modern agribusiness would bring England to.

THE MAN WHO DIED:
A COMMENTARY
(1992)

I told a number of people, some academic, that I was hoping to write a commentary for this edition[1]; and alas, met with a mixture of cynicism and commiseration, if not very plain distaste. Lawrence was third (just beaten by Dostoyevski and George Eliot, if I remember) on D. L. Mencken's list of the ten most boring writers of all time. F. R. Leavis's fine study of Lawrence in 1955 showed that the other Eliot, Thomas Stearns, was archepiscopally—and very unpoetically—dismissive of him. Sadly few of those I spoke to, and especially among the nonacademics, seemed anxious to treat him much more kindly. Lawrence, or at any rate that last-period Lawrence, was clearly no longer with it, was quite passé. Death had sunk him out of sight like a deep-diving whale, and therefore, in this ever less tolerant (and literate) world, out of mind. This is a common fate for the much-studied, of course, one of those "snatches of lovely oblivion and snatches of renewal" on the "longest journey" that wouldn't have distressed Lawrence or his once-living self. I can't imagine he ever seriously doubted that in *human* memory he would stay as fixed as a star in Heaven—or a species of flower on earth. He needed no wreaths, and knew his little ship of death would sail through all the doubts, decryings, and disparagements. As indeed, in all practical terms, it has; yet he always (he loved paradox, falling in hate as well as in love) risked rough seas for his human name, if not for his nonhuman soul.

Above all this isn't the age for sermons. We can tolerate smart slogans,

1. This essay was first printed by the Yolla Bolly Press in California, 1992. It was then reissued by the Ecco Press, New York, in 1994.

good advertising copy, fluent jargon . . . but Lawrence sometimes seems impossible. Anyone would think the man hadn't read a single word on deconstruction, or postmodern theory, or political correctness . . . or a dozen other vitally important matters. To say what you mean is hard enough; to sound as if you actually meant what you said is preposterous, ludicrously naive.

Born in 1926, four years before Lawrence himself died, I still hold some no doubt disgracefully antediluvian (to anyone smarter and younger) views on literary and other values. Words (and how they're used) continue to fascinate and haunt me. I still, dullard that I am, can't accept that since they all equally deal with signs, his poems (or Blake's, Shelley's, anyone else's) must be classed with the dullest commercial or the most abstruse scientific texts. In short, I can't discount Lawrence as seems nowadays increasingly expected of his readers. He remains to me of the dimensions, in the context of both the Victorian and our own times, of a peak in the Everest range, or of the importance of rich old cities such as Rome or Paris, or of the value of some whole botanical genus, an oak or primrose family—much too lastingly significant to be forgotten. Lawrence is very big; you may criticize and despise him, but you had better do it bigly also. Neither sniggers nor a latter-day Pecksniffianism are enough.

I am an atheist (more of that later) as to all ideas of an established and intervenient God; but not in my belief that there are comparative worths, in science as in the arts, and affecting us both as members of society and as individuals. Some objects and ideas *do* have value, though others may be as futile as a film star's fart—and only too often, as noisome. Above all I loathe the drift (a kind of fascism of the majority) that would so homogenize, suburbanize, and "democratize" life as to make it lose all its varieties and roughnesses—make it, like margarine, "easy to spread." If we attempt to destroy all distinctions, and especially those (for example in education, sensitivity, intelligence, and passion) to which we can personally lay no great claim, perhaps other people won't notice that we're actually rather dull and ordinary or that (horror of horrors) there are others who are different.

There are too many people on earth
insipid, unsalted, rabbity, endlessly hopping.
They nibble the face of the earth to a desert.[2]

---

2. D. H. Lawrence, "There Are Too Many People," in *Last Poems* (New York: Viking Press, 1933).

This difference first struck—seized—me when I went to Oxford in the 1940s. I was studying French and supposedly solely absorbed in all that, from the Chanson de Roland to Sartre and Camus; not in peculiar English visionaries such as Lawrence. Nevertheless, like many of my wartime generation, I fell on my knees with him. He said so many things we believed or didn't believe in, yet couldn't articulate; he had shocked my own parents' fuddy-duddy generation. It was obvious they were very wrong (not least, had they—and we!—but seen it, for having produced us). They'd also fathered and mothered the botched society most of us middle-class children came from. How had Lawrence (in his 1927 short story "A Dream of Life") defined it? A society full of "paltriness, smallness, meanness, fathomless ugliness, combined with a sort of chapel-going respectability!" He was writing about Eastwood in the Midlands, where he himself had been born, but he might—give or take some minor class and cultural differences—just as convincingly have been describing the suburbs where I was born myself.

Some writers *speak* to you. They can attract and fascinate; you may admire and envy them; yet somehow they never manage to establish the most serious writer-reader bond, which is a relationship almost like a marriage, and as closely intimate as an old friendship or love affair. By "speaking" we mean "writing" as if it may be assumed you are friends or lovers (or brothers and sisters) and so constitute a close human bond. I've been very aware of this "speaking" and being "spoken to" all my own literary life, both as reader and as writer. It can take place across countless centuries; it is totally indifferent to both place and time. We use "to speak" in this somewhat odd way because of a parallel with drama. We may read *Hamlet*, written about 1600. But when we see it acted, it is now, eternally now, of the very hour we see it. "Speaking" in the novel, in this sense, destroys all other "real" time between the writing and the reading, as between the acted and the written in the theater. It's by no means inevitably present, even in those writers who can and do sometimes "speak." It's by no means always present in Lawrence. He can write too much, can be a virulently judgmental bore; I can guess why Mencken so disliked him. But then, sometimes, you leap to him, or rather he leaps you with him, like the horse Saint Mawr, to an effortlessly and infinitely higher plane, almost to another planet. Then he does "speak," here, now, in the same room. To hell with time and death, the blackshirt tyrants of our helot being: Lawrence *is*.

This speaking was what first called me to Lawrence, and it is why I have always counted him as a very strong influence on my own writing, I now think a much greater one than the French existentialists, allegedly my favorites. "He was a part of me," in A. L. Rowse's phrase. But since the 1940s and my Oxford years, an unhappy shift of cultural mood has taken place in Britain. There were countless reasons for this change, not least the bitter experience of the two world wars and the loss of empire. Perhaps it is best labeled, broadly, as the collapse of a belief or faith in a positive life, a seemingly overwhelming need to denigrate and a fear of proving foolish if you do the opposite. It is (significantly) accompanied by a general ignorance of and indifference towards nature. Satire and mockery, a comic-sour doubt of the serious (curiously similar to a trait in Jewish culture, which of course has a much longer and more painful history of suffering), have since at least the 1950s been very acceptable attitudes to take or show in England, not least among the supposedly intelligent and culturally alert. When it was directed against so many patently outmoded social and political habits and notions, it was defensible, but when it began to shift to a universal disparagement . . .

Of course this oxymoronic bittersweet English culture (Keats *and* Byron, or just Byron alone, for that matter) has always had a soft, romantic side as well as a hard, satirical, or lampoon-loving one. But the current sneer or snigger on the British face, so evident in these last thirty years, has not really been able to swallow Lawrence. He is too easy to make fun of, to mock, to put down for being so preoccupied by his own ideas, so positive that all his instincts—intuition turned dogma—must be right. I can hardly blame the denigrators. Swept on in the general flood of carping, I have implicitly denied him myself (and *to* myself) for decades. I was stupidly wrong, but surely that snigger, that too-fastidious (too distorted by the zeitgeist) dismissal, weren't therefore right. Aspects of Lawrence, especially in those last years, do remain near impossible to defend or justify, indeed sometimes near the ridiculous. It is the ones that don't that we tend—if we don't positively *try*—to forget.

There are now countless critical and biographical accounts of Lawrence, and it is not my job—nor my wish—to ape an academic. I am a fellow novelist and feel a frequent sympathy and admiration for him; not a scholar-critic, desperate to amass new facts and make definitive judgments. It's not that I scorn all critics, but I know the enormous gulf between creating and judging, which has nothing—or very little—to do with comparative knowledges or intelligences, and far more with possessing a kind of religiousness . . . the need not just to teach, but to express one's finer self through teaching.

Briefly, Lawrence first saw the Mexicos, both old and new, in 1922. Some three years later, in 1925, he fell seriously ill there with influenza and malaria, and his tuberculosis was confirmed. At the end of that year he moved—it was to prove forever—back to Europe. In that last lustrum of his life (he was to die in 1930), his final spirit hardened and took shape. Again and again he tried to net the butterfly ("Farewell, farewell, lost soul!") less seen than sensed. What happens to us after death? With that was bound up another great issue. Why was humanity so ubiquitously sick, in a psychic equivalent of his own wretched state of health? It was his numerous plunges into these two dark worlds, trespassing on those of anthropology and theology, philosophy and metaphysics (to say nothing of that of politics), that were to cause the trouble. Bertrand Russell thought Lawrence led directly to the Nazis; and some of what he wrote in this period can be taken (especially if one suffers from tunnel vision and overliteralism) as highly offensive to many *now* (sixty years later) widely held views on matters such as fascism, racism, and feminism.

During Easter 1927, Lawrence and his American friend Earl Brewster, passing a shop window in Volterra, Italy, had seen a toy white cock escaping from an egg. Brewster suggested it presented both a potential title and the chance to broach the theme of resurrection. He knew he was sowing a seed in fertile ground, for they were in Volterra gathering material for *Etruscan Places* (which devotes a chapter to the little town and their visit). The old culture was already deeply attracting Lawrence.

> *The Etruscan religion is concerned with all those physical and creative powers and forces which go to the building up and the destroying of the soul: the soul, the personality, being that which gradually is produced out of chaos, like a flower, only to disappear again into chaos, or the underworld. We, on the contrary, say: In the beginning was the Word!—and deny the physical universe true existence. We exist only in the Word, which is beaten out thin to cover, gild, and hide all things.*

A result of this incident was the first part of *The Man Who Died*, called "The Escaped Cock." It was first published in *Forum* in February 1928. A further part, written that same year, was then added to the first, and the whole published, still under the same title, by the Crosbys at the Black Sun Press in Paris in September 1929. Lawrence always preferred his own original title, and never authorized *The Man Who Died* (though he "reluctantly" allowed its use on an abortive London edition). A first public edition in Britain under the new title appeared from Martin Secker in March 1931; a first American, from Alfred Knopf, six months later. The complex story of the various manuscripts and typescripts of the two parts and their publication is told at length by Gerald M. Lacy in the Black Sparrow Press edition of *The Escaped Cock*[3] and also, more simply, in Keith Sagar's introduction to Lawrence's *Complete Short Novels*.[4]

Almost everything he wrote in the later 1920s throws light on this austere last novel, but of especial value must be the *Last Poems* and *Apocalypse*, published posthumously in 1931 and 1932, respectively. An article entitled "The Risen Lord," first printed in 1929, may be read now in *Phoenix II*. Sagar felt this was so pertinent that it constituted almost a third of the novel. Of lesser but still obvious value are *Etruscan Places*, first published in 1932, and *St. Mawr* of 1925. This last is also about a resurrection of a kind, and is, to my mind, among the very best of Lawrence's last fictions. I have just read it in tandem with *The Man Who Died*, and can vouch for their closeness; though one is almost sweet sherry to the other's eau-de-vie. *The Man* is very near a sermon; *St. Mawr* remains a brilliant short novel.

There is no doubt how highly Lawrence himself valued *The Man Who Died*, whatever his feelings may have been over the title. Several letters stress its importance. After his various brushes with the police following the 1914–1918 war, most notoriously over *Lady Chatterley's Lover*, to a sick man it must at the very least have threatened still more trouble. Christ is shown resurrected and sexually potent ("I am risen"—how dare he make such an abominable pun on one of our most sacred mysteries!). He doesn't even discreetly couple, as any decent Anglo-Saxon should, with a respectable Christian woman, but flaunts his manhood with the mere priestess of some pagan cult, a shameless foreigner.

Today, these sixty-two profoundly changed and changing years later,

---

3. Los Angeles, 1973.

4. London: Penguin, 1982.

surely only the most bigoted and least imaginative could feel outraged. Anyone above that miserable level will understand that Lawrence's rejection of his early nonconformist chapel upbringing was based far more on social and aesthetic matters than on narrow sectarian ones. He asserted again and again that he was religious, indeed deeply respected Christ, at least symbolically, even if he couldn't accept much of what the Church and theology had made of him . . . and their insistence that all the faithful sheep must believe. In the last few decades we have perpetrated (and continue to perpetrate) quite enough only-too-real secular and biological crimes to make whatever blasphemy there is in *The Man Who Died* seem very mild indeed.

I am in Lawrence's case myself, having for years publicly called myself an atheist. As I said, in terms of all established religion (and most politics), I am so, with no belief whatever in either a personal afterlife or an intervening deity. To old-style believers, the world of people such as myself may seem incredibly bleak. But it isn't. For a start, our beliefs oblige us to put all reward for living—all its aesthetic point and ethical purpose, all its joys and all its duties—into life itself; and then we sometimes know, as we claim ourselves atheists, that we may also be religious, but can't say so because the word is so often assumed to be a synonym for "Christian." Lawrence transparently sensed this seeming paradox, I believe, and more acutely than any other writer of this century.

There are many eyewitness accounts (such as Cynthia Asquith's) of the almost palpable charge of life-energy he seemed to exude. He was "preternaturally alive"; there was an "electric elemental quality that gave him a flickering radiance." He was *different* from other people, and not just in degree, but in kind.

What he intensely prized was this acute awareness of being, a sensitivity like that of a Geiger counter aroused or evoked by and in all that existed, though most strongly in simple nature and the primitive worlds remotest from high culture—that is (we lack an exact word for it), the ability to feel and venerate the *existingness* in things. It isn't quite the same as Duns Scotus's medieval "haecceity" (Gerald Manley Hopkins's "thisness"), the separate individuality in all things; but much more a fundamental intuitive sense of their being. Of course we humans all imagine we have this sense; we know we're alive. But much of Lawrence's hatred of the cold, "overcivilized" north—not least of England and North America—

stemmed precisely from his feeling that we very largely lacked any true apprehension of this existingness, indeed behaved as if we couldn't believe it was there. We might have faint intimations of such a sensitivity, but we didn't, like him, profoundly treasure both it and all that provokes it. We couldn't, or we wouldn't have allowed a perverted Christianity and our maniacal pursuit of the Devil—or Mammon—and the lethally soulless machine ("Man invented the machine so now the machine has invented the man") so grossly to distort our societies and our psyches. One of his best-known attempts to convey existingness was in the short story "Sun," which also belongs to this last period and to his final return to Europe and his beloved Mediterranean.

I very much doubt if I fully understood the implications of realizing this existingness when I first fell for Lawrence. I did share it, though only slowly. It is why I became a natural historian; it is why I became a writer myself, always stumbling, despite being a novelist, after the poem; why I constantly declare myself an atheist, yet remain endlessly fascinated by religion, even by sects as remote as the Shakers; it is why, though also calling myself a French existentialist, I could never accept *le néant* and *la nausée* as one was supposed to do in those long-past years. Above all it's the existingness of things that has for me invariably dulled and diminished their other, much more obvious qualities and importances: their beauty, their social and political significance, their moral aspects . . . all have been thrown into shadow by the dazzling revelation, like some all-changing nuclear flash, that why they are or purport to be means far, far less than that they exist.

I may speak of it as if all this were (it does so seem with Lawrence) some sort of innate gift, like a musical or a color sense or one of balance. Undoubtedly it is so in part; but I very strongly believe that it is also something that can be acquired, can be learned and practiced, the susceptibility to it increased. At any rate I am sure that the manifold manners of life that most of us have given ourselves (or more often, that society gives us) are deeply hostile and inimical to this sense of existingness. Almost all our social cultures clearly see it as a threat. Our philosophies and religions, our pleasures and pastimes, both our cultural and commoner routines and habits . . . it is almost as if they were deliberately (devilishly!) designed to blur and obscure the fact that I exist—or better, that the "I" exists; and this "I" is on his or her one and only brief "holiday" from an eternity of oblivion, the *néant* of the existentialists. To begin to know, so that you may fully

accept, this—put most simply, that you both live and must die—is shattering, not least because it makes the apparent absence of any knowledge or
acceptance of it in our societies incomprehensible. Why on earth do we,
how can we, remain so ineffably stupid?

It was his acute and often raging horror at the insanely blind folly of
humankind, especially of its more fortunate and better educated, and their
total failure to see the reality of their situation, that must be seen as the
constant drive behind Lawrence through most of his adult life. It was exacerbated by the 1914–1918 war, but truly burst out in his last decade. It is
what gave him his incredible, almost supranatural energy. The less familiar
with his work sometimes shrug it off as mere egotistical vanity. It was not.
It was his essence.

Against the supposed awful pessimism of us atheists concerning the nature
of the afterlife must be set Lawrence's own recurrent notion of the
"strange flowers such as my life has not brought forth before, new blos-
soms of me." These "flowers" make up much of the *Last Poems*; in effect
they assert that there is an afterlife for the soul, though not for the "me,"
the individual ego. God breaks the loathsome, self-important ego down to
His own oblivion, but then finally sends a soul forth to take its place, a new
man on a new morning. Lawrence, of course, cannot be read for strict
common sense, narrow science, or reason; but we may go to him for feeling. Feeling is what bursts through again and again into the numerous
quasi-mantras of the *Last Poems*. He somehow can't really believe, because
he can't feel (as he might feel a pinprick), that what he is will one day die.

So much of the last work was written at a near white heat that language
is put under the deepest strain. There is perpetual war between an intellectual and a feeling Lawrence, between the someone who "wants out"
(who asks nothing, in his own words, "except to be left, in the last resort,
alone, quite alone") and the lifelong egocentric. He may conceive of an afterlife in oblivion—the great goal in "The Ship of Death"—since it sub-
merges

the obscene ego
a grey void thing that goes without wandering
a machine that in itself is nothing
a centre of the evil world-soul.

He may invite the annihilation of his own ego, yet somehow, so strong is—and remains, in this lower, latter world!—his personality, his own residual self, that his eager self-immolation is never totally credible:

> but in the great spaces of death
> the winds of the afterwards kiss us into blossom of manhood.[5]

Like Lawrence, in such matters most of us rate feeling well above reason. We wander in a mist of vaguely "religious" prejudices, of notions imbibed in childhood. It is like looking at the outside world through smeared glass, and sometimes we can barely see it. The effort of seeing it, of (in the current jargon) deconstructing it, is too much for most of us—I suspect less through lack of knowledge or intelligence than from a fear or dislike of having to face reality. Lawrence sensed this. It is one major reason he increasingly abandoned the (to him) flimsy froth of the more orthodox novel, and preferred to express himself (since he believed all his life that the novelist was superior to the poet, the philosopher, and the saint) in what was, for the previous admirers of his realism, a near-symbolic fiction. Even though what Lawrence himself always called *The Escaped Cock* was set in the Mediterranean, its techniques may seem as bare, if not as barren, as a New Mexican or Arizonan desert. In all this very last work he is repeatedly hammering nails, or one great nail, home. He hardly writes to please; he writes to teach through symbols. In short, he writes to parable.

All his life, ever since the days of the Pagans' group at Eastwood in England and the pipe dream of his ideal colony, Rananim, with its echoes of Coleridge and Southey's Pantisocracy, Lawrence had evolved a faith: the purpose of the novel was to teach. It was didactic, moral; never to merely amuse nor simply entertain. In the *Fantasia of the Unconscious* (published in 1922, just before he began *The Plumed Serpent*), he declares that "for the mass of the people knowledge must be symbolical, mythical, dynamic." This requires a "higher, responsible, conscious class"—the Lawrences of this world—to present and produce what the lower classes might absorb and learn from. As so often, Lawrence risked at best inconsistency, having so long damned modern civilization and education, and at worst the menacing tar-brush of fascism. But the underlying signal is clear. In *The Man*

---

5. See Keith Sagar's *D. H. Lawrence*, Penguin, 1986.

Who Died Lawrence was not concerned to demonstrate what he had so often proved, that he could write fine and beautiful near-realistic novels. *The Plumed Serpent* of 1926 had come out of the impact of New Mexico and his sense of his own "decayed Christianity"; but it had come also from an old self, which hadn't fully recognized the intense, burning-rapid development of the new Lawrence in the cold arms of death. I suspect this is why, like most, I count it a failure.

The new self needed the starkness and simplicity of *The Man Who Died*, *Apocalypse*, and the *Last Poems*, almost as Beethoven needed the sublimities of certain passages in the last quartets and piano sonatas. *The Plumed Serpent* hadn't made it clear enough what was wrong with Christianity, its placing of far too much stress on the Christ-Child and, especially since the 1914–1918 war, the Christ Crucified, and not nearly enough on what was for Lawrence the essential, the Christ Reborn. In *Apocalypse* he further placed the blame for the misleading of man and the corruption of true Christianity on the Revelation of Saint John of Patmos. In his 1931 introduction to the book, explaining the hostility of many intellectuals, Richard Aldington wrote, "Lawrence's fundamental heresy was simply that he placed quality of feelings, intensity of sensations and passion before intellect. In this he is the very antithesis of Bernard Shaw. . . ."

Needless to say, this novel is not faultless. There's always a danger in using euphemisms. Personally I in general prefer them to the careless crudity of so much contemporary would-be realism, but their drawback is that they can, and with time only too often do, pratfall into unintended humor. Every novelist knows the problem of sex: whom will your words please, whom will they offend? The woman-flows (*not* menstruation!), the new suns coming up, the intricate warm roses, the shutting and stirring lotuses, the scars and buds: they don't always present Lawrence at his happiest.

Nor does the element that has upset so many women in recent years, and I think quite rightly: his often rather painfully obtrusive masculinism-phallicism. This aspect of Lawrence, like his rashes of anti-Semitism, is not acceptable to many of us since the Holocaust and the rise of the feminist movement. Yet I believe that the virtues of both his writing and his personality enormously exceed the black shadows of these familiar bees in his bonnet. Lawrence is not quasi-divinely perfect, and we can't make him so.

One of those virtues is to my mind the way he finds such a simple, sometimes near-biblical, style to tell his story. The occasional flashes of his old poetry show a last relic of his acute powers of existingness: old feeling infuses skilled imagining. There is that always fertile pithiness, that flair for the striking phrase (what an asset he would have proved on Madison Avenue): "words beget words, even as gnats"; "the dread insomnia of compulsion"; "the sheer stillness of the inner life"; and many others.

I have never been able to read Lawrence for long before being plunged, besides the sympathy and affection (and pepper-grains of irritation), into thought. Part of his hyperawareness, his existingness, his soul-energy, is that he seems also a mirror for the reader. You must start searching for yourself in his texts. *The Man Who Died* needs to be read by someone fully aware of the despairing, almost hectic seriousness with which Lawrence saw mankind's deep-rooted psychological and emotional problems. Those last are what this text is essentially about, not the precise rightness or wrongness of its views concerning Christ. The human side of the world, *our* world, is very sick, and has become several times worse since Lawrence himself died; and I believe we need, desperately, whatever our own religious beliefs, to listen to his message. He isn't trying to shock us; but trying passionately, like all good preachers, to save us.

I'd like to finish with two quotations, the one from Richard Aldington's introduction to *Apocalypse*, and the other from the very last page of *Apocalypse* itself, which gives both Lawrence's living mind and his living soul.

First Aldington:

I shall only say a little about The Man Who Died. *It is intensely personal, and the saddest thing Lawrence ever wrote. It is the only thing in his work which looks like a confession of defeat, and this he promptly countered by writing* Apocalypse. *The opening part when he describes the mingled agony and gradual happiness in creeping back from death to life is full of pathos; one can't help thinking of his own sufferings as he recovered from one or other of his serious crises. Like much of Lawrence's writing, it has more than one meaning. You can take it as an expression of his latest feelings about Jesus—a rejection of Jesus as a teacher, an acceptance of Jesus as the lover. The mistake of Jesus was not in loving, but in trying to influence men by a doctrine of love. Even when he was struggling with the problem of love and hatred, Lawrence was always a great lover; his deepest and most passionate belief was in love.*

Now Lawrence:

What man most passionately wants is his living wholeness and his living unison, not his own isolate salvation of his "soul." Man wants his physical fulfilment first and foremost, since now, once and once only, he is in the flesh and potent. For man, the vast marvel is to be alive. For man, as for flower and beast and bird, the supreme triumph is to be most vividly, most perfectly alive. Whatever the unborn and the dead may know, they cannot know the beauty, the marvel of being alive in the flesh. The dead may look after the afterward. But the magnificent here and now of life in the flesh is ours, and ours alone, and ours only for a time. We ought to dance with rapture that we should be alive and in the flesh, and part of the living, incarnate cosmos.

IV

NATURE AND THE
NATURE OF NATURE

WEEDS, BUGS, AMERICANS
(1970)[1]

One thing I like about Zen philosophy is its mean attitude to words. It doesn't trust them. As soon as we have a thing named, says Zen, we start forgetting about its real nature. So labels, especially labels for very common human problems, tend to become convenient excuses for letting the problems take care of themselves. The particular stinking corpse buried beneath a word that I have in mind here is conservation.

No public figure today would dare state that he or she thinks humanity *can* support the continued cost of pollution and dying nature. Never mind what that public figure may do in private practice; he or she won't deny the most fashionable solicitude of our time. We all agree we need conservation. It is national policy, state policy, local policy, everybody's policy. And with all that interest and public concern, it's very clear that you and I don't have to do a thing about it—except pay lip service to the general principle.

There is a story about Samuel Rogers, the British poet who was a con-

---

1. I remember being given advice by a fellow writer about revising: always cut out the line or image that you judge is best. I'm very well aware that the essay that follows is nowhere near my best, so had good reason to oust it here. I have left it in because I now know United States nature a bit better and realize that there are two strange obstacles to appreciating it. One is the difficulty of grasping its enormous extent, which superficially both rejects and freezes, especially us Europeans. We all have, in effect, if we are first visitors, to go through the pioneer experience. America's very size seems to ostracize the individual; it puts us in a tight wagon-train circle surrounded by scalp-crazed Red Indians (Native Americans). The other thing that has struck me is a corollary and sadly general inability to see small, a blindness to the often exquisite beauties of countless very little objects. In that I have been greatly helped by the excellent little magazine *Xerces*, published at 4828 SE Hawthorne Boulevard, Oregon 97215, which *can* see small. It is under the aegis of the great ant-man and ecologist Edward Wilson. I deeply wish there were a comparable spirit and advocate for biodiversity in England today.

temporary of Byron and Shelley. At one of his literary dinners a group of friends were holding forth on the iniquities of slavery. For hours they poured out their fine liberal sentiments. Then one of them turned to their silent host.

"And what's your opinion of all this, Rogers? I am sure you are as deeply sorry as we for the persecuted blacks."

Rogers thought for a few moments. Then he reached in his pocket, placed a banknote on the table in front of him, and came out with one of the most curtly effective clotures on action-delaying filibuster ever recorded.

"I'm five pounds sorry," he said.

My belief is that it is high time each one of us started deciding how sorry he or she is—in terms of Rogers's bluff-calling interpretation of the word—over the contemporary rape of nature. In this case, however, the currency of sorrow needs to be expressed much more in action and changed attitude than in money. And the thing that ought to make us all feel "rich" enough to pay is the very simple fact that in most places nature is going to be saved not by official bodies but by each of us. If we don't help, if the whole social climate isn't one of active participation, right down to the personal and household level, then all ordinary wildlife is doomed. The plastic garden, the steel city, the chemical countryside will take over. The government-run parks and national reserves may still survive; but *nature in ordinary life is in the hands of people in ordinary life.*

I still live in a country (England) that has managed to maintain a comparatively healthy relationship with this ordinary nature. And though I certainly don't intend to draw a black and white contrast between a holier-than-thou Britain and an unholier-than-I America, I suspect that one major difference between the two cultures lies in the average person's attitude towards the familiar nature around him. In terms of a bad relationship, being sorry means being aware of being wrong. It is the unawareness of being personally wrong (shown both in the negative tendency to blame everything on corporate greed and in certain wrong emphases in current conservation work) that seems to me to be the weak spot in the United States. This fundamental, personal, and private relationship to ordinary nature is primarily what I want to discuss here, and in two or three rather different areas. I hope also to suggest one place, very close to home, where something can be done about the problem.

But first of all I must make one or two painful historical observations.

. . .

Why can Britain show a good deal more common wildlife in its cities, towns, suburbs, and surrounding countryside than the United States? A great deal of our happier situation is certainly due to completely fortuitous circumstances and not at all to any greater conservation conscience in the British.

American farmers are much more efficient. They change landscapes to suit their machinery. They use more poison. The British farmer has a traditional tolerance towards nature; nine out of ten are still happy to sacrifice some good farming to some good sport, to provide cover and terrain for game birds, deer, foxes, and the rest, and thus cover and terrain for many other species as well. In any case we have much smaller field systems, and they are mostly divided by that best of all natural preserves for small wildlife, the thick hedge. We have also fiercely protected our "common" land, which is traditionally unfarmed and allowed to grow wild. The great landowners of the past have left us an ecologically rich legacy of scattered woodland, and an equally rich legacy of parkland inside town limits. Even without this parkland, most British towns have grown so slowly from their medieval origins that they are often much greener and more haphazard than their comparatively instant American counterparts. Nature has never been completely crowded out. In towns and suburbs, too, there are differences in gardening practice (of which more in a moment) that favor our wildlife. But even when all allowance is made for British "luck" in the comparison, there is in my opinion a failing—though much more a passive, historically conditioned failing than an active, conscious one—on the American side.

I was reading recently one of the very first accounts of life in America, Governor Bradford's *Of Plymouth Plantation*, the story of the Pilgrim Fathers' grim early years in Massachusetts. The seeds of the attitude that many British nature lovers still sense in ordinary American life can be seen planted in his narrative. I can best describe it as a resentful hostility towards the overwhelming power of the wild land; for Bradford, natural America seems a far worse enemy than the Indians or the machinations and failings of his neighboring colonists. Of course it would be ridiculous to speak of hostility to natural America in the modern United States, but there lingers a kind of generalized suspicion about it, or else a cold indifference, as if it may have been officially forgiven the sweat and tears it exacted from the settlers and pioneers, but can't expect to be trusted, let alone loved, for a long time yet—an attitude rather similar to that of many elder fellow countrymen of mine towards the Germans.

To this very old resentment degenerated into indifference must be added later historical factors. Many nineteenth-century European immigrants (such as the Irish and the Italians) came to America with a bitter Old World experience of depressed and exploitive agricultural economies. One resolve many of them brought with their bags and bundles was a determination never to see farmland again. In sociologists' jargon, the descendants of such immigrants have developed through the years highly urbanized life-styles. Then there is the case of the intellectually dominant subculture of today's America: the Jewish. The one failing that superbly gifted race has (a failing, moreover, for which it is not to be blamed, since it springs from centuries of being herded into ghettos) is its blindness towards nature. In classical Yiddish, for example, there are very few words for flowers or for wild birds. The great writer Isaac Babel was well aware of this deficiency.

Finally, there is the intensely profit-centered aspect of the American spirit, also to be traced back to the Plymouth Colony days: the drive to maximize the financial utility of any undertaking or resource. You can't set out to rob nature of every cent it has and then still expect it to look flourishing. I admit freely that earlier Americans can be largely excused for their mistaken belief to the contrary. As every historian has pointed out, they were brought up with a sense of endless new territory to be exploited. What did it matter if you ruined the few miles around you when so much was still virgin? Even today it comes as a shock, so used have we foreigners become to thinking of the United States as one huge polluted conurbation, to see how much wild America still lies between New York and Los Angeles. Every time I fly that route, I find it harder to blame past Americans for their exploiting sins. And it isn't only the size; the image played its part. Naturally the promised land most attracted the poor. Throughout the world the poor have very understandably always been more concerned about making money than about protecting the environment. In the past, any protectionist action was invariably taken by a class of society that never went in much for emigration: the well educated and well circumstanced. Safely and comfortably back in Old Europe, they could afford such amenities and fine feelings. The emigrant poor couldn't.

But the very obvious irony of our own time is that this characteristic and forgivable poor man's view of nature is still so prevalent in the world's richest nation.

I am not belittling the energy and resources presently being devoted to conservation in the States, but for all that, I suspect that in some ways the approach is still influenced by the old conditioning. Like a certain kind of once-unscrupulous millionaire turned public benefactor, the new official protectionists are overanxious to show off their change of heart, and the problem is being tackled too much in the surely now disproved fashion first tried out on the Indians—that is, in terms of special reservations and salvation showpieces—and not enough in the way of a general reintegration of common nature in ordinary life.

The very word *common* has a vaguely un-American ring about it. It is the big things, the outstanding things, that call to the virile American heart and pocket. And perhaps this (in many other ways admirable) national habit of thinking big helps explain why so many urban and suburban environments seem to have been written off as hopeless by the professional conservationists. But these are the environments in which most people now live, and where the reintegration is most urgently needed if there is to be any essential ground change in the public attitude. What I believe is required is very simple to state: a will to foster the wildlife, *however insignificant and humble*, in the citizen's own backyard and neighborhood, and *not* to foster the illusion that nature is some large and spectacular rare bird or beast seen on a TV film or glimpsed in a remote national park during a summer vacation.

Where the British score well is at this level. They tolerate the everyday nature round them because they want it there. They may not be interested in it, but they see it as right that nature should survive and be allowed the conditions to survive. This is something barely conscious; it just seems to us—and with the full implications of the word—natural.

Another wrong (or at least suspect) emphasis in active conservation is that placed on improving *human* environmental factors, such as atmosphere and water. Very clearly, success there will help other forms of life besides the human, and it is not the end result I am questioning, but the ruthlessly pragmatic way in which conservation is sometimes presented as a unique need of social humanity, rather than as a shared need of both humanity and nature. This can turn the saving of nature into a kind of neutral by-product of the human concern. I think such an absurdity happens because conservation, though not a uniquely human need, *is* a uniquely human responsibility, and the response of man towards such responsibility has always been, "What's in it for me?"

Let me clarify with a simple analogy. I regard what are sometimes called the lower forms of nature as children, and I think we human adults of evolution have precisely the same responsibility towards them as parents towards their own human children. What I dislike in the approach that sells conservation predominantly as a road to the human Pleasant City is that it tends to orphan nature. The protection of the wildlife of the environment becomes like the protection of parentless children: something for specialized agencies and institutions to take care of, not something to concern you or me.

But enough of negative historical deductions. Let's look a little more closely at that fundamental conservation cell, the backyard garden.

I sometimes meet self-styled nature lovers who say they feed the birds in their garden, they even put up nesting boxes, for God's sake, what more can they do? Then I see their gardens—beautiful gardens, not a weed or a pest in sight among the immaculate lawns and flowers. But what I really see is what isn't there, the total absence of any plant native to the area, the poverty of thick cover (not all birds nest and roost in holes), the ubiquitous evidence of a constant use of insecticides.

What does natural life need? First, it needs privacy, even in the smallest backyard: like humanity, it wants somewhere it can sometimes go and not be seen. Many modern gardens are like glass houses without internal walls, with every function in full view. Second, since nature is a self-victimizing process, it needs a supply of victims. You can't massacre all the small nameless insect life of an area and then complain about the lack of butterflies. Plainly these needs call for a change in our whole concept of gardening and gardens. Again, I feel the British are a little ahead of the Americans in this respect—and again for mainly fortuitous, historical reasons.

Apart from anything else, the cultural pressures towards the synthetic garden are much stronger in the United States. There is the high priority put on anything that saves time. Insecticides and weed killers save time. There is the high priority put on good functioning, on neatness and efficiency. Lawns are neat. There is, in many suburban areas—and this certainly applies equally to Britain—the high priority put on conforming, on having the same plants, the same layout, though just a little bit better than your neighbors', of course. In America, freedom from crabgrass becomes a test of social acceptability; the man with the best roses walks six inches taller.

In this history of the gardening art, the *jardin anglais* has always stood for a profuse disorder. Some American visitors here suppose that the highly formal gardens of some of our Elizabethan and seventeenth-century houses represent the true old English garden. Nothing could be further from the truth, for all these are style-conscious aristocratic copies of Italian and French models. The real English garden has always been first cousin to an English hedge and an English meadow. It has always worked *with* nature, just as the artificial French and Italian styles have worked against (or in spite of) it. And this working with nature is exactly what the ecologically good garden—one honorably shared between the legal human and equally legal natural owners of the place—demands. When a bird or an insect flies into town, what it looks for from up there is a varied menu and an interesting decor, not one more neon-lit hamburger joint like fifty thousand others.

So what should we do?

Obviously the first thing to ban from the gardening shelf is all insecticide, which has been in at the start of the nastiest exterminatory chain reaction of this century. Running a very close second is the weed killer. Every "scientific" statement as to this or that product's comparative harmlessness can be treated as so much barefaced lying, since all such products aim to upset the natural balance. The next thing to curtail is the area given up to lawn. Well-kept grass gives a very poor ecological return. Much better is good evergreen cover, especially if it yields in addition nectar-rich flowers and edible fruit or berries. Such cover not only encourages birds but provides an important insect habitat. Another important consideration is the kind of ornamental flowers and shrubs that are grown. Some of the original species of mints, buddleias, ivies, daisies, and the rest may look a bit less glamorous than their modern "selected" forms, but there is no doubt which the insects find more nutritious.

If you wonder why I keep harping on about insects, the answer is very simple. Before I give it, though, I want to look at another example of the way words can become dangerously obscuring labels. Most insects fall into that slightly un-American category of mean little indistinguishable things; and just as racialists think all members of the hated race look the same, I am afraid that many Americans bury a major part of the insect universe under the label "bug." There is thus the symptomatic contemptuous usage "stop bugging me," and all the electronic-mechanical extensions: space bugs, bugged rooms, bugging devices. Under this label, all insects tend to become a kind of natural equivalent of the political Reds.

I have confirmation of this national insect phobia with every American guest I have here in England, as he or she shakes his or her head over our refusal to install screen doors in our houses. Just when, I can see them asking themselves, will these unhygienic British learn the sanitary facts of life? Well, it may be that more disease-carrying insects are flying about in the United States than where we live. But it seems more likely that we make a clearer distinction between the harmless garden and countryside insects that do often fly into the house and those that are a real danger to us. One aid to that distinction is our lack of that blanket word *bug*.

And why not bomb the bugs? Because the insect is directly or indirectly the chief food source of countless higher forms of life. If you mercilessly destroy your bugs, you build your conservation house without foundation or ground floor. You can rate your garden conservationally by checking on the abundance of insect life in it. In this context, if it's clean, it's dirty.

There is really no clearer ethical decision to make in our time: ban the insecticide from your own backyard and get your neighbors to do the same with theirs. But very clearly the process cannot stop there. The vital complement of the conservation garden is some form of local nature reserve. Although I don't doubt the honest intentions of the good people who run many of the reserves I have visited, they seem often to be founded on something of a wrong principle. In fact such local reserves should be known, and their use determined, by a now old-fashioned name for them: nature *sanctuaries*. It is absolutely essential to keep near towns and cities some such unpolluted and wild area open to nature and closed to humans; and I'm afraid that being closed to humans is not compatible with picnic areas, walk-through paths, and similar features installed in the attempt to effect a compromise between social and civic amenity and the true purpose of a wildlife reserve.

But even the conservation garden and its accompanying out-of-town reservoir of wildlife will be of little use if all the surrounding farmed country is regularly drenched with insecticide. And here I come to the crux of it. What is urgently needed is a rethinking of where conservation is most useful. Instead of thinking of the uninhabited far-off as the ideal area, we ought to reverse the process. Uncontrolled spraying is in any case safest—for humans as well as for nature—the farthest possible distance from town; and the town and its wide green belt ought to become the priority conservation zone. This situation has already arisen accidentally in many British towns. Quite a number of once-rural species have now taken happily to suburban life in protest against the pollution of their former habitats.

If hedges, small woods, and other (from the profit-oriented farmer's point of view) waste areas are to be reinstated in the landscape, it ought to be in just such conservation belts around towns and cities. If the farmers won't listen, then public authorities ought to be made to. Contrary to popular belief, many birds are extremely tolerant of traffic noise. I have even seen some of them among the scrub on the Los Angeles freeway banks and verges, only a few yards from the steel stream. But one warning: an ecologist must determine the character of the planting. Town-owned free space should be gardened for the benefit of local nature, not for civic pride or to yield a showy flower display.

I wish there were a way I could lend my own garden here in England instead of trying to say it all in words. I've attempted to practice what I preach. I won't use insecticides out-of-doors. I keep weed killers to the barest minimum. And yes, it is far from being a gardener's dream. About half of it is given over to natural scrub and cover; whatever seeds there happen to be are allowed to grow—thistle, dock, fireweed—no matter how high on the blacklist they figure. It is a town garden, and not very large by American standards. It harbors five or six breeding mammals, a dozen or so species of nesting birds with many more coming as visitors, a good variety of butterflies and moths, and a generally luxuriant insect life. A lot of hard work is saved, since I let nature look after its own part. All I have had to do is learn to bear the shocked expressions of the more orthodox gardeners who come round it. I can only report that this so-called shame is increasingly easy to bear once you have made up your mind to it. You soon realize such people are half blind. They simply don't comprehend the rewards, the richness, the sense of a harmonious creation that such disorder and laziness bring into daily life.

Nothing can annul the prior lien nature has on your property, the title it possessed long before you became the owner, long before you were, even. And there is no argument possible as to where conservation starts. It starts right there, outside your window. That is, it starts if you start, and from the moment you stop merely saying the word *conservation* in order to avoid its reality. It's no good just believing in conservation, agreeing with conservation, talking about conservation. It's one of those words that gives you only two choices. You either do or you damn.

Now let's consider the man with a gun in his hand: the hunter, the prototype of all nature exploiters. Since my views are not going to make me popular, I'd better explain that I'm not, like so many reformers, quite trying to ban the whorehouse that I've always envied the other men but never had the guts to enter myself. I spent a great deal of my youth duck hunting, and I can remember very well what it's like some winter dusk when you hear the first swift sough of oncoming wings and see the hit black shape plummet down to splash in the reeds behind you. No other game or sport I've tried has ever given me quite that thrill—or made the time wasted on it seem so endurable.

I was taught to hunt by a man named Brealey, one of the old school. I was not allowed to shoot at a bird until I had proved myself to his satisfaction on the cans and bottles he threw up as a test—and I didn't do that in a day. I was not allowed to shoot at any but legitimate and edible game. I was not allowed to shoot at that unless I could reasonably expect to kill it at that range. Another rule: you never, but never, gave up the search for a wounded bird. If night stopped you, you went again the next morning. Only barbarians used automatic shotguns; if you couldn't bring your duck down in two shots, that was your fault. You had had your sporting chance. At the time I was irked by all this punctilio. Nowadays, when I occasionally see what we in the country call town shots (city people who blaze away at anything that moves), I make silent penance to old Brealey. Like most such men, he was a good field naturalist and a sincere nature lover beyond being a crisply accurate picker of widgeon and mallard out of a dark sky. He's long dead now, but I think the world hunting community badly lacks men like him as its arbiters.

As to the rightness of one of his "laws" I can't expect to convince Americans, and especially not the gun lobby; nonetheless, I believe the repeating shotgun ought to be banned. Later in life I did use one for a time, and it seemed to me not only to make me shoot worse and to wound more than I killed, but to take a very essential element out of sport—that is, the sport itself. The thrill of hunting for pleasure is surely killing for pleasure, not just killing at any cost. A two-shot gamble ought to be enough; it's already one more than the golfer has. I have my doubts, in fact, about all the new aids to bigger bags and heavier baskets that the hunting and fishing industries have concocted. All great games depend very strictly on certain agreed limitations and restrictions; the skill lies in beating the system inside the rules. And it is time we started laying down rules on the kind of equipment and behavior hunters and fishermen can and can't be allowed. Both activities are almost purely sports now, and they need to be regulated as other sports are.

Another growing necessity is the hunting test. It seems bad enough that a man or woman can buy a gun across the counter without question, but just as bad that he or she can go straight out and immediately start firing it at any wildlife that crosses their path. I would make a certain standard of marksmanship obligatory before a hunting license was issued; I would ban minors from hunting, for reasons you will guess in a minute; I would also like to see a compulsory course in animal and bird recognition and in general hunting ethics. This is all still a good deal less than what we require of sailors, airline pilots, policemen, and other people who hold life and death in their hands.

I gave up hunting myself on the same grounds as many other men: one day I found I couldn't live with the enjoyment I got one moment from seeing birds and animals in the wild and the enjoyment I got the next from killing them. You don't just shoot a deer one evening; you also shoot a piece out of every other human being who might have seen and enjoyed the sight of it and its progeny, had it lived. As a boy I shot, out of sheer mischief (and well away from my mentor, needless to say), several buzzards and ravens—even then rarities in this part of England. Now they are virtually extinct here. I haven't heard that unmistakable deep snoring caw or kwark drifting down out of a high blue sky for years. I have to drive to Wales, a hundred miles away, to be sure of hearing it again. What that schoolboy in me helped to kill forever—or at any rate, for his lifetime— was one of the last noble and peaceful sounds in his own sky.

Another argument I have very little time for is the one that maintains that hunting helps conservation. Of course, the game the hunter wants to shoot is usually well looked after in terms of bag limitation, closed season, and protection of habitat. But everything else suffers, and especially any other wild animal or bird of prey in competition with rifle or shotgun. One of the tragedies of the British conservation story (which, I hasten to add, has many more black spots than you may have gathered from my earlier comparisons) is the abrupt disappearance of many of our once-familiar birds of prey over the last twenty-five years. Insecticides have taken their toll, but a chief enemy remains the professional gamekeeper. Although I loathe their methods—many still use the illegal pole trap and equally illegal poisoned bait—I can't really blame them. They are paid to produce gamebirds for fall shooting, and a full gibbet—the wooden rack on which they hang their "vermin"—proves they have earned their money. It is their bosses who are to blame.

In all so-called conservation for hunting there is a wide streak of tyrannical—almost puritanical—selfishness. No nonhunter would class the sight of a few fat pheasant pecking round a cornfield as any more beautiful than a peregrine stooping or a sparrow hawk slashing and tilting its lethal way down a forest clearing. But no neutral person has a say in the matter; the hunting industry decides for all of us. All this may seem a fairly harmless interference with nature and natural solitude compared with the murderous outpourings of real industry or the scorched-earth techniques of "scientific" agriculture. But the attitude *is* wrong. It perpetuates, far beyond and outside the psychology of those who actually do hunt, a wrong role of man. It treats nature not as the unfairly threatened and persecuted domain of life it has now become, but as something that is fairly preyed on. It makes killing decent, and killing is never decent; it may be necessary, but not decent. And in America above all it must strengthen the old prejudice—or carelessness—about nature: nature as something hostile, to be hunted down, ultimately down to zero, and driven away from all human settlement. To be used, in a word, at the very time when nature is so clearly asking to be saved for those who come after us.

There are two questions you ought to ask yourself if you do go after nature with a gun. One is this: "Why do I enjoy killing?" The second, and more important, is: "What have I just killed?"

The answer to that second question, let me warn you, can never be just a number and a name. In fact there is only one honest answer in this year of 1970, and only one honest action a hunter can take once he has answered.

If any group seems innocent in the rape of nature, it is that great and amorphous body of amateur natural historians, bird watchers, plant hunters, and photographers—that is, nature fans in general. The worst variety of this group, the collector, is happily today a rare specimen. One can safely assume that anyone who still collects (i.e., kills) some field of living life just for pleasure and vanity has all the makings of a concentration-camp commandant. Egg collecting, butterfly hunting, taxidermy, and all that infamous brood of narcissistic and parasitical hobbies have become so obviously evil that I won't waste time condemning them.

There is, however, a subtler sin for the amateur naturalist, one that will lead me conveniently to the core of what I want to say about our present defective attitude towards nature. I call it identification mania. It is nicely typified by that absurd new game played by some ornithologists: the species-count competition in which, on some appointed day, bird watchers drive frantically from one locality to the next to see who can accumulate the longest list. And this brings us back very close to the general human fault I started this essay with: our perverse delight in naming things and then forgetting them. If the species count were just the freakish idiocy of a clam-brained ornithological minority, it wouldn't matter. But unfortunately the philosophy behind it contaminates a great deal of our thinking, and our education, about nature.

To a professional scientist, correct identification is a basic tool of the trade. But for the nonspecialist it seems to me of very secondary importance. Seeing and enjoying nature are infinitely more important than knowing how to name and analyze it. Any trained biologist will tell you that identification expertise has about as much relation to serious biology as knowing national flags has to do with being an authority on international affairs. I put the blame for this narrow and superficial identification approach to nature squarely on the shoulders of the amateur naturalist. Nothing puts the beginner off the whole subject faster than the name-dropping conceit of this kind of expert. The tyro thinks nature must be some kind of academic memory test, a quiz show with no prizes, and quite reasonably takes up something that puts less of a premium on "experience" and know-how (or more accurately, know-what).

Almost all nature education based on the know-what approach is bad, for what goes with it is the notion that everyone ought to get an identification interest in natural history. Of course, if we did all become keen naturalists, that would solve all our problems. But if anything is certain about the real situation, it is that many people are never going to be very interested in nature either as science or as a hobby for showing off a cleverness with names. Indeed, as they have less and less contact with nature in our overpopulated world, they are very probably going to be less and less interested in it at all. What has to be done is to get this vast and growing army of the indifferent to see nature as a daily pleasure of the civilized life. It doesn't have to be named, or studied, or hunted; it just has to be there. And they have to be taught to miss it if it isn't there, the way they would miss electricity or the water supply if it were cut off.

The kind of seeing that this requires is much more aesthetic and imaginative than scientific. So for a start I should like the scientific element in our school-teaching about nature to be severely reduced and its place taken by study of the attitudes and vision of the many great painters, poets, and writers who have treated the subject. They are whom we need most to copy and to learn from, not the scientists. You can always tell the person who wants to experience nature from the one playing at being a scientist. The former will have granted equality to the whole scene, both in terms of the various families of natural life and in terms of the statistical commonness and rarity of what he is seeing. He or she won't, in short, be blind to all but his or her own field. He will know that he has to observe with both the eye of the flea and the eye of the elephant, as the Indian proverb goes. We all see too much with a human eye and to a human scale. He will see the moth's uncurled proboscis and the ancient glacier bed, the smallest and the largest; and all in one glance. He will see forms, colors, structures; see personal, artistic, and literary allusions; see whole poetries where the pseudo-scientist sees only names and matter for notes.

One of the curses of our time is that this poetic approach has come to be ridiculed as something rather romantic. It is true that without any scientific check, such an attitude can lead into the turgid bayous of "Nature Corner" sentiment or to the equally nauseating anthropomorphic scripts of the Disney nature films and the kind of commentary one hears at Marineland. If such cheap sentimentality were the only alternative to the scientific approach to nature, I should be all for science. But there is no more need to see nature *either* sentimentally *or* scientifically than there is to see paintings, or listen to music, or enjoy a game or sport in one of those two fixed manners.

And here, perhaps, there is a stumbling block particular to the American mind, with its inborn pragmatism, its demand for some immediate utility in both the object and its pursuit, and its corollary assumption that the more facts you know about a thing, the more there is likely to be in it for you. Europeans enjoy appearances. Americans enjoy things better if they know how they "work"—and of course knowing that involves knowing names. This obsession with labeling and functioning, and the corresponding impatience with the quieter pleasure of mere experiencing, is an aspect of what an American friend of mine once described to me as the single deepest fault of the national culture. He called it a lack of poetry, and then amplified the phrase by saying, "*We try to turn everything into machinery.*" Over the years I have come to see this criticism as a clue to a great deal of what is unhappy in American society.

This is not the place to discuss whether my friend was right in general. But I would choose *unpoetic* as probably the best word to describe the prevailing attitude towards natural life in the United States, just as *poetic* best describes the great exceptions to that generalization, the Audubons and the Thoreaus. Poetry, alas, is something you can't sell. All you can do is suggest that it is out there, if people will only find the time and the right frame of mind and discover for themselves that enjoyment does *not* require scientific knowledge.

Myself, I regard nature very largely as therapy. It is where I go to get away from words, from people, from artificial things. It is affection and friendship, too; the recurrence, the return in the cycle of the year, of certain flowers, beasts, birds, and insects I am fond of. It is sounds. It is curlew on a winter's evening, as I lie in bed. It is the sparrows that chirp on my roof each morning. Above all it is the familiar natural life that lives and breeds round my house—the kind of life any rarity-hunting naturalist would not even notice, it is so ordinary. But I have trained myself, partly through reading about Zen, partly through thinking on the texts of such men as Thoreau, not to take anything in my thousand-times-walked-round garden as familiar. I'm not in the least a religious person, but I suppose the process is something like prayer. You have to work at it. I once told a Benedictine monk that prayer was incomprehensible to me. "Yes," he said, "it was to me once. It becomes comprehensible only through endless repetition."

This, I am convinced, is what practical conservation needs behind it, or beneath it, if it is to work: a constantly repeated awareness of the mysterious other universe of nature in every civilized community. A love, or at least a toleration, of this other universe must reenter the urban experience, must be accepted as the key gauge of a society's humanity, and we must be sure that the reentry and the acceptance are a matter of personal, not public, responsibility. So much of our communal guilty conscience is taken up by the cruelty of man to man that the crime we are inflicting on nature is forgotten. Fortunately there seem to be many signs in the United States that this "lesser" crime against natural life at last is being recognized for what it is—not the lesser crime at all, but the real source of many things we cite as the major mistakes of recent history. You may think there is very little connection between spraying insecticide over your flower beds because everyone else on your street does the same, and spraying napalm over a Vietnamese village because that's the way war is. But many more things than we know start in our own backyards. Social aggression starts there; and so does social tolerance.

Nature is an inalienable part of human nature. We can never blaspheme against it alone. Exterminate, and you shall be exterminated. Don't care, and one day, perhaps too late, you or your children will be made to care bitterly. Evolution holds no special brief, no elect place for humankind. Its only favorite is the species that keeps its options open. The nightmare of our century is that so many of our options are closing on us. A main reason for this is that the individual increasingly lets society and its label-words usurp his or her own role and responsibility. We all know that we have to get things right between ourselves and the other forms of life on this crowded planet. What we don't, or won't, know is that the getting-right cannot be left to government, to the people who are paid to care. I make no apology for saying it again. Conservation can never be someone else caring. It is *you* caring. Now.

THE BLINDED EYE
(1971)

A sparrow's life's as sweet as ours.
Hardy clowns! grudge not the wheat
Which hunger forces birds to eat;
Your blinded eyes, worst foes to you,
Can't see the good which sparrows do.

JOHN CLARE, "SUMMER EVENING"

One September day I was standing with an American friend beside a small stream in the Massachusetts countryside. We were talking literary shop when suddenly, without warning either to him or to myself, I began running away like . . . I am afraid more like an excited ten-year-old than a bearded and not conspicuously slim man four times that age. I did not run very far because the thing I was chasing disappeared, like Hemingway's colonel, across the river and into the trees; and also because, as I could see by my friend's face when I turned, serious writers just don't break off conversations like that if they want to go on deserving the adjective.

He was not to know that I had just had my first living sight of the sublimest fancy, the summit of exquisite hope, of every British lepidopterist. During the last hundred years, 157 brave expatriate specimens of the milkweed (or monarch) butterfly, *Danaus plexippus*, have managed to get themselves netted over here; and where other small boys dreamed trains and aeroplanes, I used to dream black-veined whites, mazarine blues, and milkweeds. But though my first reaction was instinctive, I was not simply running, as my shocked friend supposed, after a large—and in the United States, quite common—tawny-brown butterfly. I was really running after a whole buried continent of memories . . . and also, I must confess, after a whole series of blind attitudes towards nature.

I began very young, as a butterfly collector, surrounded by setting-boards, killing-bottles, caterpillar cages. Then I went in for birds and compiled painstaking lists of the species I identified, an activity closer to writing down the makes of cars than to ornithology, though I suspect many misguided amateur bird watchers still think the spotting of rarities is what their hobby is about. From birds I moved on, in my teens, to botany; but I was still a victim of rarity snobbery, and for years hardly spared a second glance for any plant I had already ticked off as identified.

Then I went through a shooting-and-fishing phase, a black period in my relations to nature, and one that now, taught by Clare and Thoreau, I look back on with an angry shame. That phase ended dramatically one dusk when I was wildfowling in the Essex marshes. I winged a curlew. It fell in the mud beside the Thames, and I ran to pick it up. Curlew scream like children when they are wounded, and in too much haste I reversed my gun in order to snap the bird's head against the stock. The curlew flapped, the gun slipped, I grabbed for it. There was a violent explosion. And I was left staring down at a hole blasted in the mud not six inches from my left foot.

The next day I sold my gun. I have not intentionally killed a bird or an animal since.

Now when I observe myself, a specimen of that vicious parasitical predator *Homo sapiens*, I see that at one time or another I fell into all the great heresies of man's attitude towards nature.

First of all, I was a collector. One of the reasons I wrote—and named—my novel *The Collector* was to express my hatred of this lethal perversion. All natural-history collectors in the end collect the same thing: the death of the living. And in this age of "environmental control" (so often a barefaced euphemism for the annihilation of any species of life that threatens profit margins), collecting animate objects such as birds' eggs or insects for pleasure *must* be evil. No moral choice of our time is clearer.

Then, second, I succumbed to the heresy of destroying other life not to keep myself alive but for the pleasure of hunting and killing.

Finally, I was trapped by the subtlest temptation of them all, rarity chasing—still a form of destroying, though what is destroyed may be less the rarities themselves than the vain and narrow-minded fool who devotes all his time to their pursuit; who, in Clare's image, blinds his own eyes.

I suspect that this last abuse of nature is closely connected with the notion of nature as a "hobby." To my mind *hobby* is a deforming word—that is, it deforms anyone who uses it to describe his own relationship with natural life. Perhaps especially in Britain it has crippling connotations of the spare-time and the peripheral, of petty expertise, a clever little amateur skill at making or identifying. Only too often this hobby-mindedness engenders the vain (in both senses) attempt to ape a professional exponent in the field, and especially the established masters and ideals of yesterday—in other words, the very models and theories that any genuine contemporary professional (be he a biologist or a painter) is trying to escape, or at least to question. We can see this in the work turned out by people who go to amateur art classes. They are all trying to paint like Cézanne and van Gogh; and a great many natural-history hobbyists pick on equivalent gods, such as the great classifying naturalists of the Victorian period. Indeed, a kind of Linnaean nostalgia seems to hang over them. It is as if the whole ecological and ethological bias of the new field biology had never been developed—just as if, for the evening-class painter, Picasso (let alone Mondrian or Jackson Pollock) had never existed.

I saw recently an exhibition of an elderly woman painter's work, a genuine Essex primitive in the Grandma Moses line. The gallery owner told me that the great problem was keeping this gifted old lady away from art classes. She had no notion that her talent was remarkable precisely because it was so innocent. She thought she ought to be taught to paint better, not realizing that teaching is always teaching to imitate someone else. As she is, she is nature; and any "guidance" must be a form of pollution. This illustrates perfectly the deformation, the blinding, brought about by the hobby attitude to nature. It turns nature into a sort of golf course, where you go to amuse yourself at weekends; into the mirror in which you flaunt your skill at naming. It drains nature of its complexity, of its richness, of its poetries, of its symbolisms and correspondences, of its power to arouse emotion—of all its potential centrality in human existence. And far worse than the damage it does to the misguided natural historian is the damage it does to the vast majority who are neutral or indifferent towards nature. If this is the one avenue of approach, then it is no wonder they shrug and turn away.

. . .

Some fifteen years ago I became interested in Zen Buddhism; and among other debts I owe to that very un-European philosophy is the way it brought me to examine the Western attitude towards nature. I came to the conclusion that we ordinary nature lovers have had a miserably one-sided vision of the proper relationship between the human and the natural worlds foisted on us by our science—though rather less by our genuine scientists than by their amateur fellow travelers.

Our illusion is that nature *must* be dryly classified and its behaviorisms analyzed like so much clockwork. Or rather, since of course I am not denying the necessity and utility of this approach in its proper context, our illusion is that this is the only *serious* relationship we can have—the implication's being that any other relationship must be fundamentally superficial and dilettantish. I find this view ominously like that of our science-besotted Victorian ancestors, who thought that if you knew that *Luscinia megarhynchos* laid eggs averaging twenty-one millimeters in their longest diameter, you were far more highly evolved in your understanding of nature than poor Keats, who knew no better than to write an ode to *Luscinia*—vulgarly called the nightingale.

I believe myself that Keats's attitude to the nightingale had very arguably more *scientific* validity than that of the worthy gentlemen who pursued the bird with their brass dividers and rulers. All the hard taxonomic facts in the world don't begin to add up to the reality of the nightingale; and if a visitor from outer space wanted to know that reality, he would do much better with the ode than with *The Handbook of British Birds*. The greatness of the ode as a piece of science is precisely that it decompartmentalizes the phenomenon; it discusses manbird, not just man and not just bird. Today, with all our talk of the global village and the world environment, we ought to see its relevance; we ought to see that the lack of a right ordinary *human* attitude towards nature has become of far greater moment for effective conservation than any accurate scientific knowledge about this or that species. We know quite enough facts now; where we are still miserably retarded is in our emotional and aesthetic relationship to wildlife.

Nature is a sort of art *sans* art; and the right human attitude to it ought to be unashamedly poetic rather than scientific.

Such a bald statement may sound dangerously like the Romantic movement's theory of nature (Nature with a capital *N* as an evoker of beautiful and noble sentiments), a theory memorable when transmitted by genius but only too repulsive when couched in the purple prose of debased "Nature Corner" journalism. Ours is not the age for beautiful, noble sentiments about anything, let alone nature. For all that, I think we, in our present, vilely polluted world, had better think twice before we sneer the Romantic theory into oblivion.

It came, we might remember, as a reaction against an age very much like our own: a highly cerebral and artificial period, and one that would have raped nature quite as abominably as ourselves if it had had the technology and population to hand. And the theory did two other things. First, it reasserted the identity of humankind and nature and the dangers of splitting that identity. Most important of all, it suggested, both explicitly and implicitly, that the celebration and health of that state of identity were much more a matter for art than for science. The very nature of science is to split, to break down, to reduce to a special context; and the only human science of comprehensive reality is art. Let me give an illustration, from that famous ode by Keats I mentioned just now. These lines:

The voice I hear this passing night was heard
In ancient days by emperor and clown:
Perhaps the selfsame song that found a path
Through the sad heart of Ruth, when, sick for home,
She stood in tears amid the alien corn. . . .

Lines we all know (though we may have forgotten that here *clown*, as in my opening quotation, means "peasant" and not "buffoon"), and lines that may seem to you to have no scientific validity at all. But what I see in them, besides great verse, is a classic statement about the situation of humanity in evolution. Both science and our everyday lives make us exist in the now—horizontally, so to speak, not vertically back "down" through time. And then we are evolving much more rapidly than any other species on our planet: our thrust is ever onward and forward. Both these factors tend to detach us from the stable flow of evolution; we have lost contact with our earth, in every sense of the word. The urban world is everywhere too much with us, so that the experience of nature becomes almost a historical, "antique" sensation, like standing inside a Norman castle or an

Elizabethan house. A wry-minded New York friend put it very succinctly to me the other day in my garden, when he heard the blackbirds and thrushes singing. He saw one and turned to me. "Good God, you mean they're *not* recordings?"

Keats's point, of course, is that they are indeed in a sense recordings. My friend and I could have been taken back through two, through ten hundred years of May evening; and very probably we should have heard exactly the same sounds. More and more it is this stable evolutionary continuum that I see in nature, this plunging back like a knife through recorded time, to Ruth amid the alien corn. Nature was born not for death, but to remind us of the continuity of life. It is a kind of brake, a sanctuary, a system of landmarks in time; a check on our craze for meaningless "progress."

The practical point I am trying to make, behind all this rather abstract literary stuff, is that our education about nature remains much too oriented towards scientific views and ends. Of course, intending professional scientists must be trained; but I don't see why the rest of our children (those well-known fathers of men) have to suffer on their behalf. They need much more an education in human relationships to nature, in humanity's responsibility to other forms of life; and the clues and roads to that lie far more in the work of the countless great artists, both literary and visual, who have tried to define and expand this key relationship, than in the recognition of species and the explanation of behaviorisms.

Science may understand nature; but it can never understand what nature requires of us. Of that, poets like Wordsworth and Keats knew more in the tips of their little fingers than all the biologists in creation.

It is, alas, unrealistic to hope to persuade born name-droppers such as Europeans and Americans that knowing the name of a thing has extraordinarily little to do with its intrinsic beauty and value; and I will not attempt to plead for the extreme Zen Buddhist position, which quite simply states that the name of an object is like a pane of dirty glass between it and you. We of the West are conditioned to need some background knowledge of the objects of our appreciation. But our contemporary addiction to such information is unhealthy—as if a nameless flower cannot be worth looking at, as if this saltcellar by Cellini can't be enjoyed until we have checked in the guide that it really is a masterpiece.

I think the first thing to gain, in the appreciation of nature as well as of art, is confidence in one's ability to see beauty for oneself. This has certainly never been more difficult. Like all successful species, the human attracts parasites, and in this category I number many functions of the mass communications media. They are the lice that infect our minds, all eager to tell us what to admire, all eager to see and think for us. Just as the car and the plane have made us physically lazy and cholesterol-prone, so does all this appreciation molding induce a fatal hardening of the observational arteries. To that must be added the high program priority (especially in nature films) put upon the exotic and the rare. I look forward to the day when the BBC will spare us a trip to the Galapagos or the Great Barrier Reef and give us a series on common British garden birds; look forward to it, but don't expect it, I'm afraid. We have very little national genius for seeing the familiar with fresh eyes—another ability, let me add, more commonly found in poets than in scientists.

But here nature has at least one thing on its side. Unlike art, it is uncomposed and ever-changing, and therefore not nearly so amenable to appreciation molding. Anyone who has kept up with his or her culture will find it difficult to see famous paintings with a fresh eye; but nature inherently forces the new appreciation on us. It obliges us to make poetic judgments.

Above all, we need to learn to distinguish our total human awareness of a natural phenomenon from our specifically scientific knowledge about it. In the field, so to speak, I find that this scientific knowledge usually presents itself first. If I see a bird, its name (or my uncertainty about it) is my first reaction; then the typicality and likely explanation of its behavior, assessed against my previous knowledge of the species. But unless it or its behavior is very unusual, this scientific processing is very rapid—a second or two at most. From then on I let the poetry take over. Now, this poetry is very complex. It has to do with pure movement, sound, shape, color; it has to do with the framework, blue sky for this buzzard, bramble thicket for this warbler, in which the bird is. It has to do with what other birds are about and what flowers, what awareness of the place I have, what season it is—the migrant's arriving or departing—what mood I am in. It has also very much to do with previous history, since just as nature can take me back through time and turn history on its side, so can many species of bird, butterfly, and flower lead me back through the maze of my own life.

I will try now to describe what it is like, and I shall probably make it sound too conscious a process, a calculated system of free association. But the only really conscious part of it is my rejection of the narrowly or-nithological or botanical approach. I believe in fact that this is the natural and normal way of seeing wildlife; its effect on us, and probably in strict inverse proportion to our scientific knowledge, is largely emotive and aes-thetic.

A North London garden. Winter. A spot of cerise, gray, and black, in an old pear tree. I am standing at a window, there is snow on the ground. A cock bullfinch. A sporadic winter visitor to outlying city gardens: not un-usual. Looking for clematis or forsythia buds; or honeysuckle berries. A week ago, in Dorset, I counted twenty-seven cock bullfinches in a grove of bullace. The bullace in blossom. Bullace jam. "Whistling" bullfinch—I could do it as a boy. A Devonshire combe and our cottage there. Waking up and hearing the whistles very close and looking out and seeing six cock bullfinches sitting in the first sunlight on an apple tree. That apple tree, with its yellow-green, smoky-tasting apples no one ever knew the name of. That same bullace grove in summer. I lie in the shade there and a bullfinch sings overhead: its strange, monotonous little five-note fluting chant. Like Webern. Like a last cardinal, in the freezing wind on the dying pear tree. The future, a jet heading for Heathrow, whines over. I feel de-pressed. I have a busy day I don't want ahead. I hate cities, and summer will never come again. The bullfinch drops down into the garden. A flash of white rump. Then nothing, I can't see it anymore. A squirt of green mem-ories, like a brief taste on the tongue. But enough to keep me going, the bitter and dull day through.

Or this, something rarer. Late May, on the fringe of an Oxfordshire beech wood, sunshine, growing half-shaded under a whitebeam. A fly or-chid. I have seen this species only twice before in my life. Once during training, during the war. Flinging myself and the Bren I was carrying to the ground and there, a foot from my face, was my first fly orchid and I had twenty seconds to enjoy it before a Royal Marines sergeant (when he was drunk he used to chew razor blades, his mouth dribbling blood) shouted us up and on. The second time I saw it I was with a girl, and botany was the last thing on my mind. And now it is here again, mysteriously survived and resurrected; and when I find my fourth *Ophrys muscifera* I shall re-member this, my wife kneeling beside me, the Chiltern sunshine, the good day; and the second time again, and the first.

This highly associative and personal relationship with natural phenomena may seem, to many scientists, narcissistic and introverted. But the one thing it does not breed is selfishness; what it creates is an intense need and affection for the *direct* experience of nature. And that, in my opinion, is the only kind of soil in which a really effective general social demand for conservation can grow. It is no good the scientists' alone wanting to defend wildlife from industry and overpopulation; the human in the street has to want it as well.

Always we try to put the wild in a cage: if not a literal cage of iron, then cages of banality, of false parallels, of anthropomorphic sentimentality, of lazy thinking and lazy observation.

For this reason I am far from convinced that pet-keeping has the good educational value some teachers maintain. Personally I hate the pet mania, as I mistrust zoos and all other compromises between humans and nature in the wild. Once, in Crete, I was climbing a mountain alone. Heavy snowdrifts made me give up the attempt to reach the top, but before I began the descent I lay down on my back between two boulders in order to rest out of the icy wind. A minute passed. Then, with an abruptness that stopped my breath, I was not alone. A huge winged shape was hanging in the air some twenty feet above my head. It looked like an enormous falcon, its great wings feathering and flexed to the wind current, a savage hooked beak tilted down at me. I lay as still as stone, like Sinbad under the roc. For some ten seconds the great bird and I were transfixed, in a kind of silent dialogue. I knew it was a lammergeier, one of Europe's largest birds of prey—a species few ornithologists have seen in the wild at all, let alone from a few feet away. Ten seconds, and then it decided I was alive and swung a mile away in one great sweep on rigid wings.

Now, I could easily go to a zoo and see the lammergeiers they have there. But I have never done so. Although I accept that the bored eagles and vultures of our zoos cannot, lacking an imagination, be bored in fact, *I* suffer when I see them. I used the word *dialogue* just now. What passed between me and that splendid bird in the azure Cretan sky was simply this: Cage me, cage yourself.

I know that encaging is not the worst of our crimes against nature in this century; and that for some danger-list species it has now become the only hope of survival. Indeed I have only to go back to the woodlands I knew as a boy in the 1930s to see the greater crime: how once-common birds are now rarities, how glades once full of butterflies are now empty of them, sunlight without wings. Here, as in every other heavily farmed area in the world, the silences and motionlessnesses of a dead planet begin to steal up on us.

This guilt, which we all must share, makes it impossible now to write of nature except in terms of lamentation and sermon. I have very little hope for any form of real progress that is not broadly based on the pleasure principle. The archetypal human demand, when faced with change, has always been "What's in it for me?—that is, "What new pleasure shall I get?" And this is the strongest argument for trying to change ordinary attitudes towards nature from the pseudo-scientific to the poetic, from the general to the personal.

Poetry, then, not science; or rather, just as much science, as much knowledge of names and natural machinery, as the poetry requires. For we must learn to accept that nature is always in the end mysterious, a place where the killers and collectors and name tickers will finally see nothing, hear nothing, and understand nothing.

The deepest thing we can learn about nature is not how it works, but that it is *the poetry of survival*. The greatest reality is that the watcher has survived and the watched survives. It is the timelessness woven through time, the cross-weft of all being that passes. Nobody who has comprehended this can feel alone in nature, can ever feel the absolute hostility of time. However strange the land or the city or the personal situation, some tree, some bird, some flower will still knit us into this universe that all we brief-lived things cohabit; will mesh us into the great machine. That is why I love nature: because it reconciles me with the imperfections of my own condition, of our whole human condition, of the all that is. My freedom depends totally on its freedom. Without my freedom, I should not want to live.

One day last February I stood with Rex Cowan, two divers, and a boatman in one of the most splendid seascapes in Britain, among the reefs west of Annet in the Isles of Scilly. It was a fine day, with very little swell; just enough to give white water on the black-serried granite fangs that stretched away in all directions. A few miles west rose the brave toy pinnacle of the loneliest of all lighthouses, the Bishop's Rock; razorbills dived, gannets glided majestically overhead, all around us amiable brown faces watched from the water . . . and one young seal, a friend of the divers', yawned exactly like some dog impatient for a game. Difficult to imagine a place less tainted or more pleasurable on such a day; yet we floated in the very heart of what may well be the most terrible ten square miles in maritime history. It was not only that we were anchored even then over a wreck—the *Hollandia* of 1743, with its cargo of silver pieces-of-eight and ducatoons. We could have anchored anywhere else in that area and still been over a wreck; in some places, layers of wrecks.

Rex the well-named began to point. Every rock, every islet, every reef

1. This essay was written to introduce a book of extremely fine shipwreck photographs taken by the Gibsons of Scilly. The cover note to *Shipwreck* tells us that "Gibsons have lived on the Scilly Isles since the seventeenth century. In the early 1860s John Gibson, a seaman, taught himself between voyages to use the very recently invented camera. By 1866 John had quit the sea and set up as a professional; his son Alexander, a self-taught scholar, join[ed] him in the business a few years later at the age of fourteen. It was Alexander who brought a perfectionism to the arrangement of his pictures and often with great skill retouched his plates. Alexander's son, James, acquired all the shipwreck plates after a quarrel which resulted in his father retiring to the mainland. John Gibson died in 1920 at the age of ninety-three; and now James's son Frank carries on the tradition of photographing the sea and recording the many dramatic shipwrecks that still occur around those menacing coasts."

had its long roll of sinister honor. That lazy lash of white over a black speck was the Retarrier, where the German liner *Schiller* struck one dreadful night in 1875, and 335 men and women drowned; and there the Crebinicks, the Crims, the Gunners, the Crebawethans; Rosevean and Rosevear, where down the centuries hundreds of sailors have wished they had been drowned rather than marooned; the ill-named Jolly, Jacky's Rock, Gorregan, the Gilstone, which claimed the *Association* in 1707, heralding the worst disaster the Royal Navy has ever suffered out of action (two thousand officers and men drowned in one night) . . . it was like a great gathering of murderers. Rex talked so fast I couldn't catch all the names. Only the same monotonous verb: *struck, struck, struck*. Our boatman and the divers knew these waters better than most of us know the streets of our hometown, yet they had to join in as well, point to more reefs, add more calamities. The past agony of some places drowns all present, and forevermore.

Proportionate to their size, no islands in the world have a more lethal record than the Scillies; and few mainland coasts can, in this dark rivalry, surpass those of West Cornwall. In the case of the Scillies, the game was for long cruelly fixed against mariners. Before 1750 almost all charts, lazily copying ancient error, showed the islands ten miles north of their true position. The second black joke of the sea was not fully appreciated until very recently. An oceanic drift, the Rennell Current, sets round the Bay of Biscay and runs across the mouth of the English Channel. It is a knot an hour at most, but that is quite enough to push ships north of their supposed course. The Rennell, and not a wrong course by chart, almost certainly landed the *Schiller* on the Retarrier Ledges in 1875. All shipping to and from North Europe had and has to cope with the Scillies, and they have been nothing if not international in the toll they have taken through the centuries. A perennial problem with incoming vessels in the days of dead reckoning (that is, establishing position by log and course steered, and not by sextant) was the need to make a recognizable landfall and know which of the two great channels, the Bristol or the English, one was in. An entire East Indies fleet in 1703 expected one morning to see themselves off Portsmouth; what rose out of their dawn was Lundy. In 1758 the captain of the French man-of-war *Belliqueux* paid for his bad navigation, since the Royal Navy pounced like a cat on this foolish mouse. The *Association* fleet was forty miles north of its supposed position, established by a conference of sailing masters four hours previously, when it struck. Defoe put the situation precisely in his *Tour*: "These islands lye so in the middle between the two vast openings that it cannot, or perhaps never will be avoided"—as the *Torrey Canyon* was to discover in 1967.

The frequency of disaster, the remoteness, the atrocious economic disregard the rest of England always had for the Cornish and the Scillonians, gave rise to the very ancient occupation of wrecking. Properly the word has two meanings: wreck-inducing and wreck-plundering. The vast majority of the stories to do with the first activity—the false lights ("horn beacons" were lamps attached to a wandering cliff-top cow), the true beacons that suffered a mysterious fuel crisis when they were most needed—are poorly attested or were distorted out of all proportion by the early advocates (well-to-do gentlemen, then as now) of law and order. Hawker of Morwenstow enshrined some of the names in verse and story: Cruel Coppinger, the Killigrews, Mawgan of Melhuach, Featherstone. He wrote one of his best curses on the last:

Twist thou and twine! in light and gloom
  A spell is on thine hand;
The wind shall be thy changeful loom,
  Thy web the shifting sand.

Twine from this hour, in ceaseless toil,
  On Blackrock's sullen shore;
Till cordage of the sand shall coil
  Where crested surges roar.

'Tis for that hour, when, from the wave,
  Near voices wildly cried;
When thy stern hand no succour gave,
  The cable at thy side.

Twist thou and twine! in light and gloom
  The spell is on thine hand;
The wind shall be thy changeful loom,
  Thy web the shifting sand.

Splendid stuff; but most of the anathema from Hawker and his kind was directed against legend rather than fact—if we are speaking of the deliberately induced wreck. The second crime, of not striving officiously to keep alive, is less easy to dismiss. In earlier times every sailor wrecked on these coasts knew he had two ordeals to survive: the sea and the men on shore, with little likelihood that the second would be kinder than the first. The real criminal here was Cornish ignorance of the law of dereliction. A very old and very bad statute, whose gist in a seventeenth-century formulation ran "neither bird nor beast having escaped, for if anything had escaped alive, 'tis not to be adjudged Wreck," was taken as gospel in Cornwall long after it had lapsed elsewhere. It was to establish this definition—or invitation to murder—that first-instance survivors were sometimes knocked on the head and returned to the sea. The admiral of the *Association* fleet, Sir Cloudesley Shovell, is said to have reached land alive, and to have required a hasty redrowning—though his own press-ganged, lower-deck men are quite as likely to have done that as the Scilly Islanders. But there are two much more recent and better-authenticated stories.

One concerns a Scillies wreck of the mid–nineteenth century. Two islanders on an abandoned ship were seen to throw a dog overboard and watch it drown. When reproached for their cruelty, they claimed the wreck would not have been "dead" unless they had done it; and in his defense one of the men astonishingly quoted the relevant phrase from the original Plantagenet law. The second story is even more incredible. The steamer *Delaware* went aground during a huge storm in December 1871, near Bryher in the Scillies. Two survivors were seen to drift ashore on the uninhabited islet of Samson. Ten Bryher men—the old islanders were among the best handlers of small boats in rough seas in the world—managed, after superhuman efforts and with appalling risk to their own lives, to row a gig across to the islet. They were met with gratitude? Not at all, but by two terrified sailors with stones in their hands, convinced that their real fight for survival was still to come. Perhaps the most remarkable thing about this 1871 story is that the two men were not ignorant fo'c'sle hands, but respectively the first and third mates of the steamer.

The heroism (no isolated instance, and Bryher has a particularly fine record) of the rescuers that day is quite certainly more typical for all Cornwall, at any rate since 1800, than the stories of cold-blooded murder and deaf ears when "near voices wildly cried." The much more probable historical truth of the matter is summed up by a charming prayer—and conditional clause—composed in the Scillies in the late eighteenth century: "We pray Thee, O Lord, not that wrecks should happen, but that if any wreck should happen, Thou wilt guide them into the Scilly Isles for the benefit of the inhabitants." The girls of Tristan da Cunha had one very similar, if more frank: "Please God send me a wreck, that I may marry."

The third charge is of wreck-plundering, after the lives have been duly saved. Here, the only answer can be guilty. There are far too many eyewitness accounts of Cornish rapacity—indeed far more wreckers were themselves drowned looting than sailors murdered—to exculpate them. They would even board wrecks in the same seas that had caused their crews to abandon them. When there was wreckers' weather ("A savage sea and a shattering wind, / The cliffs before and the gale behind,'" according to an old couplet), whole villages, thousands of men and women with lanterns and axes and crowbars, with carts, wheelbarrows and sacks, would assemble like vultures; and follow a ship in trouble, for days if need be, along the coast. Even the largest vessels could be dismantled and stripped bare as a bone in twenty-four hours. The tin-miners were the most feared; no cliff, no storm, no night deterred them from getting to work once the ship had struck. Nor very often would they brook interference from magistrates or the military. . . . The gentry themselves were not proof to the mania; fine carriages as well as carts often flocked to the corpse. Even the excise men were suspect. Another story from the *Delaware* wreck of 1871 tells how the Chief Customs Officer of the Scillies prosecuted two men for looting— while his own backyard was full of drying bolts of silk. To add insult to corruption, for many months afterwards he was not seen smoking anything but fine Manila cheroots.

The most famous of all such stories concerns the parson whose Sunday sermon was interrupted by the cry of "Wreck!" outside. His congregation leapt to their feet as one man. "One moment, my friends!" bellowed the reverend gentleman from the pulpit, as he struggled frantically to remove his surplice. "Let's all start fair."

Every respectable authority dismisses the story as apocryphal; mere foreign (i.e., English) prejudice. But I suspect it is one of those inventions that are truer than the truth; and perhaps I had better mention here that I have wreckers in my own ancestry, and even living to this day an "Armada" uncle—dark-skinned, and sure proof in family legend that at least one foundered Spanish sailor ended up in a Cornish bed rather than in (another foul lie from the wrong side of the Tamar) a Cornish pasty.

More seriously, all this ambivalence about personal and legal rights goes back to the ancient importance, in a rim-of-the-world economy, of benefit of wreck. This right was a major feature in many Cornish and Scillonian rent-rolls of the Middle Ages, and gave rise to ferocious disputes, sure sign of the profits involved, over boundaries and ownership of flotsam, jetsam, lagan (or wreckage on the seabed), and the rest. I think today we may see it as a facet of the eternal struggle between the over- and the under-privileged. You cannot starve and ignore and despise a region to the permanent brink of famine and then expect it to wish the fattest ships in the world a safe journey past its shores; or to show fine scruples when some of the fat is washed up at its door. However much one respects the law, however deeply one is touched by the anguished tears of the ship owners, I think one has to see a kind of profound equity, with the sea standing in the place of Robin Hood, in the phenomenon. I do not defend wrecking; but even less could I defend the gross social and economic selfishness of the ages and central governments in and under which the practice flourished most strongly.

That these reefs and coasts remain hungry, we still have evidence every year. But in the days of sail, and even of early steam, the statistics (if not the pollutions) were far worse. Between 1864 and 1869, the Lloyd's registers give a world loss of ten thousand sailing ships. In 1856 alone, 1,153 vessels were lost round the British coasts (and the figure for British ships lost abroad in that same year is only ten less). In *one* day of a great gale in 1859, 195 ships foundered; another 298 ships were lost in the terrible November of 1893. A great lack was of lighthouses. Before 1800, there were only four in all Cornwall, and two of them were coal-cresset beacons—the Lizard and Saint Agnes in the Scillies. The most-needed light in the world, the Bishop's Rock, was not finally in operation—after an extraordinary epic of Victorian engineering—until 1858. (On April 20, 1874, in a gigantic storm, the largest waves were drowning the lantern a hundred feet above the normal sea and reflecting the light back into the keepers' eyes— the worst ordeal, the two men said, of their lives . . . and one believes them.)

Fortunately, if tragically, we know very well what it was like to be shipwrecked in the eighteenth and nineteenth centuries. Perhaps no form of human misery is so extensively recorded, and in every detail. No Royal Navy ship went down without a subsequent court-martial of the senior survivor, and of course commercial ship owners generally (but not always, for reasons I will explain in a moment) wanted full investigation from the Marine Courts. There was also the public fascination—shipwreck stories were once as popular as thrillers and sci-fi novels are today—to say nothing of the need of the survivors, and of ghostwriters with an eye for easy money, to relate their adventures. I will quote just one splendid title of the kind from 1838: *Shipwreck of the* Stirling Castle, *containing a Faithful Narrative of the Dreadful Sufferings of the Crew, and the Cruel Murder of Captain Fraser by the Savages. Also, the Horrible Barbarity of the Cannibals inflicted upon the Captain's Widow, whose unparalleled Sufferings are stated by herself, and corroborated by the Other Survivors.* I own a copy of this classic fragment of Australiana; and so also must that fine painter Sidney Nolan, who has immortalized poor, naked Mrs. Frazer in another way.

The most terrible experience must have been the catastrophe out of nowhere, at night or in fog. Again and again one reads the same story. There is a cry from forward of "Breakers ahead!"; then desperate commands to the helmsman, a wild scramble to get sails reset, to come up into the wind (which is why so many sailing ships in these circumstances first struck aft, missing stays and drifting impotently back). The masts sometimes helped if they crashed on impact and so formed a bridge of sorts, however precarious, to land. The more familiar prelude to disaster—storm—at least allowed crew and passengers to prepare themselves both psychologically and nautically for the worst.

Off mainland Cornwall the battle was sometimes prolonged for days when ships were caught inshore by a gale and fought desperately to beat out to windward. Some masters in this embayed situation would strike all sail and topmasts to reduce windage, and then anchor; but the old rope cables were not good and often parted. When the moment of truth came, all a captain could do was steer for beach or least precipitous cliff. Many times the ship struck and foundered as she came in, or, most feared of all, turned beam on and capsized. After losing all her anchors, the frigate *Anson* did exactly this in 1807 at Loe Bar, and 120 men were drowned close to shore.

I mentioned earlier that navigational techniques were only too literally hit-or-miss. The situation improved when an accurate chronometer became available in 1772, but well into Victorian times many shipmasters were far from skilled with the sextant. Then there was the condition of the ships themselves. Before Samuel Plimsoll's Merchant Shipping Act of 1876, they were often sent out criminally overladen, undermanned, and rotten-timbered. Sailors had a name for them: coffin ships. On a lee shore or in heavy seas, that was only too often precisely what they were—and also precisely what their astutely overinsured owners hoped they would be. This atrocious practice was rife, and Plimsoll deserves to be remembered for far more than his "line." The early steamships were not always much safer. Many were underpowered in relation to their size, and became unmanageable in heavy seas. Their boilers also had a nasty habit of exploding when really put to the test.

Nor in the nineteenth century was the standard of seamen good. As with the wreckers, one can discover extenuating circumstances: vile wages, peculating chandlers, brutal mates and masters. But the poor quality of the crews that the average captain had to work with gave unnecessarily steep odds. One of the finest, because so plainly written, shipwreck accounts of the period is that of Thomas Cubbin. He was the experienced master of a sound merchantman, the *Serica*, but he ran into a hurricane off Mauritius in 1868. Long before he abandoned ship, his crew virtually mutinied; they tried to get at the liquor store, they refused to work the pumps. "We're all equal now," said one of them. Yet with a single exception (that old focus of gossip and sedition, the ship's cook), his was not a particularly bad crew; the impression one gets today is that they were far more demoralized than truly mutinous.

There is, from dry land, great poetry and drama about the shipwreck; but no sailor would let me suggest that the amusement of an audience is the heart of the matter. That heart lies, as it always has lain and always will lie, in the terror and despair, in the drowned, in the appalling suffering of the survived, the bravery of the rescuers. We should never forget that; and yet . . . I should like to go now into the calmer, though deeper and darker, waters of why the spectacle of the shipwreck is so pleasing—why, in short, there is a kind of Cornish wrecker in every single one of us.

Our private attitude towards communal disaster, the joint death of other people, could be regarded as unalloyedly humanitarian only by a supreme optimist; yet I should not like to call it, short of the pathological extreme, unhealthy. There is the Christian view: we feel pity for the victims. There is the Aristotelian: we feel purged, and go away better people. And so on, until we come down to the cynical: it is all a matter of schadenfreude, and at least the population problem is relieved a little. But I'm not sure that the most important reaction is not the instinctive: thank God this did not happen to me. In other words, we derive from the spectacle of calamity a sense of personal survival—as also, however tenuously, intimations of the metaphysical sea of hazard on which we all sail.

Perhaps one should not distinguish among train and air crashes, motorway pileups, and all the other downstrokes that the traveler is prone to; yet there is something rather special about the shipwreck, and I think not simply because it usually has a longer agony and a longer aftermath than death on land and in the air. The sea seems less greedy, for a start. Humanity's ability to endure in it against all the odds is a strange and incalculable thing; so many drowned men have crawled up a beach or been picked up in small boats weeks after they were consigned by all probability to Davy Jones's bottomless locker. But more important—at least for us spectators—than this intermittent show of mercy is surely the emotional symbolism.

This springs from two things: the nature of the sea and the nature of the ship. No other element has such accreted layers of significance for us, such complex archetypal meaning. The sea's moods and uses sex it. It is the great creatrix, feeder, womb and vagina, place of pleasure; the gentlest thing on earth, the most maternal; the most seductive whore, and handsomely the most faithless. It has the attributes of all women, and all men too. It can be subtle and noble, brave and energetic; and far crueler than the meanest, most sadistic human king who ever ruled. ("I believe in the Bible," an old sailor once told Lord Fisher, "because it don't mention no sea in Paradise.") I happen to live over the sea myself; I watch it every day, I hear it every night. I do not like it angry, but I've noticed that most urban and inland people adore it so. Storms and gales seem to awaken something joyous and excited in them: the thunder on the shingle, the spray and spume, the rut and rage.

No doubt this is partly a product of a life where the elements have largely receded out of daily notice; but I think it goes deeper, into a kind of Freudian double identification, in which the wrath of the sea is interpreted both as superego and as id. It is on the one hand a thing without restraint, a giant bull in a salt ring; on the other it is the great punisher of presumption, the patriarch who cuts that green stripling, man, down to size. It is strangely—or perhaps not so strangely, in these days of the universal oil slick—as if we had committed a crime against the sea by ever leaving it in the first place; and as if we liked to be told (through convenient scapegoats, of course) that we merit retribution for our ambitious folly. In its rages we admire the total lack of reason and justice, the blindness to all but the laws of its own nature; and quite naturally, since similar feelings and desires lurk deep inside our own minds. A wrecking sea is part of what we all dream ourselves to be every night; and the ship becomes our own puny calculations, our repressions, our compromises, our kowtowings to convention, duty, and a dozen other idols of the top-hamper we call civilization. A psychiatrist tells me that a morbid obsession with disaster is a common defense against depression; its enjoyment brings a vicarious sense of manic triumph over normal reality. So the shipwreck is not only what we are thankful will never happen to us; it is also what we secretly want to happen, and finally to ourselves.

The other great nexus of metaphors and feeling is the ship itself. No human invention, with all its associated crafts in building and handling, has an older history—or has received more love. That is why we have sexed it without ambiguity, at least in the West; which in this context casts the sea, the domain of Neptune, as raper, berserker, Bluebeard. Even our judgment of a ship's beauty has tended to be that of the male upon the female—that is, we put a greater value on outward line than on soul or utility, and nowhere more than with the last of the sailing ships, that splendid and sharply individualized zenith of five thousand years' worth of hard-earned knowledge and aesthetic instinct. The vocabulary of the aeroplane seduced us for a while; but I think it is interesting that we have come back to star- and space-*ships. Jet* will do for a transport shorthand; yet when man really reaches, across the vast seas of space, he still reaches in ships. Other words may function as well; no other has the poetries.

All this leads me to believe that there is, with the kind of shipwreck I have been talking about here, a nobler constituent in our fascination: a genuine sadness. They are lost craft in both senses of the noun; they are failed hopes, ventures, destinies, but also shattered monuments to countless generations of anonymous shipwrights and sailmakers, as tragic in their way as the vanished masterpieces of great sculptors.

Just as there are found objects, so are there agonized ones. The mist comes down on the drowned *Mildred*, her masts and ultimate sails rise from the appeased water like an epitaph, a cross of remembrance, a lovely assemblage of rope construct and canvas cutout, pre-echoing Matisse and Naum Gabo. . . . We have our monuments to the Unknown Soldier; will anyone ever give us a more beautiful celebration of the Lost Ship?

ISLANDS

(1978)

The wise visitor to the Scillies does not drive straight to Penzance and board a helicopter or a ship, but instead finds time, so long as the weather is clear and the visibility good, to go out first to Land's End. And there they float, an eternal stone armada of over a hundred ships, aloofly anchored off England; mute, enticing, forever just out of reach. The effect is best later in the day, when they lie in the westering sun's path, more like optical illusions, mirages, than a certain reality. I say "they," but the appearance at this range is of one island; which has a justice in it, since in remote antiquity all the larger islands except Saint Agnes very probably were conjoined.

At Land's End you already stand on territory haunted by much earlier humankind. Their menhirs and quoits and stone lines brood on the moors and in the granite-walled fields; and even today the Scillies can in certain lights lose the name we now call them by and rebecome the Hesperidean Islands of the Blest, Avalon, Lyonesse, Glasinnis, the Land of the Shades; regain all the labels that countless centuries of Celtic folklore and myth have attached to them. Adam and Eve braved the sea, probably as long as four thousand years ago. Their burial places are scattered all over the present islands, and so densely in places that one suspects the Scillies must have been the ultimate Forest Lawn of megalithic Britain, though interment there would have been an ambition not only of the dying: the spirits of the dead could not cross water, and the living may well have cherished that thirty-mile *cordon sanitaire* between themselves and their ancestors. Whatever the reason, the islands hold an astounding concentration of nearly one fifth of all such tombs in England and Wales—far more than Cornwall, which is already rich in them.

Some of the great boulders (naturally carved by Atlantic wind and rain, split and isolated by the Ice Age) that the earliest settlers found there would have profoundly impressed, and baffled, them. They are so splendidly wrought and monumental—especially on Gugh and the south side of Saint Agnes—that it is as if some earlier incarnation of Henry Moore had played a huge joke (in one case a huge phallic joke) on posterity. The pluperfect one lies on the furze moor just above Porth Askin, exquisitely posed and pedestaled in a rainwater pool. It would grace the forecourt of any twentieth-century skyscraper; and, much higher praise, not disgrace the most fastidious Zen garden. Perhaps it was these magnificent stones that seeded the legend of the lost land of Lyonesse and the associated myth of Atlantis; of a simpler, nobler, vanished world and culture.

There is a more likely origin of the legend. The ancient Celtic inhabitants of Cornwall and the islands almost certainly had contacts with a culture if not nobler, at least more advanced, whose ships would have appeared out of the southwest, even though their homeland lay in quite another direction. The Phoenicians were the great trading, exploring, and seagoing race of antiquity. According to Strabo, they discovered the Atlantic sometime before 1000 B.C.; their colony at Cadiz dates from about that time. By an irony, they were both the most commercial and the most mysterious of ancient civilizations—mysterious because they left so few traces of their existence. Their barter-currency presumably lay most in perishable goods, which makes them the despair of archaeologists. What is quite definitely known is that they coveted tin, which they used not only as a metal but as a dye mordant (stannous chloride); and that they regarded its British source as one of their most precious trade secrets. The Phocian Greeks who colonized Marseilles in about 600 B.C. discovered this source at some later date; and Herodotus knew that the tin came from islands called the Cassiterides (from the Greek *kassyo*, "to stitch together," and *kassiteros*, "tin"), but otherwise only that they were located somewhere very far off in northern Europe. The first coherent account was by Diodorus Siculus, writing in the first century B.C.:

> *The inhabitants of that part of Britain which is called Balerium [Land's End] are very fond of strangers, and from their intercourse with foreign merchants, are civilized in their manner of life. They prepare the tin, working very carefully the earth in which it is produced. The ground is rocky, but it contains earthy veins, the produce of which is ground down, smelted, and*

purified. They beat the metal into masses shaped like astralgi *[dice] and carry it to a certain island lying off Britain called Ictis [Saint Michael's Mount].*

Strabo's report, from about the beginning of our era, runs as follows:

The Cassiterides, opposite to the West Parts of Britain, situated as it were in the same climate with Britain, are ten in number and lie near each other, in the ocean toward the north from the haven of Artabri. One of them is desert, but the others are inhabited by men in black cloaks, clad in tunics reaching to the feet, girt about the breast, and walking with staves, thus resembling the furies we see in tragic representations. They subsist by their cattle, leading for the most part a wandering life. Of the metals, they have tin and lead, which, with skins, they barter with the merchants for earthenware, salt, and brazen vessels.

Artabri is near Cape Finisterre, the northwestern land's end of the Iberian peninsula. Both Pliny and Solinus, writing a little later, confirmed the identification of the Cassiterides with the Scillies. Tin-smelting pits that can be dated to 300 B.C. have been found near Saint Just. It seems probable that the tin on the Scillies themselves was always more exposed and easily exploited, even largely exhausted by Roman times. But the island metal was still mined in the sixteenth century, and found in workable quantities as late as the eighteenth; and no doubt the islands remained a depot for the mainland "exporters" long after local supplies ran out.

In short, though positive proof is lacking, there does seem strong circumstantial evidence to suggest that mysterious strangers were descending on the extreme southwest of Britain, and regularly, from at least Homer's time, and possibly even before it. I believe myself that this is where the northern version of the Atlantis corpus of legends springs from. A comparison with the kind of myths that the conquistadors in America, or the first explorers in Polynesia, gave birth to is illuminating. Man has never liked rational explanations of why strangers are more intelligent and technologically advanced than he.

I should have made a very poor hand on Ulysses' boat, since I have never in my life gone past an island without wishing that I could have landed on it, and even in less than traditionally romantic circumstances. I had the longing only very recently, on a tour round Manhattan; would have had our launch stop at all those forsaken islets with their dilapidated warehouses and weed-jungles. In some way they put to shame the far more famous island they surrounded, and remained of their kind, where it has become a termite-heap. True islands always play the sirens' (and bookmakers') trick: they lure by challenging, by daring. Somewhere on them one will become Crusoe again, one will discover something: the iron-bound chest, the jackpot, the outside chance. The Greek island I lived on in the early 1950s was just such a place. Like Crusoe, I never knew who I really was, what I lacked (what the psychoanalytical theorists of artistic making call the creative gap), until I wandered in its solitudes and emptinesses. Eventually it let me feel that it was mine, which is the other great siren charm of islands: they will not belong to any legal owner, but will offer to become a part of all who tread and love them. One's property by deed they may never be; but humans long ago discovered, had to discover, that that is not the only way to possess territory.

It is this aspect of islands that particularly interests me: how deeply they can haunt and form the personal as well as the public imagination. This power comes primarily, I believe, from a vague yet immediate sense of identity. In terms of consciousness, and self-consciousness, every individual human *is* an island, in spite of Donne's famous preaching to the contrary. It is the boundedness of the smaller island, encompassable in a glance, walkable in one day, that relates it more closely to the human body than any other geographical conformation of land. It is also the contrast between what can be seen at once and what remains, beyond the shore that faces us, hidden. Even to ourselves we are the same, half superficial and obvious, and half concealed, labyrinthine, fascinating to explore. Then there is the enisling sea, our evolutionary amniotic fluid, the element in which we too were once enwombed, from which our own antediluvian line rose into the light and air. There is the marked individuality of islands, which we should like to think corresponds with our own; their obstinate separatedness of character, even when they lie in archipelagos.

It is not only the geologists and ecologists who feel that in the Scillies; the islanders do themselves. In the old days there were different nicknames for the men of each island. Those of Saint Mary's were Bulldogs; of Tresco, Caterpillars (perhaps for the moonlit files of smugglers); of Bryher, Thorns (all thorn trees on the Scillies are blown askew, and Bryher people were supposed to look "lopsided"). Saint Martin's men were Ginnicks, a word whose meaning R. L. Bowley says is lost, though I see Joseph Wright has it down (admittedly from a county on the opposite seaboard of England) as a synonym for "neat." On Saint Agnes you were a Turk because you looked Spanish—the imputation being against the women of that island. Saint Agnes is nearest the dreaded Western Rocks, and has given first shelter to more shipwrecked sailors than all the other islands together. It must therefore have seen Spanish Armada men, who everyone in the southwest knows may have been failures at sea but were terrors in bed. I have a "Spanish" great-aunt and uncle myself, so I believe every word of it. ("Turk" simply means "not English": that is, outlandish.)

Despite the much greater intercommunication and intermarriage of modern times, this separatism, or patriotism, has not quite disappeared. The respectively most "foreign" and most "native" of the five presently inhabited, Tresco and Bryher (though Saint Martin's might also claim the latter distinction), lie not much more than a long stone's throw apart. I sat once with a young Bryher wife. She came originally from Bristol, but she talked about the mainland's not seeming "real" anymore. Then she looked out the window and across the narrow channel. "Even Tresco," she added; and I remembered Armorel, of whom more in a minute. Armorel felt rather the same about Bryher, which in another direction lies only a slightly longer stone's throw from her own island of Samson.

Island communities are the original alternative societies. That is why so many mainlanders envy them. Of their nature they break down the multiple alienations of industrial and suburban man. Some vision of utopian belonging, of social blessedness, of an independence based on cooperation, haunts them all. Tresco is leased and managed by the Smith family, who have generally brought in outsiders to work there. I asked another native of Bryher what he thought of Tresco. He spat over the lee gunwale of his boat, which may seem ungrateful, in view of all that the Smiths become Dorrien-Smiths have done, and are still doing, for the economy and conservation of the Scillies as a whole; but the spitting was, I knew, not against man, but against principle. He was prepared to make the most of his summer living ferrying holidaymakers to the place; he allowed the charms of its modern hotel, its jolly pub, its famous subtropical gardens; but he would leave the Scillies altogether sooner than live on Tresco himself. And he used finally a phrase that was almost one of pity, as if speaking of a fat girl trying to be a ballerina: "It's not island," he said.

·   ·   ·

Of course all islanders have to be handy with boats, but genuine neso-manes are not sailors. Centuries of professional mariners have wished the entire Scillies sunk a hundred fathoms deep, and most other small islands with them. Yachtsmen may enjoy archipelago-cruising, but their true marriage is with the moving island under their feet, whereas the attachment of the fanatic is to all that the passing craft will never know. The surrounding sea is an indispensable part of the setting for this obsession, but it is not of its essence. It is the isolater, not the isolation. The ships it carries on its horizon are like arrows that have missed their target, space vehicles heading for some other planet. They may photograph the surface, but they will never know the interior.

However, it is not for nothing that since remotest antiquity the domain of the siren has been where sea and land meet; and it is even less for nothing that the siren is female, not male. Something deeper than aboriginal sexual chauvinism—the fact that ship-handling was always a man's affair—lies behind this. It is odd, if you think about it, that Ulysses should feminize both his bulwark and its age-old greatest enemy, the reef, the rock, the uncharted shore; almost as if being wrecked were the result of a quarrel between women, eternal destroying Scylla versus eternal launching Helen of Troy.

I think we must read here a paradox about possession, or possessibility. Good sailors have always married their ships as well as their wives. A recent book showed that even those sailors in stone ships, offshore lighthouse-men, can still enter into a very curious emotional relationship with their towers; not at all the sort of thing that the economic view of man as mere smoke in the wage-labor wind allows for. But of course to possess is always to want to possess more. No earlier man ever went voyaging for fun, or risked the sirens for the sheer hell of it; he went to find land, food, tin, gold, trade, lebensraum . . . power of some kind. His voyage was undertaken in what he already possessed, though never as securely as he wanted, and towards what he wanted to possess in addition, though never as certainly as he imagined. Eons of empty marriages to pretty faces lie behind the siren; Adam may have delved in the literal earth, but he never scratched much beyond the surface of Eve's mind and nature. It was she, after all, who provoked the very first voyage, outward bound from Eden with her dimwit of a husband.

. . .

The historically very abrupt discovery of the charms of the seaside has always seemed to me one of the most bizarre happenings in the cultural history of Europe. Before 1750, it is almost as if everyone felt about coasts as many people feel today about airports. Of course one goes to them if one has to travel by air; of course one lives by them if one's livelihood depends on it or if other circumstances oblige; but who in their right mind would ever go to an airport from choice, just for idle pleasure? The analogy may seem absurd, but that makes our apparent long blindness to the very real pleasures of the seaside even more mysterious. It is true that well up to 1700 most foreign tourists descending on European beaches came with cannon trained and cutlass in hand. The last place to pass a happy holiday in the summer of 1690 would have been on the Dorset or Devon coast. Admiral Tourville's French fleet spent most of that season cruising close inshore looking for towns to sack; Teignmouth was burned to the ground, and other places bombarded. And it is also true that the very notion of "holiday" was, in all but its original and literal sense, for most of the world a late-Victorian invention. Yet a mystery does remain: how can something so nice have been ignored for so long?

The change came, like most major human changes, from a conjunction of two factors. Humans can follow reason against pleasure, and pleasure against reason, but when the two combine, they are irresistible. In this case the medical profession and the first Romantics spoke as one. The doctors discovered the medicinal value of sun-bathing—and even sea-drinking, in the early days. The Romantics discovered nature and the picturesque. The sea was therefore judged good for both body and aesthetic soul; for me, in a word. The annual conferences of the Amalgamated Union of Sea Sirens must have been gloomy affairs in the early eighteenth century; everywhere they were being declared redundant by the new lighthouses, the improved navigational methods. Then suddenly a miracle: they had a brilliant idea. Instead of combing their tresses and facing out to sea, they would comb their tresses and face inland. Instead of corrupting sailors, they would pervert the landlubbers.

This abrupt acquisition of new victims can be very accurately dated in the case of my own town of Lyme Regis. Here there was a third factor involved as well: international politics. Again and again during the first decade of the eighteenth century, Lyme was beseeching Her Majesty in

Council, and the Duke of Marlborough, to send cannon and powder against the "insults of enemy privateers." Then followed thirty years of silence on the matter. In 1740 John Scrope was sent by the Privy Council to inspect the town, and reported that "by the long peace their Fire Arms have been so much neglected that upon a late inspection of them there was not a musquet in the Town that could be fired, so that the town is in a neglected and defenceless condition." Six nine-pounders were sent, so Lyme was no longer defenseless; neglected it remained, but in that "long peace" salvation had been brewing.

By 1750 the place was moribund, a warren of hovels, with all but two of its former opulent medieval and Tudor houses in ruins. Its harbor was in decay, an early victim of gigantism, far too "tight" and shallow for the merchant ships of the time. Its one other ancient industry besides sea trading, serge-weaving, was being throttled—as everywhere else in the west of England—by the better-organized and more competitive north of the country. Nobody ever visited it, nor easily could visit it even if they wanted to, since there was not a single carriage road. It was as near dead as one can imagine; and our coasts were sick with hundreds of towns in an exactly similar state.

But in 1770 an alert, farsighted, and exceptionally generous man descended on the corpse. He was Thomas Hollis, a benefactor of Harvard and an early socialist before the name—a radical, a *philosophe*. He told Lyme that its only hope was to make itself a little more presentable, and showed it the way to start. He bought the hovel property in the town not to profit from it, but simply to have it sledgehammered to the ground. He cleared a little central square (now lost again; such is human progress); he proposed an assembly room. He suggested to the astounded natives that it was pleasant to stroll by the sea, and made a start on a marine parade; and he did even better by pulling off a great publicity coup, persuading the most famous Englishman of his time to bring his sickly young son—one day to be as famous as his father—to Lyme for the air and climate. If it was good enough for the Earl of Chatham and young William Pitt, it was very soon good enough for many others. Hollis, a much greater human being than either Pitt, performed this small miracle in only four brief years, before his death in 1774.

By 1800 the main industry of Lyme had become what he foresaw and what it has remained ever since: catering to those who came, and come, to the sea for pleasure. It took place as suddenly as this, between 1750 and

1780, in countless other small coastal towns all over Britain. The sea, its water, its air, the light and relief it gave landscapes, became the rage. Lyme had its most famous literary visitor in 1803 and 1804, when Jane Austen arrived with her family, and it is interesting to note the contrast between her judgments of the place itself and of its society. The latter got very low marks indeed from the mercilessly fastidious young woman, but she grew positively Wordsworthian—if not downright brochuristical—when it came to the natural setting. The lift, the allegro that takes place in *Persuasion* when the action moves to Lyme is completely typical of the people of this time. They had discovered what we are now taught to covet and love from infancy. I think there has been no nicer sea change in social taste— even though in 1800 it was still reserved for the well-circumstanced—in our history.

The hidden intention of that invisible turned-round siren installed on every beach was not at first perceived. For many decades sea-bathing remained what it had been to Jane Austen, a medicinal activity. Quite probably even fewer were actually bathing in the sea than at the very beginning of the mania, since along every promenade and front had sprung purpose-built interior (and warmed) sea-baths; and those who still braved Neptune direct did it from wheeled cabins. But the Victorian spirit was dominant long before 1836, and it was that age which began to see the siren plainly—that is, to sense the always implicit eroticism and sexuality of the beach.

No one saw those qualities more clearly than the Reverend Francis Kilvert, who loathed the "detestable custom of bathing in drawers" and twice—and delightedly—shocked public beaches by refusing to wear them. In 1873 he wrote (one may take his "ignorance" with all the salt in the English Channel), "I had in my ignorance bathed naked . . . however some little boys who were looking on at the rude naked man appeared to be much interested in the spectacle, and the young ladies who were strolling near seemed to have no objection." Two years later he was on the Isle of Wight during July:

> *The morning was blue and lovely with a warm sun and fresh breeze blowing from the sea and the Culver Downs. As I walked from Shanklin to Sandown along the cliff edge I stopped to watch some children bathing from the beach directly below. One beautiful girl stood entirely naked on the sand, and there as she half sat, half reclined sideways, leaning upon her elbow with*

her knees bent and her legs and feet partly drawn back and up, she was a
model for a sculptor. There was the supple slender waist, the gentle dawn and
tender swell of the bosom and the budding breasts, the graceful rounding of
the delicately beautiful limbs and above all the soft and exquisite curves of
the rosy dimpled bottom and broad white thigh. Her dark hair fell in thick
masses on her white shoulders as she threw her head back and looked out to
sea. She seemed a Venus Anadyomene fresh risen from the waves.

But the Lolita-haunted Kilvert was a century ahead of his time in erotic honesty, and few others of his age would have admitted such thoughts, let alone committed them to paper. Still, they must have harried even the most timid and conventional. One may dress against other eyes, but not against the caress or shock of water on the most private skin. Decent Christian gentlemen and advisers of youth made such a thing of the manly cold bath because they feared terribly what might go on in a warm one. As late as 1882 the town council of Lyme was still threatening severe penalties for any male degenerate who dared venture within fifty yards of the ladies' cabins.

Our museum has a very revealing family album of 1886. It gives a delightfully vivid picture of what a seaside holiday was like in that year: prawning, mackereling, tennis, walking, fossiling, sandcastling, sketching, photographing, making fun of the locals . . . but not a single word about taking one's clothes off and swimming. The one other thing just as conspicuously absent, to our own age's eyes, is symptomatic: despite the many—and evidently lively and attractive—young people of both sexes in the family, there is also not the faintest hint of any romantic attachment, even jocularly expressed.

"Sea-bathing tends to invigorate the whole nervous system," pronounced *Modern Etiquette* in 1889. "However, as an agent for promoting the softness and delicacy of the skin, and the bright hues of the complexion, it is inferior to the warm or tepid bath. It is better not to bathe in the sea until two hours after a meal, and the circulation should be promoted by friction and the aid of a good, brisk walk." The lady authoress goes on, too, to warn against "exposure to the ray of the sun in summer. It is very injurious to the skin, causing it to tan." This latter concern probably explained why the fashionable months for sea-bathing in Jane Austen's time were October and November: one had at all costs to preserve one's ability to blush. Nothing was more erotic to nineteenth-century man than a milky cheek turning pink.

But all this middle-class nonsense was doomed. The seaside jaunt had become more and more of a national habit, ever since Sir John Lubbock's Bank Holiday Act of 1871. Even *Modern Etiquette* had to confess, and approve of, the fact that "of late ladies have taken very much to rowing." *Punch*, for its part, had been hinting at the sexual charms of the seaside since at least 1864, when that trendsetting (and trend-mocking) Parisian George du Maurier joined its staff; and even then, he was only taking up a line that late-Georgian cartoonists such as Rowlandson and Cruikshank had been as frank about as our own age. It was fully accepted by the 1890s. The jolly opportunities for studying the female form, for having the chance encounter, constitute the main theme of that charmingly illustrated series on popular European coasts by the French artist Mars—a series aimed quite as much at Anglo-Saxon audiences as at Gallic ones. All those hiked skirts and peeping lower calves, that wind-disheveled hair, young Belle Epoque beauties in disarray . . . from there it was only a short step (facilitated by Tommy Atkins's discovery of French popular art in his brief reliefs from the horror of the trenches) to the splendid vulgarities of the kind of postcard that George Orwell immortalized. I suspect we have still not fully recognized the debt that sexual—and perhaps political—liberation owes to the seaside holiday.

The beach has now become the principal public pleasure area, closer and closer to the bedroom, of all advanced Western—and Eastern—societies. It is where one goes to spoil one's own naked body, to find sex and romance, to release; for an oblivion on all routines, fixed hours, formalities. It may have become increasingly difficult to escape the world at the seaside of high summer; but even there, workaday identity at least can be lost. All through every August I listen to the sound of children's voices floating up from the beach into my own seaside garden. They are within a quarter-tone of being screams of extreme terror; but they remain screams of extreme pleasure. The subtle siren plies her trade, and meets very little resistance now.

Since the proximity of the sea melts so much in us, the island is doubly liberating. It is this that explains why indigenous small-island communities, at least in the long-discovered temperate zones, are on the whole rather dour and puritanical in their social ways and codes. They have to protect themselves against the other perennial temptation of the island: dropping the necessary inhibitions of mainland society. Islands are also secret places, where the imagination never rests. All isolation, as the cold-bath merchants also knew, is erotic. Crusoes, unless their natures run that way, do not really hope for *Man* Fridays; and islands pour a stronger wine of forgetfulness than any other place on all that lies beyond the horizon. "Back there" becomes a dream, more a hypothesis than a reality; and many of its rituals and behaviors can seem very rapidly to be no more than devices to keep the hell of the stale, sealess, teeming suburb and city tolerable.

The puritans, from Homer on, have always suspected islands, and wished their addicts the fate allotted Odysseus and his men. William Golding repeated the ancient warning in *The Lord of the Flies*: such literal isolation will breed swine—self-destruction—whether through lotus-eating or through loss of mainland law. I think it is significant too that the most self-revealing novel Thomas Hardy ever wrote, *The Well-Beloved*, is set on the quasi-island of Portland. It is a story full of incest, of repressed eroticism, of narcissistic guilt on the part of its tortured author. He makes much play between the pagan and the Christian view of life, the illicit and the licit; and makes it very clear that the illicit inhabits the old Portland (and his own complicated psyche) precisely because of its detachment from the mainland, both physically and psychologically.

I have always thought of my own novels as islands, or as islanded. I remember being forcibly struck, on my very first visit to the Scillies, by the structural and emotional correspondences between visiting the different islands and any fictional text—the alternation of duller passages, "continuity" in the jargon of the cinema, and the separate, island quality of other key events and confrontations—an insight, the notion of islands in the sea of story, that I could not forsake now even if I tried. This capacity to enisle is one I always look for in other novelists; or perhaps I should say that none I admire lacks it. It is a capacity that lies quite literally at the heart of what has often been called the first modern novel, Defoe's *Robinson Crusoe*; and it lies equally at the heart of the very first novel of all. The island remains where the magic (one's arrival at some truth or development one could not logically have predicted or expected) takes place; and it rises strangely, out of nothingness, out of the onward dogwatches, mere journeying transit, in the writing.

The Scillies have a Victorian novel partly devoted to them. This is Sir Walter Besant's *Armorel of Lyonesse*, first published in 1890 and not possible much before that date, since it shows the "new" young woman of the time in all her brave and earnest glory. One must in art derive the species from the Pre-Raphaelites, but the vogue for her sturdy, glowing cheeks, her impetuous frankness, her comparative emancipation, probably began with another novel ten years earlier than Besant's, Sabine Baring-Gould's *Mehalah*. The similarly eponymous Mehalah is also an expert oarswoman and girl-mistress of an island, though of a very different kind from Armorel's Samson. The two books, like their two once-famous and now-forgotten authors, make for an interesting contrast. Baring-Gould, an embittered High Anglican clergyman, took the puritan view of islands, which allowed him to write a much darker and finer story. Swinburne noted its powerful echoes of *Wuthering Heights*, another essentially "island" book, for all its geographical setting; and I have sung Mehalah's praises elsewhere myself.

Besant was a better man than he was a writer: a lifelong champion of the underprivileged, and a patron saint to all American and British authors, since he was the first to campaign consistently and effectively for their legal and commercial rights. The London scenes in *Armorel* are rather too full of stock characters and stock melodrama to make the book any but a very minor work of its period. Yet for thirteen chapters in the beginning, when Besant describes the life of his young heroine on the now-uninhabited island of Samson, he does achieve something better, a strange sea-idyll, or island pastoral; he even achieves a genuine echo of a much more ancient girl on an island, and not only because that far more famous idyll, which I shall come to, also begins with the saving of a selfish, handsome stranger from drowning.

We may smile today at the passionately idealistic tomboy Armorel, who is several light-years removed from our own notions, both political and physical, of the aware and attractive young woman; but something of the honesty and independence that islands bestow, and of their ancient magic, does glow through these pages . . . one doesn't forget Armorel, or her spirit, indeed one may even regret them, since the conditions of solitude and of self-dependence in which such character can emerge are now gone from the world. But they are, still today, a little less lost in the Scillies than anywhere else in Britain south of the northern isles.

The first novel in world literature is woven of islands and the sea, and of solitude and sexuality, which is why it has had a greater influence on subsequent storytelling, both thematically and technically, than any other single book in human history. It also first demonstrates (with a complexity and subtlety that still escape all probability) the value for the form of the archipelagic structure I spoke of earlier. A novelist can no more afford not to be steeped in it than can a Christian in the Bible, a philosopher in Plato, or a Socialist in Marx. It is the sine qua non of all serious study or practice of fiction.

I am one of those heretics who believe the *Odyssey* must have been written by a woman. The heresy is not new among authors. Samuel Butler believed it, and produced some convincing circumstantial evidence; and so did Robert Graves in our own time. Whoever did write it seems to have been markedly more knowledgeable about domestic matters, the running of a large household, than about nautical ones. The one bit of showing-off in the latter field—the description of the boat Odysseus builds to escape from Calypso's island—is shipyard stuff, not seagoing expertise; and in the very first pages nothing is more striking than the loving detail bestowed on the *provisions* for Telemachus' voyage, and the total absence of such detail when it comes to the craft itself. Throughout history it has been man who worships and polishes the vehicle, and woman who packs the suitcases.

Transparently also the writer is obsessed by all the things—especially young female things—that keep husbands away from their proper place at home. There is that repeated, vivid eye for the interior decor and life of the palaces of Nestor, Menelaus, and Alcinous—how guests are received, how they are bathed, how dressed, how fed, even how the laundry is done—that ubiquitous sympathy for the feminine ego, from the glittering grande-dame entry given Helen of Troy to Calypso's sadness; the love of describing clothes and jewelry; the kindness shown older women, and the flagrantly greater interest, in the Land of the Dead, taken in the female ghosts. . . .

Butler, who was no Kilvert, decided that the authoress was hiding behind the nicest (morally) of the waylaying island girls, Nausicaa. If the writer must be hidden behind a character, I should plump myself for Penelope, or rather, for the theory that Scheherazade was not the first woman to know that letting a man hear all he imagines is one very good way to put him under your spell. Who would want the cold, salt reality after such a telling?

Here as in so many other matters, and for obvious physical and social reasons, it seems probable that if man went out and brought home the raw material, it was always woman who cherished, "cooked," and wrought it. With men, it was always the challenge of getting; with women, the elaboration of the got. We know that women tend to be the main "carriers" of folk song and folklore among primitive peoples. Men must perforce have a closer knowledge of external reality, however superstitious they are; and women a closer knowledge of the internal imagination, of the storeroom of the reported image, not the directly apprehended one. Weaving and embroidery lie at the heart of all storytelling, as they do at the root of all decoration. The Greeks knew it. Their very word for a recited epic, *rhapsody*, means simply "stitched song." Plaiting the real with the imagined defines all art; and I think it no coincidence that (like Circe and several other women in the book) Penelope takes to weaving as both her pastime in her long wait and her excuse for her fidelity.

The more one looks at the internal evidence, the more convincing it becomes. Who steals the very first chapter of the great story? For whom is most sympathy evoked? Not the absent Odysseus, but his abandoned wife and all her domestic problems, most strikingly that of a son well on his way to becoming another Orestes. And what is the emotional climax? The night of reunion in book 23, when even dawn is delayed in awe, on the command of the divinity who has finally brought patient wife and wandering husband together again—another woman, the wisdom-goddess Athene. (The actual final book, 24, is a mere tidying up of loose ends.) No man who has ever risked or provoked the shipwreck of a marriage by his own selfishness has ever doubted the profound affirmation of *female* wisdom in that climactic passage; or for that matter had to wonder why the ancients personified wisdom as a woman. Even more significantly, Athene is a pre-Greek deity. She was the protectress of palaces in the Mycenean age in which the story is set, and also the goddess of arts and crafts . . . a women's goddess, if ever was.

We know that behind the Homeric legend of the Trojan War lay a very real conflict in the last centuries of the second millennium before Christ, over trading power and land to settle. It was between a loose confederation of Mycenean pirate-kings and the holders of the gate, the Bosporus, to the coveted Black Sea. We also know that "Homer" was writing several centuries after these events and by no means (though one may argue over how conscious the irony is) with undivided admiration for the Mycenean part in them. Few of the male heroes—human or divine—are very attractive, or allowed to be happy, and especially when they are away from home. Zeus and Poseidon move only to punish; moving men *invite* punishment. Penelope's suitors are continually being told to go home; and refusing to do so, duly meet their end in a bloodbath, a mirror-image of the agonies that Odysseus, the sole survivor of his Ithacan squadron, has been through on his own travels.

What bouquets there are for men go to those who have either stayed or resettled at home: Menelaus, Nestor, Alcinous, the prince-shepherd Eumaeus, Old Man Laertes. The enigma, of course, is Odysseus himself. In one light he is the least attractive character of them all, with his compulsive lying, his suspiciousness, his infidelity, his vindictive anger—but then his very name means the "one with enemies," the "victim," or in modern terms, the paranoiac. In this aspect it is difficult not to see him inside a much more recent myth, against a background of tiny islanded townships in that other wild ocean of the American West; and most certainly there not with the face of the noble sheriff, but much more with that of a Lee Marvin or a Jack Palance—the unscrupulous, pathological killer. Dryden found two perfect adjectives for this aspect of him in his translation of Virgil's *Aeneid*: "dire" and "insatiate" Odysseus.

If that were all there was to him . . . but there remains his courage, his onwardness, his questing, his surviving, his shrewdness, his humor, his fallibility; his quintessential maleness, with all the faults and virtues, as close-woven as the shroud-cloth on his wife's loom, of that biological conditioning. One has only to compare him with the heroes of the other ancient Greek travel-sagas: Heracles, Perseus, Bellerophon, Jason of the *Argo*. Those men are myth-puppets from the nursery of the imagination. Odysseus is real, and human, however mythical and supernatural the circumstances in which he finds himself. If his vice is that he cannot stay out of the game, his own cheating—mainly done merely to survive—is petty compared with that of the other players, the gods who control the way things are; which makes him universal man, and justifiably paranoiac.

The *Odyssey* is fundamentally an analysis of the mechanism and the justice of this paranoia. Odysseus' greatest and most implacable enemy, Poseidon, is the god of the great medium of his temptation, the sea. His return from Troy is therefore both a penance for past sins and a running demonstration of why they came about. Again and again he or his men have their agony prolonged because of their own greed or pointless aggression. His one virtue is his longing to return home, to find Penelope—that is, wisdom—but (despite the night of reunion) Homer puts a great question mark over this. The savage massacre of the suitors, the hanging of the corrupted maids, the mutilation ("with a sharp knife they sliced his nose and ears off, they ripped away his privy parts as raw meat for the dogs, and in their fury they lopped off his hands and feet") of the shepherd Melanthius, all suggest that the paranoia remains. And there is a famous thread left lying loose at the end, the fact that Odysseus knows from Tiresias that he must make one more voyage still: "till you reach a people who know nothing of the sea and never use salt with their food." That is, he must travel forever, on this planet, in search of an unattainable, his own landlocked, peace. The sea, the invitation to the unknown, will remain his unassuaged demon.

The *Odyssey* has always strongly reminded me of one side of a later literature, also written in a time of struggle for power and search for lebensraum, of quasi-ritualized aggression, of brute male greed for prestige and property, and all in the context of another line of ambitious sea-pirates. The period following the Norman Conquest was also that in which the first women writers of our era began to use storytelling—based, as with Homer, on material from long before their own time—gently to suggest better ends in life to their menfolk. The key vehicle for this new worldview was once again the story of wandering adventure, though their protagonists' sea was more often the forest than the literal one. But true sea voyages and islands are by no means absent from these tales, and I have already suggested that the parallel between the old, vast, mystery- and wolf-filled forests of Europe and the sea was very strong.

What is significant is that writers such as Marie de France and Christine de Pisan chose to send out so many latter-day knightly versions of Ulysses on their voyages of self-discovery; and that their very frequent final demonstration was that true wisdom always lay at home, or quite certainly not in the overt original purpose of the journey. It is very instructive to read the *Odyssey* and Marie de France's stories side by side, not just for the central similarity of attitude to the quest theme, but for the common little touches of humor, the psychological accuracy underlying the delight in the fabulous (the ability to make fabulous beings behave humanly), the obsession with domestic behavior and domestic objects, the preponderant role played by the relationships between men and women—a shared set of sensibilities and preoccupations that we know, in the latter case, did not belong to a man.

Even if one must take the orthodox scholarly view, and make Homer the male bard that tradition has always maintained he was, it seems to me certain that he was composing quite as much for a feminine audience as for a masculine one, and from an essentially feminist point of view—that is, a civilizing one—using very much the same techniques as those early-medieval writers. Scholars have delighted in seeing the *Iliad* and the *Odyssey* as anthropological crossword puzzles all of whose clues lead to solutions in obscure religious symbolisms: Penelope becomes the center of a duck-goddess cult, Odysseus a sacrificial king, and so on. Of course that is a part of it. But I think no one who has wandered round the palace complexes of Knossos or Mycenae can believe that even in that time (long before Homer's own), there cannot have been, behind the picturesque sacred groves and golden boughs, ordinary men and women with practical social problems; and quite sophisticated enough mentally (if their artifacts are anything to go by) to distinguish at least some of their contemporary relevance from their mythical representation.

Archaeology has time and time again proved that the Homeric descriptions of artifacts and techniques were very far from mythical; and the continuous and highly realistic central theme running behind all Odysseus' ordeals and adventures is the predicament of the wife left to rule in her husband's absence. This must have been a very familiar one in an age of universal piracy. No theme is more often repeated in the *Odyssey* than the upset wreaked on the economy of Odysseus' palace—that is, on any island-state without a firm hand in control. There was, of course, within the chronology of the story, a very recent example of just this problem not far from Ithaca—the adultery of the queen of Mycenae with Aegistheus, their murder of her husband, Agamemnon, on his return from Troy, their own murder in turn by Orestes . . . forced marriages, usurpations of power, internecine and family strife, endless petty war. And why? Very largely because of male stupidity and arrogance, that inability to be satisfied with what one has, that perpetual lust to amass more, possess more, score more—and that last in a very modern sense, since female slaves were a not-unimportant part of the Mycenean marauder's hoped-for booty.

The sea was the road to this lust; and also an escape from wisdom and the wives at home. Odysseus exists in a web of women of all sorts, both the wise and the wicked; and again and again he is saved from the wicked ones by Penelope and Athene. The vivacious, game-playing, and deliciously polymorphic goddess can be read as a spirit version of Penelope, an Ariel to her Prospero, since she is obviously half in love with Odysseus herself, reproachful of his other women, yet not for a moment jealous of his wife. She even makes the latter more beautiful than she already is, using a divine cosmetic to bleach her skin "whiter than ivory." She is a wish fulfillment of the woman left at home, in other words; or of the writer and his or her audience.

The sea and its islands thus become the domain of what cannot be controlled by wisdom and reason; the laboratory where the guinea-pig Odysseus must run through the mazes; where the great ally of reason, the conscious, gives way to the rule of the unconscious and the libido, that eternal and oceanic unsettler of domestic peace and established order. Since it is Odysseus' own unconscious that drives him on, its sea-domain is peopled by women. There is perhaps no more brilliant antedating of Freud in all ancient literature than that meeting Odysseus has, on the dark shores of the River of Ocean at the end of his furthest voyage, with his own dead mother, Anticleia.

As my mother spoke, there came to me out of the confusion in my heart the one desire, to embrace her spirit, dead though she was. Thrice in my eagerness to clasp her to me, I started forward with my arms outstretched. Thrice, like a shadow or a dream, she slipped through my arms and left me harrowed by an even sharper pain.[1]

In that brief image lies the genesis of all art: the pursuit of the irrecoverable, what the object-relations analysts now call symbolic repair.

---

1. All quotations from the *Odyssey* are taken from E. V. Rieu's translation, published by Penguin Books. I may also recommend Robert Fagles's new translation (London and New York: Penguin, 1996).

· · ·

In many ways, in the cunning structure of the Odyssey, the novel actually begins with Odysseus and Calypso on Ogygia. The name Ogygia may be related to the word ocean; it carried a connotation for the Greeks of great antiquity, primevality. But the island was also highly sinister because it lay in the west, perhaps in the Atlantic. I suppose that today the west, because of the association with summer holidays (or in America, with the notion of new frontiers and California), bears a generally pleasant sense, but it was not so as recently as Elizabethan times, when the west wind was the evil wind, the bringer of storm and disease; and it was even less so in ancient times. The best trading and colonizing opportunities undoubtedly lay westwards for the eastern Mediterranean peoples; but the very word for "west" in Greek, skaios, has an evil, threatening sound. The ancient Egyptians associated the direction with death. Greek ornithomancers faced north to ply their craft, and good bird omens always passed on the right, or eastwards. This explains the antediluvian deseil, the Mithraic equivalent of the Christian's sign of the cross before some difficult enterprise: the sunwise or righthand turn. Ships used to make it, sometimes three turns, before a long voyage. All journeys "to the left" were inherently dangerous.

Athene makes this danger very clear when she delivers a report on Odysseus during a cabinet meeting on Olympus.

> *The island is well-wooded and a goddess lives there, the child of the malevolent Atlas, who knows the sea in all its depths. . . . It is this wizard's daughter who is keeping the unhappy man from home in spite of all his tears. Day after day she does her best to banish Ithaca from his memory with false and flattering words; and Odysseus, who would give anything for the mere sight of the smoke rising up from his own land, can only yearn for death.*

This, of course, represents Athene-Penelope's official view of the wicked girl, whose name is Calypso. Odysseus himself backs it up when he comes to tell the story of his time on Ogygia later in the text. Calypso, he says, was "wily"; "never for a moment did she win my heart." But then he immediately plunges on: "Seven years without a break I stayed. . . ." Now, this is far longer than he stays anywhere else—even the voluptuous Circe rates only one year—and indeed accounts for over a third of his two decades of wandering.

Furthermore, between these two unkind reports on the girl in book 1 and book 7, we actually meet her in book 5, where Homer gives us a rather different story. Athene has nagged at her father again, and Hermes is dispatched to Ogygia to tell Calypso she must give Odysseus up, as the gods have further plans for him. Taking the form of what sounds suspiciously like a gannet for the journey (further evidence that the island is either in the extreme western Mediterranean or in the Atlantic itself), he steps on shore "from the blue waters" and walks along the strand to the great cave where Calypso lives. What greets his eyes is very similar to what Besant's hero sees when he first visits Armorel's farm on Samson; and if it is meant to turn the reader off, it is singularly unsuccessful.

> *A big fire was blazing on the hearth and the scent from burning logs of split juniper and cedar was wafted far across the island. Inside, Calypso was singing in a beautiful voice as she wove at the loom and moved her golden shuttle to and fro. The cave was sheltered by a verdant copse of alders, aspens, and fragrant cypresses, which was the roosting-place of feathered creatures, horned owls and falcons and garrulous choughs, birds of the coast, whose daily business takes them down to the sea. Trailing round the very mouth of the cavern, a garden vine ran riot, with great bunches of ripe grapes; while from four separate but neighboring springs four crystal rivulets were trained to run this way and that; and in soft meadows on either side the iris and the parsley flourished. It was indeed a spot where even an immortal visitor must pause to gaze in wonder and delight.*[2]

But not this immortal visitor. After the usual civilities and a cup of tea (brewed ambrosia), the major god and very minor goddess get down to distinctly barbed business. Let me forsake the translation of E. V. Rieu for a moment and put it in more modern, multicorporation terms.

"How nice to see you," says Calypso, "and to know that after all the head office hasn't completely forgotten I even exist."

"My dear girl, if you imagine I'd ever come to a godforsaken place like this of my own free will, you're out of your mind. I've never had a more boring journey in all my life. You provincials don't realize what a desert you live in." He looks round and yawns. "It's this miserable what's-his-

---

2. Here I shall perhaps cite the name of a charming little orchid I was shown in Oregon the same spring that I wrote this essay. It is *Calypso bulbosa*.

name fellow you've taken on. The Old Man has other ideas for him. I'm instructed to tell you to remove your tiny claws. Right?"

Calypso springs to her feet, hands on hips.

"You miserable sods! Just because he's not in the company. And I am. I haven't even hidden it, we're as good as married." Hermes shrugs, says nothing. "The sheer gall of it! When everyone knows you all spend your life at the head office having affairs and chasing secretaries. You're such hypocrites; you do this all the time. And you needn't think I don't know why. One of those ghastly old female department heads has been nosing around again. They're just jealous." Hermes examines his fingernails. Calypso is near tears. "Look, he would have drowned without me. I rescued him, I nursed him, I fell in love with him. I'm even teaching him how he can apply to join the company." Hermes raises his eyebrows. Calypso stares, sighs, at last surrenders. "All right. But the Old Man can damn well find the transport himself. I'm not going to."

Yes, I am vulgarizing a sacred text; but not travestying a very attractive touch of mutinous hurtness in Calypso during that exchange. Hermes leaves. She goes out to find Odysseus moping as usual on the shore, staring out to sea, and realizes her cause is lost just as much with him as at Olympus; and there and then, like Circe, she decides to give him up with gentleness and good grace. She will help him build a boat, provision it for him, send him a fair wind to start out with. The ungrateful man is immediately suspicious: there must be some trick. Will she swear by the Styx (the one oath that even the gods could not break) that it is all aboveboard?

She tells him, behind a half-teasing mask, one or two much-needed home truths then. He lets his cunning mind rule his human heart, she says; he ought to know that pity can be greater than sexual desire, that the truest love can sacrifice its own existence. She does swear by the Styx, but turns quickly away. Homer says that Odysseus walks after her. Let us hope that it is, for once in his life, to make an apology.

Calypso makes one last attempt, at supper that night. She warns him that more suffering is to come if he leaves; and promises that if he stays with her, he will gain immortality. They can live together till the end of time. And finally she asks how he can keep thinking of the aging Penelope when he has a warm young goddess at his side. Odysseus is diplomatic and runs down his wife's looks. True, she's only mortal, but the sea calls, and as for the suffering . . . "Let this new disaster come. It only makes one more."

It grows dark, and they have one last night of love. The next morning he is allowed to start building his escape boat.

The Calypso interlude is one of the most endearing in the whole *Odyssey*, a conflict between a dream and a reality, a case of a lonely woman hopelessly in love with a lonely man helplessly in love with his own destiny. It is also one of the most striking cases in all literature of humanity in the writer overcoming the inhumanity of convention. Calypso (whose name holds the *skl* in cipher) should by all the rules of myth be evil. The "good" characters in the story report her as evil, the hero spurns her sexually, even her fellow gods sniff at her . . . I remember, the very first time I read the *Odyssey* as a schoolboy, hating Odysseus for leaving her. After many rereadings, despite my knowing that both inner and outer logic must make him leave, I still cannot quite forgive him; and that forked feeling, I am convinced, was not created by a man. At any rate I know how much I owe, as a writer of fiction, to the Calypso-Penelope dilemma; it has haunted my own and countless other novels, and always will.

Odysseus heads for Phaeacia, or Skeria, the modern Corfu. But Poseidon, furious that Olympus has relented (if not the authoress furious that her hero has forced her to write that he leaves Calypso's island "with a happy heart"), dismasts the boat in a violent squall. It drifts in the gale; then another monster wave sinks it. Odysseus strips and swims for it. On the third day he comes to the coast of Corfu, but there is a huge surf, nothing but cliffs. He is carried onto the rocks: "He clung there groaning while the great wave washed by. But no sooner had he escaped its fury than it struck him once more with the full force of its backward rush and flung him far out to sea. Pieces of skin stripped from his sturdy hands were left sticking to the crag, thick as the pebbles that stick to the suckers of a squid when he is torn from his hole."

Once more Athene comes to his aid and helps the exhausted man swim along the coast to the sandy cove at a river's mouth; and there at last he can drag himself ashore. He covers himself in leaves under an olive, and sleeps. The next morning the daughter of the king of Skeria-Corfu, Nausicaa, comes with her maids to wash clothes at the river. They play with a ball, and Odysseus wakes. Quick as ever to find his feet, he seizes a branch to cover his nakedness and steps out with a flowery speech addressed to the beautiful princess. Yet another affair seems about to begin; but this time Odysseus is home. He is befriended by the king and queen and lent a ship to take him to Ithaca, where he will execute his bloodthirsty revenge. Even there, though, since he is in disguise to begin with, the odysseys do not cease: he keeps inventing new ones as a "cover" for his presence, stories of Egypt and the Phoenicians. His old friend the shepherd Eumaeus tells another: a king's son by birth, his life too was ruined by the sea and by piracy. Everywhere, then, the cruel, separating sea; and the folly of sacrificing all to it, when the only tangible and endurable Calypso-Circe-Athene is the one the sailor left behind in the first place, on his own safe home island and kingdom of Ithaca.

In my own first novel, *The Magus*—written, like all stories of its kind, under the vast aegis of the *Odyssey*—I used a famous quotation from T. S. Eliot's *The Four Quartets*:

> *We shall not cease from exploration*
> *And the end of all our exploring*
> *Will be to arrive where we started*
> *And know the place for the first time.*

This does not happen to Odysseus when he at last lands on Ithaca, by a grim irony at the cave of Phorcys, one of Scylla's putative fathers. He fails to recognize his own birthplace, partly because Athene has thrown a mist over the spot where he finds himself. In fact he is plunged into gloom. He doesn't know what the people will be like, he doesn't know where to hide the presents that Nausicaa's parents have given him. He wishes he had never left Skeria-Corfu. He has obviously been tricked and marooned on some desert island. His first and supremely typical positive action is to check that none of the presents has been stolen by the Corfiot crew during the landing. (They have left, only to be turned into a reef on their homeward trip by Poseidon, in one last fling of rage.) He starts to weep on the barren shore. Only then does a handsome young shepherd—Athene, in disguise once more—appear and tell him where he truly is.

But that first anticlimax, like the curious hesitation on Penelope's side when she does at last recognize him, before the emotion comes, is enormously shrewd; and it does, I think, put a vital accent on the hopelessness of Odysseus' case, on his incapacity to do anything but undergo the experience, the turning of the wheel, even though it finally comes to rest exactly at the point where it started. Odysseus may be the wiser for it, but dire and insatiate, he is still condemned to sail on and on, round and round, from island to island, from experience to experience.

The only land where people "know nothing of the sea" is death; and for better or for worse, the only answer to the mysteries of life lies in the voyage to the islands. In that long penultimate passage of the greatest novel, and greatest homage to the *Odyssey*, of our own century, another sailor, Leopold Bloom, is put to the dry question on his own return to Ithaca, at the end of his Dublin day. This is how its crux runs:

Would the departed never nowhere nohow reappear?

Ever he would wander, selfcompelled to the extreme limit of his cometary orbit, beyond the fixed stars and variable suns and telescopic planets, astronomical waifs and strays, to the extreme boundary of space, passing from land to land, among peoples, amid events. Somewhere imperceptibly he would hear and somehow reluctantly suncompelled, obey the summons of recall. Whence, disappearing from the constellation of the Northern Crown he would somehow reappear reborn above delta in the constellation of Cassiopeia and after incalculable eons of peregrination return an estranged avenger, a wreaker of justice on malefactors, a dark crusader, a sleeper awakened, with financial resources (by supposition) surpassing those of Rothschild or of the silver king.

What would render such return irrational?

An unsatisfactory equation between an exodus and return in time through reversible space and an exodus and return in space through irreversible time.

What play of forces, inducing inertia, rendered departure undesirable?

The lateness of the hour, rendering procrastinatory: the obscurity of the night, rendering invisible: the uncertainty of thoroughfares, rendering perilous: the necessity for repose, obviating movement: the proximity of an occupied bed, obviating research: the anticipation of warmth (human) tempered with coolness (linen), obviating desire and rendering desirable: the statue of Narcissus, sound without echo, desired desire.

That is Odysseus: the voyage in the mind. The real Ulysses is whoever wrote the *Odyssey*, is Joyce, is every artist who sets off into the unknown of his own unconscious and knows he must run the gauntlet of the island reefs, the monsters, the sirens, the Calypsos and the Circes, with only a very dim faith that an Athene is somewhere there to help and a wise Penelope waiting at the end. No recurrent symbolism in the *Odyssey* is more pertinent than the long and deliberate stripping its hero undergoes: of his ships, of his men, of his hopes, of his clothes, even of his very skin on the cliffs of Corfu. Perhaps the only hope of self-escape for the "statue of Narcissus, sound without echo, desired desire" lies in that *moly* bloom which Hermes hands the sailor at Circe's door; and which James Joyce places ("shall I wear a white rose") at the very end of his mistress-piece in his own Molly Bloom: "yes he said I was a flower of the mountain yes so are we flowers all a woman's body yes that was one true thing he said in his life and the sun shines for you today."

I should like now to tell the story of a much later real-life Odysseus and his crew, and of the fortunate islands that they discovered. In view of the treasure their voyage eventually brought to light, I am delighted that the tale begins very close indeed to where I write: to be precise, in Lyme Regis, during bad Queen Mary's reign. In 1554 the wife of a tradesman, John Somers, gave birth to a fourth son, who on April 24 was christened George. A decade later another citizen of Lyme, John Jourdain, also had a son, christened Silvester.

George Somers went early to sea, and by the 1590s had become a typical buccaneering Elizabethan captain with many Atlantic voyages and beard-singeing exploits to his credit. Thomas Fuller in his *Worthies of England* reports that he was a "lamb on the land . . . a lion at sea"; and at least part of his prowess was due to his excellence as a navigator. But by 1600 Somers seems to have settled for the lamb's side of it and retired with his laurels, and loot, to Lyme and his wife. She was a local girl, Jane or Joan Haywood, and they were married in 1582, when she was eighteen. In 1603 he became a Member of Parliament for the town and was knighted. In 1604 he was elected mayor. But evidently, like any true Odysseus, he could not just live by the sea, he had to sail it.

In 1609 Somers, a founding member of the London or South Virginia Company, was appointed admiral of the fleet that was to take a new injection of settlers to the troubled colony. On April 23 he made his will, and a few weeks later sailed in the accurately (if variously) named *Sea Adventurer* or *Sea Venture* (three hundred tons), with nine other ships. Not only were the sailors and settlers Ithacan in their number—about five hundred—but the settlers, at least, sound identical in spirit, being (there were also women on board) mostly "youths of a most lewd and bad condition." The majority were to take one look at Virginia and return to the fleshpots of England at the first opportunity. Also on board the *Sea Venture* were Sir George's nephew Matthew, Silvester Jourdain, and very probably a number of other Lyme seamen.

However, long before they reached America, the *Sea Venture* parted company with its little flock. Here I will put the story in the capable hands of Lyme Regis's first historian, George Roberts.

On the 25th July, the admiral's ship, with the other commanders and their commission, and 150 men, parted company in the tail of a hurricane. The ship worked so much, and became so leaky, that the water rose in the hold above two tiers of hogs-heads. With all hands ba[i]ling and pumping for three days and nights without intermission, still the water seemed to increase. At last, all being spent with labour, and seeing no hope, they resolved to shut down the hatches. In this extremity, those who had "comfortable waters" drank to one another as taking their last leaves, till a more joyful and happy meeting in the other world. Sir G. Summers [sic], the skilful seaman, sat all this time on the poop, scarce allowing himself leisure to eat or sleep, steering the ship to keep her upright, or she must have foundered. He unexpectedly descried land: upon the news all ran up, and from ceasing to [bail] nearly caused their destruction. They spread all sail, though they knew the land to be Bermudas—the land of devils and spirits, then dreaded and shunned by all men. The ship soon struck upon a rock, but a surge of the sea cast her off, and so from one to another, till she was most luckily thrown up between two, as upright as if she had been on the stocks. The wind having calmed, they got out, people, goods, and provisions, in their boats, and arrived in safety without the loss of a man; though some say a league, others half a mile from the shore.

Fallen into a land of plenty and pleasantness, the strangers were lavish in their praise of it. Sir George Summers, like another Aeneas, procured food for the whole company by catching fish with hook and line. They killed thirty-two hogs, which abounded there, said to have swam ashore from a Spanish ship, called the Bermudas, *which was carrying hogs to the West Indies.*

The Bermudas were first sighted, before 1515, by the Spanish sailor Juan de Bermudez. They were first named Virginiola by the shipwrecked men, then Somers or Summer Islands (the latter probably because of the mild climate, but perhaps also because "Summers" is a common alternate spelling of Somers in Lyme documents of the time), and only later acquired their present name.

The Englishmen, as Englishmen will, attributed their good fortune to the fact that they were English; the island's malevolence clearly extended only to wicked Catholic foreigners like the Spaniards and the French—though they were at first puzzled, it is true, by the mysterious noises at night, and worried, as superstitious seamen might well be, by the ubiquitous pigs. However, they quickly developed a fancy for their enforced home, despite its evil reputation, and in fact behaved exactly like Odysseus and his crew on Circe's island of Aeaea after that first little contretemps, also having to do with pigs. The climate was delicious, there was wood and fresh water, palm-leaf for roofing and walling, seafowl (apparently petrels or shearwaters) "full and fat as . . . partridge," turtle, fish "dainty as salmon"; and the pork had "more pleasant and sweet a taste than mutton in England." Even the Bermuda crow had "as white flesh as a chicken." Readers of contemporary travel-agency literature may notice a certain familiar ring ("superb seafood, endless unspoiled beaches") in these similes, and they will be quite right. Most of the gentlemen reporters on all the early American "ventures" had a heavy financial stake in their success; if they did not quite yet show the monstrous blind eye exhibited by some Victorian emigrant-recruiters in Europe, they were very decidedly not interested in turning customers away.

The idyllic side of this first involuntary holiday in the Bermudas was short-lived. The soldiers, sailors, and settlers of the *Sea Venture* had scattered among the various islands, and quarrels and mutinies soon developed. In the first escape attempt, fourteen men set out in one of the *Sea Venture*'s boats for the American mainland. They were never heard of again. Somers then built two small boats, probably using a mixture of the *Sea Venture*'s timbers and the local juniper (Bermuda "cedar"). On May 10, 1610, the two pinnaces set out for Jamestown. They made the six-hundred-mile passage in only thirteen days, thanks once again to Somers's seamanship and expertise in navigation; but they landed only to find the rest of the original expedition much less happy with their unshipwrecked lot. They were starving, and they had Indian troubles.

Somers eventually agreed to sail back to the Bermudas in company with Samuel Argall, the later kidnaper of Pocahontas, to fetch meat and fish for these less-than-brave New Worlders. He was separated from Argall, but arrived back in Bermuda in early November—only to die there on November 9. The cause of death was a "surfeit of pig." His last order to his nephew Matthew was to take a cargo of the "black hogs" back to Jamestown. Perhaps the crew mutinied at the thought of taking live pigs on board and once more turning their backs on home; perhaps the new captain decided to have a grim revenge on their superstitiousness. At any rate, having buried his uncle's heart and entrails in the islands, he secretly sealed up the presumably well-salted corpse in a juniper box, smuggled it aboard, and set sail for Lyme.

The ship made the voyage safely, in spite of its dark cargo. Sir George's remains, carried "athwart and first ashore" if tradition was obeyed, were interred on June 4, 1611, with full military honors, and lie to this day beneath the vestry floor in the church of Whitchurch Canonicorum. Somers had a manor farm in the parish, on a hill overlooking the sea and his birthplace. His wife, I am afraid, proved no Penelope. An entry in the Whitchurch parish register records that on July 12, 1612, "Lady Sumers" married a certain "William Raymond, Esquire"—no doubt a buccaneer of a different, safer kind . . . or perhaps a fool. When the will was proved in November of that year, it turned out that Matthew had inherited all of his uncle's considerable real estate. It was evidently not quite pure piety that had made him risk Scylla's fury by bringing that indisputably dead body back.

Silvester Jourdain had meanwhile sailed in another ship straight back to England from Virginia. It carried an official dispatch to the Company patentees, which was to be rewritten and published later that year as *A True Declaration of the Estate of the Colony in Virginia*. This was drafted by William Strachey, another of the Bermuda survivors, who had also written a private—and much more truthful—account from Virginia in a letter dated July 10, 1610, which remained unpublished until 1625. But Jourdain evidently sniffed a scoop; or perhaps he wanted to play the mini-Homer. As soon as he was back, he rushed out a pamphlet entitled *A Discovery of the Barmudas, otherwise called the Isle of Divels*; and this was the first publicly available account of the extraordinary adventure.

Quite apart from his anxiety to get his pamphlet out, nothing is more probable than that Jourdain would have been in London in 1610 to tell the

story to the many backers of the Virginia adventure. One person in particular who would have wanted to question him was the Earl of Southamp-
ton, a patron of the Weymouth and Harlow voyages to Virginia earlier in
that decade, and another founder of the Company; and in the Southamp-
ton circle was a sharp-eared and myth-prone playwright with as good a
nose for the topical as Sir George Somers had had for magnetic north. He
was also no mini-Homer, though he had had some trouble adapting his
gifts to the new fashion for the pastoral, a form concerned primarily with
the contrast between nature and culture . . . the debit and credit of human
progress and civilization. Like all men of his time, he had had a long love-
hate relationship with the symbolism of the sea-voyage, and a particular
obsession with death by water. It had first declared itself nearly twenty
years before, in one of his earliest plays, and he must, in that winter of
1610, have remembered the relevant passage. A man recalls a nightmare:

> Lord, Lord! methought, what pain it was to drown!
> What dreadful noise of waters in mine ears!
> What ugly sights of death within mine eyes!
> Methought I saw a thousand fearful wracks;
> Ten thousand men that fishes gnaw'd upon;
> Wedges of gold, great anchors, heaps of pearl,
> Inestimable stones, unvalued jewels.
> All scatt'red in the bottom of the sea;
> Some lay in dead men's skulls. . . .

All through history, literary scholars have searched externally for
sources, which approach is not necessarily wrong, but overlooks one very
simple fact that any practicing author could tell them. The major influence
on any mature writer is always his own past work. The tyro dramatist from
Stratford may, in the lines above from *King Richard the Third*, superficially
have been trying to out-Marlowe Marlowe; but he was also sowing a seed
for future germination. He knew the *Aeneid* much better than he did the
Odyssey, but Odysseus' experience already haunts this passage: the onward
hubris and vaulting ambition of the voyage, the black stasis of shipwreck
and drowning, the gateway beyond of ultimate revelation. Clarence's
dream stayed dry tinder, waiting for the Bermudan spark.

I must not let local patriotism run away with me. In fact Shakespeare
seems to have taken rather more from Strachey's letter, which he must have

been shown, than from Jourdain. It is not at all unlikely that he met one, or even both, of them. But the key figure in the story is really the man whose bones lie under the vestry floor; who kept the *Sea Venture* afloat, who maintained some sort of order during that difficult winter on the islands, who organized the escape and brought it and the two writers he had aboard to a successful conclusion. I think it is to him, the only begetter in nonliterary reality, that we most owe the one other exploration of the island metaphor that stands shoulder to shoulder with the *Odyssey* and *Robinson Crusoe*.

Like so many geniuses of the first order, Shakespeare seems to me to have saved his profoundest work till the very end. *The Tempest* (its first known performance, before the king, took place on November 1, 1611) may not have the greatest poetry, or the greatest penetration of human character. Its brevity (it is the shortest but one of all his plays), its enormous compression in time and space, its cuts, leaps, and discontinuities— all these can make it seem lightweight, no more than a sketch. But its lightweightness is that of Cézanne's last watercolors or of the arietta from Beethoven's last piano sonata: whatever such art may lack in substance, it gains, like a sublime thistledown, in altitude. The brusquenesses, even the clumsinesses, are those of supreme mastery, of a man sailed far beyond the barrier of mere technique; to where those lines I earlier quoted from T. S. Eliot assume their greatest force and justification.

The Tempest floats free in a way that no other of that formidable chain of masterpieces of the seventeenth-century years of Shakespeare's life quite manages. Those others are for the world at large; this is for each. And that is why Shakespeare made his overriding metaphors the island and the sailor stranded in a place that he cannot fully understand . . . which both bewitches and is intensely cruel; which can hold both Calibans and Ariels, Antonios and Mirandas; which can be only too savagely "real" and yet still an insubstantial pageant. Of course Prospero's island no more lies in the Bermudas than it is, according to the story, set between Tunis and Italy— though the latter location strongly echoes those of both the *Aeneid* and the *Odyssey*. *The Tempest* is a parable about the human imagination, and thus finally about Shakespeare's view of his own imagination: its powers, its hopes, its limits—above all, its limits. The play's true island is our planet, in its oceanic sea of space.

Any specific and realistic shape the island location took in Shakespeare's consciousness must have derived from his knowledge of the Strachey,

Jourdain, and other, associated pamphlets, and I am not for a moment proposing the Scillies as an alternative; yet they were far more on Elizabethan and Jacobean minds than they are on ours today. This was because of their vital strategic importance during the chronic Armada scares of the period, which by no means began or ended with the debacle of 1588. In August 1601, the mayor of Lyme was urgently ordered to "set forth a barque . . . for the discovery of the Spanish fleet"; there was a major panic as late as 1628, when many Scillonians fled to the mainland. Given the difficulty of sailing in convoy, the Spaniards were well aware that they needed an offshore rendezvous before launching a final attack, and the Scillies were the obvious place for it. The problems of fortifying the islands (an effort first undertaken in 1548) and exploiting their value as an early warning system crop up continually in the State Papers of the period. The very notion of an ordained ruler's having the would-be usurper wrecked and brought to justice would have remained highly attractive to anyone who had lived through the worst years of the Spanish threat. But there is something else on the Scillies that does bring us, symbolically, much closer to the play.

Two summers ago I spent a few days on one of the least-known and most beautiful of the larger European islands, the queen of the Baltic, Gotland. By pure chance one morning, out walking, I came through some fir trees on the edge of a remote strand on its eastern coast and stumbled on something that took me immediately back to the Scillies: a maze of beach pebbles laid in concentric rings, as if by some playful group of idle teenagers. But I knew I was staring down at something much more ancient and haunting than that. There is just such a maze on the western side of Saint Agnes, also standing on a little slope above the sea, and looking out towards the ships' graveyard and seal-city of the Western Rocks.

It is near a farm called Troytown; but that name comes from the maze itself. *Troy-fair* and *Troy-town* are very old dialect words meaning "a mess," "a confusion" . . . "a maze." These particular pebble mazes, usually of ten to fifteen yards in diameter, are found mostly in Scandinavia, where they have a very close association with coasts and islands. According to Geoffrey Grigson, they usually carry similar names there: Trojeburg, Tröborg, and so on. There is another famous one on Gotland, at Visby. R. L. Bowley says the Saint Agnes maze has been recorded for two hundred years and was "probably originally constructed by a bored lighthouse keeper"; but I think, with Geoffrey Grigson, that the evidence is very much against this. We know the Vikings knew Scilly, and the similarities with indisputably much older sea mazes in Scandinavia are too great.

We shall never know what ritual significance these mazes had for the Vikings, but in both Celtic and Mediterranean Europe the maze appears to have been associated with the tomb, and escape from it, with reincarnation. This is what lies at the heart of the Daedalus legend: the real labyrinth he escaped from in Crete was the maze-pattern of the very ancient spring fertility or "partridge" dance (more accurately, the dance of the migratory and corn-field-haunting quail, still a prime harbinger of summer on every Aegean island). It certainly predated Minoan Crete, and was probably originally performed on literal threshing floors, and only later on the symbolic threshing floor of the maze.

I have a fragment of antiquity standing beside me as I write this: a fat old pot from the third millennium B.C., excavated in one of the mountain plains just north of ancient Sumeria. In a kind of strip cartoon round its shoulder, stylized two-headed birds peck and bob in a field of corn; and among them one can see the most famous of Minoan-Cretan symbols, the *labrys*, or so-called double-headed axe. But the two triangles of which the latter is formed are in fact simply even more stylized headless birds. Another highly stylized symbol on the pot, of four inward-pointing triangles, is related: this stands for four deer, or cattle, running round a pool. A case in the British Museum is devoted to the elaboration of this design.

The *labrys* that supposedly guarded, or warned against entering, the labyrinth is no axe, but a dancing-bird symbol of fertility, or food. *Labrys* is not a Greek word, but I believe its origin can be plausibly guessed. One has only to say *labr-* to feel the mouth and lips move to peck in and gulp. There is a Greek adjective, *labros*, that means "forceful and greedy"— "gluttonous," by extension. Another word, *labbax*, denoted a sea-wolf. *Labrum* is Latin for "lip"; and the Romans' *labor*, our "labor," is based on an ancient sense of slipping away and its consequent suffering and anxiety (which we retain in the "labor" of childbirth). The need to eat, the need to work to eat, the need to propitiate the forces that control fertility and climatic conditions . . . these are what the ancient labyrinth or maze truly signifies. Even the monster at its Cretan center, the bull-man Minotaur, is a fertility symbol. I know that the maze on Saint Agnes was first built not by a bored lighthouse-keeper of the eighteenth century, but by a Phoenician sailor two and a half thousand years earlier; and know equally well that no serious archaeologist would for a moment support such a hypothesis.

The maze is also a very ancient symbol of ingenuity in craftsmanship, of the ability to fabricate, to sew and weave, beyond ordinary skill—in other words, it is the prime proof of the artificer, or artist. If Minos stood for sea power, or exploitive commerce, and Scylla stood for its greatest enemy, hostile nature and the shipwreck, Daedalus stands for the producer who inspires the endless conflict between profit and its loss. Nothing could be more poetic, both symbolically and in justice, than the end of the Daedalus-Minos legend.

Minos keeps the great artificer and his son, Icarus, prisoners on Crete. Daedalus invents flight, but his son goes too close to the sun and ends up a victim of the first fatal air crash. Daedalus buries him, then flies on to Italy, and eventually to Sicily, where he works for King Cocalus (another ominous-sounding sea-name). Minos, not one to accept brain drain, sets out to find his disobedient inventor. He knows the fugitive is in hiding, so once arrived in Sicily, he sets a problem that he knows only Daedalus will be able to solve: the passing of a linen thread through the complex convolute chambers (the maze symbolism again) of a Triton shell. Daedalus is tempted and, by a brilliant piece of what Mr. Edward de Bono would call lateral thinking, solves the problem. Minos now knows the scent is very warm. But King Cocalus's daughters warn Daedalus, and a plot is made, neatly echoing the fate that Minos once callously left Scylla to meet. He is persuaded to take a bath. Daedalus constructs an ingenious pipe; as soon as the sea-emperor is in the tub, it is flooded with boiling water (or pitch, in another version), and he (Cretan sea power) is done for. *Omnia vincit ars*; and what are all the Somerses, Southamptons, Jourdains now but skulls and bones in Shakespeare's cellar? It is not Odysseus who finally survives, but Daedalus. "O, my name for you is the best," cries Buck Mulligan to Stephen Dedalus at the beginning of *Ulysses*. "Kinch, the knifeblade."

All of which may have escaped Shakespeare's little Latin and less Greek; but mazes he would have known. They were much commoner—especially in the unicursal, as opposed to multicursal, form of the one on Saint Agnes—in the England of his day. They were usually made of turf, not shore pebbles. In another play drenched with magic, *A Midsummer Night's Dream*, Shakespeare already has Titania lamenting their disappearance (*quaint* carries its old sense of "ingenious" or "cunning" here, not its modern one):

The nine-men's-morris is fill'd up with mud:
And the quaint mazes in the wanton green,
For lack of tread, are undistinguishable.

No doubt it was the Puritans who were historically responsible for the loss, at about this time, of the old morris floors and turf-mazes, with their superstitious associations. One explanation of Prospero's final-curtain speech holds that it is a tacit apology to King James for the play's references to magic, witchcraft, mazes, and demonology in general. It is not an explanation that satisfies me, though such "material" may well have been suspect for the pious and conventional of the period. What is certain is that Shakespeare did deliberately plant the maze symbolism in *The Tempest*. The very structure is circular and mazelike, and there are a number of direct references. "Here's a maze trod indeed," groans old Gonzalo, "through forthrights and meanders!" Then Alonso in the last act: "This is as strange a maze as e'er men trod,/ And there is in this business more than nature/ was ever conduct of." At the very end, when Gonzalo blesses Ferdinand and Miranda, he adds, "For it is you that have chalk'd forth the way/ Which brought us hither." All of us have found ourselves, he says in conclusion, "Where no man was his own."

It must be remembered too that the verb *amaze*, also used at key places in the play, had a far more literal connotation then—of trance, of almost total loss of normal bearings and physical capacity. "Half sleep, half waking" is how Shakespeare himself glosses *amazedly* in *A Midsummer Night's Dream*. Men of his time knew where the real monster lay in the labyrinth: not at its center, but in the difficulties of finding the right path to it. To the more sophisticated Elizabethans and Jacobeans, the maze bore a close analogy to the ring-diagram of the Ptolemaic universe (with its anthropocentrism) and to astrology, where each planet-path symbolized an aspect of psyche; and perhaps also to the tortuous search for the philosopher's stone. When Prospero says, "Now does my project gather to a head" near the end of the play, he is certainly using the jargon of alchemy. The maze center represented true self-knowledge.

One of the naive cuts in Francis Quarles's *Emblems* of 1635—perhaps the most popular book, after Foxe's *Martyrs*, of that soul-searching century— shows this interpretation very clearly, and even includes the association with the sea. Anima, the pilgrim soul, stands at the maze center, holding a cord thrown down by an angel on a lighthouse with a burning cresset. At the beginning of the maze, a blind man follows his dog, and just outside it, drowning men raise their arms for help; two others try to clamber up the rocks on which the lighthouse sits. There are ships on the horizon. It is a very strange picture, since the maze (in this case of the multicursal type) seems set in the sea, with its passage cut in water. A stanza of the accompanying poem explains this bizarre conceit. The "labyrinth" is the world:

> *This gyring lab'rinth is betrench'd about*
> *On either hand with streams of sulph'rous fire,*
> *Streams closely sliding, erring in and out,*
> *But seeming pleasant to the fond descrier;*
> *Where if his footsteps trust their own invention,*
> *He falls without redress, and sinks without dimension.*

And Gonzalo:

> *All torment, trouble, wonder and amazement*
> *Inhabits here: some heavenly power guide us*
> *Out of this fearful country.*

The proving maze in *The Tempest* is constructed by Shakespeare's imagination, hiding behind the mask of Prospero. At one level, it is very similar to our most familiar contemporary use of the word, in the laboratory maze for testing learning ability and behaviorism in animals; and as has been often pointed out (and like, I am afraid, a good deal of laboratory testing), it does at this level little but underline the obvious. True, two nice young people fall in love, but out of their own natures, not through magic. A fuddleheaded but kind old man, Gonzalo, remains fuddleheaded and kind to the end; two cynical, scheming politicians demonstrate by their final bitter silence that they will always be so; two seamen-buffoons and an Indian "savage" stay unredeemed. Even the spirit Ariel seems anxious to be freed from playing assistant to any more such futile experiments. Only Alonso, who conspired in the usurpation, shows any plausible repentance; but he has very little to lose by changing sides—it is mere shrewd diplomacy—when his son is to marry the heiress to Milan.

It is certainly not difficult to read, even in Prospero himself, a suspicion that he has in vain tried to surpass that other sea-magician and pig-maker hiding behind Caliban's Bermuda-inspired mother, Sycorax (from Greek *sys,* "sow," and *korax,* "crow")—that is, Circe. The "every third thought shall be my grave" that he prophesies of his return to Milan is hardly a happy final note. He forgives, as Circe and Calypso forgive their visitor (his last command to Ariel repeats their last gift to Odysseus, the provision of a fair wind), but the forgiveness is also like theirs in its air of forced circumstance, of noblesse oblige. No hearts have changed.

I spoke earlier of Homer's humanity's overcoming convention in the treatment of Calypso, and I sense something similar in *The Tempest*: a wise sadness seeping into the ritual happy ending. The play may outwardly demonstrate true culture, or moral nobility, triumphing over both false culture and culturelessness; but it throws strange doubts and shadows on its own message and on its very form. The conflict revealed is the oldest in all art, and it takes place inside the artist: between the power to imagine and the use of imagining. *Cui bono?* To what purpose? What will it change? The question haunts every constructor of worlds that are not the one that is the case. Solution is not helped by that other secret every artist nurses, all the incommunicable pleasures of maze construction, of sea voyaging, of island discovering, that may be infused in the final product, but are never explicit in it. The truth is that the person who always benefits and learns most from the maze, the voyage, the mysterious island, is the inventor, the traveler, the visitor . . . that is, the artist-artificer himself.

I believe this is precisely what Shakespeare realized during the course of creating *The Tempest*: a terrible solipsism underlay the play. Who benefits most is the maker of it, Prospero-Shakespeare; and what he learns most is the dubious efficacy of the demonstration to all who merely undergo it, as opposed to the one who designs it. This is one major reason the maze running changes so little in the basic nature of the guinea pigs, and why there is that famous reference to Prospero's drowning his books and turning his back thenceforth on magic. Three times Caliban tells Stephano and Trinculo that Prospero's books must be destroyed before he can be murdered.

Of course this may seem supremely unimportant to the outsider, to all of us in the audience; enough that the maker here is a great poet and dramatist. *The Tempest* now has the status of a personal myth become universal; and like all myths, it allows of countless interpretations, maze upon maze, which makes it additionally delicious meat to an age so besotted by analysis and dissection, so devoted to daedalizing Daedalus. The growing tendency of our century is to reify, to put learning above living. It is even a fault in Prospero himself. We sometimes forget how he first lost his dukedom in Milan; here is his own notoriously stiff and knotted (in syntactical and metrical terms) account to his daughter. His reign in Milan was

> . . . *for the liberal arts*
> *Without a parallel; those being all my study,*
> *The government I cast upon my brother,*
> *And to my state grew stranger, being transported*
> *And rapt in secret studies.*

He goes on:

> *I, thus neglecting worldly ends, all dedicated*
> *To closeness and the bettering of my mind*
> *With that which, but by being so retir'd,*
> *O'er priz'd all popular rate . . .*
> *. . . Me, poor man, my library*
> *Was dukedom enough. . . .*

And the books that had been his downfall were, it will be remembered, secretly smuggled by old Gonzalo on board the boat that took him into forced exile. The "books" are his imagination, and he cannot be parted from that, whatever the final talk of drowning, "deeper than did ever plummet sound."

The climax of the self-doubt lies in that very last speech of the play, despite its surface flatness and near banality. One can take it as the trite request for applause, as much expected at the time as the flowery dedications to rich patrons that began most books. But it reads rather differently if we posit that Prospero really stands for Shakespeare's own power to create magical islands of the mind; and that what has gone before (and far beyond *The Tempest* itself) raises very considerable doubts about the ability of that power to change human nature in any but very superficial ways.

> *Now my charms are all o'erthrown,*
> *And what strength I have's mine own,*
> *Which is most faint: now, 'tis true,*
> *I must be here confin'd by you,*

Or sent to Naples. Let me not,
Since I have my dukedom got
And pardon'd the deceiver, dwell
In this bare island by your spell;
But release me from my bands
With the help of your good hands:
Gentle breath of yours my sails
Must fill, or else my project fails,
Which was to please. Now I want
Spirits to enforce, art to enchant;
And my ending is despair,
Unless I be reliev'd by prayer,
Which pieces so, that it assaults
Mercy itself, and frees all faults.
As you from crimes would pardon'd be,
Let your indulgence set me free.

What is striking here is the repeated reference to imprisonment and release. The illusion, the magic, is over; but the innermost meaning, the conclusion from the maze heart of the imaginative power, is not. The prison for Shakespeare is in having failed to communicate ("I must be here"—in the marooning artifice of the medium, on the stage—"confin'd by you") that the power to affect, and effect, by imaginative means is strictly dependent on precisely that same *active* energy of imagination in the audience that lay behind the work's creation. The "spell" is the audience's literalness, or blindness. What makes the island "bare," the ending "despair," is the putting of art in the "bands" of parenthesis, in the treatment of it merely as ingenious maze, external form, surface of text and image, entertainment.

It is almost as if Shakespeare had foreseen the very recent neo-Freudian theory of language and literature as the prime alienators of self from reality, a universal exploitation far worse than the social and economic ones. Something castrating haunts both the Greek and the Latin words for "I write"—*grapho* and *scribo*—which have a shared Indo-European origin meaning "to cut." It is seen in all the ancient magical uses of the sign or symbol that forbids or proscribes. The text may demand action; but something in its external, objective, "other" nature is always inherently alienating of action in all who did not perform the original action of its creation.

In simplest terms, and at even the very highest level, it is someone else's magic.

We are, in that epilogue, eons beyond the make-believe world of benevolent wizards and cowslip-dwelling sea nymphs. Only one wind will ever fill those sails, if the barrenness of our planet-island is ever to be truly left behind; and it is beyond even Shakespeare's power to provide it.

But that the vital motive power must lie in the imagination of the beholder is implicit in the piece. It has, I think justly, been interpreted as a play with a cast of one; that is, its eleven main parts can all be seen as aspects of the one mind, as so many planets of different humors mazing and circling round a central earth. The central earth of *The Tempest* is clearly Prospero-Ariel, the imagination and its executor, the writer and his pen, forced to cohabit with all the other dispositions of the mind . . . and all stranded, like a schizoid Crusoe, on the island of the each. *Hamlet* and *Lear* and *Macbeth* are dreams of men. *The Tempest* is a dream of the only divinity men are allowed, and a statement of how literally island-small, compared with the all-controlling power of the gods of myth, it is—and always will be until it is shared and understood.

Every child who visits Saint Agnes has a hop round the Troytown maze; and I hope will long continue to do so, for I should hate to see it fenced in and museumized like Stonehenge. But to anyone who has lived for longer than a summer holiday on a remote island, I trust it will always mean rather more than a minute's amusement—or amazement. Most who have been through that experience will know that the maze began at their first step ashore; and I should be surprised, even though the center (given the present world shortage of Prosperos and Ariels) was not reached, if any in retrospect regret the exploration.

I first began to feel the releasing power of *The Tempest* when I lived on my island in Greece: the lack of a Prospero, the need of a Prospero, the desire to play Daedalus. It is the first guidebook to take for anyone who is to be an islander; or since we are all islanders of a kind, perhaps the first guidebook for anyone at all, at least the self-inquiring. More and more we lose the ability to think as poets think, across frontiers and consecrated limits. More and more we think—or are brainwashed into thinking—in terms of verifiable facts, such as money, time, personal pleasure, established knowledge. One reason I love islands so much is that of their nature they question such lack of imagination; that properly experienced, they make us stop and think a little: why am I here, what am I about, what is it all about, what has gone wrong?

Modern wreck-divers use the word *crud*, a dialect form of *curd*, to describe the coagulated minerals that form round any long-sunken metal object, and that have to be laboriously chipped and leached away before it can be exposed to sight again. Islands strip and dissolve the crud of our pretensions and cultural accretions, the Odyssean mask of victim we all wear: I am this because life has made me like this, not because I really want to be like this. There is in all puritanism a violent hostility towards all that does not promise personal profit. Of course, the definition of profit changes. "It may be thought," wrote Cromwell to the House of Commons after he had helped reduce the city of Bristol in 1645, "that some praises are due to those gallant men, of whose valour so much mention is made: their humble suit to you and all that have an interest in this blessing is that in the remembrance of God's praises they be forgotten." The profit then lay in eternity, and the ticket to what was to be bought by an arrogant extreme of self-denial.

We have in our own century lost all faith in the remembrance of God's praises. The profit now is tallied in personal pleasure; but we remain puritan in our adamant pursuit of it. Purveying recipes for pleasure has become a mainstay of popular publishing and journalism: where to go, what to enjoy, how to enjoy, when to enjoy, to such a clogging, blurring extent that our modern duty to enjoy is nowadays almost as peremptory—and destructive—as the old Puritan's need to *renounce* pleasure, to ban the play, the dance, the graven image, and everything else that makes present life agreeable. It is all very well to create a permissive society. But we have not created the essential corollary of a pagan mind.

The true pagan mind, from Homer on, always knew that the laws of pleasure had very little to do with endless consumption, endless exhortation to experience, endless attempts to tell the individual in what his pleasure consists and to guide him through the labyrinth whose deepest values can only be self-discovered. We cannot all be labyrinth makers; but we can all learn to explore and trace them for ourselves. There used to be a guide to the famous maze at Hampton Court that showed the quickest route to take. Nobody who used it ever reached the center, which lies not in the unraveled, but in the unraveling.

We have helicopters, motorboats, guided tours; all the facilities, all the knowledge. Shakespeare, despite that gold ring in his ear, very probably never saw a remote sea-island in all his life, so his is merely charming fantasy, overintricate and increasingly incomprehensible, like his rich language in this tired, etiolated period of our own; and he himself merely the world's greatest dramatist, safe-throned on the peak of Parnassus, at a very great and alienating distance from you, me, and anything else relevant today. . . .

But now I am hopping into a sermon, and that will never do. Like all good islands, the Scillies can play their own pulpit. To those who cannot go there, will perhaps never go there, I can at least recommend Fay Godwin's photographs, which represent very exactly what that wise visitor I began with will look for: the elemental compound of sky, sea, sand, rock, the forms and textures of simplest things, the cleansing, as the sea itself will cleanse, of overartifice, overknowledge, and overcivilization from the mind exhausted by our age's mania for the secondhand, mechanical image. Our century has rightly learned to admire the Zen gardens of Japan for their austere simplicity; and most of Scilly remains one huge Zen garden of the Atlantic.

A medieval master of that faith was once asked by a novice which plant in a garden most pleased the Buddha. The old man thought, then answered:

"The mirror."

"But master, a mirror has no leaves, no flower, no fruit."

My sincere hope is that the slap the novice then received was freighted with every ounce of force still lying in the sage's arm.

LAND

(1 9 8 5) [1]

I have first of all to confess to a considerable dislike of photography as everyman practices it. I detest the sight of bands of tourists armed with cameras, snapping everything into nonexistence, like so many piranha-fish. The disapproval comes, needless to say, very largely from the fact that I was just such a photographer myself for many years. Then as now, my knowledge of photographic techniques was, and remains, a close cousin to total ignorance. I did once dabble with an enlarger, but it very rapidly mastered me instead of the reverse, and I gave up the darkroom with relief. I took the experience at the time as one more proof of a personal inability to cope with machines, but I now see there was a more obdurate cause: photography and novel writing are deeply antipathetical activities, and inherently hostile—indeed by nature almost blind—to each other's virtues.

What disqualifies me even more plainly is that I am doubtful of landscape photography as generally practiced. It is certainly very far from what I seek myself in landscape, which is the personal and direct experience of it, in both a temporal and a physical sense—the very opposite of a photograph, in sum. I do not even like landscape itself very much, as most people think of the word: the large general view, the wide expanse of country. There is an illusion that all country people adore the long tramp, adore striding over hill and dale, enjoying the air and reveling in the prospects. Nothing could be more wrong in my case, and I regard this idea

---

1. This essay was written as a preface to Fay Godwin's remarkable photographic work on British land-scape. The book in which it first appeared—*Land* (London: Heinemann, 1985)—is a testament to her wordless eloquence.

of use of the countryside as a purely urban (and largely literary) one, something gone in for only by town-dwellers who happen to find themselves in the country through retirement or on holiday. The long walk may be an eminently healthy pastime, but like jogging and many other activities of that kind, it is for me also one of the most boring.

I have heard Fay describe the formidable walks she does in pursuit of her remoter subjects, and they secretly make my soul flinch. I am much more a peasant loafer and hedge-poker; an idler, a lingerer. What interests me in a landscape is above all its natural history, its flowers, trees, birds, spiders, insects, creatures of all kinds, and a walk that does not both require and allow one to stop and examine at leisure every ten yards is no amusement for me. My truest and dearest kind of landscape is very small indeed, never more than a field or one hillside, and usually much smaller still, no more than an odd corner. All more distant landscapes seem to me to taunt, to invite the close entry of the kind I like, yet at the same time to make it clear that such entry is impossible; and this is even more taunting with the photograph, which makes such entry doubly impossible. Fay once asked me why I was staring so at one of her prints—was there something wrong with it? I had not the courage to tell her I was trying to recognize a flower in it, which she had very carelessly, in her obsession with the right composing of the view, left too far from the lens to make identification easy.

This attitude is eccentric, I know; yet I believe it was shared by a number of artists and writers close to nature, and close to my heart, such as Thomas Bewick and John Clare. To most people landscape is very much bound up with the idea of grandeur, or extended space. My view of it is much more as a succession of living, and no more than room-sized, vignettes. What fascinates me is the particularity of the nature at one's feet, being able both to touch it and to know it in all its scales, which in this country are seldom matched to those of the human body or to the time-consecrated interests and purposes of the landscape artist.

Then there is my worst grumble of all: the deadness, the fixity—or fixingness—of the photographic print. It is not only that everything is held like a fly in amber. One cannot even hold the fixed fly in one's hand, and turn it round, see it from any other angle or distance. I sometimes feel an almost metaphysical horror before photographs, that they freeze time so, snatch their fractions of a second from it and then set them up as the ultimate reality of the thing photographed. I am, as I write, at the early stage of going through material for another photographic book, of views of

Thomas Hardy and his world, taken by photographers of his own time. I know that many of these photographs are of great historical interest, are at the least valuable archival material, and that we should be grateful they have survived . . . which is indeed to be the tacit point of that book. But as I look at them, I feel a resentment. Here is Hardy standing with his new bicycle, in the late 1890s, on the lawn in front of Max Gate. But what happened five seconds before? What happened five seconds after, when the photographer (Hardy's friend the scholar-parson Thomas Perkins) took his head from beneath the black cloth and announced that the very recent present was now eternal future?

All our knowledge of the world, even in the living present, is very small; and perhaps this fundamental animus I have against the photograph is due to the fact that it reminds us of that so much more vividly than any other art form. Its glimpses make us greedy for more, and simultaneously forbid any more, like a lid smashed down on stealing fingers. Because photographs are so close to visual reality and to the illusion of actually being there, we feel our deprivation far more sharply than with a painting or a description in words. This is why for me there is no substitute, with landscape, for being there in reality; for choosing one's own way through it, discovering and experiencing it fully and directly.

I suppose I am really complaining of the impossible: the lack of narrative in the still photograph. I mentioned in my novel *Daniel Martin* a literary account of a particular landscape that has deeply appealed to me ever since I first read it. The writer is Restif de la Bretonne, in his romanced autobiography, *Monsieur Nicolas*. His father was a well-to-do farmer in the Auxerre region of France, a hundred miles southeast of Paris, and young Restif-Nicolas—the date was about 1744, when he was ten—was allowed to look after the family flocks as they grazed. The description of what he calls *les bons vaux*—I have given it as the "sacred combe," but the literal sense conveys richness and abundance—runs over several pages. Here is the beginning of it:

> *Opposite to the vineyards of Mont Gré and behind the wood of Bout-Parc was a still lonelier valley which I had never yet dared enter: the high bordering woods gave it a somber look that frightened me. On the fourth day after the Nitry vintage, I ventured to go there with all my flocks. At the bottom of the valley were bushes for my goats, growing on the edge of a ravine, and greensward where the heifers could graze as in the Grand-Pré. Finding my-*

self there alone, I was filled with a secret horror, caused by Jacquot's tales of the excommunicated being changed into beasts; but the horror was not wholly unpleasant. My fourfold flock grazed about; the smaller pigs found an abundance of a kind of wild carrot, and rooted in the earth, while the larger ones, their mother leading, moved towards the wood. I was following to prevent them from entering it when, under an old oak covered with acorns, I saw an enormous wild boar. I trembled with fear and delight, for his presence there added to the wilderness which gave the place such charms for me. I came as near to him as I could. He saw me but, proudly disdaining a child, continued his meal. By a lucky chance, the sow was in heat; she went to the boar, who ran at her as soon as he smelled her. I was drunk with joy at the spectacle they presented to me, and held back my three dogs so that the boar should not be disturbed. At the same moment a hare showed itself, and a roebuck; and I thought myself transported into fairyland; I hardly breathed. I gave an inarticulate cry when a wolf appeared, and was forced to loose my dogs against this common enemy; the fear that he might attack the herd destroyed the charm of his presence (for all wild animals added to this in my eyes). My dogs frightened away hare, roebuck, and boar; all vanished into the wood, but the spell remained; it was even strengthened by a beautiful hoopoe coming to perch among two pear trees, of a kind the folk call honey-pears, because their fruit is so sweet and sugared that wasps and bees devour them when ripe. I knew the fruit well, for the parents of my friend Etienne Dumont had a honey-pear tree at the bottom of a field very near to my father's house, and he would sometimes take me to eat the little fallen pears. But how delicious were these, my very own, and on free ground! Add to this that they were ripe and plump, and that I owed no man for them, for the trees grew on the wild sward that bordered the ravine. . . . I looked with admiration at the hoopoe, the first I had ever seen, and ate some pears, while I filled my pockets with a feast of them for my young brothers and sisters.

This passage is imprecise in almost all the ways that a photograph must be precise; yet for me it has an emotional vividness, an accuracy with regard to an experience that every child has known, the first discovery of a secret place or landscape, which photography—even cinematography—is eternally barred from. The effect here is gained not just because the writing is sequential, describing a series of events, thoughts, reactions, but above all because it is so vague in its general detail that no reader will envision the place in the same way. It is both "so far" and intensely close at the same time, like the memory (as of course it really is) of an older person; and this, I believe, is a faculty beyond exact representation. That is, even if exact representation of the *bon val* had been possible—had Restif also been a ten-year-old genius with a pencil—it could only have diminished, not enhanced, the experience. One can go blind with seeing, in more ways than one.

By chance, a few years ago, I had my own camera stolen in Italy. I now regard it as a beneficent misfortune. I have not replaced it, and am the happier for it, like a sinner by chance brutally weaned of his sin. The main reason I am happier concerns this harm that I think the exact image does to memory. Human memory is a wise thing, and nowhere more than in what it chooses to forget. It knows best not only what we need humanly and emotionally to remember, but more subtly, *how* we should remember it, sometimes closely, sometimes dimly and fleetingly. We may imagine we would be more satisfied, richer beings if we remembered everything fully and precisely, "as in a film." We would not. Our memories also have soft-focus lenses, excluding and selecting mechanisms, and a genius (which cameras in themselves do not possess) for knowing in which details the richest meaning and symbolism lie for us. The trouble with the precise mental image, which we so often covet, or lament the absence of, is that it destroys all but one transient, time-fixed aspect of reality, whether it be that of a face, a place, or an event. It no more gives the whole truth of a marriage, say, than does a formal wedding photograph.

I used to enjoy photographing flowers in particular; now I prefer to remember them in a much vaguer way, and yet, perhaps strangely, what seems a more present one, compared with what I might feel if I had a photograph before me. The photograph dates, makes past, inalienably now dead. (This is why I dislike my piranha-fish tourist photographers, because they so often photograph in order not to have to look; as if recording for the future that they were there were more important than the being there itself.) In my mind, the plants can still grow, and I have learned not to worry about all those rare orchids and the rest that I might have remembered if only I had taken a photograph, but that I have actually forgotten. This applies to much else—to faces, landscapes, events, all one's past.

There is a parallel with overexact research in novel writing. The writer's vague recall will generally marry to the reader's imagery much better, and finally acquire, in the context of fiction (which depends so vitally on the reader's imagination), a greater reality and richness.

This must seem a strange and crotchety preamble; so I must, before I rule myself totally out of court as an introducer, admit that I write the above in a rather perverse sort of way. I have acquired these instinctive prejudices and doubts at least in part because serious photography does—by that other sort of perversity, perhaps, which draws all of us to contraries—attract and interest me. I discovered this attraction when Fay and I collaborated on another book, *Islands*, in 1978—though we in fact collaborated very little, since we agreed that we should both do our own thing as regards the general subject, the Scilly Isles. Her contribution impressed me very much by its austere purity, its almost fierce concentration on the elemental aspects of the Scillies; she managed to lend a paradoxical air of the abstract, from the worlds of Henry Moore and Ben Nicholson, to many of the shots. It was not how I see (or then saw) the islands; but it was of quite sufficient force to make me think again, and respect her very different vision of them.

I said just now that the camera has no genius for finding where the richest symbolism lies; that does not mean that the photographer may not possess such a power, and Fay handsomely proves that some photographers do. But that is not all. Her work since *Islands* has significantly developed not only in an artistic but in what I feel inclined to call a moral way. For reasons I will come to, the photographer's attitude towards British landscape has become a fraught and difficult question; and (putting matters very baldly) one clear answer to it is that the conventionally beautiful photograph *is* enough in itself. It is when we are given nothing else that things go wrong.

Fay is an inveterate pursuer of ancient roads: the Ridgeway, the drover roads of Wales, the whisky roads of Scotland, the Saxon Shore Way round Kent, the journey through Romney Marsh, most recently in Wessex. I must believe that all this walking and photographing to a prescribed itinerary has instilled in her a more than physical respect for the ancient road, indeed a kind of metaphysical one in terms of her art—that is, the finding also of a right road in terms of portraying landscape. Here she has, over these last few years, discovered that essential something else, beyond the capacity to take beautiful photographs: a feeling, an intuition, a personal philosophy—whatever it is that converts the good technician into the true artist.

Fay began with a camera in the mid-1960s, when she was already well into her thirties. This late start, much more normal with novelists than in her own profession, had its advantages; as did the fact that she is self-taught, and so was spared all the dubious conditionings of an art-college education. She has said that her own self-teaching was "painful and expensive," but I do not take her regrets very seriously. She would have been a far less unexpected photographer than she is if she had been spared that pain and the expense. Nor, since her father was a diplomat, had she spent many of her formative years in Britain, and she therefore came unusually fresh, when she began to concentrate on it, in 1974, to British landscape as well.

Moreover, she began her working life not in photography, but in publishing, and remains noticeably at home with writers, very much as aware of their craft and its problems as she is of hers and its own. She has worked with a number of us, on the strict understanding, which we all accept (though many reviewers haven't, alas), that it is truly an equal collaboration: no question of Fay's being treated as an inferior, a mere illustrator. In this book her work is indisputably the major contribution, and I am delighted to play second fiddle to it.

Being known mainly through books is a very mixed blessing for the photographer. Publishing realities mean that often poor, and always too small, reproductions—compared with the exhibition prints—are inevitable penalties. The difference between many of Fay's photographs, seen cramped and wrongly toned on the page, and then much larger, as they come from her darkroom, is often depressingly great. But her decision to risk this has had one recompense: a great variety of work and experience in the field, and I suspect a far clearer insight into what she is doing (or should be doing) than a more idealistic photographer might have.

She herself defined her aims in a characteristically forthright interview in 1983:

I don't have an academic approach to photographs, and I'm not very interested in theory. I'm much more interested in working. The old question about whether photography is an art is a silly question. I've been called a Roman-

*tic photographer and I hate it. It sounds slushy and my work is not slushy.
I'm a documentary photographer; my work is about reality, but that
shouldn't mean it can't be creative.*

Deep down I also share with Fay—despite my love of aspects of it that
neither still nor moving camera can record—a fascination with the special
character (I will define it as "usedness") of British landscape. It is a plati-
tude that ours is one of the most worked (and now rapidly becoming one
of the most abused) landscapes in the world. The working of Britain began much earlier than we generally think. A surprisingly high proportion
of now-farmed land was already being farmed at the time of the Domes-
day Book, and no less than 93 percent of land under the plow in 1914 was
also being tilled in 1086. Historians estimate the national population before the plague came in 1349 to have been between five and seven million,
the latter a figure not to be regained until the early eighteenth century.
Moreover, soil exhaustion was a perennial medieval problem, and far more
outlying land was brought into use to counter it than we may imagine.

It is this human working and reworking of small Britain from Stone
Age times that is its peculiarity. Englishmen (not least as colonial Americans) have seemingly been intensely acquisitive ever since the Norman
Conquest, and long before the Protestant work ethic officially came into
being. Something in them has always hated the sight of unused—or unusable—land, a hatred now applied perhaps more to land not used and prof-
ited from to the maximum. It is the technically less efficient farmers in
Europe, such as the French, who increasingly benefit their countries in
ecological terms. If I want to see the flowered meadows, the abundant butterflies, the beautiful arable "weeds"—cornflower and corncockle, poppy
and heartsease—of my childhood, the Continent is where I have to go;
they have been virtually exterminated in superfarmed Britain.

There lies over much of our land a formidably dense accretion of
knowledge of this past use, a local history unparalleled anywhere else in
the world. It is the fruit of many things: of folk history and legend, of Victorian (sometimes rather painfully sentimental and belletristic) fascination
with the past, of hard modern archaeological and historical scholarship
and research. I look after the history of one very small town and its close
neighborhood in Dorset, and all I have really learned about it is that it is
hopelessly too immense and detailed, too flush with sources, too open to

differing interpretations—in a word, too rich—for one person to hope to master. We are certainly now, and have long been, a grossly overcrowded country. If we were ever somewhere near balance (in aesthetic terms of human-landscape) in our more recent history, it was in the late eighteenth century, in the England of Moritz's *Travels*. One still has a sense there of a harmony, a form of green paradise. But that is as irrecoverable as a dream.

A photograph is neither a history nor a guidebook, and cannot tell us of all the human facts behind a landscape; yet it can suggest this deep *use*, or hidden human past, behind what the print outwardly shows. Here I believe Fay is peculiarly, if not uniquely, successful among her contemporaries. Several photographs in this collection demonstrate this. One that I am particularly fond of shows, from the snowed cliffs above Dover, two Channel ferries leaving the harbor—in itself, so stated, a banal snapshot subject. Yet this photograph has always given me, since I first saw it, an acute sense of an age-old and elemental yesterday spying on today. It has something to do with the depth given to these cliffs in the foreground, with their greater sharpness of detail and tone, against the slightly misty ships in the background below; but it also suggests some strange reversal of time. Today, the twentieth century, becomes the dream; and endless yesterday, the reality.

Eastern Docks, Dover is very far from being the only such time-questioning photograph here. I have seen words like *simple* and *straightforward* used of Fay's marked gift for composition and viewpoint, and it does often imply an honesty as "natural" as Atget's. But I think something much more complex is going on in shots such as this, with their juxtapositions of time. Their effect, in the throwing-together of modern and ancient, or man-made and primeval, is often enigmatic, almost sphinxlike. We are not quite sure what the photographer wants us to see, or why we have a sense that we may have missed the point.

The photograph from Dover Cliffs is also for me a kind of stumbling by accident on a crime: not one I could easily define, and certainly something far more complicated than the mere rape of nature or all the other sins against the land and sea that humanity has been forced into committing through its technological cleverness and stupidity in so many other areas of life. It conveys perhaps above all a sense of loss, a sadness that we have misused, or misunderstood, so much. I do not know what Fay's own feelings were when she took the photograph, but there is here for me, as in almost all her best work, an unmistakable undertone of warning melancholy, as if she knew she was photographing relics, places or feelings lost, like the faces of dead friends, to most of us.

I am being romantic? But we are now, in hard fact, on the bleak threshold of losing much of our old landscape. The camera cannot really reveal the grim truth that now lurks in the fields, the copses and woods, the distant valleys and hillsides of contemporary Britain. We have done unimaginably dreadful things to our countrysides in these last fifty years. We have destroyed an incalculable number of hedges; profoundly changed 95 percent of our natural lowland meadows, with their once-countless flowers, and 80 percent of our chalk and limestone grassland, the most beautiful of all; got rid of at least half of our heathlands and fenlands, between a third and a half of our ancient broad-leaved woods, and a third of our upland moors and rough pastures. The farmers' ever-increasing use of herbicides and pesticides keeps well ahead of the inflation rate, in financial terms. We are, says the Nature Conservancy Council, down to rock bottom in terms of providing suitable habitats for the continued existence of a frightening number of species of mammals, birds, insects, plants. It is only here and there along our coasts and on the really high hills and mountains that the old richness of natural life is not yet in danger.

In short, we have let scientific agriculture, or agribusiness, perform with its poisons and (idiotically so called) grass enrichers what we would call, in a human context, a holocaust. If many do not realize this, it is largely because so much of it is concealed from the nonspecialist. It is not as if, to someone traveling quickly through it, our average countryside would seem much changed. It stays green, while large areas still seem remarkably uninhabited to the casual eye. The spoilation and decimation are not in the least the result of rural overpopulation, or of the encroachment of the sprawling city and ribbon development that people feared between the two wars. By an irony it often appears least in the smaller nature, or in that view of it, that the passer-through most notices: the roadside verge and hedge. The true horror lies beyond and away from any road, in the endlessly "improved" or monoculture fields, the meadows whose former wildflowers can sometimes still be glimpsed, a handful of last survivors, here and there in surrounding hedges. In most cases they, and their dependent birds and insects, have disappeared forever.

It is not the farmers who are really to blame for the green deserts they have created, but rather the profit-driven greed and overpopulation of our species as a whole. The beauty of the land and the security of other species of life are no more than feathers on those scales. Recently a federal court in America allowed a river to bring a suit against a polluting city—that is, it allowed the river to become a human person, with maintainable rights whose breach was spoken for by human attorneys. We are lost until this outrageous idea (that a beach, a field, a stream, a threatened species, may have legal rights) becomes part of our own law, and an accepted part of human ethical thinking.

To my mind, this terrible situation poses a problem for any artist whose work involves the portrayal of country or natural life. Of course, as every holiday brochure and glossy magazine shows, enough still survives for only the beautiful (or the peaceful and lonely, with the twentieth century carefully censored) to be shown. But such work comes increasingly to seem in dubious moral taste. Rather like the rococo of the late eighteenth century, it may provide us with pretty objects, but only inside a dangerously narrow excerption from reality. Readers may think I exaggerate, but their grandchildren, in their green Sahara, will know better.

More and more I am out of sympathy with artists who monotonously purvey the pretty, the conventionally attractive, side of life and landscape outside our towns and cities, as if nothing had changed; and not least because their work is so popular, so endlessly provided for and bought by the public. I have turned down many offers from publishers to do various kinds of popular countryside books. I complained to one that there were already at least half a dozen good volumes on what he proposed; he totally misunderstood my objection, and answered that the market was virtually bottomless, so I need not worry about sales. The fault is not, of course, in finding beauty in nature, but in suggesting that all is well with it. We forgive, indeed expect, exaggeration in the holiday guide; but we seem oblivious to the same exaggeration in many of those charmingly illustrated and produced nature and landscape and rural-reminiscence books that sell in their hundreds of thousands, and especially to urban buyers. Part of their attraction is no doubt good, in that it recalls an ideal myth of the countryside and attaches people afresh to it; but a greater part, I very much fear, hides the reality of what is going on there. In effect, this kind of soft art and the wide public it caters to are unconsciously conspiring to perpetuate part of the ideal myth, that nothing really changes in the countryside.

Ever since people grew sentimental over the countryside and its landscapes, and it became a source for provoking emotion, a gymnasium for the sensitive, it has become more and more difficult to be honest about it. It has become too convenient, too lucrative, for the majority of artists not to distort it; to beautify, soften, make elegant, to garden it to suit public taste. One of the greatnesses of Thomas Bewick was that he managed—in his famous end-of-page vignettes—at least partly to counter this; to remind people that rural life could be obscene, stupid, and cruel, to both man and beast. The hanged human suicide over the stream is matched by the hanged dog; the thin ewe chews the besom's twigs in the snow outside the deserted Highland croft, while her lamb tries to get milk from her; the dog pisses both on the doctor's coat and on the hay the donkey eats; the members of the traveling fair troupe walk with their performing dogs, their monkey and their bear, beside the gibbet; the men outside the beerhouse are happily lost in the savage cockfight. . . . This is a hard, often bitter world, observed with humanity but not sentiment.

It is this unsentimental side that I find lacking in many of Bewick's followers in this century. They may equal him in mastery of technique in their various arts; but in honesty, very rarely. Their work perpetuates the rural dream of countless gentle intellectuals in this harsh century, whose real forebears were such escapist artists of the last century as Morland and Birket Foster: the creators of the cozy myth of the contented cottager, the countryside as humble idyll, for the delectation of those, mostly urban, who preferred to ignore agricultural and rural reality. Over them hangs too great a sweetness, too nostalgic an interest, too comfortable a tranquillity in the past, in tradition, in flowing with the stream. I think it must be said that it is a characteristically middle-class, privileged way of proceeding: always try to please people, never try to shock or shift them.

I do not mean that *épater les bourgeois* is a nobler thing, nor in itself a sounder recipe in creating; this century has given manifold evidence in all the arts that it is not, especially when it comes to mean that technical skill and a craftsman's knowledge of the medium are at best irrelevant, at worst proof of reactionary politics. Nevertheless, I do not believe this is a time when pure tradition, even done with all the skill in the world, can be enough. It is enough for the world at large, in both commercial and aesthetic terms. But it is not enough in any art that is based on our relation with nature. That relationship has never been good, and it is now in a desperately bad way, and I do not see how a polite, traditional, "classical" practice of it can any longer fit with the idea of the serious artist. A huge majority of the other members of our species are murdering nature and natural landscape the world over, and some reflection of this must be seen.

This is indeed precisely what I see, and increasingly, in Fay's work. She calls it documentary realism; I would rather call it creative honesty, a seeing that her obviously traditional and beautiful face, most strikingly displayed in *Remains of Elmet* (1979), must be sometimes abandoned. It is where, for me, she becomes an important photographer, not just a naturally gifted one.

The word *landscape* first appeared in English at the very end of the sixteenth century. It came from the Dutch *landschap*, meaning "province" or "region," and was first Englished as "landskip," which, if only unconsciously, suggests it was a rather trivial notion. The Catholic scholar Thomas Blount hardly improved on that low estimate in his *Glossographia* (a book "interpreting all such hard words, of whatsoever language, now used in our refined English tongue") of 1656:

> *Landskip, Parergon, Paisage or By-work, which is an expressing of the Land, by Hills, Woods, Castles, Valleys, Rivers, Cities, &c as far as may be shewed in our Horizon. All that which in a picture is not of the body or argument thereof is Landskip, Parergon, or bywork.*

This long counting of landscape as *parergon*—subsidiary work, mere accessory—is an odd aspect of European cultural history, and sadly revealing of a much older fault in man: his belief that nature is there purely for his use, and so either hostile towards or of deep indifference to him in its wild or unusable state. This is betrayed in that favorite medieval motif the *hortus conclusus*, the closed or walled garden, as emblem or symbol of the land cultivated and brought under control by man, in which the equally symbolic Virgin and her tamed unicorn may safely sit. Truly wild landscapes are normally, and significantly, seen only as background to hermit and Hell pictures. Much of this jealously anthropocentric view of the world can undoubtedly be blamed on the Bible and the teachings of the Church (the wild is also a good hiding place for sinners and outlaws); and I should like to think we may at root attribute it to an archetypal and in earlier times understandable fear on the part of humankind for its own safety and survival. But except when they serve as entertainment in a zoo or on television, a general dislike of most nonhuman species and wild landscapes of this planet still characterizes our world as a whole; yet without the old reason, in most areas of it, of any very present danger to society. So I believe we must look deeper, to a profound narcissism, or obstinate inability to comprehend or tolerate anything not in human shape, or not at least humanized by us.

It is striking what a good sense we have put upon that verb "to humanize." "To make gentle, tractable and familiar" is how it was defined in the seventeenth century; and this returns us to the earlier concept of man as God's steward over all other nature. That is why we put such a great value, in birds and beasts, on their amenability to being stewarded. How else could one of the most solitary and aggressive of species ("never two robins in a bush") become far and away the most popular, and the most sentimentalized, bird in European folklore? The trouble, needless to say, is that man continues to play far less the steward than the Nazi storm trooper or the slave-master in regard to all that vast part of nature that declines humanization, or hampers profit.

The only proper subject for painting in Blount's time was man and his works—his cities, his houses, his wars and ceremonies, his saints and gods (even these last had to conform to his image). I was struck by this at a recent exhibition in London, "The Genius of Venice." The art critics, and many of my friends, all seemed to consider it a very great exhibition indeed. I thought it a melancholy and wretched one, precisely because it was so obsessively man-centered. I do not recall a single picture from it that did not emphatically announce that landscape and nature were *parergon*, mere background filling. Many painters, both in the sixteenth century of the exhibition and later, did not even bother with this boring part, but employed apprentices and hacks to do it for them.

At last the Romantics came, and wild landscape gained its long-awaited due—sometimes to a distinctly absurd degree—with natural features' being treated almost as honorary humans. This was certainly a step on from the censorship of the past, but it also, it seems to me, subtly removed such features from reality. It is as if we could make them into main subject, or *ergon*, promote them from their former humble background status, only by once again humanizing all these mountains, torrents, streams, rocks, and woods, and using them as substitutes for the human face and human emo-

tions. We talk of an artist's "capturing" a likeness, and forget the old magical power, the secret possession, implicit in the expression, and plain in
Paleolithic art. In capturing nature in our far more conscious art, we also
once again declare it our servant. This too is better than the direct exploitation and destruction of it, but history has shown that reproducing its
beauty in our guise has done singularly little to stop its rape and pollution
in the real world outside art. We have deigned to notice nature and we
have deigned to use it for our own edification: that is quite enough.

I am not for a moment saying that many landscapists do not have a very
genuine love and feeling for the subjects of their work. Yet this very attachment hides a trap, beyond that already mentioned, the obvious lure of
pleasing and cashing in on public taste. If you want to portray something
for which you have deep feelings, then of course you will try to take it at
its best; and this must involve, however fine the motives, yet another distortion of reality, a tacit attempt to sell in the way that manufacturers sell
their products, by putting them in the best possible light. Nor am I saying
that landscape artists should start producing deliberately ugly work; but I
am suggesting that they are faced with a dilemma. They instinctively avoid
the ugly, the common, the monotonous; or where the subject is intrinsically beautiful, the poor angles, light, weather conditions, and the rest.
Even at the humblest amateur level, we struggle to "lose" telephone wires,
cars, people; all that spoils our highly conventional ideal of the good photograph. But this is an extremely selective process, and can soon degenerate into the photographer's pitting his or her wits and expertise, however
slight, against the truth of the landscape to be captured.

Too often, with the more skilled, it leads to a sin that I think of as making landscape *perform*, in the animal-training sense: showing how clever the
trainer is in what he has taught his animals (most commonly, to perform in
a way that runs deeply against their real nature). Dogs stand, elephants
dance, dolphins leap on land; and human fools applaud. I regard all this
trained-animal performance for entertainment as concealed human exhibitionism. Its equivalent in photography is the hideously obtrusive and
narcissistic determination to see the photographer's ego, rather than the
thing photographed: "Here is a remarkable landscape—because I took it."
It reaches a nadir in that form of conceptual art that must actually change
the landscape itself by draping plastic sheeting off a cliff or across a countryside, and then photographing it. The fault comes from various other il

lusions of our self-obsessed century: the beliefs that worthwhile art must be "new," which most often condemns it to be extravagant, and that self-advertisement, not representation, is what matters for the artist.

Fay's work is conspicuously free of this sort of pseudo-expressionist showing-off, and may be firmly recommended to those in love with unusual lenses, exposure tricks, shock angles, darkroom games, fancy titles, and all the other toys and gimmicks of the trade. There are branches of photography that can use the artificial and flagrantly technical tour de force. But landscape seems to me a peculiarly unsuitable subject for this approach, and I admire Fay's almost puritanical sobriety in it.

At least we should surely require, in any photographer whose work we are to respect, an awareness of these problems of landscape photography; and I must confess I very rarely detect it in many of her contemporaries. It is a very delicate tightrope for the artist to walk. But the single-minded pursuit of the most striking, or newsworthy, or conventionally beautiful, photograph leads always, to my mind, to a fall; certainly not to the truest or most honest work.

Liking in landscape must tell us as much about a person as taste in food or clothes; and when such preferences are widely shared, as much about an age. Lacking very often seems as significant as liking—that is, lack as represented by the presence of some marked opposite to the landscape where one lives, almost an antidote to it. This is often peculiar. Quite what the Victorians of the genteeler city suburbs, for instance, found so deeply satisfying in mournful Highland glens and even more mournful Highland cattle defeats the (or at least *my*) imagination.

I remember just such a Highland glen-plus-cattle canvas, a long way after Landseer, from the 1930s. It used to hang—in my childish memory the animals were terrifyingly life-size—in my grandmother's flat at Westcliff-on-Sea, a suburb of Southend at the mouth of the Thames. It was as remote from the actual flat "Dutch" landscape, or mudscape, of the huge river estuary outside as something from another planet, as remote indeed as the literal other-planet landscapes, all city-machine and vast perspective, that are popular with the young today. It was equally remote from anything I know of my grandmother's actual experience, and was, I think, the first landscape I took violently against. I did not like the look of the shaggy, long-horned cattle one bit (any more than I like the grotesque automata with their laser guns of Space Art); while the gloomy treeless landscapes behind suggested a profoundly tedious and unpleasant place to be.

Yet there the wretched picture stood, obscurely symbolic of a nobler, purer life: a place where you somehow ought really to prefer to be, the Garden of Eden and Paradise all in one. It was rather like the related American legend of the Wild West, another case of an impossible dream's completely trumping all probable reality. In some strange way the Scottish painting sternly rejected this soft, compromising southern and suburban world in which it was. Perhaps that is what the Victorians found so fulfilling in the genre: above all, it reprobated the here and now.

I did not as a child note something else about the painting. It was in technical terms extremely, if not quite photographically, realistic; yet in all human and psychological terms, not least in its place of honor on my grandmother's wall, exactly the reverse. An older person might have seen there a far better ground for disliking it—that is, a very clear example of the ancient human fault of allowing the representation of a thing to excuse us, or distract us, from its reality. All art carries this danger, of course, however seemingly objective and realistic its technique. It never gives a fully objective view, always a subjective one. Some theorists have maintained that photography is an exception to this rule, that ever since the days of Niepce, Daguerre, and Fox Talbot, it has at least potentially allowed its practitioners to exorcise the demon Subjectivity from their work. But I believe this view—the notion that total realism of appearance equals total reality—to be an equally total delusion.

Yet it remains a common one in this "visual age," where we all become more and more dependent on one form of photography or another for much of our daily knowledge of the outside world. In my view it was already a damaging fault in the Pre-Raphaelite movement, itself influenced by the recent discovery of photography. The betrayal or perversion of reality by realism is more obvious and naked in painting, perhaps; but it is more persistent in photography, because of the latter's superlative powers of exact mimesis. To photograph is by no means necessarily to photograph the reality; only too often it is, for both photographer and audience, to photograph a myth. And one, moreover, that may be as absurd and truth-hiding as those Highland cattle.

Professional photographers suffer particularly from this absurdly egalitarian fallacy. Their photographs have to be very exceptional to convince most people that they could not have done just as well, given the same camera and the same darkroom facilities. Yet no one feels this before a good painter or draftsman, or any other kind of image maker. Allied to it is another myth, that there is no true creativity in photography; that it is without imagination, merely copying what is there, operating a mechanical eye and an automatic printer. This position may grant a small flair for selecting points of view, but that is all; all the rest is a matter of tools, papers, chemicals. It is the camera that does the real work, not the person holding it.

The only truth in this is that the camera does restrict the true photographer rather more than the tools of any other art; and that he or she is confined inside that purely mimetic view of reality that matches human vision. Drawing a somber or laughing (or any other emotional adjective) landscape is child's play compared to photographing one, because of the license to exaggerate and invent that we grant the older visual arts. It is the tacit contract the photographer has with external reality—to work with it alone—that is the prison. A landscape must be dour or smiling in reality, a subject and a mood "out there," before the artistry can begin. In many ways this seems to me to make photography the most classical—that is, the most caged by restrictions—of all the arts. Its difficulty also requires a very special sort of patient perseverance. Truly good landscape photographs are a little like *objets trouvés*, natural objects worn and reshaped only by time and the elements; they are objects worn only by the photographer's age and experience of the right angle, the right light, the right mood and moment. Even a totally wild landscape is humanized once it is photographed; but finding that point on the right road, the exact place, the exact time, where the humanizing is almost forgotten, so that the final print seems almost a natural object itself—that requires the greatest skill of all, and I believe it is a noble one.

Fay has that skill, and gives me a humbler kind of reassurance as well, in that she can so frequently deny all those no doubt quirky personal doubts I have concerning photography, which are in turn a product of my general fear of the machine; of its passive inhumanity grown active antihumanity. A number of her pictures I know by heart, yet look at again always with renewed pleasure. Almost all her finest ones are jealous with their secrets. It is certainly so for the one I should count as my own most cherished favorite, that superbly balanced field, tree, cloud in *Large White Cloud near Bilsington, Kent*. I have had it beside me all through this writing,

and I am convinced it is a very great photograph. Yet I am hard put to analyze why it satisfies and pleases me so much; how it says things I know
I could never write, epitomizes so many unspoken feelings. It is like a
certain kind of poem, unalterable, perfect in its every syllable. Here lies a
subtle eye; and an even subtler human spirit.

COLLECTORS' ITEMS:
INTRODUCTION[1]
(1996)

I came to nature through hunting it with both gun and rod, and later by assembling mementos of my "victories" over it. I don't think I realized that it was as if we were at war, just as the whole country had been with the Nazis. I might pretend to myself that my justification was partly scientific, but I am afraid that the sacred relics—the buzzard's talon, the flash of jay's blue primaries, the raven's beak, the pinned rows (obscenely like soldiers on parade) of butterflies and moths—were all lies. Only too common, but still ugly falsehoods. The amassing of such hunting trophies has grossly and fatally misled generations of us, far more male than female, ever since Paleolithic times.

All humanity is victim in a matter that I rather brush by in "The Nature of Nature," though that essay does begin with a very pertinent quotation from that clear-sighted paragon of Scots poets, Norman MacCaig. In the "balancing that shakes my mind" that he speaks of in his poem "The Equilibrist," he is referring to that permanent tightrope that all of us now more or less consciously have to stumble along. It lies between the countless insistences of that part of us which is unique and individual, and the demands of the equally greedy one that is social—between each individual ego and the Communist, Christian, or whatever we publicly choose or are chosen to be. Society wants us to function as "efficient" social cogs or cooperative units, yet something in us wants very deeply to behave as what we believe we are—to be in all senses *selfish*, accepting that we the

---

1. An introduction to two excellent essays by Kate Salway and Marina Benjamin, *Collectors' Items* (London: Wilderness Editions, 1996).

preyers are really the preyed-on, the lonely victims of deeply conflicting drives. Living both with and in this profound dichotomy or schizophrenia is the balance we humans must hope to achieve; its learning has given birth to most of our greatest art, while its reality leaves most of us trying to exist and balance as if we were in a dense fog.

Natural history has always very largely involved collecting. The endless opportunities there to indulge self-esteem and display vanity have long brought out the very worst in man—and stifled the best, which lies in his saving ability to grasp the transience of being. My own painfully slow progress from the sick days of my own little schoolboy *Wunderkammer* during the *entre-deux-guerres* has shown me that nature is in fact not about collecting at all, but about something infinitely more complex and difficult: being.

I believe the loophole that led me out of such a plainly wrong attitude towards all nature was less botany than gardening. I am in general very "suspicious" of the latter activity, especially of the kind I term "municipal"—the growing of plants simply to exhibit a rather pompous civic pride, showing off (rather like my own father, in truth) by means of the more flauntable species and vaguely implying their aristocratic origin— and the more studied "bourgeois" sort, whose secret motive (also shown in many other things) is generally to demonstrate one's own very great taste in life-style by establishing what the new poststructuralists term "use values."

This will perhaps outrage countless "serious" and enthusiastic gardeners; nonetheless I feel that gardens and the feelings they arouse in us are very much revealers of this profound fundamental unbalance between each individual "private" self and its very different communal-social opposite. In a way we make them all serve, like their wild equivalents, as our cabinets of wonder, where we feel we best show—as with our clothes, our furniture, our foods, our conversations, our literary and artistic interests, our private hobbies and obsessions—what we are (and that we are!) in this cruelly Fascist, individual-hating and -suppressing world we are "unfairly" forced to inhabit, as a penal colony.

In Kate Salway and Marina Benjamin we have two acute, perceptive, and sensitive female voices, clearly well versed in the lamentably cruel and brutal history of our attitude towards nature, of man's sickening perversion and distortion of what it should and might be for him into so many "use values"—as with those Stone Age ornaments he has so idiotically and childishly worn through almost all cultured creation to pamper his own ego and ensure survival in this most precarious and least stable of worlds. Neither woman comes to a happy conclusion; nor does David Quammen in his recent *The Song of the Dodo*,[2] a skilled scientific account of island bio-geography and our only too present age of extinctions. Evolution leads us clever—but not clever enough—apes into a seemingly near-inevitable darkness and nullity. The black shadows of these two essays gain their intensity from a simple fact: man, the male of the species, is historically, psychologically, anthropologically, and very, very clearly, the more guilty gender. I am truly delighted that both the authors here are female, and that they are, if only symbolically, doing what mothers of children foolishly playing on cliff-edges have always done.

2. New York: Scribner, 1996.

THE NATURE OF NATURE
(1995)

Noticing you can do nothing about.
It's the balancing that shakes my mind.

NORMAN MACCAIG, "THE EQUILIBRIST,"

FROM *COLLECTED POEMS*

(LONDON: CHATTO & WINDUS, 1990)

I am now nearly seventy, and no longer fully trust my brain, but I should like to try to give some of my feelings about the cruise, as I tend to think of the experience of living on this planet—"cruise" because it seems artificial, not quite real in terms of the countless moral, philosophical, and religious past assertions I've read about it; and not quite real because it is deeply imbued for each one of us by something I'll mention later: *keraunos*, or hazard. I'm well aware that my own voyage has not been unpleasant, and that I am, especially in view of the far worse experience life has both now and in the past given to so many others, fortunate. There have been some descriptions of the "cruise" in all my novels, but perhaps more relevantly, certainly as regards nature, in an essay I first published in 1979, "The Tree." I'd like this present tangled nest of memories and thoughts to be read in association with that. Perhaps "The Nature of *My* Nature" would be a more honest title.

A year or two ago I was asked, with others, to reevaluate C. P. Snow's well-known essay of 1959, *The Two Cultures*. The history of that upset in stock intellectual thinking may be read in Stefan Collini's account of the affair in his introduction to the work as published by the Cambridge University Press.[1] Like many at the time I was torn, reproached, and confused

---

1. *The Two Cultures* (Cambridge: Cambridge University Press, 1993).

by it. I knew I was not, and would never be, the "true" scientist Snow appeared to recommend; and I felt some sympathy for his best-known opponent, the formidable Dr. Leavis. I saw the necessity for science on countless technological and economic grounds and realized only too well the cost of ignoring it, the blindness of which Snow accused us on the artistic side. I was clearly, in his terms, a drone.

Although I have called myself a natural historian all my life, I am more precisely (though in something inherently imprecise) a nature lover. I wouldn't now pretend to be a scientist at all; if I were truly one, I suspect I'd even deny I was primarily a writer. I certainly know that I see literature far more as an expression of feeling conveyed through poetry, drama, and fiction than as any sort of serious scientific statement about reality. I seem closest to a clever octopus, a mere—to us humans—feeler. This does not mean that I reject or am rejected by serious science; though I am banned from or dismissed by much of it purely because of my own stupidity and lack of ability to concentrate. An academic friend, I hope not meaning to be too critical, very recently told me that I was "tangential and Coleridgean," expensive adjectives to indicate "tangled" and "disorganized."

I acknowledge the often vital importance of scientific knowledge as a part of my own deep attachment to nature. Yet I somehow felt that the quasi-revolution Snow provoked in our culture was being fought on a wrong field (or a defective map) and in a biased cause. It failed to realize the importance of the individual and the aesthetic, and seemed largely unaware of the key element of the now and its existential reality. Snow's essay seemed to respond to something that was oceanically subtle and complex with a shout as foolish and implicitly Fascistic as Canute's unsuccessful command to the tide.

I soon scribbled some notes when I began to collect my thoughts about The Two Cultures recently. One was this: *Science tries always to dismiss and discount feeling.* The other: *Marrying feeling and knowing, that is the problem.* Of course it is preeminently the problem because feeling is for individuals, between a you and a me. Each of us is always, at heart, however apparently similar, inalienably *not* anyone else. Knowing is for society as a whole; it always intends and wishes to be "final," certain, eternal—all that we know we and our personal lives may never be. I wasn't happy with the attitude (in public, in Snow, and in myself) of these two transmitters respectively of feeling and of knowledge. At the same time I recognized the separate importance of each in the whole. Snow was quite right to recognize or publicize the fact that feeling (so often expressed through the arts) had long tried to suppress or omit the facts (the science) from any intelligent view of our human life. But just as women have long been grossly and selfishly misunderstood, slighted and exploited by men, so has the feeling by the knowing. I abhor the crassness of my own sex, abhor how ineptly, not to say cruelly, it has behaved on the voyage since the Bronze Age. Intelligent history has almost constantly linked the feminine gender with the more personal mode of apprehension, and most men do now have a sense at least of the apology owed for their gender's having historically encouraged a slavish adherence to convention—the past—and made it (only too often brutally and brutishly) the social norm. But the guilt of our whole species over our previous slighting and despising of science is rather different. The leap to now demanding a near hegemony for it, to invite it so wholly to invade and occupy our societies, lives, and minds, seems headstrongly rash. Not to know becomes a kind of crime; only to feel, a sort of sin.

My "problem" may seem irrelevant, because insoluble; but its two constituents are so interwoven, so symbiotically one, that to separate them risks, as sometimes with Siamese twins, destroying both. Society and school, the way the world trains and conditions its young termites through politics and education, are hell-bent on keeping these vital modes or functions separate. One is not supposed to feel and to know at the same time, though of course one may (if less commonly) feel what one knows and (much more frequently) know what one feels. The problem lies in trying to get the two systems of information exchange, each ruled by a fundamentally different ethos, to marry and bear fruit. It seems only too obvious, in this world of 1995, that in general, knowing is cock of the roost. Feeling is the runt of the litter.

This must sound as if I were spoiling to damn all science as distasteful and foreign, like Dr. Opimian in Peacock's *Gryll Grange* of 1860, or like the writer himself, a skeptic as to most of what progress has brought to my own culture and civilization; but I'm not, to use Snow's language, a Luddite. I am grateful for almost all of the saner scientific discoveries since (and especially those put forth by) Darwin, and not least for the so-called information revolution. I may be technologically illiterate, near helpless, even by average standards, as I can neither drive a car nor use a word processor, but this isn't something I am in the least proud of. I know it's because I'm digitally clumsy and disciplinarily lazy.

. . .

I never much liked C. P. Snow as a novelist. His stories seem a little too hard to excavate and cleanse from the coagulated strata of all his academic and class snobberies, as pointed out by Collini. The rancorous spat with Leavis now seems to me near primitive and ill judged on both sides. As with so many writers in English on this side of the Atlantic, Snow's middle-classness, his craving to become a pundit, cling to him like rust on some ancient suit of armor left out in the rain. If I had to rate novelists and essayists by their knowledge of science, and their intellectual pungency, let alone by the quality of their own fictional writing, I should certainly place the ferretlike Arthur Koestler well above him. But murdering the already dead is akin to tomb-robbing, very rarely a defensible pursuit, as well as being only too clear a proof that most of "educated" humanity grossly undervalues the now. The now is a delicate plant. Almost everything in society forbids or denies the climate and conditions in which it may flourish.

I now come to something far worse in the mea culpa line. That concerns my distinctly shabby claims to any real science myself. I know just enough to trick the even more ignorant than myself; novelists are like conjurors, always expert at misleading. To a true believer in the scientific process and its basic ethos I must seem preposterous: that horror of horrors, a mere glib amateur, little more than an irritating poseur. The way I invent names, both Latin and English, for some of the plants whose true "labels" I have forgotten in my own ill-kept garden . . . such shameless misleading of innocent visitors is unforgivable.

Yet I do passionately love nature. I never really understood why I loved my now-dead wife, yet I did; and long ago realized that the not-knowing (the emotion's prevailing over common sense and reason) can become a mysterious part of the love.

Some reference books have me down as an atheist; and certainly, as regards any established deity or religious figure, I am so, and all the more resolutely when some god or goddess is presented with purely human qualities such as being kind or merciful, and possessing listening and intervenient powers. Such fairy-tale figures are for children; my universe is, or appears, infinitely bleaker. I do respect and sometimes admire many religious images and icons, sects, theologies, and what lies beyond them, but I am by trade an inventor of fiction, almost a professional liar. I appreciate the countless virtual realities that the religious create; and what drives them to claim, sometimes with a savage fervor, that their plausible fictions are unique truths. The religious instinct is in essence a great novelist.

So. If I'm not at all religious in any conventional sense, what am I? To try to pass my view off as a philosophy would, at this date and among so much infinitely more sophisticated thinking on such matters, be ridiculous. I'd prefer a more human term. My *feeling* about human existence on this uncontrolledly sprouting planet is that its perceptible reality, and its destiny, waver and zigzag amid a triangle of opposing yet counterbalancing factors. Physically and mentally we individuals bounce, carom, and ricochet like pin-table balls. I call (rather in the way I rebaptize plants) these beliefs or views among which we collide by classical Greek names: *sideros, keraunos, eleutheria*. Iron necessity, lightning hazard, freedom.

The first pin off which the ball (our soul) bounces is iron necessity, which projects all those inevitable facts, only too real, that curtail or limit our freedom. A ubiquitous example of these is death. A slightly less obvious—to us self-obsessed humans—one is the cell we are all obliged to inhabit. Its walls are formed by eachness and ego, our difficult individuality. We imagine disciplines, efforts of ascesis, that may exceptionally seem to grant us a sort of freedom from these two tyrants; but generally we know we must, like grubs in their cells, inhabit the cramping structures our biology and psychology—and that odd computer we call the brain—have evolved for us. We can then devote our imprisonment to becoming (at least in the West) distinguishable and—we hope—distinguished. That latter seems the only plausible way we shall partly avoid the certain final oblivion of the primary iron necessity.

The second and most random course-changing pin is the one I typify as *keraunos*, "the thunderbolt." This is pure hazard. It shows as much in fatal air crashes as in exciting lottery wins, in many dire tragedies and in as many shocks of happiness. Its results may be hoped for, expected, predicted, dreaded; but they are never certain, *real*, until after they have occurred. Yet very few would have it otherwise. Bliss, hell; the good cries to the bad, while the *keraunos* makes a nonsense of that dark iron necessity, the arrow of time.

The last pin or shoulder off which we spring on our loxodromic way is *eleutheria*. Freedom springs from our instinct to revolt against iron necessity and from our perpetual doubt as to whether we can possess any verifiable freedom of will, or whether everything is not, finally, determined for us. Because our individuality and so much else (like our eventual death) is imposed on us, we crave escape. Almost all we think of as progress is this *eleutheria*. It destroys all stasis. We may call it rebellion, revolution, a thousand things, many of them seen (especially if one is comfortable with how and where one lives) as evil. But evolution itself is a form of terrorism, a civil war against stasis. We don't realize it because its bombs take a demi-eternity, compared with the brevity of our human lives, to explode. Freedom has long had a deep and powerful fascination for humankind. Its effects may be good or bad; those of iron necessity are almost all counted outwardly as the latter. For us humans, *sideros* lies in shadow; *eleutheria* in light.

I found one indispensable first rung onto the ladder of natural history: an interested uncle. He was in charge of practical biology at the local preparatory school to which I went, and I associate him with almost all my early red-letter days. My father had been totally disgusted by wild nature ever since his agonies in the trenches of the First World War; to him it was intrinsically hostile and useless, except in his own small garden. It was to my uncle that I owed the thrill of hunting for lappet caterpillars among the sloe thickets of the Essex seawalls near where we lived. To him I owed the vaguely roulettish pleasures of "sugaring"—the practice of creeping round Leigh-on-Sea and Westcliff, torch in hand, patrolling at his side various wooden fences and tree trunks anointed with the sweet gunge he concocted for attracting moths. One day, he entrusted me with a great rarity, the huge larva (it was near pupation) of a death's-head hawkmoth, which some neighboring farmer had found in his potato field. Oh the joys of that, the gloating countless times a day over its jam jar, the stroking that induced the poor thing to peep—a miracle, an insect that "spoke"! All nature seemed human, its diverse forms puzzlingly near . . . cousins.

I had a highly eccentric real cousin on the other side of the family, who also encouraged me to *see* nature. Among other things, Laurence ran long-distance for the England team, abhorred all onions, and collected scarce clarets, but even more oddly still he traveled all over the world and worshiped, almost as he might have a guru, Donisthorpe the myrmecologist. In later years a recurrent nightmare of my life became that Laurence might die and leave me his huge collection of spirit-bottled ants. It was groundless, for some Australian museum has them now. What I did get from him was a dose of Darwin's disease: perpetual curiosity.

These two men lit a spark in me, though I believe it was alive even earlier, almost *ab ovo*. I'd been fascinated since my earliest years by nature's mysterious otherness, its belonging, though "related," to a world where things happened in different ways than in our human one, seemingly often governed by the fortuitous. This charming innocence was to be worsened, indeed corrupted, by Oxford, where I studied French. I later went to live in France, and plunged even deeper into sin, having a passionate, life-changing affair with a shatteringly beautiful and rich young woman. I found her only in the remoter countrysides. I had glimpsed her in England, though never quite declared my fascination, already sensing that her true home was further south, in the Mediterranean. I called this lovely creature *la sauvage*, "the wild." Of course I'd been taught something of France's arts, her society and culture, her peoples and cities (and been hooked, like many of my generation, by Camus's existentialism), but they have all paled before the naked, generous breasts, the languorous limbs, the exquisite jewelry, the sensuous underclothes, the sheer abundance, of this charming persona. I have ever since sought by preference *la sauvage* in every country in which I have lived or traveled and judged most events and persons in its light. It is that aspect of wild nature beyond all that we normally attach to culture and civilization, the naked reality of the *rus* far beyond all *urbs*.

In France I also became deeply enamored of a distinctly un-English notion of *liberté*. This was a freedom chosen far less on "correct," democracy-loving grounds than because it so happily promoted and encouraged the pleasing of myself. That rather selfish freedom—I had first suffered from it on being evacuated to rural Devon at the start of World War Two—did seem to be implicit in nature itself, but my passion for it (or her) was unashamedly hedonistic. It liberated me, a little as France itself had just been liberated from the Germans, from the crippling polio of English Puritanism, or what its later zealots had made of the original. The natural life of France still remains for me a marvelous memory of a release, a little like a visit to a high-class restaurant for a gastronome: delight and variation, endless surprise. If France was a sort of mistress, Greece (where I next lived) was half Circe, half mother. I am trigenic, of three motherlands, a matriot for all, and far from sure where I truly belong.

With my third progenitress, England, I had long grasshoppered from insects to other creatures, but I went into that in the transparently worst (though I suspect sometimes more heuristic than truly damaging) way. Whenever I could, as well as watching, I hunted and fished. All Nimrods get to know their nature, both outwardly and inwardly, along with their prey. My one excuse was the 1939–1945 war, the rabbits, pigeons, and trout that I could sometimes bring home; but I also killed other creatures, and some of them have haunted and still haunt me in this present appalling dearth of so much other English nature. One bird I shot (though only once) was later to become my totem. Its august, benign and quasi-mythical—like the Persian *simurg*—presence in a landscape has in my eyes and ears long condoned, or by its absence condemned, much else. If I see or hear ravens, something in me always rises with and to them. I'm lucky, where I live now, to know of a pair that still breed only a few miles away. That is more the reason I still live here than the sobriety my seniority sometimes pretends. I remember loathing Los Alamos, knowing its history, when I first saw it many years ago. But as I stared grimly past its boundary warnings there was a *kwark*, a call from the very soul of freedom, high in the blue sky over it. I might perhaps have taken that as darkly, sickly, and "symbolically" as Poe did, as implying that all was death and desolation in this world. But in that black speck two or three miles away I saw life, and "evermore."

In botany I soon realized I particularly cherished wild orchids (*la sauvage* at her most seductive). Some of them became rather like the ravens, whose presence or absence in an area profoundly changes it. My special paradises were the Causses, or limestone plateaux of southern central France and Greece, especially Crete. I have now hunted wild orchids over most of Europe, and by proxy (in Luer's books) over the United States also. The hothouse millionaire's orchidomania I despise, as I do bird-twitching and most of the other collecting and hoarding activities; all seem to me sick, however useful they may claim to be scientifically. A few years ago I had a small stroke and ended up at the Royal Free Hospital in Hampstead, London. I made up a mantra in my very first days there: it was *tenthredinifera, tenthredinifera, tenthredinifera*. . . . Only two years before I had stumbled, near the top of a Cretan mountain, on a loosely scattered cluster of the sawfly orchid (*Ophrys tenthredinifera*). This is a very beautiful relation of our own English bee orchid, but my cri de coeur (based on a conviction—not yet disproved—that I should never again tread that or any other Cretan mountain) was really a lament for a delectably plant-rich island.

I haven't quite finished with my own inconstancy over natural knowledge. Before my aversion to London (indeed to all large cities) finally drove me away from it, I was one day in the early 1960s summoned to the Old Bailey on jury duty. The case the twelve of us had to decide concerned incest. It was diabolically, obscenely nasty, as accreted with falsehood and human bestiality as a pigsty with dung. Its victims and even the accused were so stupid and illiterate that the real people who should have been in the dock were we jurors, guilty of having allowed our own culture to sink to such abysmal depths. I remember standing outside the court with my jury duty fee in my hand when we were dismissed. I came to an instant decision: I would go straight to the nearest large bookshop and perform an *acte gratuit*, buy something as remote from my own insufferably disgusting species as I could find. I ended up with Lockett and Millidge's *British Spiders*, the standard textbook of the time. For many (too many) years I then spent an absurd amount of time peering down an entomological microscope and looking for infinitesimal *trichobothria* or trying to decipher, like some insane papyrologist, the exact shape and outline of both male and female sex organs (by which alone the vast majority of smaller spiders can be surely identified). It was during my pursuit of spiders that I was infected by an eventually overwhelming doubt. But this is not quite the end of what must seem a sadly fickle story.

In 1978 I became curator of our little museum here at Lyme Regis in Dorset. Lyme is above all famous for its mainly Jurassic—and also Cretaceous—fossils. This collector of "ologies," despite the several foundered voyages that littered his past, now decided he was lured by yet another wreckers' beacon: paleontology. But as I have hinted, I had by that time been bitten by a tarantula of doubt over what most of the general public still supposes to be a foundation stone of true science. I'd often been harried by academics over my own writing, and probed over what they evidently saw as a noisome paradox, a lamentable deficiency, in my work. I might keep claiming that natural history (as I knew it) was behind all my fictions; yet where was there any real evidence of that? I might say I admired Gilbert White, Thoreau, Richard Jefferies, and many others, but I seemed totally disinclined to try to emulate them. This was at least half true. I have always regarded nature as peculiarly sacrosanct. It was Jefferies who first pronounced it "ultrahuman," or beyond humanity. D. H. Lawrence, nowhere near as misguided as Snow made out during his vendetta with Leavis, reached nearest—especially in his poetry—to penetrating that strange otherness about it. The experience is nearly impossible to describe in prose, but I will try.

The acutely sensitive Virginia Woolf stated my own general difficulty quite plainly: "Nature and letters seem to have a natural antipathy . . . they tear each other to pieces." I have always felt, from long before I became a practicing writer, very nearly the same thing. As soon as we start, an angry "Trespassers are forbidden" or *Noli me tangere* springs up. I know I adore nature; yet must feel myself as regards expressing that love, when faced with it, a eunuch. I may seem to go where I want, but in reality I may not, because I cannot.

With paleontology (and our fossil-rich local cliffs, quarries, and beaches in Dorset) I soon realized I was faced with not only an enormously complicated field but a still-shifting one, by no means definitively fixed. Science, hypnotized by Linnaeus, was still announcing new species, sometimes whole new genera, because of the enormous lacunae left by the as-yet-undiscovered. Only if near-infinite multiplicity is desirable—its classifications endlessly fluid, elastic, and mobile—can this become anything but a labyrinthine nightmare.

This brings me to the giant tarantula lurking in its subterranean lair and waiting to pounce on my would-be dalliance with science. Its fangs first struck towards the end of my obsession with spiders: put simply, why was I so mesmerized by the binomial system? In Uppsala, some years before, I had offended some worthy Swedish literary professors by selecting the wrong visit of the two that they had offered. They could happily show me some of the precious early manuscripts in the university library, or, since it was one of his almae matres, I could (if I must) walk around Linnaeus' original garden. I had no doubt. To hell with the great library and its treasures; I wanted, and duly got, Linnaeus' curious little walled and parterred patch.

I have described elsewhere (in "The Tree") the "heresy" that began there. It does not surprise me at all that the poor doctor was half crazed by the end of his own life, drenched and drowned in the enormous flood of names, names, names he had unleashed. When I took over the museum in Lyme I soon saw that I stood on the same terrifying cliff brink, about to fall into a sea of fog. I tried to relabel some of our collection of ammonites and other fossils; it was like walking through the distorting maze of a fun fair, walls bizarrely lengthening or shortening, incomprehensible elisions and hiatuses, ends to all previous assumptions. After a few years of stumbling and pratfalling in the dark wings, I turned my back on this theatrical maze.

In so many sciences this endless cataract of new names and knowledges has created an awesome new Frankenstein, otherwise known as the specialist. Specialization may focus, as a lens the rays of the sun, on the knowledge of one generally very small field and subject. But it also has an unfortunate habit of focusing not just on the subject but on the specialist as well; and can sear him or her into desiccation like an autumn leaf. In plain language, nothing can more distressingly dehydrate, isolate, and detach.

I was long a victim of the myth of the polymath. Knowledge is encyclopedically vast. Nowadays it can be mastered only through cybernetically controlled computers; by a single man or woman, a single consciousness, never. Yet we former mythomanes are reluctant to give up the idea that all may be held in one small brain. Personally, I have abandoned all hope of mastering the specific details in the various fields of which I used to boast—I'm afraid sometimes to flaunt—knowledge. More and more I take a far humbler comfort in at least knowing a little at the generic level; and I grope after something beyond all species.

What my refusal of too dry an obsession with spiders and fossils, indeed with much else of nature, has provided is a kind of parallel view. One perspective remains not unscientific. If I had to praise one book from recent paleontological literature, it would be Stephen Jay Gould's *Wonderful Life* of 1989,[2] about the Canadian—and Cambrian—Burgess Shales. It doesn't worry me that some of his fossicking through the deeper significance of evolution remains in dispute; it is still a marvelous example of what my myrmecological cousin always sought beyond his eccentricities: the stimulation and (at least temporary) satisfaction of curiosity. The other, humbler view springs from what used to be called the amateur approach—

---

2. London: Hutchinson Radius, 1990.

much more the liking and being interested than the being totally immersed. I love the mucking about for "gold" in the panoplies of both past and present time to be found in the Dorset world about me, or indeed wherever I am.

I do now accept the necessity of a binomial system for all academic specialists and many professional people, even for some skilled amateurs. But I mistrust such obsessive particularization for myself and the vast majority of mankind and womankind. I long ago half realized that while names in one way make us see, in another, like clouded glass, they blind. We all know our world is grossly overpopulated in human terms; it's just as intolerably overcrowded by names, by tickets and labels. That is why so many can't, or don't, see nature: among the brainwashed, if a thing is nameless, it is invisible. Social, economic, and architectural factors all conspire to induce such myopia. We are equally dim-sighted as to time, being unable to see so much of the past and believing we must live in the present (though so seldom seeing what I'll speak of in a moment, the now). We use our general insensitivity to time as a censor does his scissors: to remake the world around us not as it is, but as it suits us and our societies to believe.

In any case there is, due to our appalling inability sanely to administer the environments about us, less and less nature to see. I keep a kind of funeral register of the plants, birds, insects, and animals that I knew *were* present in my garden here in Dorset, and not uncommonly up to far less than my own lifetime ago. They are now, it seems irrecoverably, gone; or at best on the brink, "endangered" species locked in a desperate fight for survival against the planet's most viciously selfish and greedily dominant one, man.

Nature in England, if still more in danger of dying than actually dead, is nonetheless in a parlous state; we slowly slide into the zero of extinction. To many foreigners, conditions on this cramped island may appear far worse than those in their own (in this context) far richer and happier countries . . . and perhaps, in view of our blundering imperialistic past, this is deserved. Our virtuous Protestantism, though for long shocked by and suspicious of *la sauvage*, hasn't of course allowed this sad decline in (or indifference to) nature without attempts at prevention.

I don't wish to dismiss such protests, as I certainly don't want to suggest that the state of the whole planet, the prolix rattishness of humankind, its plague, don't make me often despair. We seem either blind (lacking in elementary knowledge and common sense) or evil (deliberately harmful and self-destructive). Fine language will not save or reorient us; as well give space vehicles to peasants and expect them to fly at once to an unknown tomorrow. One obvious underlying cause of the countless wrongs, pollutions, and deprivations we inflict on our world is the atrocious overpopulation our species permits itself, a hypertrophy infinitely worsened by what we may think of as our special grace, our individuality, the fact that each one of us is unique. Despite that raven at Los Alamos, unless some great change in humankind occurs (unblinds, converts, transmogrifies), our gross stupidity and apathy will one day doom the Earth.

Yet here my savage old mistress pulls me back from total gloom. My study in Lyme Regis looks out on a green May garden over the English Channel and evokes both present and past. The past . . . both my own and the world's. My reason tells me that so much, not least the terrifying random *keraunos*, sudden all-changing fate beyond prediction, must seem to consign not just our, but all, species to oblivion. I have no belief at all in any divine power that might save us from this threatened nostricide or the total hazard of the *keraunos*. Yet something in wild nature, though often dumb, masked, or hooded, has on occasion, as just now, touched my individual soul. It is a perhaps foolish optimism, a memory of how one escapes through what Sir Thomas Browne called the "postern of resipiscence"— the recognizing of past error. I am; very well, I shall one day die, knowing I've failed to do anywhere near enough to halt the folly, to try to reduce it before it becomes too late; but I will not believe that all sentient, intelligent being must end.

This brings me to beingness, existingness. It is the best example of that complaint about the lethal enmity between words and nature that Virginia Woolf noted. D. H. Lawrence seems to me to have come closest in this century to touching it, and I have written about this in my commentary on *The Man Who Died*. I doubt if I understood the implications of realizing this existingness when I first fell for Lawrence, but as I have said in that commentary, "I did share it, though but as a candle to his sun. It is why I became a natural historian; it is why I became a writer myself, always stumbling, despite being a novelist, after the poem. . . ."

Illness has kept me even more alone than usual these last two years, and brought me closer to being, though that hasn't always been very pleasant for my body. What has struck me about the acutely rich sensation of beingness is how fleeting is its apprehension. It's almost as transient, as fugitive, as some particle in atomic physics: the more you would capture it, the less likely that you will. It refuses all attempts at willed or conscious evocation, it is deaf to pure intelligence alone, it envelops you in a double or twinned feeling. One is of intense nowness, the other of realizing that you (oneself) alone, in *your* individuality, are infinitely fortunate to experience it, perhaps in nothing so much as its seeming to fall from something whole and *unindividual* on your separateness. It is being, being, being . . . a perpetual miracle, so vivid and vital that ordinarily we cannot bear it; always rare enough to be a shock, no similes or metaphors can convey it; like a sudden nakedness, a knowing of oneself laid bare before a different reality. There looks to be nothing; then, as with the thunderbolt, all.

Only yesterday I bought a new, posthumous, unfinished novel, *The Double Tongue*.[3] The publishers discovered it among William Golding's papers. Unfinished, yet it seems to me a subtle weighing (or "feeling"!) of both this world and the ancient one by a very wise old philhellene (no Nobel in recent years was more deserved). Something on its very first page caught my eye. Golding describes the Pythia, the famous female oracle at Delphi in ancient Greece and the central character and "message" of his fiction: "Blazing light and warmth, undifferentiated and experiencing themselves . . . there was no time, even implied. So how could it be before or after, seeing that it was unlike anything else, separate, distinct, a one-off. No words, no time, no even I, ego . . . naked being without time or sight. . . ." My revered brother novelist would have known what I'm speaking of here. Among other things this intense awareness of being makes the pointless destruction of other life (whether of other species or of other human beings) seem as unthinkable, as wicked, as some Eastern religions and famous European "feelers" such as Saint Francis have long maintained it to be.

It is this experience of existingness, of having both possessed and known it free of all the usual cloying detritus of religion, superstition, and mysticism, that makes me profoundly grateful that fate allowed me to become at least something of both an artist and an aesthete. It is the realizing that I have been set, not by any special effort or diligence or because I deserve it, but by what seems almost total chance, on a right path—right not just to foster my own pleasure, but far more importantly, right for the bet-

---

3. London: Faber and Faber Limited, 1995.

terment of my entire species. If I had to prescribe a future type for humankind, the writer (reflective of ego) and natural historian (seeking beyond it) would rank high above the technologist and computeromane. I am not at all happy that a pseudo-scientific quirk in me once demanded, like a dictator, that I must know in one approved scientific way alone.

I fear I'm not making the main tenor of this essay very clear. I am distorted by science, unable to think or write outside its bias. Just as Jefferies coined the word *ultrahuman*, so we need an *ultrascientific* (beyond its own terms, vocabulary, and logic). To try to portray feeling only in and by "proper" scientific terms and methods is like using the long-stuffed or the dry skin to evoke the moving, or representing the living by the still, color by black and white: it is an approximation, not the reality.

This "feeling" part of our being, this other self, is the shadowed one, and in some ways the more primitive, though in countless others the more complex. Many might consider it yet another thing, like religion, to be relegated to the lumber-room of history. Such a comparison seems to me terrifyingly wrong. We desperately need its counterweight to all the autocratic excesses, encroachments, and ukases of knowing.

All writers make up their own private slang as to what goes on when they write. An important term—at any rate for me, in my own practice—is the *fork* (as in a path), by which I mean a fairly continuous awareness of alternatives, both "learned" (remembered) and "fortuitous" (wild), in what is done. This possibility-mongering may vary intellectually and emotionally in the shape of narrative, in dialogue, through moral and descriptive passages, down to individual words. One thing eternally "on sale" is the blue pencil: omission. This fertile awareness is far subtler than a mere crossword quickness at hitting on synonyms, and derives in part from the green embryo without clues constituted by the pristine, unformed, barely conceived text. The polycistronic ("producing more than one gene") and polyfunctional capacities of the imagination invent both the clues and the final answers to any work of art. This can lead the artist nearer to something he or she may profess not to credit: God, or a simulacrum (in my own case, once, a muse).

This two-edged power of hypothesization can very easily transfer itself from the text to ordinary life. Every time I fly, I know I shall crash and be killed; every time (even at my age!) I meet an attractive woman, I imagine love will follow . . . even though I'm only too certain it neither will nor can. A puritan might equate the freedom to invent with being given the luxuries—in both senses—of a Mogul emperor, a perpetual license. But my intention here is to suggest that being allowed to exist within such an infinity of possible variations, the endless bifurcations of the alternative, forms the reality, like some difficult differential equation, that most serious artists have either to worry or rejoice over.

Alas, the world seems determined to abolish and destroy living feeling by stifling its existence with dead knowledge. I have doubted recent attempts both to scientize something so compounded of irrational feeling as litera-ture and to presume it might be explained by the language and methods of a patently hostile *Aschauung*. We writers have recently been told that be-lieving there is such a thing as an autonomous individual self is ridiculous and that the very corrupt nature of the words we use—not just our art but the language we couch it in—is suspect also. We are eternally behind bars, our tongues are tied, our words by being words kill all chance of verity.

This is why, while not denying the vast utility of science in the count-less practical and technological spheres where it now dominates our lives, I still think that Snow and his kind were gravely wrong when they main-tained that in the infinitely complex and *still*-unsounded reality of what we are, "feeling" (the old aesthesis, the world of the emotions and the arts) is so much less important than "knowing."

What did Jeans once say? The world is not just stranger than we think; it may be stranger than we *can* think. We must allow not only for countless "scientific" fresh truths but for equally countless new evaluations of their comparative importance. The world has changed prodigiously since I was born, in 1926; knowing it fully, in all its scientific diversity, is already im-possible. Yet the feeling about it of each "I," that obstinately unassimilable and irreducible one, is and always will be relatively possible to ascertain. The unique individual must, by very virtue of his or her uniqueness, real-ize that things can be judged and decided only partially—that is, on what *it* alone chooses or is chosen to sense and perceive. Science strives after to-tality; it wants always to know more. Habitually, in strict scientific terms, wrongly, feeling is stoical. It knows enough.

Any true scientific knowing is always, like feeling, only partial. How much we know—or ignore—depends largely on hazard. Our human free-dom lies in allowing or admitting that this hazard is like rain in our lives.

We seldom realize how vital to us this both exquisite and baneful uncertainty is. Cruel, painful, even death-dealing though it may be, we could not live in this world without its sheer incomprehensibility.

What frightens, bewilders, and enchants me about the *keraunos*, the thunderbolt of pure chance, is the constancy of its occurrence. It is a beyond-science, an antithesis of all that normal science, with its mechanical fixities, has led and leads us to foresee. This unexpectability remains a main source of every individual's energy, physical and psychic.

Both art and science, behind the clumsy fixed classifications and etiologies out of which that latter tries to construct a supposedly ultimate truth, are in eternal chaos. We need to institute an oscillation between the two sides, like a heartbeat; to understand not just the nature of things, but the nature of understanding them. This will never be clear to science, by mere knowing alone. The unnecessary border war, as foolish and futile as most others in human history, is aggravated by the artistic side's pandering (sometimes very debasedly) to its audience's pleasure. The old Puritans sternly maintained that the seduction of our animal side distracted from what they considered to be the unique and only proper truth. Something in the arts must therefore (especially in a Protestant-leaning culture) make them seem inherently the more selfish and wicked; and the sciences the more sober, serious, and decent. The arts establish their realities far less quickly, despite the instant communications of the global village; yet these slower fruits of feeling frequently affect and alter the general course of the "cruise." The seeming-blind, hesitant, octopod gropings of the arts towards a more general sense of fulfillment ("purpose") for humanity are not all to be dismissed. Poets and writers (like painters and musicians, saints and philosophers) are in precisely the same situation as Columbus, knowing neither quite where they are going nor what they will find—or how their discovery will later develop.

Both the knowledge and the feeling "maps" of our contemporary world are in effect little more adequate than those primitive geographical notions (the crude maps we now tend to smile at) of the Middle Ages. This is because we suppose that feeling (as shown in things like taste, conviction, and opinion) must be essentially a personal matter, very private and individual; therefore, in a world of general laws crying for ubiquity and fearing all exception, unimportant. Actual science may have cast huge doubts, a pervasive skepticism, on all the old gods. Yet religion remains a warm blanket to cover man and woman against the hideous frosts of death and space. Science has, in proclaiming such authority and power, secretly usurped divinity.

I may be, as George Steiner warned, a mere word-helot: imprisoned in the past, or far more in it than in any future. But in this I prefer to be guided by what I have learned scientifically, creatively, and existentially from nature. I accept that I am ludicrously unfinished, that I constantly lose my balance (or that sense of *eukosmia*, "decency and right order," which fosters it). This is what the excellently shrewd and sharp-eyed Scots poet Norman MacCaig speaks of in the quotation that opens this essay. I know now that I shall never have children, that I betray the apparent fundamental biological purpose for existing. I shall die hopelessly short of entelechy and bitterly regret that fate bore me when it did (I thank hazard it was not historically earlier, and wish it had been later); yet would rather have been created at any time than not at all. While I live I would hope to conserve my own powers of feeling and knowing, defective though they often are. This is not selfishness but awareness of the reality of both the *sideros* and the *keraunos*, necessity and chaos, and of how short our individual cruise is . . . or seems, towards its end.

It pains me that such a *galimatias* as this must express me, that I can say no more about all that has said so much to me. Perhaps you will count me as a peculiar outcast, an exile from normality. I hope you will credit that I truly venerate, behind my inadequacies, the wild; and pity the ignorance of all those who deem themselves so superbly evolved that they judge they can do without it. Such seem to seek extinction; like this, they shall find it.

A large garden owns me—not the reverse—here in Lyme. I behave there as I do with texts, pursuing alternatives. Most plants, both wild and cultivated, have dates of epiphany. They may vary little from year to year, yet when they explode, they appear at their most fulfilled, most perfect, most fit to be contemplated *à la japonaise*, in the Zen Buddhist way. Their epiphanies are when their existences most crave to be seen.

It is a beautiful June evening. I shall walk down the hill to the bottom of my steep plot, past the cream-white furbelows, bee-loud and brave against an azure sea, of the acacias. In a secret corner there, a few stems of *Ophrys scolopax*, the woodcock orchid, grow. Woodcocks come from the Mediterranean and are not meant to flower as far north as this island, but in the warmth of our south-facing coast they do. They have become my every summer's secret joy, an apotheosis of the recurrent green universe. I cherish them empathetically so much they would make me cry, if I were the crying kind. I look at them now, knowing they are and that I am, in love and silence.

V

AN INTERVIEW

AN UNHOLY INQUISITION

JOHN FOWLES AND DIANNE VIPOND[1]

(1995)

DIANNE VIPOND: *You call this an "Unholy Inquisition"; don't you like being closely questioned?*

JOHN FOWLES: About as much as a resistance fighter being interrogated by the Gestapo or an atheist by the Inquisition! But I don't, as some seem to think, just blindly disregard academics. Certainly not so much as that little gibe I put in the dedication to the "Behind the Magus" essay ("For CIRCE and all the other tomb-robbers") might suggest. The Circe there is real—the charming Kirki Kephalea, who teaches at Athens—but by the "other tomb-robbers," I was sniffing like a raccoon at other academics. Most academics want facts, facts, facts, and of course I know that their pursuit is profoundly useful. It's just that my daily, present world sometimes seems very remote from theirs. Novels are like old love affairs—there is so much, not all bad, that one doesn't want to talk about, so much one can't. A great deal of all novels' beauty and excitement *for the writer* lies in the *now* in which they were or are being written. Like most, I am a bit manic-depressive, though the poles for me seem to lie much more between a writing self and a nonentity. One self knows profoundly that it is neither important nor socially relevant at all; another, far

---

1. Dianne, a Canadian who teaches English at UCLA (Long Beach), is too much a friend to make a proper academic—though of course she is—and I am much more fond of her than perhaps I, as a mere subject, should be. Among other things she has led me over much of Los Angeles as, in a different way, has that strange, sharp, but gifted Italian-American writer John Fante (1909–1983). (Fante's novels and correspondence have all been republished by the Black Sparrow Press, Santa Rosa.)

rarer, seems sometimes possessed. I feel identity with the average tribal shaman.

DIANNE VIPOND: *How do you feel about the state of the arts, especially the novel, at the end of the millennium?*

JOHN FOWLES: I should guess I'm more optimistic than most. I don't like the way pessimism—the black, absurdist view—has so often become fashionable during this century, a supposed proof that the artist really understands the world. This isn't to dismiss its only too real and manifold cruelties and horrors, just to question whether the black view isn't being exploited because it's so much easier to maintain and defend than its opposite. Optimism, however slight, always relies on an element of the rational, of realism. I don't believe we shall ever achieve valid art through formlessness and unthinking hazard. We need less would-be all-comprehending vision, and more honest craftsmanship.

Darwin, Freud, and Nietzsche sent this century, almost as much by being misunderstood as the reverse, through a prolonged typhoon, but there seem signs that the planet is trying to right itself from the wreckage. Many of our changes of direction already seem wrong in retrospect, and we now realize better what a dangerous, evil-fascinated species we are. I am torn, believing the arts *must* be allowed to evolve. Attempts to stop that are futile. At the moment I'm just reading a very good new poetic novel, Philip Marsden's *The Bronski House*, about the history of Poland during this century: its endless invasions and catastrophes, the destruction of all stable family life . . . yet somehow something seems to survive amid the horrors and holocausts. In a way this history resembles that of the poor old novel, how in spite of the countless "invasions" by the visual arts it still makes a nonsense of that silly question I've been hearing most of my adult life: "*Is the novel dead?*" Like Poland, it isn't!

DIANNE VIPOND: *In the past, you have indicated that you have half a dozen or so unfinished novels. If I recall correctly, Daniel Martin once fell into such a category. Do you have any plans for revising and publishing any of these? Your readers are anxiously awaiting the next Fowles novel. Do you have any plans for a new novel?*

JOHN FOWLES: I can't pretend I sit on a hoard of unfinished books and am obsessed with being published. I should loathe being so bound. There are two "possibilities." I have talked publicly of one, usually a sure way of aborting any project. It is a novel set in a quasi-mythical Balkans. I've been fiddling with that for nearly a decade now, and my feelings towards it remain impossibly mobile and fluid. I reconceive it every month or so. This is a pleasant experience for a unique and only reader (myself) but a nightmare for anyone else, including publishers. I experience this book (temporarily titled *In Hellugalia*) as I might a living dream. There is another, *Tesserae*, a sort of existentialist mosaic of what it was like in the 1950s to be poor, unfocused, and unpublished; but I think Kerouac and his "movement" did all that more brilliantly. I really don't have much normal literary vanity—or perhaps it is that I know my actuality miserably fails what I secretly wish for it. Almost all writers write to be known, to become a distinct flavor. I should prefer to be a sort of folk remedy. I'm not a Buddhist, but I dislike most of the typical egocentricities of artists and intellectuals, the thinking classes, both in Europe and in America.

DIANNE VIPOND: *What role do the female characters play in your fiction?*

JOHN FOWLES: I consider myself a sort of chameleon genderwise. I am a novelist because I am partly a woman, a little lost in midair between the genders, neither one nor t'other. I certainly think that most novelists are a result of not being clearly typed sexually. I'm just reading Margaret Drabble's excellent new life of the English novelist Angus Wilson. He was very much such a typical masculine-feminine writer.

DIANNE VIPOND: *There seems to be a compulsion on the part of the artist to create—in the case of a writer, the need to write, to tell, to reveal, to question, to record, to leave a verbal trace. Does this reflect your experience? If so, how?*

JOHN FOWLES: This trace-leaving used to be an obsession with me. I am these days much more occupied with savoring the present. I generally admire other writers who have the same mania for recapturing the fleeting "now." Poets do this best, of course. The tragedy of my own life is that I am not a great poet. I deeply envy both T. S. Eliot and Philip Larkin, in England our two technically finest poets of this century; yet I much dislike other aspects of the nature of both. Two other British poets I more fully admire are Seamus Heaney and the Scot Norman MacCaig. That last should be much better known than he is.

DIANNE VIPOND: *Insofar as you are a wordsmith of the first order, what does language mean to you? Does it reveal? conceal? represent an attempt to impose order upon chaos?*

JOHN FOWLES: I adore language, and especially English with its incomparable richness. I think of that richness less as a doomed attempt to impose order on chaos than as an attempt to magnify reality. I have no time for the old Socialist belief that you must avoid all rare words and communicate by lowest common denominators alone. As well say you must use inferior tools.

DIANNE VIPOND: *You have mentioned the influence of Alain-Fournier's* Le Grand Meaulnes *on* The Magus *and of Claire de Duras's* Ourika *on* The French Lieutenant's Woman, *two of your major novels. As a student and translator of French literature and an English writer, what do you see as the most significant differences between the two languages from an artist's perspective?*

JOHN FOWLES: I've always been glad I studied French at Oxford. It introduced me (through the Romance languages in general) to the other great culture of Europe and much of America. I am English, yet I would guess myself closer to the other side of Europe than most other English writers—with some obvious exceptions, of whom Julian Barnes is a current example. Again I feel a bit of a midair person about this . . . and happily so. This doesn't mean I speak French well at all; but I *read* it sufficiently. I had my say on this in my essay "A Modern Writer's France."

DIANNE VIPOND: *What aspect of writing do you find the most challenging? In the past, you have mentioned tone of voice and dialogue.*

JOHN FOWLES: Easily the hardest thing is saying what you *feel*, partly because so few of us really know what we truly feel. That is clearly connected with "tone of voice." I'm no good as a mimic, unlike quite a number of well-known writers. Perhaps that's what makes me think dialogue, the playwright's skill, so important. I deeply envy people like Harold Pinter for their brilliant minimalist use of both spoken speech and its silences. One of the greatest arts of the novel is omission—leaving it to the reader's imagination to do the work.

DIANNE VIPOND: *You refer to the other arts quite often in your novels, notably painting in* The Collector *and* The Ebony Tower, *and more specifically the work of the Pre-Raphaelites in* The French Lieutenant's Woman *and a Rembrandt self-portrait in* Daniel Martin. *Music seems to be more prevalent in* The Magus. *How would you characterize your use of the other arts in your novels?*

JOHN FOWLES: The visual arts, from the cinema to painting, absorb me most; music far less, though I do like some in my life. At the moment it's a new CD I have of Condon's Chicago jazz, another marvelous tape of Turko-Greek music from Istanbul, and a new record of Bach's unaccompanied cello sonatas. Almost all music interests me, but especially (almost exclusively) that performed on a solo instrument—the orchestral and choral somehow calls far less.

DIANNE VIPOND: *You have written about the work of Thomas Hardy and that of D. H. Lawrence. Do you see your work, in any way, as continuing in this particular tradition of the English novel? I'm thinking of Hardy's meliorism and romance and Lawrence's social critique and depiction of male/female relationships.*

JOHN FOWLES: Hardy interests me privately because he is, so to speak, a dead neighbor. I see his "country" from my study window. I adored Lawrence when I was a student in 1940s and have recently, though so many nowadays find him politically incorrect, discovered a deep recrudescence of sympathy for his almost metaphysical attitude to the now—the importance of conveying the immediacy and reality of the present. I am worried far less by his sometimes cockamamy views on society and man-woman relations. I feel closer to that obsessive, intensely self-absorbed line, in which I'd also put Golding, than to any other in Britain. We all know we've been born in prison; must accept the bars, yet crave freedom.

DIANNE VIPOND: *You have written about your father's fascination with philosophy in* The Tree. *Do you attribute any of your own interest in the world of ideas as represented in your fiction and* The Aristos *to his influence?*

JOHN FOWLES: Yes, I think so. He had been trained as a lawyer and approached all philosophy like a prosecuting counsel. But above all he made me realize that the suburban view of life was crippling and hideously insufficient.

DIANNE VIPOND: *Your essay "Hardy and the Hag" refers to Gilbert Rose's psychoanalytical theory, in which he posits that the love interest in most novels—that is, the male character's pursuit of an idealized young female—masks the novelist's sense of separation from and loss of the original mother/child bond, perhaps Oedipal in the Freudian sense. You have written about your father in* The Tree, *but I don't recall any reference to your mother. Do you attribute any particular aspect of your own artistic development to your mother's influence?*

JOHN FOWLES: I found Rose's use of separation-and-loss theory useful, but to say that it has deeply influenced me is not really true. As always I am driven back to a natural-history image. A common small fly of trout streams over here, the caddis (*Trichoptera*), builds a case for its chrysalis out of the grit in streambeds. I've been the same over countless theories and views of existence and literature. I have made them a part of me, but never the whole of me.

As for my mother, now several years dead, I have slowly grown into a realization of how much I owe her—I think above all for her maternal normality, in a way her sheer conventionality. I have also a guilt that I never fully acknowledged this to her, indeed never had a shadow of Christian patience towards her faults, among which, poor woman, were her logorrhea and her triviality—believing that life consisted of its trivia. She hardly affected me artistically, and as a young Oxford snob I thought most of her views on art beneath notice. But psychologically I now realize, almost every day of my life, that she did make me. I *am* her. I am happiest that she came of Cornish—or Celtic—stock.

DIANNE VIPOND: *You are obviously someone who is sensitive to words both semantically and phonetically. Is there anything to the observation that more than a few of the titles of your novels have the letters "MA" figuring prominently in them—*The Magus, Daniel Martin, Mantissa, A Maggot—*as do several words that seem to be central to your work: maze, mask, magic? A kind of maternal muse, perhaps?*

JOHN FOWLES: Writers are often blind to clues like this about their work. It had never occurred to me before. But yes, I see I am indeed M-dominated. Perhaps in part through my attachment to feminism.

DIANNE VIPOND: *You have said that you find Jung's theories most congenial to the purposes of the literary artist, and numerous references to Freud appear in your work. You have also noted the childlike qualities of the artist. The observations of mothers, infants, and children by the English pediatrician Donald Winnicott have been developed into theories about the real or true self, the "child within" of current psychoanalytical literature. Do you find these hypotheses of any relevance to your concept of the artistic personality?*

JOHN FOWLES: Fragments of Freud and Jung have long helped me make my chrysalis case, especially the latter. I've always said that if I knew myself to be deeply disturbed, I'd rather go to a Freudian psychoanalyst, but that Jung is infinitely more valuable for an artist. One of the Eranos yearbooks[2] was important for *The Magus*. I know very little of Winnicott.

DIANNE VIPOND: *How do you decide upon titles for your novels and choose names for your characters?*

JOHN FOWLES: I suspect I generally go to the subconscious, again partly to the worlds of Freud and Jung. I remember discovering that Alison (or Alysson) means "without madness" in classical Greek, long after I had given her that name, knowing she would be the central character of *The Magus*. It was for me a kind of proof that whatever had made me originally pick her name was deeply *right*.

DIANNE VIPOND: *When you were interviewed by Michael Barber, he suggested that Daniel Martin seemed to be Nicholas Urfe twenty-five years later; you agreed that this was precisely what you had intended. Is Henry Breasley another projection of this character at a later stage in life, with all of them together comprising portraits of the artist as young, middle-aged, and older man?*

JOHN FOWLES: No. Breasley is in no sense meant to seem "related" or autobiographical, but much more a separate character sketch. Years ago, as a student of French, I was deeply impressed by the *Caractères* of La Bruyère, his whole concept of that way of entering the world of ideas *and* commenting on social custom. I am going to be contradictory here: in another sense they are all self-portraits.

DIANNE VIPOND: *You have revised both* The Aristos *and* The Magus, *which is somewhat unusual for a writer to do. They each hold a rather significant place in*

---

2. New York: Pantheon Books, 1955.

your work as a whole; the former a work of nonfiction that clearly outlines your personal worldview, the latter your "first" novel in the truest sense of the word. Your revision of these books seems to confirm this. Would you agree? Do you subscribe to the theory that a work of literature is never really finished but simply abandoned at one stage or another?

JOHN FOWLES: I think the need for sales, for money, makes most writers eschew revised versions. But in all perfect or quasi-ideal worlds we are never truly satisfied with what we have done. It's always wanting another shot in a lottery; like a mania for exquisitely fault-free typography. Most works of literature have always been left at some stage of imperfection.

DIANNE VIPOND: *The word* silence *recurs throughout your fiction. Are you using it in the same way that a musician uses silence as the backdrop to his or her composition? What role do these lacunae of silences, both implicit and explicit, play in your novels? Are they invitations to the reader to participate in the text, in the heuristic process that is the fact of reading?*

JOHN FOWLES: I'm a deep believer in silence—the "positive" role of the negative. Yes, certainly it can be an obvious way to oblige the reader to help form and to experience the text. Although I feel no ambition to imitate them, I have long had sympathy and respect for writers like Beckett and Pinter. I feel very strongly that reading should almost always be a heuristic (that is, a "teaching by revealing self") process. I like it that in the Middle Ages, literature was the domain of the clerics or clerks. Of course that religious parallel can lead to mere preaching, a boring didacticism, but I cherish the reminder that we writers have inherited a moral, ethical function.

DIANNE VIPOND: *Most readers would agree that there is an element of eroticism in your work. In* The Uses of Literature, *Italo Calvino writes, "In the explicitly erotic writer we may . . . recognize one who uses the symbols of sex to give voice to something else, and this something else, after a series of definitions that tend to take shape in philosophical and religious terms, may in the last instance be redefined as another and ultimate Eros, fundamental, mythical, and unattainable." Do you think this applies to your work? What about to* Mantissa?

JOHN FOWLES: I confess to your "element of eroticism." I did once (very spasmodically) collect eighteenth-century "pornography." Certainly France taught me that the usual Anglo-Saxon and American unbalance over sex (in both their obsession with and their puritanical prudishness over it) was ridiculous. I happen to like Calvino's fiction very much, indeed class him with Borges and Saul Bellow, two other writers I much admire, but I don't quite know what he meant by the "other and ultimate Eros." I don't for instance have much time for texts like De Sade's *120 Days of Sodom*. I'd rather say I am *implicitly* erotic!

DIANNE VIPOND: *In* The Magus, *you write about the "characteristically twentieth-century retreat from content into form, from meaning into appearance, from ethics into aesthetics." Is this a reference to the tendency towards reification that many postmodernist texts seem to exhibit? What does this statement have to say about your intentions as a writer?*

JOHN FOWLES: I suppose I hanker after a more Victorian attitude. I really don't like total obsession with form, with the "look of the thing." By "content" I suppose I mean seriousness. All writers are rather like prostitutes: they know they have to sell by physical appearance, though underneath they may have far more serious intentions and meanings.

DIANNE VIPOND: *On several occasions, you have quite modestly claimed only partial knowledge of French critical theory. This comes as something of a surprise from someone who studied French literature, reads French, has written a philosophical book himself, is familiar with Barthes and Robbe-Grillet, among others, and writes novels that constantly seem to test the current boundaries of the novel form. To what extent do you see the relationship between theory and the practice of writing as a dynamic, dialectical one? Has theory played any part in the tasks you have set yourself as a writer? or influenced your thinking about the contemporary novel in any way?*

JOHN FOWLES: As I have repeatedly said, I wouldn't count myself even remotely an academic. I really don't know the poststructuralists and deconstructionists at all well. But I suppose my partial knowledges of Barthes, Kristeva, and so on are like bunkers on a golf course—by being there, they do slightly direct where you drive. But I'd doubt if anyone plays golf just to think about bunkers. I'm not unaware of them, but I don't feel they have much to do with the art of writing. I dislike in any novel a too-overt use of theory. I'd say more realism, not more fantasy, sci-fi, and all the rest, is what is needed in the next century.

DIANNE VIPOND: *During your discussion of* The Tempest *in* Islands, *you raise the question of whether art has the power "to change human nature in any but very superficial ways." Yet in your own work you consistently seem to engage in social critique in one form or another as you chronicle the second half of the twentieth century. You have described yourself as "broadly socialist." What opinions do you hold about the relationship between art and social change? between literature and politics? about (his)story—that is, the relationship between narrative and history?*

JOHN FOWLES: I have always felt much closer to socialism, even the old Marxism, than to its right-wing and Fascistic opposite. I'd say that what is wrong with most European socialism, as with the Democratic party in the United States, is that it is too static, too trammeled by past—and partly unionist—theory. I'm afraid socialism has never understood the vital importance of art: how important the avant-garde is as a cultural barometer, yet how it must partly cling to tradition. Art may change human nature, but only very generally . . . very slowly, also.

DIANNE VIPOND: *Considerable attention has been given to low self-esteem as a cause of individual acts of violence and aggression. What does your concept of the* nemo *as described in* The Aristos *have to say about this?*

JOHN FOWLES: Man is wedged between being a social creature and being an individual. I think the nemo, the sense that you are nothing or nobody, can drive all of us to violence and unreason. Through all human history it has been the hidden motive—that unbearable desire to prove oneself *somebody*—behind countless insanities and acts of violence.

DIANNE VIPOND: *Novels have been described as elaborate lies, yet most serious writers appear to be trying to get at some sort of ineffable truth through writing. What kind of truth do you strive for?*

JOHN FOWLES: Every writer knows this dilemma—that for a novelist, his or her trade demands the ability to lie, and yet something in him or her is yearning to express a whole truth about the human condition. The one I hope for is the Socratic: partly skeptical, often cynical, but always looking for an ethical truth. I find that the truth seldom lies too far from socialism and Marxism.

DIANNE VIPOND: *In* Islands, *you have written, "The truth is that the person who always benefits and learns most from the maze, the voyage, the mysterious island, is the writer . . . the artist-artificer himself." Is this psychographic self-exploration distanced by invention and the intervention of fictional characters a form of self-creation? Is it another version of "Madame Bovary, c'est moi?"*

JOHN FOWLES: Yes, I'd agree with that. Above all, you are in search of yourself. The trouble is that so often you lose track, through vanity. Vanity is the nightmare haunting every writer's step. Of course, most audiences don't help at all. They take a writer's self-absorption unto themselves. He or she does what they imagine they secretly want to do themselves.

DIANNE VIPOND: *To what extent do you believe that complete self-knowledge is possible? Is this similar to the "whole sight" to which you refer in* Daniel Martin? *The quest for selfhood, the journey of self-discovery itself, seems to be as important as—if not more important than—any of the conclusions that your protagonists tentatively reach at the end of your novels. Is this a gesture in favor of process over product?*

JOHN FOWLES: Yes, that is what I meant by "whole sight." This thoroughness of vision is more important than any seeming recipe for success in life . . . being a Socialist or anything else. We still haven't beaten Socrates' most famous piece of advice: *Know thyself.*

DIANNE VIPOND: *In* Daniel Martin, *Jenny observes that Daniel's real mistress is loss. You have also repeatedly mentioned the impact of Alain-Fournier's* Le Grand Meaulnes *(another novel that centers around the motif of loss) on your writing of* The Magus. *In* The French Lieutenant's Woman, *Charles's quest lies in his loss of Sarah. You have written in* Islands *and in several other contexts that the "genesis of all art lies in the pursuit of the irrecoverable, what the object-relations analysts now call symbolic repair." Would you comment on this?*

JOHN FOWLES: I agree with all this. It seems so obvious it needs no commentary. Deep down, I write today because I shall die tomorrow—the final loss!

DIANNE VIPOND: *You quote from* Ourika, *"Ideas are the only motherland." This seems to get at something that in part may account for the international appeal of your work. You have been described as a novelist of ideas. How important are ideas, and what part do they play, in your fiction? Could* The Aristos *be regarded as something of an intellectual/philosophical blueprint for the concerns of your fiction?*

JOHN FOWLES: Ideas, right down to the symbolic aspect of objects, that whole vast and peculiar city of being, are all vital to me. Yes, certainly *The Aristos* was an early attempt to explain both this and myself. I would still very largely hold by what I said there—if not always with *how* it is said!

DIANNE VIPOND: *With the publication of* Daniel Martin, *you described yourself as a humanist, yet existentialism seems to be as much present in that novel as in any of your earlier ones. What is the relationship between these two worldviews as you employ them? Are you using "humanism" in a broad rather than a narrow philosophical sense? What does humanism mean to you?*

JOHN FOWLES: For me, humanism is essentially the holding of a dislike or contempt for violence. It is in one sense a philosophy of compromise. The present world is a disturbed wasps' nest, socially, politically, *and* personally. For me humankind's most obvious fault, not least in its appalling attitude to other species, is its lack of humanism.

DIANNE VIPOND: *How would you describe the tension between free will and determinism in your writing?*

JOHN FOWLES: I wouldn't, and couldn't! But I know it exists.

DIANNE VIPOND: *Are individual freedom and self-conviction antidotes to the abuse of power? To what extent is the responsible use of power a motif in your fiction?*

JOHN FOWLES: To the second question, I think very much so; to the first, I should hope always, if analyzed. "Power" seems always Fascistic, potentially. It always kills true thought and feeling. That is why individual action and at least seeming free will are so important. The irresponsible interests me far more. As every decent journalist knows (most novelists also!), abuse and indecency yield much more, are far spicier, than use and decency.

DIANNE VIPOND: *Your nonfiction, which is often about a subject other than art, frequently reveals your own aesthetics. Why do you choose these vehicles to discuss artistic concerns in general and sometimes your own art in particular? Are these books masked volumes of literary criticism?*

JOHN FOWLES: It's just that I venture to suppose that my general views of art, and even the little novel reviewing I do, will be of some general interest. I never approach someone else's book without thinking that this will be a little square of mosaic in my general portrait. This is very vain. I am aware of that.

DIANNE VIPOND: *In the foreword to your book of poems, you suggest that the "crisis" of the modern novel is its self-consciousness. Do you think metafiction is a natural stage in the evolution of the genre as a literary form?*

JOHN FOWLES: Well, I suspect there was such a crisis until fairly recently. Whether it was a "natural" stage or one leading to eventual extinction, who knows? But I strongly feel that the novel is *not* dying. And that the greater complexity of technique caused by its added self-consciousness does or can fulfill the ultimate purpose of both explaining and teaching more.

DIANNE VIPOND: *You have been called a protean novelist—always breaking molds, trying something new. Is part of your reason for employing various types of novels as vehicles for your fiction an effort to be true to the original meaning of the word* novel, *"new"? Do you consciously set out to experiment with narrative form, or does the narrative itself dictate its structure? How does your experimentation with form represent an expression of artistic freedom, a refusal to be categorized? To what extent does your preference for multiple endings indicate a refusal to conform to the dictates of tragedy or comedy? an incorporation of chance/hazard?*

JOHN FOWLES: I am a great believer in freedom, but I don't like totally irrational freedom, or anarchy. I remember that when I studied French, I really didn't get on with what most of my teachers assured me was true greatness, as manifested in Racine and Corneille. I found a far greater depth in Molière. Simply, I just don't like very constricting, mathematical symmetry and forms. Disbelieving in set form is how I feel free.

DIANNE VIPOND: *The* Doppelgänger *motif is ubiquitous in your fiction. Twins, sisters, parallel characters, and often the dynamics of male-female relation-*

ships all seem to point to the "double." Your poem "The Two Selves" also deals with the idea of a dual persona. Could you comment on your use of the double?

JOHN FOWLES: I honestly don't know what it signifies, but I suppose it's a sort of longing for an impossible freedom. I have some sympathy for those suffering from that psychiatric illness, I think they call it multiple-personality disorder. I often wish I were someone else, and very much so with some other forms of nonhuman life. This is another reason that I adore nature.

DIANNE VIPOND: *Both in* Daniel Martin *and in* The Tree, *you make a distinction between "looking for" and "looking at," in each context with specific reference to orchids. "Looking at" seems to be the favored stance. But doesn't one need to look* for *before one can look* at? *Something on the order of a kind of marriage of the Western quest (looking for) with the Eastern, Zenlike contemplation (or looking at)? Is this the psychological work that most of your protagonists are engaged in during their quests for selfhood?*

JOHN FOWLES: Of course one begins to "look at" very often by first "looking for." "Looking for" I do vaguely attach to science, to wanting to increase scientific knowledge. "Looking at," in a full sense of existential awareness of the now, is an art we have more or less lost in the West, which is far more common with peasants and, I'd guess, with women than with intellectuals of either gender. I do try to suggest a realization of that. I called it a sense of existingness in a recent essay. It is abominably difficult to define, but I think both D. H. Lawrence and Virginia Woolf—and indeed Golding in his last and posthumous novel, *The Double Tongue*—at least sensed it.

DIANNE VIPOND: *In* The Tree, *you write, "The key to my fiction . . . lies in my relationship with nature . . . in trees." You refer to the journey into the artist's unconscious, which is never fully comprehensible but yields the artistic product and is experienced secondhand by the audience. You liken the choices of the artist to the choices of paths that one could take during a walk in the forest. "Behind every path and every form of expression one does finally choose lie the ghosts of all those that one did not." Is there any connection here with the concept of loss to which you have referred as a necessary condition for artistic creation? How does this relate to the sacred combe, le bon val?*

JOHN FOWLES: The knowledge that you haven't explored, *can't* explore, every path is part of the sense of loss—all that you've missed seeing. Perhaps what I said to Susanna Onega in Spain puts this best:

> *I am, I suppose, a wanderer or a rambler. A person who strolls and deviates through life. I always think the notion of the fork in the road is very important when you are creating narrative, because you are continually coming to forks. You don't exactly know where you are going, but you have deep principles or feelings that guide you very loosely. On the actual page you often do not know when a scene is going to end, how it is going to end, or, if you end it in this or that way, how it is going to change the future of the book. This is a state of uncertainty, or in terms of the modern physics, indeterminacy. . . .* [3]

DIANNE VIPOND: *In your essay "The Nature of Nature," you suggest that your inability to write about nature in any profound way is due to your perception of it as sacrosanct—that your experience of nature is not translatable into words. Are you intimating that despite your inability to write about nature per se, your perception and experience of nature are somehow mysteriously related to your creativity as an artist?*

JOHN FOWLES: Yes, very much so; others such as Woolf have also felt this.

DIANNE VIPOND: *Your attribution of the* Odyssey *(with Butler and Graves) to a woman writer, your praise of the* lais *of Marie de France, and of course your generally strong, grounded female characters all suggest an egalitarian attitude towards gender. You have aligned men with external reality and women with internal imagination. Is there a hint here of an attempt to reconcile the world of ideas with the realm of the imagination? intellect with art? the Jungian anima and animus? the male and female attributes that are inherent in each individual but that society so often misshapes for its own not always honorable ends?*

JOHN FOWLES: There seems a general tendency to associate "ideas" with the male sex and intuitive imagination with the female. It's always secretly surprised me that so many of the artists we now consider great were *not*

---

3. *Form and Meaning in the Novels of John Fowles* (London: VMI Research Press, 1989), 179.

feminine. I'm afraid the well-known historical bias towards my own gender can't be balanced by supposing there are countless women who haven't yet been recognized. I don't think there are. One much more likely explanation may be that so many male artists do have a deep feminine element in both their subconscious and their conscious. Perhaps we assess the artists of the past too clumsily by using mere animal-sexual definitions. I'd love to think that Homer was a very feminine ancient Greek male. A homosexual?

I have sympathy with Lou Salomé's view after her relationship with Rilke, that male artists, while better than mere men, are at best no more than imperfect women.

DIANNE VIPOND: *Are there any specific models for your female characters? You once mentioned that your wife, Elizabeth, was the inspiration for some of them.*

JOHN FOWLES: I've often said that I've written about only one woman in my life. I often feel when writing that the heroine of one novel is the same woman as the heroine of another. They may be different enough in outward characteristics, but they are for me a family—just one woman, basically. In my own life that woman has been my wife, Elizabeth, who died in 1990. I've thought about trying to do an account of her but so far haven't, knowing she lies so close behind many of my characters.

DIANNE VIPOND: *You have claimed to have a feminine mind. Could you elaborate on this?*

JOHN FOWLES: I'll quote a previous answer, from 1977:

> The women in my books are usually standing for other things. I've used a phrase in Daniel Martin, "right feeling," which I derived from Jane Austen, that central moral position that hovers behind all her scenes. Women enshrine right feeling better; a comprehensiveness of reaction to the world. It suits me to set that in women characters only because I am a male writer. If I were a woman writer, I think I would simply reverse the situation as many women writers do, as Emily Brontë does in Wuthering Heights. Reason and right feeling are not quite the same thing.

DIANNE VIPOND: The French Lieutenant's Woman *has been described as a feminist novel. Do you see yourself as feminist writer? Is it possible to be a feminist writer if one's female characters are essentially symbols as opposed to fully integrated, individuated characters in their own right?*

JOHN FOWLES: I hope I am a feminist in most ordinary terms, but I certainly wouldn't call myself one compared with many excellent women writers. Part of me must remain male. Masculinity is like the old pea-soup fog, a weather condition I remember from youth. It takes you a long time to realize not only where you are but where you ought to be. True humanism must be feminist.

DIANNE VIPOND: *You have said that you rather admire the Victorian novelist Sabine Baring-Gould, though you accept that he is now counted as minor, and in 1969 you introduced his 1890 novel* Mehalah, *a drama set in the Essex salt marshes. Your emphasis on individual freedom is particularly applicable to women. Like Baring-Gould's title character Mehalah, Sarah Woodruff is characterized as a "new woman" of the late Victorian period. One critic, Pamela Cooper, has suggested that your female characters are essentially passive, that they are objects of male desire or inspirational muse figures but not independently creative themselves. Is there any reason that you seem to take them to the brink of artistic creativity but never over the threshold?*

JOHN FOWLES: This reproach is probably justified. In part it's because woman remains very largely a mystery to me—or perhaps I should be more honest and admit that this mysteriousness has always seemed to me partly erotic. It's certainly not because I resent their artistic skills. If I ever do finish *Hellugalia*, the central character will be female.

DIANNE VIPOND: *Your characters are often preoccupied with making sense of the past. You don't write historical novels per se but rather novels set during earlier periods of history that must be understood in terms of their relationship to the present, which makes them contemporary rather than historical novels. Do you see your role as a novelist in any kind of historical terms?*

JOHN FOWLES: I don't feel there's much point in any historical novel that doesn't have considerable contemporary relevance. True history is best left to the historians. I do enjoy their work, but rather as I enjoy traveling abroad.

DIANNE VIPOND: *In your essay "Notes on an Unfinished Novel," you write, "History is horizontal." Can you explain what you mean by this?*

JOHN FOWLES: I was trying to emphasize the importance of the now. The nowness of any given point in time is pure and virginal. You don't begin to understand ordinary history until you have at least some sense of this staggering perpetual yet evanescent nowness.

DIANNE VIPOND: *In* Islands, *you write, "The major influence on any mature writer is always his own past work." In what ways has your own past work influenced your writing?*

JOHN FOWLES: Academics always seem to wish to explain everything in a writer in terms of past influences. There are of course very good teaching reasons for this—keep the little devils quiet—but as I grow older I more and more deeply see myself as one being, not the several beloved of deconstructionists. The hazards and incidents of life are far too complex for me to think someone—some writer or idea—can ever have been a "major influence." Chance (what I call in a recent essay the *keraunos*)—the countless other artists and theories that I have bumped into or that have bumped into me—has made me.

DIANNE VIPOND: *What kinds of changes do you see in your writing over time?*

JOHN FOWLES: There are some, a kind of hardening of fixed views, as I grow older. But I am very, very conscious that I must stay open—that is, remain capable of judging other values, both in literature and in normal experience.

DIANNE VIPOND: *How do you feel about your novels' being taught in English classes?*

JOHN FOWLES: A great deal of pity for the poor devils. But more seriously, I believe the literary process is fundamentally beneficial, both for its artists and for its audiences, and especially when it widens their concept of freedom, both personal and social. I like feeling that a vast stream of artists is both behind and ahead of me. One can't stand on the bank. One is willy-nilly in the stream; one *is* the stream. And by "one" I mean both writers and readers.

DIANNE VIPOND: *Know thyself. . . . How do you think the future may best know you?*

JOHN FOWLES: Perhaps through my diaries, which I hope will one day be published.

DIANNE VIPOND: *Tell me about them.*

JOHN FOWLES: They are so loose and disconnected they're not really what most people think of as diaries. Indeed for many years I've called them "disjoints." They're in no sense a coherent account of what I've said and thought, or proper records of what I've done. I am nonetheless a total believer in the value of such private scribblings for all writers, above all the young ones. At best they become the mirror in which he (or she, of course) learns himself; of his own faults, hypocrisies, and dishonesties. I have kept mine very erratically, but at least ever since I went to Oxford in 1947. Often they seem about someone I hardly recognize these days; sometimes they make me smile, or their sheer stupidity and self-ignorance makes me grind my teeth. I cringe. Writers aren't even remotely like scholars and professors, you know. We have to live with the constant knowledge that we change, that all changes; and that most of us writers are cripplingly burdened by our vanity. I suspect that's why so very few people "keep" diaries honestly.

DIANNE VIPOND: *Recently you seem to have been writing essays rather than fiction. Is there any particular reason for this?*

JOHN FOWLES: I feel squeamish about the element of lying in all fiction. Just as I wish I could have been an excellent poet, I also perhaps secretly wish I had been, like my father, a sort of philosopher.

DIANNE VIPOND: *Trust the teller or the tale?*

JOHN FOWLES: Neither. Being human means automatically, given the nature of individuality and the cosmos we inhabit, that we are fallible.

Everything is relative. No absolutes, except our—both your and my—final ignorance. We may pretend we know, but we never do. Least of all how lucky we are still to dwell in the now.

Still . . . still. I exist *still* as I write this, you exist *still* as you read it. Can't you sense a mystery, a precious secret told to you alone, in that word?

ACKNOWLEDGMENTS

The essays collected here have appeared previously in the following publications, although frequently in quite a different form:

"I Write Therefore I Am": *Evergreen Review*, August–September 1965.

"Notes on an Unfinished Novel": Copyright © 1968 by *Harper's Magazine*. All rights reserved. Reproduced from the July issue by special permission.

"Foreword to the Poems": "Foreword" from *Poems*. Copyright © 1973 by John Fowles. Reprinted by permission of The Ecco Press.

"Of Memoirs and Magpies": *Bookmarks*, edited by Frederick Raphael (London: Jonathan Cape, 1975). Reprinted by permission of Jonathan Cape.

"The Filming of *The French Lieutenant's Woman*": Foreword to *The French Lieutenant's Woman: A Screenplay*, by Harold Pinter (Boston: Little, Brown, 1981).

"A Modern Writer's France": *Studies in Anglo-French Cultural Relations*, edited by Ceri Crossley and Ian Small (London: Macmillan, 1988). Reprinted by permission.

"Behind *The Magus*": *Behind The Magus* (London: Colophon Press, 1994). Reprinted by permission.

"The J. R. Fowles Club": "The J. R. Fowles Club" from *Who's Writing This?: Notations on the Authorial I with Self-Portraits*, edited by Daniel Halpern. Copyright © 1995 by The Ecco Press. Reprinted by permission.

"Greece": First appeared in Kirki Kephala, *E Ellenike Empeiria (The Greek Experience)* (Athens: Olkos, 1996). Reprinted by permission.

"The John Fowles Symposium": Previously unpublished.

"On Being English but Not British": *The Texas Quarterly*, Autumn 1964.

"Gather Ye Starlets": *Holiday*, June 1996.

"The Falklands and a Death Foretold": *The Guardian*, August 14, 1982, *The Guardian* ©, and *The Georgia Review*, Winter 1982.

"My Recollections of Kafka": *Mosaic: A Journal for the Interdisciplinary Study of Literature*, Volume 3/4 (Summer 1970), Special Issue: "New Views of Franz Kafka."

"Conan Doyle": Foreword to *The Hound of the Baskervilles*, by Arthur Conan Doyle (London: John Murray and Jonathan Cape, 1974). Reprinted by permission of Jonathan Cape.

"Hardy and the Hag": *Thomas Hardy After Fifty Years*, edited by Lance St. John Butler (London: Macmillan, 1977). Reprinted by permission.

"Eliduc": From *The Ebony Tower* by John Fowles. Copyright © 1974 by J. R. Fowles Limited. By permission of Little, Brown and Company.

"The *Lais* of Marie de France": "Foreword" by John Fowles, copyright © 1978 by John Fowles, from *The Lais of Marie de France*, translated by Robert Hanning and Joan Ferrante. Used by permission of Dutton Signet, a division of Penguin Books USA Inc.

"Molière's *Dom Juan*": This article first appeared in April 1981, in the program for the National Theatre's production of Molière's *Dom Juan*, translated by John Fowles and directed by Peter Gill in the Cottesloe Theatre.

"Ebenezer Le Page": Introduction by John Fowles (approximately 3,750 words, pp. 7–16) to *The Book of Ebenezer Le Page* by G. B. Edwards (Hamish Hamilton, 1981). Introduction copyright © J. R. Fowles Ltd, 1981. Reproduced by permission of Penguin Books Ltd.

"John Aubrey and the Genesis of *Monumenta Britannica*": Foreword to *Monumenta Britannica or A Miscellany of British Antiquities (Parts One and Two)* (Boston: Little, Brown, 1982). Reprinted by permission of Dorset Publishing Co.

"Golding and 'Golding'": From *William Golding: The Man and his Books*, edited by John Carey. Compilation © 1986 by John Carey. Essay © 1986 by John Fowles. Reprinted by permission of Farrar, Straus & Giroux, Inc.

"The *Lost Domaine* of Alain-Fournier": Afterword to *The Lost Domaine (Le Grand Meaulnes)*, by Alain-Fournier, translated by Frank Davison (Oxford: Oxford University Press, 1986), by permission of Oxford University Press.

"Thomas Hardy's England": From *Thomas Hardy's England* by John Fowles. Introduction copyright © 1984 by J. R. Fowles Ltd. Text copyright © by Jo Draper. By permission of Little, Brown and Company.

"Commentary on D. H. Lawrence's The Man Who Died": Originally appeared in *The Man Who Died*, a limited edition by The Yolla Bolly Press (Covelo, Calif., 1992).

"Weeds, Bugs, Americans": *Sports Illustrated*, December 21, 1970.

"The Blinded Eye": *Animals*, Vol. 13, No. 9, January 1971.

"Shipwreck": Introduction to *Shipwreck*, photographs by the Gibsons of Scilly (Boston: Little, Brown, 1975). Reprinted by permission of Jonathan Cape.

"Islands": *Islands*, photographs by Fay Godwin (Boston: Little, Brown, 1979).

"Land": Essay for *Land*, photographs by Fay Godwin (Boston: Little, Brown, 1985). Reprinted by permission of Heinemann.

"Collectors' Items: Introduction": *Collectors' Items*, photographs by Kate Salway, text by Marina Benjamin and Kate Salway (London: Wilderness Editions, 1996).

"The Nature of Nature": Originally appeared in a limited edition *The Nature of Nature*, published by The Yolla Bolly Press (Covelo, Calif., 1995).

"An Unholy Inquisition: John Fowles and Dianne Vipond": First appeared in the special John Fowles issue of *Twentieth-Century Literature*, 42: 1, Spring 1996.